D1607155

Robert Frost

A Descriptive Catalogue
of Books and Manuscripts in
the Clifton Waller Barrett Library,
University of Virginia

Robert Frost  *A Descriptive Catalogue of Books and Manuscripts in the Clifton Waller Barrett Library University of Virginia*

COMPILED BY JOAN ST. C. CRANE

Published for
the Associates of the University of Virginia Library

by the University Press of Virginia
Charlottesville

Contents

Illustrations

On Collecting Robert Frost

THERE is a fascination about book collecting that, once experienced, fastens itself on an individual so firmly that it is difficult to shake off. Indeed, the serious collector almost invariably arrives at the point where he has not the slightest desire to rid himself of this delightful incubus. Of course, the various fields of book collecting are so numerous that volumes could be written on this subject alone. They range from subjects such as early medicine and science, art, music, the literatures of peoples and nations, political economy, history, fine printing, bindings, and so on, ad infinitum. One of the most frequent manifestations is the single-author collection.

In my own case, a career of some thirty-five years has been devoted to forming a comprehensive assemblage of American literature from the beginnings of the Republic to the present day. In doing so I have engaged in gathering some 1,000 single-author collections with the intention to make them as complete as possible. Robert Frost, preeminent poet of our times, stands high in the ranks of these American writers, and accordingly, much time and attention has been devoted to the gathering of as complete a collection of his books and manuscripts as possible. Herein lies one of the most exciting activities of the collector: the location and acquisition of great rarities. The thrill of the chase grips the collector, and when success crowns his efforts he naturally has a euphoric feeling of accomplishment. The pursuit of the sole surviving copy of Robert Frost's first book, *Twilight*, occupied ten years from 1950 to 1960, as will be described further on, and it might be said that the acquisition of the unique first book of a world famous poet is the supreme experience of a collector.

One may be sure that the collector derives a benefit from knowing personally the creator of the books and manuscripts he is so assiduously gathering. Certainly, this was my experience with Robert Frost. For me the benefit has been twofold. In the first place, Robert encouraged me to seek out certain rarities that seemed unobtainable, and he advised me of the location of various runs of his letters. In addition, he provided me with some of his own manuscripts that are among the chief ornaments of the collection. Second, it was a rare privilege for me to be exposed to that strange, baffling, always interesting personality. My acquaintance with the poet over some fifteen years ripened into what I like to consider a warm friendship, and the times I spent in his company were invariably exciting and rewarding.

In 1950 I delivered an address entitled 'Bibliographical Adventures in Americana' at the annual meeting of the Bibliographical Society of America, which was subsequently published in the Society's *Papers*. I ventured the opinion that the three leading American writers of our time were Eugene O'Neill in the drama, Willa Cather in fiction, and Robert Frost in poetry. This essay came to the attention of Robert Frost, and I received a friendly, jocular message thanking me for placing him in such a high category.

Some time before, I purchased my first Frost item, the first issue of *A Boy's Will* (London, 1913) from James F. Drake and Co., a fine copy in the first binding of gold-colored pebbled cloth. As the years passed I acquired several additional copies of this key volume, all presentation copies from the author.

In 1950 the famous Earle Bernheimer sale was held at the Parke Bernet Galleries in New York. I had heard a good deal about the Bernheimer Frost Collection, and I examined the catalogue eagerly. What a wealth of manuscripts and, wonder of wonders, the sole surviving copy of Frost's first book, *Twilight*; two copies had been printed and one destroyed. The redoubtable Captain Louis Henry Cohn represented me at the sale, and it proved to be one of the most exciting I have ever attended. The upshot was that we made a clean sweep of the manuscripts. In the excitement I committed an egregious blunder. I let *Twilight* get away. Within hours I was lamenting the loss of that unique volume. It was not until ten years later that the book came my way. At the sale it had gone to Mr. Roy V. Thornton, an old friend of Frost's and the owner of a choice Frost collection. In 1960 Robert was staying with us in New York shortly before the dedication of the Barrett Library at the University of Virginia, where he was to be one of the star attractions. I was telling him about the Frost items that would be on display. He asked, 'How about *Twilight*?' I said, 'The man won't sell.' Robert thought for a minute and replied firmly, 'Tell him I would like to see *Twilight* at the University of Virginia.' The next morning I called on John Kohn, who had heard that Thornton was in a selling mood. At my request, John called Thornton and told him of Robert Frost's wish. The reply was, 'I won't sell *Twilight*, but I will sell the whole collection.' Thereupon, John negotiated the purchase, and it was a heartwarming sight at the dedication ceremony to see the silvery head of the great poet bent over his first diminutive offspring.

In 1951 my wife, Cornelia, and I made a pilgrimage to Boston with Louis and Marguerite Cohn to spend the weekend in Robert Frost's company. We put up in style at the Ritz Hotel, and on Saturday night the Cohns entertained at dinner in Robert's honor. This was my first opportunity to have an extended visit with the poet, and I found him at his talkative, genial best. My acquisition of the manuscripts at the Bernheimer sale had given me a standing in the Frost world, and Robert was delighted to hear that their destination was the University of Virginia Library. He spoke feelingly of his great friendship with James Southall Wilson, Chairman of the English Department, and he was deeply interested to learn that Professor Wilson had been my mentor in encouraging me to embark on the building of a comprehensive collection of American literature for Mr. Jefferson's University. On Sunday there was a sudden snowstorm. We had been invited to visit Robert at his home in Cambridge, half of a two-family dwelling. On arriving at the house, we found the poet sweeping the snow off his porch and front steps. Robert took us to a small French restaurant the name of which I have forgotten, but I remember well the delicious repast. On this occasion I inquired about the manuscripts of *A Boy's Will* and *North of Boston*. Robert laughed and said they were probably swept up off the floor of the David Nutt publishing office in London. I naturally expressed my distress at the untimely end of these precious manuscripts. A few weeks after my return to New York I received a small bundle of holograph transcripts of all the poems in these first two books with some added ones and the statement that they were written out for Waller Barrett because he would have them so.

One of my most cherished acquisitions during this period was the gathering of family documents that concerned Robert's father and mother. There is a letter from Robert's father, William Prescott Frost, Jr., which probably contains the very first mention of Robert. The letter was written about seven months after his birth on March 26, 1874. The letter reads: 'we are all well, particularly the little boy, who, in fact, has never seen a really sick day in his short life. Belle says she is going to have his picture taken this week, and then you shall have a chance to see how much like his father and grandfather he is. . . .' This acquisition led to my first acquaintanceship with Robert's daughter, Lesley, who has since become a warm and valued friend.

A little later I came into possession of the letters of Robert to his friend the poet Robert Hillyer. Hillyer was the brother of another good friend, Ethel Medina, wife of the celebrated Judge Harold Medina, whose book, *The Anatomy of Freedom*, I edited for Holt, Rinehart and Winston. These letters came from John Fleming, who has established a high reputation on his own achievements as successor to the renowned Dr. Rosenbach.

To my thinking, George Goodspeed of Boston is the premier bookseller of New England. From him I obtained many a choice Frost item. He and Robert were very friendly. On one occasion George invited me to attend a dinner at the St. Botolph Club in Robert's honor. I remember the evening so vividly because I heard Robert read the poem 'The Gift Outright' for the first time. It made quite a hit. As Robert stepped down from the dais, he handed me the original manuscript from which he had read. Out of the corner of his mouth, he said, 'Here's something for you—you like to pick up the scraps.' The 'scrap' showed the title as 'We Gave Ourselves Outright,' changed in Frost's hand to the title under which the poem was published, 'The Gift Outright.' At the foot of the page were the words, 'My history of the Revolutionary War which was the beginning of the end of Colonialism. R. F.' Quite a scrap!

I mentioned previously the publishing firm of Holt, Rinehart and Winston. Henry Holt became Frost's publisher in 1915 when he returned from England, and the company has acted in this capacity ever since. I became a Director in the early fifties and thus had the opportunity to become closely associated with Alfred Edwards, later President of the concern. Edwards was one of Frost's closest friends and contributed valuable assistance in the publication of his books. This aid extended to Frost's personal business arrangements. Edwards's services for Robert can only be compared to those of Kathleen Morrison, who as amanuensis, confidante, and arranger of his daily life performed so notably in smoothing his path in his later years.

As time went on, the collection grew in bulk and importance. Some 270 letters from 1912 to 1962 furnish an invaluable autobiographical commentary on Robert's life for fifty years. Among the more important of these is the Bartlett group of 55 letters from 1912 to 1949. My first sight of these letters was in the Bender Rare Book Room of the Stanford Library at Palo Alto. Terry Bender (no relation to the donor) was the Curator. He told me the letters were on deposit from Mrs. Margaret Anderson, daughter of John and Margaret Bartlett, close friends of Frost in the early pre-England days. Stanford naturally coveted the archive but had no funds available. When I returned to the East, I consulted Robert. He said 'Buy them, but be generous to the daughter of my old friend.' I returned to California, interviewed

Mrs. Anderson, and arranged the purchase. I was interested to learn that she was the daughter-in-law of Melville Best Anderson, the translator of Dante whose version I had recently perused with enjoyment. Mrs. Anderson wished to publish a book based on the Frost letters. I suggested that she come east to meet Frost's publisher, Holt, Rinehart and Winston. She did so, and her book was accepted. These letters and the accompanying material form one of the most important sections of the collection. Among the items are the corrected proof sheets of the original printing of *A Boy's Will*. I suppose these are as close as we shall ever get to the original manuscript itself.

Two books about Frost have led to rewarding associations. The first is *The Trial by Existence* by the late Elizabeth Shepley Sergeant. Lunching with Miss Sergeant at her charming miniature abode with a pocket-handkerchief lawn directly overlooking the Hudson River was a source of frequent pleasure for my wife and me. The guests, Van Wyck Brooks, Thornton Wilder, Katherine Cornell and others, provided wealth of stimulating conversation. Miss Sergeant's book was published by Holt in 1960, and we gave a reception at the Grolier Club in New York to celebrate the event. Robert was in his element with a gay throng of admirers. After the reception there was a small dinner in the Council Room of the Club. The guests included Mark Van Doren, Marianne Moore, Monroe Wheeler, Judge Medina, Isable Wilder, Glenway Wescott, and Alfred Edwards. There had been an oversight in the invitation list. Robert's old friend, the renowned poet and critic, Louis Untermeyer, had not received his invitation to the dinner. I hurried upstairs and squeezed in a chair. Louis was adamant—he would not attend a dinner to which he had not been invited. Robert finally convinced him that his presence was necessary to make the occasion a success. He relented to the extent of agreeing to go upstairs but declined to partake of the feast. During a colloquy with Robert, he absent-mindedly tasted a dish and soon was consuming viands and wines with gusto. Robert was right—he added a great deal to the party.

There have been many books written about Frost, and there will be many more. Elizabeth Sergeant's *The Trial by Existence* will, in my opinion, always stand high among them. A proper Bostonian and a writer of charm and talent, she had known Robert for some thirty-five years and had indeed written the first important essay on the man and his work. This was published in 1927 in a book entitled *Fire under the Andes*. Before she died, arrangements were completed to bring her extensive Frost archive to the University of Virginia Library.

The other book in which I have been deeply interested is the biography

of Frost by Lawrance Thompson of Princeton, also published by Holt. I
had many meetings with Larry during the composition of this work.
Needless to say, all the material in the collection was freely at his disposal.
To date, two volumes of the biography have been issued. Tragically, Larry
was stricken with a serious illness in the course of writing the third and
final volume. He struggled manfully to complete this work before his death
and succeeded in leaving a substantial corpus that will be published. As is
well known, the second volume won the Pulitzer Prize. By arrangements
concluded many years ago, Larry Thompson's archive is at the University
of Virginia.

Perhaps one of the most satisfying experiences in collecting Frost has
been the acquisition of family letters. Beginning with letters of his father
and mother, we have secured a substantial number of letters from Robert to
his sister-in-law, his daughter Lesley, and his grandson William Prescott
Frost III. Together with these are letters of Elinor Frost to various mem-
bers of the family. Most of these letters have been published recently under
the guidance of Lesley Frost Ballantine.

Of my experiences with Robert, one that stands out is his visit to the
University of Virginia in October 1952. We had come down early to make
arrangements and had engaged rooms in the Thomas Jefferson Inn for
ourselves, Robert, and Lesley and Joe Ballantine. The evening of the Frost
address was cold and rainy. We all went by automobile to Cabell Hall or as
near thereto as we could get and continued the rest of the way on the Lawn
under dripping umbrellas. The area was completely deserted. A lingering
doubt entered my mind as to whether my idol had the pulling power he
had shown so convincingly time after time. We entered the building and
made our way to the auditorium. All doubts were instantly resolved. The
place was packed to overflowing—everyone had come early to make sure of
a seat. I introduced the speaker, and he regaled us with an hour and a half
of fun and poetry.

A later occasion on which I had the privilege of making the introduction
was for one of the distinguished poetry readings at the Young Mens' He-
brew Association in New York. I encountered Robert behind stage and the
following dialogue took place:

Frost: 'I hear you're introducing me.'
Barrett: 'That's right.'
Frost: 'What are you going to say about me?'
Barrett: 'I have it here.' (displaying a two-page typescript)

Frost: 'Let me see it.'

Barrett: 'I can't. They want us on stage.' (We move to the wings.)

Frost: 'Now, I want to know what you're going to say.'

Barrett: 'I can't tell you. The chairman is signalling me to introduce you.' (I go on stage. The introduction lasts six minutes. I return to the wings to the echo of thunderous applause.)

Frost: 'What did you say?'

Barrett: 'I haven't time to tell you. They're calling for you out there.' (Frost goes on stage and returns after an hour and fifteen minutes with repeated encores.)

Frost: 'Now, let me see that introduction.'

Barrett: 'I'll tell you what I'll do. I'll trade my manuscript for one of yours.'

Frost: 'I should think you would.' (The chairman enters and hands me an envelope.)

Frost: 'What's that?'

Barrett: 'It's my honorarium for introducing you.'

Frost: 'You get paid for doing that? How much is it?' (I open the envelope and find a check for $25.)

Frost: 'That's all right. I get a lot more.'

After the reading we all repaired to the apartment of Ann and Joe Blumenthal, two special people to whom Robert was very much attached. Joe, an outstanding typographer, designed many of Robert's productions and was the innovator in the printing of Frost poems annually as Christmas cards. His work at the Spiral Press created an appropriate milieu for Robert's poetry in the sensitive adaptation of format to the tone of the poems.

One of the most interesting occasions with Robert was the celebration of the fortieth anniversary of the Pulitzer Prize arranged by the Grolier Club. All of the winners of the Prize over that period in fiction, poetry, and drama were invited. The spouses, male or female, were also cordially invited. As chairman of the affair, I had to struggle with the knotty problem of place seatings. As a four-time winner, Robert sat on the President's right, and as the winner of three awards, Thornton Wilder sat on his left. Everything went swimmingly until the arrival of a distinguished dramatist who had regretted for his wife. He entered with an eye-filling blonde on his arm. His eminence had dictated his presence on the dais. I had the unwelcome duty to inform him that his companion, as he described the young lady, would be obliged to sit at one of the subsidiary tables. He objected violently, but eventually decided to remain. His companion more than earned her way by keeping her table in gales of laughter. Another crisis developed in connection with Robert Frost's granddaughter, Robin, a beautiful girl of twenty who, as previously arranged, accompanied her grandfather. Robin was promptly waylaid by a red-bearded poet who suggested, *sotto voce*, that she duck the party and go with him to his apartment. My antennae picked up the thread of his remarks, and I intervened with the statement that Robin was here with her grandfather and would most surely remain. The poet admonished me to mind my own business, but when he realized that I was adamant, he departed from the gathering with scarcely concealed disgust.

The climax of the evening was a champagne reception at the Grolier Club House. Robert was seated with a large group at his feet and all was going well when Thornton Wilder approached me with the suggestion that we all repair to his suite at the Plaza and continue the celebration. It was well after midnight, and I told him that Robert had arisen at six that morning in Boston, taken the train to New York, and made a radio and television broadcast. In addition he had been a guest at a gala luncheon and had been on his feet a great deal at the Pulitzer dinner and reception. I felt that he must be exhausted and that I should take him home promptly to my apartment. Wilder measured me with a withering look and said, 'In the first place you're a spoil-sport and in the second place, you don't know Robert very well. Good evening!' I took Robert home and as we entered the apartment, he said, 'I don't want to go to bed now. Give me a very light nightcap and we'll have a good talk.' At three A.M. he retired and I staggered off to bed thinking how right Thornton Wilder had been.

During Robert's last illness I was kept constantly informed of his condition, but my last earthly connection with him came about some three years after his death. One day in my mail I spied an envelope addressed to me in that well-known handwriting. I gave a start at what seemed to be a voice from the dead. I opened it and found inside a letter four years old enclosing the manuscript of a poem we had been discussing at the time. Robert had written the letter, sealed and stamped it. He had apparently forgotten to mail it, and it was among his papers when he died. The person who found it merely placed it in the nearest mailbox.

Nowadays as I look over the vast array of items in the collection, I feel a sense of gratitude for the privilege of knowing an extraordinary personality and a very great poet. I have, too, a sense of fullfillment at having had the good fortune to bring together so many of the original documents relating to Frost's life and poetic career. I cherish the hope that these materials will prove an inspiration and provide impetus to generations of students and scholars.

C. WALLER BARRETT

Preface

WHAT satisfaction, what innate pleasure, goes into the gathering of a collection, any collection. I recall my own excitement as a child in a collection of quartz pebbles, with their variant colors from white-white to rose-rose. Then there were butterflies from the Derry meadows; shells from the Rye beaches; autumn leaves for pressing (crab apple and sugar maple, willow and birch); 4- and 5-leaf clovers, which I still surprise between the yellowing pages of a long-ago favorite book; my father's collection of ferns, for which he had me scaling the cliffs of Mt. Pisgah, Lake Willoughby in Vermont for the rare *Woodsias*.

In England, with paternal assistance (and teaching), we collected fossils from the Jurassic rock, prehistoric echinoderms (starfish, sea urchins) from the chalk pits of Buckinghamshire. Still later came Carrol's geology display of rocks from the dead river beds and mountain peaks of New England.

Collecting would seem to be an emotional response to form, an instinct to shape. Poetry of course is a clear answer to it. As my father put it:

> Let chaos storm
> Let cloud shapes swarm
> I wait for form.

Forms!—so many beautiful forms: the wild geese responding to the migration V; 'the crows above the forest call. Tomorrow they may form and go'; the bees to the comb; the spider to his web; snowflakes to their primordial crystals. Or to quote from Robert Frost's great essay, 'The Figure a Poem Makes':

Just as the first mystery was how a poem could have a tune in such a straightness of meter, so the second mystery is how a poem can have a wildness and at the same time can have a subject that shall be fulfilled. It should be the pleasure of the poem itself to tell how it can. The figure a poem makes. It begins in delight and ends in wisdom. The figure is the same as for love.

Which brings us to another important way mankind keeps in form. The museums, galleries, libraries are the repositories of the great collections of paintings, sculpture, and literature that restrain civilizations from becoming uncivilized, great men from being forgotten. This bibliography of the C. Waller Barrett–Robert Frost Collection does both. Mr. Barrett has been gathering the collection over the years and presenting it to the University of Virginia. It has, of course, been available to researchers at all times. However, this volume brings it within easy access to scholar, researcher, and reader alike. I stress the reader. From the acquisition of *Twilight* on out, the book reads like a detective story, a search and find of the rare editions, manuscripts, letters of Robert Frost.

Take just the letters—letters and more letters! When I am asked, as I so often am, where and when my father did his writing, my answer has been that he wrote after midnight, that until midnight (even after) he walked and he talked. He walked to meditate, and he talked with all who agreed with him that there is 'a time to talk.' Way back when, before we children knew he wrote, he played games with us—jackstraws, croquet (my mother's favorite sport, at which she excelled), baseball, hoop rolling, tennis, Hearts. Otherwise he could most often be found reading aloud to the assembled family, or to my mother in particular. Now I discover that he also wrote letters, and again I am faced with the question of where and when. However, here are the letters—as circumstantial evidence.

When awards are given for this remarkable compilation, one way of shaping the literary and personal life of Robert Frost, they will include the dedicated staff of the University of Virginia's rare archives. For here are the facts, the indisputable facts, and didn't my father say, 'The fact is the sweetest dream that labor knows.'

For me there are meanings within meanings within the book itself. But above and beyond all else, it expresses the abiding friendship that came into being between the poet and the collector, thus sealing the collection with my father's blessing and, speaking for his family, mine also.

LESLEY FROST BALLANTINE

Bibliographical Introduction

In the perennial debate between literary scholars, book collectors, bibliographers, rare book curators, and booksellers, the constant theme is the need for the dissemination of information about the exact contents of major collections. The Barrett Collection of the University of Virginia Library has always been open to visitors who wished to make use of its extraordinary range of materials in American literature, whether or not these visitors had informed themselves before coming to Charlottesville of what is to be found here. But the value of a great national collection goes beyond making raw bibliographical and literary material available to visitors on request. A collection finally justifies itself when those in charge of its accumulation and preservation make a thorough analysis of its holdings for the direct purpose of contributing new knowledge to the subject. A collection is at its best a working collection for its staff as well as for outside visitors. The results of these informed investigations, in published form, can then be spread across the world for further identification and study by all interested students.

This first bibliographical catalogue of a series to make public the nature of the Barrett holdings is thus an original contribution to our knowledge of the work of a great American poet, Robert Frost, as well as the record of a superb collection. Book collectors and bibliographers will find here the first ordered chronological examination of the complex history of the issues and variants of—for example—*A Boy's Will* and *North of Boston*. The biography of Frost, as well as the history of his publication, is enriched by the identification of the printer of the two copies of *Twilight* and the publisher of *The Gold Hesperidee*. The letters to his daughter Lesley contain firsthand information of extreme frankness about Frost's relations with his publisher Holt and his negotiations with Harcourt, Brace. The numerous association copies provide a picture of his relations with his friends. The printed Christmas cards are curiosa of considerable personal interest as well. Frost's drive for recognition is oddly illustrated by the correspondence in 1912-13 with John Bartlett about a review which has survived in few copies of the original printed version, represented here by a fine example. Frost's interests are strikingly bared in the annotated copy of his own 1949 *Complete Poems* which he carried with him on his lecture tours in 1951–53 and in which he wrote down lists of his subjects for talks and of ideas for later development. The literary critic and the student of the development of Frost's texts will find here a unique gathering of what Frost preserved of his working drafts, intermediate manuscripts, and galley proofs with alterations, as well as newly discovered variants within his book publications.

A final and more comprehensive bibliographical assessment will be made in the future, of course, for it is of the first importance that the works of this poet should be studied, their variants identified and assessed, and every point in their publication, no matter how small, analyzed. To this eventual compilation the present detailed analytical catalogue will unquestionably make a major contribution. In part this contribution is in its own right, for this is a thoroughly researched and admirably written series of bibliographical descriptions brought to life by equally informed discursive notes that have an independent interest. In part, however, its contribution will be the stimulation of fresh research when owners of Frost's writings check their copies against these descriptions and cumulatively add to the weight of the evidence as well, one hopes, as discovering further new facts from previously unassessed material not in the Barrett Collection. For the first time literary scholars will know in detail what material is extant in this core collection. This bibliographical catalogue brings together collecting and scholarly interests in a fine blend. It is a happy beginning to a series that will make an important contribution to the history of the writing and publication of a number of American authors of concern to our national heritage. No better choice for this beginning could have been made than that found in the riches of the Barrett Robert Frost collection.

FREDSON BOWERS

Cataloguer's Note

THIS volume attempts to describe a specific collection in bibliographical terms. Description of the printed work follows a systematic method recommended by Fredson Bowers for a collection checklist. One ancillary intention is to provide a bibliographical aid to the works of Robert Frost until publication of the definitive bibliography.

The major printed works are given full description in sections A and B, first appearances of poems in books and periodicals are listed without detailed physical description in section C, and prose works are similarly listed in section D. In all sections the arrangement is chronological; however, later significant editions of individual titles are listed with the first edition of that title in section A. In each section, Barrett copies are enumerated with their acquisition numbers beneath separate title listings.

Only the cream of the Barrett Frost collection of printed works is described here. We do not include secondary editions of collected works, foreign editions, later printings of individual poems, books about Frost, music, reviews, and pictorial material—all represented in the collection in depth with many copies signed or inscribed. A full listing would triple the bulk of the catalogue and seem to imitate the completeness of a bibliography which no catalogue of a single collection can presume to do.

For purposes of color identification, ISCC-NBS Centroid numbers are used for overall binding colors and significant color printed elsewhere. If the exact shade, hue, or color value is not essential to identification, a simple subjective color designation is provided. If two varying printed colors are seen in different copies of the same edition, Centroid numbers are used; otherwise, not.

In quasi-facsimile transcriptions of matter printed in more than one color, the initial lettering is black unless otherwise designated. Varying colors are identified in brackets preceding the lettering in that color and a return to black is then similarly identified in brackets.

The manuscripts and letters (sections E and F) represent the complete holdings of Robert Frost manuscripts in the Barrett Library as of Summer 1973. Unpublished material is so identified, and the published source is located for published material. The arrangement of manuscripts in section E is chronological by date of composition as nearly as can be determined. A full physical description of each manuscript is provided. All textual variations between manuscripts of individual poems and the published texts are keyed to the edition edited by Edward Connery Lathem, *The Poetry of Robert Frost* (Barre, Mass., 1971), which contains line numberings. The letters in section F are not described physically beyond designation as typed or holograph. The letters are arranged in substantially chronological sequence beginning with papers relating to Robert Frost's parents, followed by Frost family letters and Robert Frost's letters to others arranged chronologically; however, more than two letters to one person are listed as a group. The Frost family letters have recently been published in *Family Letters of Robert and Elinor Frost* (Albany: State University of New York Press, 1972), edited by Arnold Grade. Mr. Grade kindly supplied a calendar of the letters prior to publication.

Though we claim the integrity of the collection as the first source of information contained here, such information would have been impossible to evaluate and confirm without the help of scholars whose specialized knowledge of Robert Frost and his work far exceeds that of the migratory worker in the archival field. This catalogue would have been much the poorer without the encouragement and expertise of John S. Van E. Kohn and Newton F. McKeon, former Librarian of Amherst College. Others who gave information generously were Frederick B. Adams, Mrs. Lesley Frost Ballantine, Josiah Q. Bennett (Lilly Library, Indiana University), Joseph Blumenthal (The Spiral Press), Fredson Bowers, Herman Cohen (Chiswick Book Shop), Mrs. Marguerite Cohn (House of Books, Ltd.), John A. Griffin (Lawrence Public Library, Lawrence, Mass.), Edward Connery Lathem and Walter W. Wright (Dartmouth College Library), Mrs. Kathleen Morrison, J. Richard Phillips (Amherst College Library), Winifred D. Sayer (The Jones Library, Amherst), Richard H. Templeton, Lawrance Thompson, and Jacob Zeitlin (Zeitlin & Ver Brugge). The index was the work of Clinton Sisson, Research Librarian, Alderman Library.

The task of providing historical background for much of the material would have been very difficult without constant reference to the two published volumes of Lawrance Thompson's biography of Robert Frost and the *Selected Letters*, edited by him. The 'Bibliographical & Textual Notes' section in Edward Connery Lathem's *The Poetry of Robert Frost* (Barre,

Mass., 1971) was the single most valuable source of information on the publishing history of individual poems after 1937. Descriptions of printed works before 1937, of course, lean heavily on the authority of W. B. Clymer and Charles Green's bibliography of Robert Frost. Alfred C. Edwards, executor and trustee of the Robert Frost Estate, made it possible for us to print and reproduce in facsimile the unpublished manuscripts which are among the chief treasures of the collection.

Shortly after completion of this text, Mr. Barrett acquired the books and papers of Robert Frost's biographer, Lawrance Thompson. This remarkable assemblage of letters, manuscripts, association copies of first editions, and Mr. Thompson's own notebooks and journals of his relationship with the poet over a period of twenty-five years adds an important new dimension to an individual author collection already extraordinary in scope. The Thompson material arrived too late for full description in this catalogue; however, a few major pieces have been incorporated in the text and an addendum following section F provides a calendar of the Thompson letters and manuscripts.

Clifton Waller Barrett's intimate knowledge of the books and manuscripts and his recollection of friendship with the poet have been invaluable. To him go first and last thanks as begetter of this great collection and the catalogue that describes it.

JOAN ST. C. CRANE

Key to Abbreviations

ABW	A Boy's Will	MI	Mountain Interval
AFR	A Further Range	NOB	North of Boston
AWT	A Witness Tree	SB	Steeple Bush
ITC	In the Clearing	WRB	West-Running Brook

Clymer & Green. Clymer, W. B. Shubrick, and Charles R. Green, *Robert Frost: A Bibliography* (Amherst, 1937)

Thompson, *The Early Years*. Thompson, Lawrance, *Robert Frost, The Early Years, 1874–1915* (New York, 1966)

Thompson, *The Years of Triumph*. Thompson, Lawrance, *Robert Frost, The Years of Triumph, 1915–1938* (New York, 1970)

Thompson, *Selected Letters*. Thompson, Lawrance, ed., *Selected Letters of Robert Frost* (New York, 1964)

RF & JB. Anderson, Margaret Bartlett, *Robert Frost and John Bartlett: The Record of a Friendship* (New York, 1963)

Part I

Printed Works

A   Books and Pamphlets

American and English Editions

A1   1894 TWILIGHT (First and only edition)

[Twilight. Lawrence, Mass.: American Printing House (?), 1894]

Collation: [1]⁶; pp. [1–12] = 6 leaves.

  Note: This copy, the only one known to exist, has an excised leaf, 1₂ (pp. 3–4), which contained (according to Robert Frost's statement) a contemporary inscription by the poet to Elinor White [Frost] on recto and verso. The leaf is presumed a blank, though its position indicates the possibility that it was the title-leaf. A perfect copy would consist of a single gathering of six text leaves enclosed in a gathering of six blank leaves on different paper; three preliminary and three terminal leaves with the first and final as pastedown endpapers, all twelve leaves stitched at the center fold.

Contents: p. 1: half-title, 'TWILIGHT'; p. 2: blank; pp. 3–4: blank (?); pp. 5–11: text; p. 12: blank.

Text Content:

Twilight	The Falls
My Butterfly	An Unhistoric Spot
Summering	

Paper: Heavy wove antique-vellum paper with no visible watermark; endpapers and flyleaves of a lighter wove vellum paper watermarked with a shield containing the date '1850', over a Gothic 'G', surmounted by an arm-and-scimitar crest. Beside the pictorial watermark, the word 'LINEN'. Leaves measure 146 × 97 mm. Edges trimmed, stitched.

Binding: Red-brown (55.s.Br) pebble-grained calf (the original binding). A double blind border rule (rule endings intersect and extend to the edges of the cover), gilt-stamped at the center of the front cover, 'TWILIGHT'. Back cover blank with double blind rules as at front.

Publication: *Twilight* was Robert Frost's first book. Beyond the information supplied in Frost's inscription to Earle J. Bernheimer on the first flyleaf recto of this copy, nothing is definitely known of the printing history: 'I had two copies of Twilight printed and bound by / a job printer in Lawrence Mass in 1894 probably / out of pride in what Bliss Carmen [*sic*] and Maurice / Thompson had said about the poem in it called My Butterfly. / One copy I kept for myself and afterward destroyed. / The other I gave away to a girl [Elinor Miriam White; later, Mrs. Robert Frost] in St. Lawrence / University to show to her friends. It had no success / and deserved none. But it unaccountably survived / and has lately leaped into prominence as my first / first. A few scattered lines in it are as much mine as any I was ever to write. I deliver it into your / care my dear Bernheimer with the last request that / you be not too fondly selfish with it, but consent to lend / it once in a long long time to some important exhibition / of my works as at the Jones Library in Amherst or the Baker / at Dartmouth. Boston February 1 1940 Robert Frost'.

A connective thread of evidence exists that makes it possible to conjecture on the identity of the 'job printer' who printed *Twilight*. In 1891 Robert Frost was elected Chief Editor of the Lawrence High School *Bulletin*. Lawrance Thompson (*The Early Years,* p. 114) gives an account of Frost's dealings with the printer of the *Bulletin*: 'The preparation of the December, 1891, issue . . . was a major literary accomplishment for Robert Frost; at least, it seemed to him to be an enormous tour-de-force, as he tossed off piece after piece on that day in the printer's office, until he had enough to make up the required eight three-column printed pages.'

The Lawrence High School *Bulletin* for 1891–1892 lists only one advertisement for a printer in its section of advertisers: The American Printing House, job printers for the American Publishing Company of Lawrence, who published the *Daily American* (for which Frost worked as a reporter for a short time in 1895). It would not be unreasonable to assume that the only printer to advertise in the *Bulletin* was its printer.

Further evidence that the American Printing House was the Lawrence High School printer is to be found in a commencement exercise program for 1892 (Frost's and Elinor White's graduating class) which employs an unusual stylized uncial font on the front cover. The identical font is used in the advertisement that appears for The American Printing House and also in the Latin motto that is used on the front cover of the October 1891 issue of the *Bulletin*. As Chief Editor, Frost would have had frequent dealings with the printer, as the excerpted paragraph above demonstrates. When he decided to have *Twilight* printed in an edition of two copies only, he would have gone to a printer he knew well; one who would be likely to accept such an eccentric and (to the printer) unprofitable order as a friendly favor. Of the fourteen job printers listed in the Lawrence city directory for 1894, evidence points strongly to The American Printing House as the printer of Robert Frost's first book, *Twilight*.

On the second flyleaf recto of this copy is a more recent inscription: 'Sixty years [1954] later signed / over to my friend / R. V. Thornton / at Chicago. / Robert Frost'. At the terminal flyleaf verso are lines in Frost's hand: 'Lave of trees chafing interlocking / And a woodpecker knocking'. This phrase is not identified in the concordance of RF's poetry.

Frost sold this copy to the collector Earle J. Bernheimer. In the sale of Bernheimer's books (Parke-Bernet Galleries, 11–12 December 1950, cat. 1207) it was purchased by House of Books, Ltd., and subsequently sold to the collector Roy V. Thornton. Frost himself acted as liaison for C. Waller Barrett in the purchase of the book from Thornton in 1960.

A facsimile of *Twilight* was printed in 1966 for the Barrett Library in an edition of 170 copies by the Reynolds Company of Charlottesville, Va.

In 1947 Earle Bernheimer had a facsimile of one of the poems, 'The Falls,' printed by the Ward Ritchie Press in an edition of 60 copies to use as a Christmas card.

Barrett Copy: On the evidence of Robert Frost's statement, the only copy in existence.

A2   1913 A BOY'S WILL (First Edition)

A BOY'S WILL | BY | ROBERT FROST | [orn.] | LONDON | DAVID NUTT | 17 GRAPE STREET, NEW OXFORD STREET, W.C. | 1913

Preliminary Note: There are two issues of the first edition of *A Boy's Will* in four variant bindings. Within the four genuine bibliographical combinations (see below), 70 of 100 copies of the third binding and all copies of the fourth binding contain a manually introduced variation in the form of a rubber-stamp on p. iv. In addition, the last 135 copies of the fourth binding were signed and numbered by the author, creating another nonbibliographical variation that nevertheless needs to be identified. Since 1937 the points of true issue, binding variants, and manual alterations have been lumped together and incorrectly given the designations of six 'issues' in an illogical attempt to conflate issue in the sense of bibliographical differences in sheets, issue in the sense of binding, and illegitimate issue in the sense of matter introduced outside the printing shop. However, this surface simplicity clashes with established bibliographical principles; hence, we supply here a new set of designations for both *A Boy's Will* and *North of Boston* in which we propose to list the bindings chronologically within the major categories of issue, identify the manual insertions as secondary characteristics, and thus restore chronology of true bibliographical issue.

FIRST ISSUE

Collation: $[A]^8(-A_{4.5})$ B—D^8 $E^2(=A_{4.5})$; pp. $[\pi i–ii]$, [i–vii] viii–ix [x], [1] 2–50 [51–52] $=$ 32 leaves.

Note: Final signature E^2 is identified as originally integral with the first gathering, A, by the rough-cut openings at the top edges which correspond with the openings of A_1 and A_8, making these leaves $A_{4.5}$.

Contents: pp. πi–ii: preliminary blank leaf; p. i: half-title, 'A BOY'S WILL'; p. ii: blank; p. iii: title-page; p. iv: blank; p. v: dedication, 'TO | E[linor]. M[iriam]. F[rost].'; p. vi: blank; pp. vii–ix: contents; p. x: blank; pp. 1–50: text (on p. 50, 'PRINTED BY | SPOTTISWOODE AND CO. LTD., COLCHES-TER | LONDON AND ETON'); p. 51: 'Certain of these poems are reprinted by | courteous permission from:—*The Forum, The | Independent, The Companion.*'; p. 52: advertisement, 'THE 1s. SERIES OF MODERN POETS.' (17 titles).

Text Content:

Into My Own	In Neglect
Ghost House	The Vantage Point
My November Guest	Mowing
Love and a Question	Going for Water
A Late Walk	Revelation
Stars	The Trial by Existence
Storm Fear	In Equal Sacrifice
Wind and Window Flower	The Tuft of Flowers
To the Thawing Wind	Spoils of the Dead
A Prayer in Spring	Pan with Us
Flower Gathering	The Demiurge's Laugh
Rose Pogonias	Now Close the Windows
Asking for Roses	A Line-storm Song
Waiting	October
In a Vale	My Butterfly
A Dream Pang	Reluctance

Paper: Rough wove cream paper, endpapers of heavier rough wove cream paper. Leaf measurements vary with the binding variants and will be provided with binding descriptions.

Bindings:

Binding A (sold by Nutt, 1913): Bronzed brown (75.dp.yBr, but with a bronze sheen) pebbled (*i.e.,* sand) cloth. Gilt-stamped on the front cover, '[within a blind border rule frame] A·BOY'S·WILL | [orn.] | ROBERT·FROST | [orn.].'. Spine and back cover blank. Leaves measure 193 × 128 mm.; edges rough-cut.

Note: An article by H. B. Collamore in the *New Colophon*, NS 3, no. 3 (1938), 354–56, asserts that there are two varieties of bronze cloth binding: (1) 'dark brown shiny bronze with pebbled surface,' and (2) 'orange-brown shiny bronze with a more wavy pebbled surface.' The orange bronze is described as the more scarce, though Collamore assumes that the brown bronze was used to bind the first books that appeared. No copy in orange-bronze cloth is in the Barrett Collection; however, the first Barrett copy (592588), in brown bronze, is a review copy and should, therefore, serve to indicate priority of the brown-bronze binding if priority exists.

Binding B (sold by Nutt, *ca.* 1917): Cream vellum-paper boards; lettering and decoration identical with that of binding A, but stamped in red (13.dp.R), including the border rule. Spine and back cover blank. Leaves measure 185 × 122 mm.; edges trimmed.

SECOND ISSUE

Collation: [A]^8($-$A$_{1.8}$, A$_{4.5}$) X^2($=$A$_{8.1}$) B–D^8 E^2 ($=$A$_{4.5}$); pp. [i–vii] viii–ix [x–xii], [1] 2–50 [51–52] $=$ 32 leaves.

Note: In the second issue, the collation is altered by folding A$_1$ (the preliminary blank leaf in the first issue) back to form a single unsigned gathering of two leaves with its cognate A$_8$ (pp. ix–x) as the first leaf. Folded thus, X$_2$ becomes pp. xi–xii, a blank leaf preceding the text.

Contents: As in the first issue, but with the altered order of pagination effected by the position of the blank leaf, X$_2$ (pp. xi–xii). Also, 686 of 716 copies of the second issue (bindings C and D) have 'Printed in Great Britain' rubber-stamped on the blank title-page verso (p. iv).

Text Content: As in the first issue.

Paper: As in the first issue, but without endpapers; the wrappers are glued to the sheets at the spine. Leaves measure 185 $\times$ 122 mm. and are cut flush with the edges of the binding.

Bindings:
Binding C (bound for Simpkin Marshall): Cream linen-paper wrappers; lettering identical to that of bindings A and B, but stamped in black without a border rule. Spine and back cover blank.

Binding D (sold by Dunster House, Cambridge, Mass., 1923): Cream linen-paper wrappers; lettering as on all previous bindings, but in a similar, heavier font without a horizontal bar surmounting the letter 'A' and lacking the border rule. The ornaments are 4-petaled flowers formed of four circles; beneath are two dots and a thin perpendicular wedge in descending order. The ornaments of the preceding bindings are 8-petaled flowers; beneath the lower, a single dot from which descend three leaflike slashes.

Publication: The publishing history of *A Boy's Will* parallels that of *North of Boston*. Both books were published by the London house of David Nutt, which went into bankruptcy after the First World War. Remaining unbound sheets of the two books were acquired by Simpkin Marshall & Co. of London, acting for the trustee in bankruptcy of the Nutt firm. In 1923 the major portion of these sheets and some copies bound for Simpkin Marshall were purchased from them by Dunster House Bookshop, Cambridge, Mass. A detailed account of the circumstances surrounding this transaction and of Robert Frost's part in it is given in Thompson's *The Years of Triumph* (p. 587): 'The other important event which involved RF, during this visit to the Boston area [October 1922], occurred when he visited the Dunster House Bookshop and made arrangements with the owner, Maurice Firuski, to perform the odd task of selling large numbers of two scarce books.

'Back of this proposal was the fact that when the firm of David Nutt and

Company went into bankruptcy, in the spring of 1921, RF's friend J. W. Haines wrote to him from Gloucester, England, explaining the situation. He said that some bound copies of the first editions of *A Boy's Will* and *North of Boston* were in danger of being reduced to pulp, together with several hundred unbound sheets of each book, and that Haines had found ways to protect them until RF expressed his wishes in the matter. Several months later, on 20 Sept. 1921, RF wrote to Haines (copy, DCL): "I'm going to send you in a few days all the money I can raise to buy in those poor old first editions of mine with David Nutt. I may ask you to store some of the books somewhere until I think what exactly to do with them. Some of my friends think they might be worth something here."

'Lincoln MacVeagh apparently suggested that Firuski, at the Dunster House Bookshop in Cambridge, might handle the entire matter for RF; hence the visit to Firuski in Oct. 1922. Haines, hearing nothing from RF during the next few months, bought all the bound copies and sheets of both books, and notified RF of what he had done. On 14 Dec. 1922, RF wrote to Haines (copy, DCL): "I have found a bookseller in Cambridge, Mass named Maurice Firuski who thinks he can undertake to handle all the North of Bostons in stock over there and all the Boy's Wills too." The arrangement was carried out, after considerable correspondence. As a result, some extremely complicated bibliographical points were created for those who chose to collect the various issues of the first editions of *A Boy's Will* and *North of Boston*.'

One thousand sets of sheets of *A Boy's Will* were originally printed, according to the report of the printer, Spottiswoode, Ballantyne & Co., Ltd., to Clymer & Green. Of these, Clymer & Green deduce that no more than 350 copies were bound up for distribution by David Nutt between 1 April 1913 and the time of the company's dissolution. No records were saved; hence definite numbers cannot be assigned the binding variants released by Nutt. Copies in binding A were bound by the Leighton-Straker Bookbinding Co. before 1 April 1913. The binding B copies were bound during the war.

There is strong reason to believe either that the numbers assigned the copies in the Nutt bindings (350) and copies bound for Simpkin Marshall (reported as 100 in binding C) are incorrect or that more than 1,000 sets of sheets were printed. Information supplied by Frederick B. Adams, Jr., from his file of the Haines-Firuski correspondence (concerning the transfer of surplus sheets and bound copies from Simpkin Marshall to Dunster House) clearly indicates that 70 of the 100 copies bound in cream wrappers for Simpkin Marshall were purchased by Dunster House together with 616 sets of sheets ordered to be similarly bound (binding D) in England before transfer was effected. A total of 686 bound copies were therefore sent to America, rather than 616 reported by Clymer & Green. Add to these the 30 remaining Simpkin Marshall copies and the original 350(?) Nutt copies, and the number of sets of sheets printed totals 1,066. There is no logical reason why, many years after the fact, the figure of 1,000 sets of sheets reported by the printer should be doubted. If we accept this figure and the figures set forth in the Haines-Firuski correspondence as correct, then fewer than 350 copies were released by David Nutt. Accounting for the 100 copies bound for Simpkin Marshall, the number of original Nutt copies dwindles to 284.

Copies to be sent to America in 1923 were rubber-stamped 'Printed in Great Britain' on p. iv.

In 1943 Herman Cohen of the Chiswick Book Shop, New York, bought the stock of Dunster House when that shop went out of business. In the stock he found 135 copies of *A Boy's Will*, second issue, binding D. Cohen consulted Captain Louis Henry Cohn of The House of Books, Ltd., New York, whom he knew to be a close personal friend of Robert Frost. Captain Cohn asked Frost to sign and number the 135 copies, and Frost agreed to do so. The Parke-Bernet Galleries sale catalogue of the Earle J. Bernheimer Collection (11–12 December 1950, cat. 1207, no. 76) contains evidence of this arrangement: 'Tipped in one copy [of *A Boy's Will*, signed and numbered] is a typed letter . . . by Capt. Louis H. Cohn to Mr. Bernheimer in reference to the above copies: ". . . When Frost was here you know I spoke to him about signing and numbering all the copies of the Fourth Issue [*sic*] of *A Boy's Will*, in fact, he had an idea that they should be bound up to make a Fifth Issue. . . . Mr. Frost decided a short time ago to sign and number these copies and the disposition of them has been entrusted to us as the Fifth Issue. . . ."

'Tipped in copy "1" is an A.L.s. by Robert Frost . . . Cambridge, Mass., Dec. 20, 1942. To an unnamed correspondent: "I am to sign the first edition of A Boy's Will for Captain Cohn's client—a hundred [*i.e.*, 135] copies at fifty cents apiece. Its an irony of time that they should come round to me the way they have. The whole lot of A Boy's Will and North of Boston. . . ." '

Information about the last 135 copies signed and numbered by Robert Frost has been generously corroborated by Mrs. Marguerite Cohn and Herman Cohen.

The 1,000 bound copies of the first edition of *A Boy's Will* may be distinguished chronologically and bibliographically as follows:

First issue, binding A: 1913 Nutt. Bronzed brown cloth.

First issue, binding B: *ca.* 1917 Nutt. Cream vellum-paper, red lettering.

Second issue, binding C: 1922 Simpkin Marshall. Cream linen-paper wrappers.

Second issue (rubber-stamp), binding C: 1923 Simpkin Marshall / Dunster House.

Second issue, binding D: 1923 Dunster House. Cream linen-paper wrappers, variant lettering. All copies rubber-stamped on p. iv.

Second issue (signed and numbered by Frost), binding D: 1943 House of Books for Chiswick Book Store. All copies rubber-stamped on p. iv.

Barrett Copies:

590316. Galley proofs with 'FIRST REVISE' rubber-stamped on p. 1 and p. 33. On the half-title: '[in an oval rubber-stamp] From Spottiswoode & Co., Ltd. . . . | 30 Jan. 1913'. Lacks the dedication leaf and the final printed leaf, 'Certain of these poems are reprinted. . . .'. 'Contents' p. viii is misnumbered 'vi'; p. ix is misnumbered 'vii'. The galley text (G) differs from the first edition (F) thus: page 1, line 13: them] G; they] F

5, line 8: The line is incorrectly justified to the inner margin in G; properly indented in F.

32, line 4: golden lid.] G; golden lid,] F

32, line 8: command.] G; command,] F

46, line 2: sun−assaulter] G; sun-assaulter] F

Holograph corrections and marginal notes in Frost's hand:

page 1: 'they' (for 'them' in line 13)

3: 'Youth Companion' (at the end of the poem, indicating the first printing of 'Ghost House')

4: 'Forum' (at the end of the poem, indicating the first printing of 'My November Guest')

5: 'This line should be carried in.' (line 8)

7: 'Two or three you may have seen before.' (at the end of the poem)

31: 'Independent' (at the end of the poem, indicating the first printing of 'The Trial by Existence')

32: ',' (at line 4); ',' (at line 8)

33: 'A variant' (at the end of the poem)

42: 'Transcript' (at the end of the poem, indicating the first printing of 'Now Close the Windows')

44: 'New England Mag.' (at the end of the poem, indicating the first printing of 'A Line-Storm Song')

45: 'Youth Companion' (at the end of the poem, indicating the first printing of 'October')

46: 'hyphen' (at line 2)

48: 'Independent' (at the end of the poem, indicating the first printing of 'My Butterfly')

50: 'Youth Companion' (at the end of the poem, indicating the first printing of 'Reluctance'); 'The feeling here is that the better things never go into magazines.'

592588. A review copy of the first issue, binding A. Rubber-stamped on the dedication page, 'With the publisher's compliments'.

592589. First issue, binding A. Inscribed on the front open endpaper recto in Frost's hand, 'John and Margaret [John T. and Margaret Bartlett] / Outcasts of Lulu Flat / from / E. M. F. and R. F. / Castaways on an Island'. John T. Bartlett was Frost's favorite pupil at Pinkerton Academy in 1906. They remained lifelong friends. 'Lulu Flat' refers to Lulu Island, Vancouver, where the Bartletts lived in 1912.

592592. First issue, binding A. Inscribed on the front open endpaper recto in Frost's hand, 'Wilbur E. Rowell / from / R. F. / Beaconsfield, Bucks. / October 4 1913'. Rowell was an attorney and executor of Frost's paternal grandfather's estate.

592822. First issue, binding A. Inscribed on the open endpaper recto in Frost's hand, 'Leona [Leona White Harvey, Frost's sister-in-law] / from / Rob & Elinor / July 1914 / Ledbury Eng.' A second inscription on the recto of the preliminary blank in the hand of Leona White Harvey, 'To Vera−May 10−1931 / From her Mother / Leona White Harvey'.

592590. First issue, binding B. With the ownership signature on the front open endpaper recto of John Freeman, poet, critic and biographer of Herman Melville. A few penciled marginal notes in Freeman's hand.

592587. Second issue (rubber-stamp), binding C. Signed 'Elinor Miriam Frost' in Mrs. Frost's hand on the dedication page. On the verso of the blank leaf following the contents, Frost has written a fair copy of 'To the Thawing Wind,' which appears printed on p. 12. The holograph poem contains two textual variations: line 8: as the ices go] F; as the ice will go] MS

    12: pictures on the wall] F; picture on the wall] MS

Beneath the poem, in Frost's hand, is 'For Earle Bernheimer'.

Uncatalogued. The Lawrance Thompson copy. Second issue (rubber-stamp), binding C. Inscribed on p. 1 with lines 7–8 of 'The Trial By Existence.' Signed beneath, 'Robert Frost / To Lawrance Thompson'. The poem is on pp. 29–31 of the book.

592591. Second issue, binding D. Inscribed on the front open endpaper recto in Frost's hand, 'To Robert Partridge / from / Robert Frost'.

592593. Second issue, binding D.

592586. Second issue (signed and numbered by Frost), binding D. Signed 'Robert Frost / 127' beneath the half-title.

A2.1   1915 A BOY'S WILL (First American Edition)

A BOY'S WILL | BY | ROBERT FROST | AUTHOR OF "NORTH OF BOSTON" | [publisher's device] | NEW YORK | HENRY HOLT AND COMPANY | 1915

Collation: [1–4]⁸; pp. [i–vi] vii–ix [x], 11–63 [64] = 32 leaves.

Collation: [1–4]^8; pp. [i–vi] vii–ix [x], 11–63 [64] = 32 leaves.

Contents: p. 1: half-title, 'A BOY'S WILL'; p. ii: blank; p. iii: title; p. iv: blank; p. v: dedication, 'TO | E. M. F.'; p. vi: blank; pp. vii–ix: contents; p. x: blank; pp. 11–63: text; p. 64: 'Certain of these poems are reprinted by courteous | permission from:—*The Forum. The Independent, The | Companion.*'

Text Content: As in the first edition (English), differently paged.

States: The first printing has a misprint, 'Aind', on the last line of p. 14. This was corrected to 'And' in the second printing. Copies of the first state with 'Aind' have been seen only in the earliest binding with white endpapers (see *Binding* and *Paper* notes below); however, second state corrected copies have been seen in both bindings with white and buff endpapers.

    All copies of the first edition (English) and the first American edition have the misprint 'wich-hazel' for 'witch-hazel' at p. 62, line 16. This was corrected in *Selected Poems* (1923), and the word appears correctly spelled in all subsequent printings of the poem 'Reluctance.'

Paper: White wove paper; endpapers of heavier white wove paper. Leaves measure 192 × 132 mm.; top edge trimmed, other edges uncut. Some later copies have endpapers of heavy buff (76.1.yBr) wove paper. The white endpapers are usually in combination with the fine cloth binding; buff endpapers with the coarse.

Bindings: Blue (187.d.gyB) fine linen cloth with white endpapers. Gilt-stamped on the front cover: '[within a thick-thin double rule frame] A BOY'S WILL | [acorn orn.] | ROBERT FROST'. Spine gilt-stamped: '[thick-thin rule] | A | BOY'S | WILL | [acorn orn.] | ROBERT | FROST | [thin-thick rule] | HENRY HOLT | AND COMPANY'. Later copies are bound in a coarser blue (187.d.gyB) linen cloth with buff endpapers.

Dust jackets: Contrary to Clymer & Green's (pp. 27–28) statement, 'Later copies appeared in glassine dust wrapper,' the earliest Barrett copy with 'Aind' for 'And' is jacketed in glassine. A later corrected copy bound in coarse blue linen has a jacket of drab paper (77.m.yBr), lettered in black. Front cover: 'A BOY'S WILL | By | ROBERT FROST | *Author of "North of Boston"* | 75 Cents Net | *This is Mr. Frost's first volume of poetry.* | [within a single rule: a 4-line blurb from *The Academy* (London) and a 3-line blurb from *The Dial*]'. Spine: 'A | BOY'S | WILL | By | ROBERT | FROST | 75 Cents | Net | [Holt device]'. Back cover and flaps blank. According to Clymer & Green, 'The early dust wrappers exist in three states. The first two showed the price on the spine and the front cover as 75¢. The third had the price blacked out with a rubber stamp and replaced by "$1.00." The earlier of these carried nothing on the back cover whereas the other carried advertisements of *North of Boston* and *A Boy's Will*. Later copies appeared in glassine dust wrappers.'

Publication: The first American edition of *A Boy's Will* was published in a first printing of 750 copies by Henry Holt and Co. in April 1915, one month after the American edition of *North of Boston*.

Barrett Copies:
592594. Fine blue linen, white endpapers, glassine dust jacket. 'Aind' for 'And' at p. 14. On the open endpaper recto, Frost has written a fair copy of the poem 'Stars,' in which there is no textual variation from the printed poem at p. 18 of the book. Beneath he has signed his name and 'For Earle Bernheimer'. An extension of the note was appended later, 'and from him / to R. V. Thornton / with my approval / R. F.'
709277. Coarse blue linen, buff endpapers, p. 14 corrected. On the open endpaper recto, Frost has written a fair copy of 'Nothing Gold Can Stay,' signed and dated 'Ann Arbor May 1922'. This poem was first printed in the *Yale Review* (October 1923) and later included in *New Hampshire* (1923). When it was inscribed here, it was as yet unpublished, with readings that vary thus from the published first edition (1st):
line 3: Her early leaf's a flower] 1st; Her early leaves are flowers] MS
  4: But only so an hour.] 1st; But only so for hours;] MS
  5 Then leaf subsides to leaf.] 1st; Then leaves subside to leaves.] MS

6: So Eden sank to grief,] 1st; In autumn she achieves] MS

7: So dawn goes down to day.] 1st; A still more golden blaze,] MS

8: Nothing gold can stay.] 1st; But nothing golden stays.] MS

These textual variations occur in no printed versions of poem and represent an earlier form of the text copied into the volume.

592595. Coarse blue linen, buff endpapers, p. 14 corrected.

528937. Fine blue linen, white endpapers, p. 14 corrected, dust jacket (as described above).

A2.2   1934 A BOY'S WILL (Second American Edition)

A BOY'S WILL | BY ROBERT FROST | [woodcut vignette of a fence-post by Thomas W. Nason] | HENRY HOLT AND COMPANY | NEW YORK

Collation: [1–4]⁸; pp. [i–iv], [1–8] 9–56 [57–60] = 32 leaves.

Contents: pp. i–iv: blank; p. 1: title; p. 2: 'FIRST 1934 EDITION | COPYRIGHT 1934 BY HENRY HOLT AND COMPANY | PRINTED IN THE UNITED STATES OF AMERICA | BY THE SPIRAL PRESS · NEW YORK'; p. 3: dedication 'To E. M. F.'; p. 4: blank; pp. 5–7: contents; p. 8: blank; pp. 9–56: text; pp. 57–60: blank.

Text Content: In this edition, 'In Equal Sacrifice' and 'Spoils of the Dead' have been omitted. 'Asking for Roses,' omitted from the 1930 *Collected Poems*, is included here; however, 'In Hardwood Groves' (added to the *A Boy's Will* section of the 1930 *Collected Poems*) is not included.

Paper: Fine white wove paper, endpapers of the same stock. Leaves measure 222 × 139 mm.; edges trimmed.

Binding: Very fine tan (79.1.gy.yBr) linen cloth. Front cover: 3 intertwined scythes stamped in gilt on a brown (81.d.gy.yBr) panel framed in a brown (81) rule. Spine: on a brown panel, in gilt, '|| A BOY'S WILL by ROBERT FROST ||'. Back cover blank.

Dust Jacket: Ground color is pale beige (lighter than 90.gyY) printed overall in olive gray-brown (113.OlGy). Front cover: '[within a single-line rule] A BOY'S WILL | [vignette as on title-page] | BY | ROBERT FROST'. Spine: 'A BOY'S WILL by ROBERT FROST'. Back cover: '[within a single-line rule] Poetry by ROBERT FROST | [list including Frost's published work] | [Holt imprint]'. Inner flap: 'A BOY'S WILL | by | ROBERT FROST | [13-line blurb] | [Holt imprint]'. Back flap: 'COLLECTED POEMS | OF ROBERT FROST | [11-line advt.]'.

Barrett Copy:
592596. Inscribed by Frost on the front open endpaper, 'To Earle Bernheimer / any newness there / is in this edition. / Robert Frost'.
Uncatalogued. The Lawrance Thompson copy, inscribed on the front open endpaper recto, 'Lawrence [*sic*] Thompson / from his ever / Robert Frost'.

A3   1914 NORTH OF BOSTON (First Edition, first issue)

NORTH OF BOSTON | BY | ROBERT FROST | AUTHOR OF "A BOY'S WILL" | LONDON | DAVID NUTT | 17 GRAPE STREET [top of vertical rule] EDITORIAL | NEW OXFORD STREET [bottom of vertical rule] 6 BLOOMSBURY STREET | W.C.

Collation: [A]⁸ B–I⁸; pp. [i–vi] vii [viii] ix [x], 11–143 [144] = 72 leaves.

Contents: p. i: half-title 'NORTH OF BOSTON'; p. ii: blank; p. iii: title-page; p. iv: '*First edition*, 1914'; p. v: 'TO | E. M. F. | THIS BOOK OF PEOPLE'; p. vi: blank; p. vii: '*THE PASTURE*' (8-line poem in italics); p. viii: blank; p. ix: contents; p. x: '*Mending Wall* takes up the theme where | *A Tuft of Flowers* in *A Boy's Will* | laid it down.'; pp. 11–144: text. On p. 144, 'Printed by BALLANTYNE, HANSON & Co. | at Paul's Work, Edinburgh'.

Text Content:

Mending Wall	After Apple-picking
The Death of the Hired Man	The Code
The Mountain	The Generations of Men
A Hundred Collars	The Housekeeper
Home Burial	The Fear
The Black Cottage	The Self-seeker
Blueberries	The Wood-pile
A Servant to Servants	

Paper: Cream wove paper; endpapers of white wove paper. Leaf measurement varies with the binding variants and is provided with binding descriptions.

Preliminary Binding Note: The first edition, first issue of *North of Boston* appears in five binding variants distributed over a period of eight years (see *Publication* note). The first edition, second issue (i.e., first American publication, see A3.1) was issued in 1914 in the United States in what is designated chronologically as binding B.

Binding A (sold by Nutt): Olive-green (127.gyOlG) coarse linen cloth measuring 195 × 154 mm. Leaves measure 191 × 145 mm.; top edge trimmed, other edges uncut. Gilt-stamped on the front cover: '[within a single blind border rule]

NORTH OF BOSTON | [oval dot] | ROBERT FROST'. Spine stamped in gilt: '|| NORTH | OF | BOSTON | [oval   dot] | ROBERT | FROST | D.   NUTT ||'. Back cover blank.

Binding B (sold by Henry Holt): See A3.1 (second issue).

Binding C (sold by Nutt): Dark yellowish green (137.d.yG) fine linen cloth measuring 189 × 145 mm. Leaves measure 185 × 136 mm.; all edges trimmed. Stamped in blind on the front cover: '[within a single blind border rule] NORTH OF BOSTON | [oval dot] | ROBERT FROST'. Spine stamped in gilt: '|| NORTH | OF | BOSTON | [oval   dot] | ROBERT | FROST | D.   NUTT ||'. Back cover blank.

Binding D (sold by Simpkin Marshall): Light blue (181.l.B) fine linen cloth measuring 200 × 145 mm. Leaves measure 196 × 136 mm.; all edges trimmed. Stamped in dark blue (183.d.B) on the front cover: 'NORTH OF BOSTON | [oval dot] | ROBERT FROST'. Spine stamped in dark blue (183): 'NORTH | OF | BOSTON | [oval dot] | ROBERT | FROST | NUTT'. Back cover blank.

Binding E (sold by Dunster House): Grass-green (125.m.OlG) coarse linen cloth measuring 200 × 145 mm. Leaves measure 196 × 137 mm.; all edges trimmed. Stamped in gilt on the front cover and spine as in binding A, but with the blind rule at top and bottom only. Back cover blank.

Binding F (sold by Dunster House): Grass-green (125) coarse linen cloth measuring 195 × 150 mm. Leaves measure 191 × 145 mm.; top edge trimmed, other edges rough-cut. Lettered as on bindings A and E, but with the blind rule at top and bottom only as on binding E. Back cover blank.

Publication: As noted previously, the publishing history of *North of Boston* parallels that of *A Boy's Will*. Of 1,000 sets of sheets originally printed, approximately 350 copies were bound up in coarse green cloth (binding A) and sold by the firm of David Nutt in 1914. Early in 1915, 150 sets of sheets were sold by Nutt to the American firm Henry Holt and Company. These were supplied with a cancellans Holt title-leaf and bound in cloth-backed tan boards (binding B) for sale in the United States. During the war, Nutt bound up approximately 200 more copies for sale in fine green linen cloth (binding C). Nutt went into bankruptcy after the war, and the remaining sets of sheets were sold to Simpkin Marshall, London. Of these, 100 copies were bound in light blue cloth (binding D); probably for sample when the stock was offered for sale to the Dunster House Bookshop, Cambridge, Mass., in 1922. Fifty-nine of the copies bound in blue were rebound (in the same size) in coarse green cloth to resemble the original Nutt binding. The remainder of 200 sets of sheets were bound uniformly, but the dimensions varied slightly from those of the rebound Simpkin Marshall copies. The blue-bound copies (and therefore the copies rebound in green) are taller and narrower, whereas the last 200 copies are almost identical in dimension with the original Nutt copies which were being imitated. Similarities of cloth and gilt-stamping in binding A and bindings E and F indicate that the work was done by the same binder in England before the later copies were sent to America.

All 259 copies sold to the Dunster House Bookshop were rubber-stamped 'Printed in Great Britain' on p. iv.

The 1,000 bound copies of the first edition can be distinguished chronologically and bibliographically as follows:

First issue, binding A: 1914 Nutt, ∓350 copies. Coarse green cloth.

First issue, binding C: *ca.* 1917 Nutt, ∓200 copies. Fine green cloth.

First issue, binding D: *ca.* 1922 Simpkin Marshall, 41 copies. Blue cloth.

First issue, binding E: 1923 Dunster House, 59 copies. Rebound binding D, coarse green cloth. Rubber-stamp on p. iv.

First issue, binding F: 1923 Dunster House, 200 copies. Coarse green cloth. Rubber-stamp on p. iv.

Second issue, binding B: 1914 Holt, 150 copies. Cloth-backed boards. With cancellans Holt title-leaf (see A3.1).

Barrett Copies:

592823. Binding A. Inscribed on the front open endpaper recto in Frost's hand, 'Leona [Leona White Harvey, Mrs. Frost's sister] / from / Rob & Elinor / Ledbury / July 1914'.

592728. Binding A. Inscribed on the front open endpaper recto, 'Professor Stuart P. Sherman / from / Sidney Hayes Cox.' Beneath, in Frost's hand, 'Robert Frost Jan 7 1951 / Cambridge'. Sidney Cox met RF in 1911 when they were both teaching in Plymouth, New Hampshire. Their lifelong friendship is described in Cox's book, *A Swinger of Birches* (New York, 1957).

592825. Binding A. Inscribed 'To Mother— / with a wish for many / happy returns of the day / From / John and Margaret [John T. Bartlett and his wife] / January 15, 1915', on the front open endpaper recto.

592722. Binding C.

592721. Binding D. Signed on p. 1, 'Sincerely yours / Robert Frost'.

592729. Binding E. On the front open endpaper recto Frost has written and signed a fair copy of 'Why Wait for Science' (published in *Steeple Bush,* 1947). The poem contains no variant readings from the first edition. Inscribed 'To Russell Alberts / October 16 1945'.

592718. Binding F. Signed on the front open endpaper recto, 'To Russell Alberts / from his friend / Robert Frost / Cambridge / 1946'.

Uncatalogued. The Lawrance Thompson copy. Binding F. Inscribed on the front open endpaper recto, 'To Lawrence [*sic*] Thompson / if he will promise / not to be too hard / on Longfellow / Robert Frost'. RF refers to Thompson's book, *Young Longfellow* (1938).

A3.1   1914 NORTH OF BOSTON (First Edition, second issue [for American publication])

NORTH OF BOSTON | BY | ROBERT FROST | AUTHOR OF "A BOY'S WILL" | [publisher's device] | NEW YORK | HENRY HOLT AND COMPANY | 1914

Collation: [A]⁸(±A₂) B–I⁸; pp. [i–vi] vii [viii] ix [x], 11–143 [144] = 72 leaves.

Contents: As in the first edition, first issue; but with the Holt cancellans title-leaf; verso printed '*First edition, 1914*'.

Text Content: As in the first edition, first issue.

Paper: Cream wove paper; the cancellans title-leaf on heavier wove stock. Leaves measure 202 × 145 mm.; top edge trimmed, other edges uncut. Endpapers of heavy white wove paper.

Binding (binding B): Drab gray-brown boards (79.l.gy.yBr) backed with brown (77.m.yBr) cloth. A cream paper label measuring 57 × 91 mm. on the front cover, printed in black: '[within a thick-thin double rule] NORTH OF BOS-TON | [acorn orn.] | ROBERT FROST'. A cream paper label measuring 48 × 17 mm. on the spine, printed in black: '[thick-thin rule] | NORTH | OF | BOS-| TON | [acorn orn.] | ROBERT | FROST | [thin-thick rule]'.

Dust Jacket: Gray-brown (79.l.gy.yBr) wove paper, printed in black. Front cover: 'NORTH OF BOSTON | By | ROBERT FROST | $1.25 NET | [5-line blurb followed by seven review quotations within a single-line rule frame]'. The excerpted quotations are from reviews in the *London Outlook, London Bookman, London Nation, English Review, London Times, New Weekly* and by Ezra Pound in *Poetry*, 5, no. 3 (Dec. 1914). Spine: 'NORTH | OF | BOSTON | BY | ROBERT | FROST | $1.25 | Net | [publisher's device]'. Back cover and inner flaps blank.

   Note: In the *London Times* review excerpt, the word 'faint' is correctly spelled. The first American edition has 'fain' (see A3.2 on jackets of later reprints).

Publication: See the account of the publishing history of the first edition, first issue. Although the date 1914 appears on the Holt cancellans title-leaf and on the copyright, the correspondence between Holt and the firm of David Nutt between 12 September 1914 and 23 March 1915 supports the conclusion that the 150 sets of sheets for American publication were not actually published in America until 20 February 1915. A full account of the correspondence is given in Edward Connery Lathem's *Robert Frost, His 'American Send-off' – 1915* (1963). On 5 October 1914 Holt sent Nutt a firm order for 150 sets of sheets and enclosed copy for their own imprint and 'an electro of the [Holt] owl cut' for use on the American cancellans title-leaf. The sheets did not arrive until January 1915, and prior to the February publication date, Holt had enough orders to exhaust the small edition (cf. Thompson, *The Years of Triumph*, pp. 5–6). On 19 February 1915 Holt immediately cabled Nutt for 200 more sets of sheets. There was a delay, and on 23 March 1915, Holt wrote again: 'We published "North of Boston" on February 20th, and our first supply was immediately exhausted. Now we find ourselves without any supply for a month, and piracy threatened. So to protect your interests and those of the author, we are forced to reset both of Mr. Frost's books here in order not only to forestall piracy but also to take advantage of the present interest in Mr. Frost's work.' On 17 March 1915 Alfred Harcourt of Holt wrote to RF, 'we have been out of "North of Boston" practically ever since the day of publication. . . . We have had no reply to our cable of February 19th to David Nutt ordering a further supply or to our letter of the same date to them. In this situation, in order to protect your interests from piracy, rumors of which we hear, we are proceeding to set up "North of Boston" and "A Boy's Will" and hope to be able to have our edition of this on the market by the first of April' (Thompson, *The Years of Triumph*, pp. 573–74). This was the first American edition (see A3.2) of which 1,300 copies were published, probably in late March 1915.

Barrett Copies:
592719. In original dust jacket. With the bookplate of Thomas B. Mosher.
592720. Inscribed on the front open endpaper recto, 'To Waller Barrett / from / Robert Frost / Cambridge / January 7 1951'.
592723. Henry Holt's copy with his ownership signature in pencil, dated February 1915, on the front open endpaper recto.

A3.2   1915 NORTH OF BOSTON (First American Edition [the first edition printed in America])

NORTH OF BOSTON | BY | ROBERT FROST | AUTHOR OF "A BOY'S WILL" | [Holt device] | NEW YORK | HENRY HOLT AND COMPANY | 1915

Collation: [1–9]⁸; pp. [πi–ii], [i–viii] ix [x], 11–137 [138–142] = 72 leaves.

Contents: pp. πi–ii: blank; p. i: half-title, 'NORTH OF BOSTON'; p. ii: blank; p. iii: title-page; p. iv: '*First edition*, 1914 | *Second edition*, 1915'; p. v: dedication, 'TO | E. M. F. | THIS BOOK OF PEOPLE'; p. vi: blank; p. vii: '*THE PASTURE*' (8-line poem in italics); p. viii: blank; p. ix: contents; p. x: '*Mending Wall* takes up the theme where | *A Tuft of Flowers* in *A Boy's Will* | laid it down.'; pp. 11–135: text; p. 136: blank; p. 137: '*GOOD HOURS*' (16-line poem in italics); pp. 138–142: blank.

Text Content: As in the first edition, with the addition of 'Good Hours' (p. 137), which is not included in the contents (p. ix).

Paper: Rough wove white paper; endpapers of a smoother, heavier white wove stock. Leaves measure 193 × 128 mm.; top edge trimmed, other edges uncut.

Binding: Dark gray-blue (186.gyB) fine linen cloth lettered and decorated in gilt. Front cover: '[within a double thick-thin rule frame] NORTH OF BOSTON | [acorn orn.] | ROBERT FROST'. Spine: '[thick-thin rule] | NORTH | OF | BOSTON | [acorn orn.] | ROBERT | FROST | [thin-thick rule] | HENRY HOLT | AND COMPANY'. Back cover blank.

Dust Jacket: Heavy gray-brown (63.l.brGy) wove paper lettered in black. Front cover: 'NORTH OF BOSTON | By | ROBERT FROST | $1.25 NET | [5-line blurb] | [7 excerpts from English and American reviews: the *New Republic*, *London Outlook*, *London Bookman*, *Chicago Evening Post*, *English Review*, *London*

Times, New Weekly]'. Spine: 'NORTH | OF | BOSTON | BY | ROBERT | FROST | $1.25 | Net | [Holt device measuring 16 × 12 scant mm.]'. Back cover and inner flaps blank.

Note: The review excerpts from the *London Times* on the front cover has the reading, 'Poetry burns up out of it as when a fain [*sic*] wind breathes upon smouldering embers.' The original printing of the review in the *London Times* has 'faint'. This is correctly reproduced as 'faint' in the same excerpt on the dust jacket of the first edition, second issue (binding B). In all examined copies of dust jackets on reprints of the present edition, the incorrect spelling 'fain' persists. The size of the Holt device on the spine, however, is noted either as 19 × 16 mm. or 16 × 12 mm. (as above). A copy of the first printing is reported by John S. Van E. Kohn of Seven Gables Bookshop, New York, as having a jacket with the correct 'faint' and the Holt device on the spine measuring 19 × 16 mm. Kohn also owns a copy of the October 1915 reprint with a 'fain' jacket and the larger device.

Publication: See A3.1 *Publication* note. Thirteen hundred copies were published in late March 1915.

Barrett Copies:
592724. In the original dust jacket.
592726.
592727.

A3.3   1919 NORTH OF BOSTON (Second American Edition)

NORTH | OF | BOSTON | BY | ROBERT | FROST | PICTURES   BY | JAMES | CHAPIN | HENRY HOLT AND | COMPANY—NEW YORK

Collation: [1–16]⁴ [17]⁶; pp. [πi–ii], [i–viii] ix [x], 11–138 = 70 leaves.

Contents: pp. π i–ii: blank; p. i: half-title; p. ii: blank; p. iii: title; p. iv: blank; p. v: dedication, 'TO | E. M. F. | THIS BOOK OF PEOPLE'; p. vi: blank; p. vii: '*THE PASTURE*' (8-line poem in italics); p. viii: blank; p. ix: contents; p. x: '*Mending Wall* takes up the theme where | *A Tuft of Flowers* in *A Boy's Will* | laid it down.'; pp. 11–135: text; p. 136: blank; p. 137: '*GOOD HOURS*' (16-line poem in italics); p. 138: blank.

Illustrations: Frontispiece portrait of Robert Frost facing the title-page (p. iv) and fourteen illustrations on coated paper, each with a heavy smooth protective tissue, inserted facing pp. 11, 20, 24, 32, 46, 54, 56, 66, 76, 90, 102, 114, 128, 136. Each is signed in the plate by the artist, James Chapin.

Text Content: As in the first American edition.

Paper: Heavy white laid linen-rag paper, watermarked 'BRITISH HAND MADE' in a belted oval; above is an anvil on a stump, a hammer raised over it.

Endpapers of the same stock. Leaves measure 216 × 147 mm.; top edge trimmed, other edges uncut.

Binding: Dark green (151.d.gyG) paper-covered boards; shelfback of darker green (152.blackish G) cloth. On the front cover is a label of gold Chinese paper measuring 84 × 42 mm., lettered in black, 'NORTH | · OF · | BOSTON | : : : BY | ROBERT | FROST'. The spine lettered in gilt, '|| NORTH | OF | BOS-TON | · · · | ROBERT | FROST || HENRY HOLT | AND COMPANY'. Back cover blank.

Dust Jacket: Dark green (151) heavy paper (as the binding). Front cover lettered in gold, '[within a gold frame rule] NORTH | OF | BOSTON | BY | ROBERT | FROST | PICTURES BY | JAMES | CHAPIN | HENRY HOLT AND | COMPANY—NEW YORK'. Spine lettered in gold, '|| NORTH | OF | BOS-TON | · · · | ROBERT | FROST || HENRY HOLT | AND COMPANY'. Back cover and inner flaps blank.

Publication: Five hundred copies of this edition were printed. Though the book is undated, the publisher's records give 1919 as the year of issue.

Barrett Copies:
592730. Inscribed on the front open endpaper recto, 'To R. V. Thornton / from / Robert Frost / Chicago / December 4 1953'.
592731. Inscribed on the front open endpaper recto, '[The first three lines of 'Mending Wall'] Robert Frost / For Remsen Bird / September 27 1932 / And now to Earle Bernheimer / May 9 1942 / And now to R V Thornton / Dec 4 1953 by R. F in Chicago'. Inscribed on the half-title (p. i), 'This book I prize as one of my chief / possessions — because of my great / affection for Martha Foster Abbot who / gave it to me — because of the poems / so full of the richness and reality / of New England the land of my fathers / and because the beloved author wrote / in it the three lines which are the / most important to me — I give this book, though wanting to keep / it, to my new friend Earle / Bernheimer, overcome with / the greater desire that he should / add it to his collection — I / give it as we plan with Louis / Mertins and Benjamin Steeter / the coming of Robert Frost / to California —— / Remsen Bird / Feb — 16 — 1942'. Remsen Bird was president of Occidental College in Los Angeles.
Uncatalogued. The Lawrance Thompson copy. The frontispiece portrait signed by RF; inscribed on the front flyleaf by the artist, James Chapin.

A4   1916 MOUNTAIN INTERVAL (First Edition)

MOUNTAIN INTERVAL | BY | ROBERT FROST | Author of "North of Boston" | [Holt device] | NEW YORK | HENRY HOLT AND COM-PANY

FIRST STATE

Collation: [1–6]⁸ [7]⁴; pp. [i–ii], [1–6] 7–8 [9–10] 11–99 [100–102] = 52 leaves.

Contents: pp. i–ii: blank; p. 1: half-title 'MOUNTAIN INTERVAL'; p. 2: '*By* ROBERT FROST | "An authentic original voice in literature."|—*The Atlantic Monthly* | NORTH OF BOSTON | Cloth, $1.25 net; limp leather, $2.00 net | HENRY HOLT AND COMPANY | Publishers   New York'; p. 3: title-page; p. 4: 'COPYRIGHT, 1916, | BY | HENRY HOLT AND COMPANY | [short rule] | Published November, 1916 | THE QUINN & BODEN CO. PRESS | RAHWAY, N.J.'; p. 5: dedication, 'TO YOU | WHO LEAST NEED RE-MINDING | [6-line dedicatory text]'; p. 6; blank; pp. 7–8: contents; p. 9: '*THE ROAD NOT TAKEN*' (20-line poem in italics); p. 10: blank; pp. 11–98: text; p. 99: 'THE SOUND OF THE TREES' (25-line poem in italics); pp. 100–102: blank.

Text Content:

The Road Not Taken	The Hill Wife
Christmas Trees	I. Loneliness—Her Word
An Old Man's Winter Night	II. House Fear
A Patch of Old Snow	III. The Smile—Her Word
In the Home Stretch	IV. The Oft-Repeated Dream
The Telephone	V. The Impulse
Meeting and Passing	The Bonfire
Hyla Brook	A Girl's Garden
The Oven Bird	The Exposed Nest
Bond and Free	'Out, Out—'
Birches	Brown's Descent or the Willy-Nilly Slide
Pea Brush	The Gum-Gatherer
Putting in the Seed	The Line-Gang
A Time to Talk	The Vanishing Red
The Cow in Apple Time	Snow
An Encounter	The Sound of Trees
Range-Finding	

States: On p. 88 (in the sixth gathering), the sixth and seventh lines of the poem both read 'You're further under in the snow—that's all—'. This was corrected to 'Sounds further off, it's not because it's dying; | You're further under in the snow —that's all—'. On p. 93 (in the same gathering), line 6 from the bottom reads ' "When I told her 'Come,' "'; corrected in the second state to ' "When I told her 'Gone,' "'.

It should also be noted that three distinct weights of paper are found in the six Barrett copies of the first state and one of the second state examined. No pattern in the use of light, medium, and heavy paper for various gatherings can be discovered, and it would seem that the different weights of paper have been used arbitrarily. However, the American editions of *A Boy's Will* and *North of Boston* are printed on the same manufacture of paper as *Mountain Interval* and reveal no such variation in paper weight, being uniformly on medium weight paper. The discrepancies in copies of *Mountain Interval* are noted below in the *Barrett Copies* section.

Paper: Rough wove white paper. Leaves measure 192 × 134 mm.; top edge trimmed, other edges uncut. Endpapers of smooth wove cream paper.

Binding: Dark blue (187.d.gyB) fine linen cloth lettered and decorated in gilt. Front cover: '[within a thick-thin rule frame] MOUNTAIN INTERVAL | [acorn orn.] | ROBERT FROST'. Spine: '[thick-thin rule] | MOUN-|TAIN | INTER-|VAL | [acorn orn.] | ROBERT | FROST | [thick-thin rule] | HENRY HOLT | AND COMPANY'. Back cover blank.

Dust Jacket: Rough gray wove paper printed overall in black. Front cover: 'MOUNTAIN | INTERVAL | By | ROBERT FROST | *Author of "North of Boston" and "A Boy's Will"* | $1.25 net | [22-line blurb]'. Spine: 'MOUN-|TAIN | INTER-|VAL | ROBERT | FROST | $1.25 | net | [Holt device]'. Back cover: ' "An Authentic Original Voice in Literature." – *The Atlantic | Monthly.* | ROBERT FROST | The New American Poet | NORTH OF BOSTON | [4 statements and excerpts from reviews by Alice Brown, *New York Evening Sun, Boston Transcript, Brooklyn Daily Eagle*] | A BOY'S WILL Mr. Frost's First Volume of Poetry | [excerpt from a review in *The Academy* (London)] | [price list] || [Holt imprint]'. Inner flaps are lacking from the dust jacket in the Barrett collection.

Barrett Copies:

592700. On medium paper with gathering 4 on heavy paper. Inscribed on the front open endpaper recto, 'Otto the Great friend / from / R. F.' Otto Manthey-Zorn was professor of German at Amherst and a neighbor of the Frosts'.

592696. On medium paper with gathering 5 on light paper. On the front open endpaper recto is a fair copy of 'Fragmentary Blue,' signed 'Robert Frost / Arlington 1919'. This poem did not appear in print until July 1920 in *Harper's Magazine*. It was later printed in *New Hampshire* (1923). There is no textual variation between this and the printed versions save for the absence of four commas in this holograph version. At front is a bookplate with the name Gilchrist. According to a statement of Frost, Mrs. Gilchrist was president of the Poetry Society of Vermont. Her pencil notes occur throughout the volume, showing an intimate knowledge of Frost's work and his character. On p. 99, above the poem 'The Sound of the Trees,' she has written 'Written at Lascelles Abercrombie's house, The Gallows, Dimmock, England.' Page 88, line 6 has been corrected in Frost's hand.

592697. On medium paper with gathering 3 on heavy paper. Inscribed on the front open endpaper recto, 'Wilbur E. Rowell / from / Robert Frost / with sincere regards'. Pages 88 and 93 corrected in Frost's hand. Wilbur E. Rowell was an attorney and executor of Frost's paternal grandfather's estate.

592695. On medium paper with gatherings 5 and 6 on light paper. Inscribed on the blank flyleaf recto, 'To Waller Barrett / from his friend / Robert Frost / Cambridge / January 7 1951'.

592698. On medium paper with gatherings 3, 4, and 7 on heavy paper. Inscribed on the front open endpaper recto, 'For Richard Cabot / with our love and grati-tude / Robert Frost / Carol Frost'. Pages 88 and 93 corrected in Frost's hand in pencil.

592701. On medium paper with gatherings 2 and 7 on heavy paper. Inscribed on the front open endpaper recto, 'Leona / from / Robert & Elinor'. In dust jacket. Pages 88 and 93 corrected in Frost's hand.

Uncatalogued. The Lawrance Thompson copy. On medium paper with gather-ings 2, 3, and 5 on heavy paper. Inscribed on the front open endpaper recto with lines 5–12 of 'Pea Brush,' but with the title 'A Spring Day in a New Clearing'. Signed beneath, 'Robert Frost / To Lawrence Thompson'. The poem is printed on p. 41 of the book.

SECOND STATE

Collation: $[1-5]^8$ $[6]^8$ ($\pm 6_5, 6_8$) $[7]^4$; pp. [i–ii], [1–6] 7–8 [9–10] '11–99 [100–102]: 52 leaves.

Note: Leaves 6_5 and 6_8 are both cancellans; 6_5 is tipped on a stub, 6_8 pasted at the inner margin to leaf 7_1. On leaf 6_5 verso (p. 88) the sixth line is corrected to 'Sounds further off, it's not because it's dying;'. On leaf 6_8 recto, 'Come,' in line 6 from the bottom is corrected to 'Gone,'.

Contents, Text Content, Paper, and *Binding*: as in the first state.

Publication: Four thousand copies were published November 1916. This number includes both first and second states. An alleged third state with the corrected leaves integral in the sixth gathering has not been located.

Barrett Copy:

592695. On medium paper with gathering 2 on heavy paper. The cancellans leaves are also of heavy paper. Inscribed on the front open endpaper recto, 'When there was no more lantern in the kitchen / The fire got out through crannies in the stove / And danced in yellow wrigglers on the ceiling / Robert Frost /To Russell Alberts'. These are lines 201–3 of 'In the Home Stretch,' first printed in *Century Magazine* (July 1916) and included in *Mountain Interval*.

A4.1   1921 MOUNTAIN INTERVAL (Second Edition)

MOUNTAIN   INTERVAL | BY | ROBERT   FROST | [Holt   device] | NEW YORK | HENRY HOLT AND COMPANY | 1921

Collation: $[1-5]^8$; pp. [1–8] 9–75 [76–80] = 40 leaves.

Contents: p. 1: half-title, 'MOUNTAIN INTERVAL'; p. 2: '[within a single rule frame] *By* ROBERT FROST || "An authentic original voice in litera-|ture."

—*The Atlantic Monthly* | NORTH OF BOSTON | A BOY'S WILL | MOUN-
TAIN INTERVAL | || HENRY HOLT AND COMPANY | Publishers   New
York'; p. 3: title-page; p. 4: 'Copyright, 1916, 1921 | BY | HENRY HOLT AND
COMPANY'; p. 5: dedication, 'TO YOU | WHO LEAST NEED REMIND-
ING | [6-line dedicatory text]'; p. 6: blank; pp. 7–8: contents; p. 9: '*THE ROAD
NOT TAKEN* | [20-line poem in italics]'; p. 10: blank; pp. 11–75: text; p. 76:
blank; p. 77: publisher's advt., 'SOME RECENT POETRY | [works of 12 poets
listed] || THE HOME BOOK OF VERSE | [6 lines of description] || [Holt im-
print]'; pp. 78–80: blank.

Illustration: Photographic portrait on white coated paper of a plaster bust of Frost
within a thick-thin rule frame inserted facing the title-page. Lettered beneath the
portrait, '*Copyright, Henry Holt and Company* | ROBERT FROST | From the
original in plaster | by AROLDO DU CHÊNE'.
    Note: Clymer & Green state that there was also a 1921 edition of identical for-
mat, but without the frontispiece.

Text Content: As in the first edition.

Paper: Heavy wove cream paper measuring 227 × 146 mm. Top edge trimmed,
other edges uncut. Endpapers of smooth wove white paper.

Binding: Gray green (151.d.gyG) paper-covered boards; dark olive green (128.d.
gyOlG) fine linen shelfback. Front cover stamped in gilt, 'MOUNTAIN IN-
TERVAL | ROBERT FROST'. Spine stamped in gilt, '[thick-thin rule]
| MOUNTAIN | INTERVAL | ROBERT | FROST | HENRY   HOLT | AND
COMPANY | [thin-thick rule]'. Back cover blank.

Barrett Copy:
592702. With the frontispiece.

A5   1923 SELECTED POEMS (First Edition)

SELECTED   POEMS | BY | ROBERT   FROST | [Holt   device] | NEW
YORK | HENRY HOLT AND COMPANY | 1923

Collation: [A–D]⁸ E⁸ [F–I]⁸ [K]⁴; pp. [i–viii] ix–x, [1–2] 3–143 [144–146] = 78
leaves.
    Note: The fifth gathering only is signed with an alphabetical designation. The
other gatherings, unsigned, have therefore been given alphabetical rather than
numerical identification to maintain collational consistency.

Contents: p. i: half-title, '[at the upper right corner] SELECTED POEMS'; p.
ii: '[within a single rule frame] *By* ROBERT FROST || "An authentic original
voice in liter-|ature."—*The Atlantic Monthly* | NORTH OF BOSTON | A
BOY'S WILL | MOUNTAIN INTERVAL || HENRY HOLT AND COM-

PANY | Publishers New York'; p. iii: title-page; p. iv: 'COPYRIGHT, 1923, | BY | HENRY HOLT AND COMPANY | *March, 1923* | PRINTED IN THE U.S.A.'; p. v: dedication, 'TO | HELEN THOMAS | IN MEMORY OF ED- WARD THOMAS'; p. vi: blank; p. vii: 'PUBLISHERS' NOTE | *The poems included in this volume are | reprinted from "Mountain Interval," "North of Bos- ton," and "A Boy's Will."* '; p. viii: blank; pp. ix–x: contents; p. 1: section-title, 'I'; p. 2: blank; pp. 3–143: text; pp. 144–146: blank. Section-titles with blank versos at pp. 5, 45, 51, 71, 101, 111, 137. Those at pp. 51, 71, and 101 have printed pagination; all other have implied pagination.

Text Content:

The Pasture	In the Home Stretch
The Cow in Apple-Time	The Road Not Taken
The Runaway	The Oven Bird
An Old Man's Winter Night	A Vantage Point
Home Burial	The Sound of Trees
The Death of the Hired Man	Hyla Brook
A Servant to Servants	My November Guest
The Self-Seeker	Range-Finding
The Hill Wife	October
'Out, Out . . .'	To the Thawing Wind
Putting in the Seed	A Time to Talk
Going for Water	The Code
Mowing	A Hundred Collars
After Apple-Picking	Blueberries
Birches	Brown's Descent
The Gum-Gatherer	Revelation
The Mountain	Storm-Fear
The Tuft of Flowers	Bond and Free
Mending Wall	Flower-Gathering
An Encounter	Reluctance
The Wood-Pile	Into My Own
Snow	

The only new poem, collected here for the first time, is 'The Runaway.' It was printed first in the *Amherst Monthly* (June 1918); later in *New Hampshire*.

Paper: White laid paper with vertical chainlines 24 mm. apart, unwatermarked. Leaves measure 194 × 128 mm.; top edge trimmed and stained dull green, other edges uncut. Smooth cream wove endpapers. One Barrett copy has the top edge unstained.

Binding: Dark green (147.v.d.G) paper-covered boards. The paper is impressed with a pebbled pattern, and both covers are decorated with a recurring wreath design stamped in gilt. Backed with very dark green (152.blackish G) fine linen cloth lettered on the spine in gilt, 'SELECTED | POEMS | [Holt device] | FROST | HENRY HOLT | AND COMPANY'.

Dust Jacket: Gray-green (150.gyG) heavy wove paper printed in green (146.d.G). Front cover: '[within a decorative border rule frame consisting of a bar and three circles in a continuing pattern] SELECTED POEMS | ROBERT FROST | [Holt device in lower right corner]'. Spine: 'SELECTED | POEMS | FROST | HENRY HOLT | & COMPANY'. Back cover blank. Front inner flap: 'By | ROBERT FROST | [listings for *Mountain Interval, North of Boston, A Boy's Will*, followed by a list of six titles by Walter de la Mare] | HENRY HOLT AND COMPANY'. Back inner flap: '[orn. rule] | A | SHROPSHIRE | LAD | by | A. E. HOUSMAN | *AUTHORIZED EDITION* | $1.50 | [7-line blurb] | HENRY HOLT AND COMPANY'.

Publication: One thousand twenty-five copies were printed and the book was published 15 March 1923.

Barrett Copies:
592612. Top edge stained green.
592611. Top edge unstained. Signed on the front open endpaper recto, 'Robert Frost / June 1924'.

A5.1   1923 SELECTED POEMS (First English Edition)

SELECTED POEMS | BY | ROBERT FROST | [Heinemann device] | LONDON: WILLIAM HEINEMANN LTD. | NEW YORK: HENRY HOLT AND COMPANY

Collation: [A]⁸ B–I⁸; pp. [i–viii] ix–x, [1–2] 3–132 [133–134] = 72 leaves.

Contents: p. i: half-title, 'SELECTED POEMS' (at the upper left corner); p. ii: blank; p. iii: title-page; p. iv: '*First published*, 1923. | Printed in Great Britain'; p. v: dedication, 'TO | HELEN THOMAS | IN MEMORY OF | EDWARD THOMAS'; p. vi: blank; p. vii: 'PUBLISHERS' NOTE | *The poems included in this volume are | reprinted from "Mountain Interval," | "North of Boston," and "A Boy's Will."* '; p. viii: blank; pp. ix–x: contents; p. 1: 'I' (section division); p. 2: blank; pp. 3–133: text; on p. 133, '*Printed in Great Britain by | Billing and Sons, Ltd., Guildford and Esher*'; p. 134: blank. Section divisions with printed Roman numerals I–VIII are at pp. 1, 5, 41, 47, 65, 93, 103, and 127; versos blank.

Text Content: As in the first American edition.

Paper: Rough white wove paper; endpapers of a lighter, smoother white stock. Leaves measure 188 × 126 mm.; top edge trimmed, other edges uncut.

Binding: Dark gray-blue (187.d.gyB) fine linen cloth. Covers blank. The spine has a white paper label measuring 22 × 41 mm., lettered in red-orange (35.s.rO), '[orn. rule comprising three winged cherub heads] | Selected | Poems | Robert | Frost | Heinemann'.

Dust Jacket: Light gray-blue (190.l.bGy) linen paper, lettered overall in dark gray-blue (186.gyB). Front cover: '[within a multiple border rule frame comprising a thick-thin rule frame enclosed in a thin-thick-thin rule frame] *Selected Poems by* | ROBERT FROST'. Spine: 'Selected | Poems | by | Robert | Frost | 6s. | NET | [Heinemann device] | Heinemann'. Back cover: '[within a thin-thick-thin frame] *'New & Recent Poetry* | [advt. of 13 lines in italics for works by Robert Graves, John Masefield, Dorothy Wellesley, Muriel Stuart, Isaac Rosenberg, Iolo Williams, and an anthology of Italian poetry selected by Mme. Lorna de Lucchi] | *Heinemann'*. Front inner flap: 9-line blurb on Frost. Back inner flap: 12-line Heinemann advertisement in italics (imprint beneath) within a single-rule frame.

Barrett Copy:
592613. In dust jacket.

A6   1923 NEW HAMPSHIRE (First Edition)

NEW HAMPSHIRE | A POEM WITH NOTES | AND GRACE NOTES BY | ROBERT FROST | WITH WOODCUTS | BY J. J. LANKES | PUBLISHED BY | HENRY HOLT | & COMPANY: NEW | YORK; MCMXXIII [title in facsimile hand-lettered capitals]

Collation: [1–8]^8; pp. [i–viii] ix–x, [1–2] 3–113 [114–118] = 64 leaves.

Contents: p. i: blank; p. ii: '*By* ROBERT FROST || A BOY'S WILL | NORTH OF BOSTON | MOUNTAIN INTERVAL | SELECTED POEMS | NEW HAMPSHIRE ||; p. iii: woodcut vignette of a tree in the lower right corner; p. iv: frontis. woodcut; p. v: title-page; p. vi: 'COPYRIGHT, 1923 | BY | HENRY HOLT AND COMPANY | *Printed October, 1923* | PRINTED IN | THE UNITED STATES OF AMERICA'; p. vii: dedication, '*To* | VERMONT AND MICHIGAN'; p. viii: blank; pp. ix–x: contents; p. 1: half-title, 'NEW HAMPSHIRE'; p. 2: blank; pp. 3–16: text of 'New Hampshire'; p. 17: woodcut vignette of tree in the lower right corner; p. 18: woodcut illus. of pine trees under stars; p. 19: 'NOTES' (section-title); p. 20: blank; pp. 21–75: text of 'Notes' section; p. 76: woodcut illus. of country path; p. 77: 'GRACE | NOTES' (section-title); p. 78: blank; pp. 79–113: text of 'Grace Notes' section; p. 114: woodcut vignette of grindstone beneath a tree from which hangs a scythe; pp. 115–116: blank.

Illustrations: Four woodcuts by J. J. Lankes printed on leaves integral with the text as described above; vignette woodcuts.

Text Content:

New Hampshire
A Star in a Stone-Boat
The Census-Taker
The Star-Splitter
Maple
The Axe-Helve
The Grindstone
Paul's Wife
Wild Grapes
Place for a Third
Two Witches
   I The Witch of Coös
   II The Pauper Witch of
     Grafton
An Empty Threat
A Fountain, a Bottle, a
   Donkey's Ears and Some
   Books
I Will Sing You One-O
Fragmentary Blue
Fire and Ice
In a Disused Graveyard
Dust of Snow
To E. T.
Nothing Gold Can Stay
The Runaway
The Aim Was Song

Stopping by Woods on a
   Snowy Evening
For Once, Then, Something
Blue-Butterfly Day
The Onset
To Earthward
Good-Bye and Keep Cold
Two Look at Two
Not to Keep
A Brook in the City
The Kitchen Chimney
Looking for a Sunset Bird
   in Winter
A Boundless Moment
Evening in a Sugar Orchard
Gathering Leaves
The Valley's Singing Day
Misgiving
A Hillside Thaw
Plowmen
On a Tree Fallen Across the
   Road
Our Singing Strength
The Lockless Door
The Need of Being Versed in
   Country Things

Paper: Rough white wove paper; endpapers of mottled tan wove paper treated for the mottled effect on one side only. The front open endpaper verso and terminal open endpaper recto are plain cream through which the mottling can be seen. Leaves measure 219 × 141 mm.; top edge trimmed and stained a very light green (122.gyYG), other edges uncut.

Binding: Dark gray-green (151.d.gyG) paper-covered boards, backed with dark green (147.v.d.G) linen cloth. A gold paper label measuring 88 × 46 mm. mounted on the front cover, lettered in black, 'NEW : . | HAMPSHIRE | : : : BY | ROBERT FROST | [orn. vignette of a tree]'. Spine lettered in gilt, 'NEW | HAMPS | HIRE | [leaf orn.] | ROBERT | FROST | [Holt device]'. The 'S' in the second line is a long 'swash' letter that extends diagonally from top right of the second line to bottom left of the third line, preceding 'HIRE'. Back cover blank.

Dust Jacket: Very pale green (121.p.YG) coated paper, lettered and decorated in dark green (138.v.d.yG). Front cover: 'NEW HAMPSHIRE | [woodcut country scene of road, house, tree, and mountain] | ROBERT FROST'. Spine: 'NEW |

HAMPS|HIRE | [leaf orn.] | ROBERT | FROST | $2.50 | [Holt device] | Henry Holt | and | Company'. Back cover blank. Front inner flap: '*By* Robert Frost | NEW HAMPSHIRE || A POEM | With Notes and Grace Notes | *With Wood Engravings* | *by J. J. Lankes* || [27-line blurb, followed by the price, $2.50, and Holt imprint]'. Back inner flap: '*By* ROBERT FROST || [5 titles, followed by the Holt imprint]'.

Publication: Though the date of the first printing is given on the copyright page as October 1923, the publisher's records state that the first edition was published on 15 November 1923 in an edition of 5,350 copies. The second printing was January 1924; the third, May 1924; the fourth, November 1924.

Barrett Copies:

592712. In dust jacket. Inscribed on the front open endpaper recto, 'Robert Frost / Amherst December 1923 / Robert Frost / Chicago December 1953 / Now for Roy Virgil Thornton'.

592709. Inscribed on the front open endpaper recto with a fair copy of 'Nothing Gold Can Stay' (which appears on p. 84), signed 'Robert Frost / For Russell Alberts / October 18 / 1943'.

592711. Inscribed on the front open endpaper recto, 'For Leona [Mrs. Frost's sister, Leona White Harvey] from Robert / and Elinor'.

592710. Second printing. In dust jacket. Inscribed on the front open endpaper recto, 'Robert Frost / Amherst June 1924' and, on p. iii, 'For S. V. Smith / the best wishes of his classmate / Robert Frost'.

592708. Fourth printing. With the bookplate of Hugh Walpole. Inscribed on p. i with a fair copy of 'Atmosphere: Inscription for a Garden Wall' (published in *West-Running Brook,* 1928), signed 'Robert Frost / For Hugh Walpole. / South Shaftsbury Vermont U.S.A.'

Uncatalogued. The Lawrance Thompson copy, inscribed on the front open endpaper recto with a fair copy of 'The Aim Was Song' (p. 86); signed beneath, 'Robert Frost / For Lawrence [*sic*] Thompson'.

LIMITED EDITION

Note: The collation, contents, and text content of the limited edition are as in the trade edition, but with the addition of an inserted leaf preceding p. iii. This is the limitation leaf with blank recto. Verso: 'Of this edition, Three Hundred and | Fifty copies only have been printed. | This copy is Number [supplied in ink] | [in RF's hand] Robert Frost'.

Paper: Heavy cream laid paper without watermark. Chainlines measure 31 mm. apart. Endpapers of heavier light-tan wove paper showing a heavy line in the weave. Leaves measure 227 × 153 mm. Top edge trimmed and gilt, fore-edge uncut, bottom edge rough-cut.

Binding: Black buckram with beveled edges. Lettering and decoration stamped in gilt. Front cover: 'NEW HAMPSHIRE | [vignette duplicating the final woodcut on p. 114 of a grindstone beneath a tree]'. Spine: NEW | HAMPS ['swash'

S extending diagonally from top right to bottom left of following line] | HIRE |
[leaf orn.] | ROBERT | FROST | [Holt device]'. Back cover blank. In a white
paper-covered board box (the paper is patterned with a grosgrain design) with a
cream paper label measuring 113 × 75 mm., lettered in black, '[within a thick-
thin rule frame] NEW : . | HAMPSHIRE | : : : BY | ROBERT FROST | [vi-
gnette of a tree] | *Limited Edition* | *Autographed*'.

Barrett Copies:

592706. Inscribed on p. iii with the final 4 lines of 'Stopping by Woods on a
Snowy Evening' (printed on p. 87) and signed 'Robert Frost / For Crosby Gaige'.
455605.
592707. Inscribed on the front open endpaper recto, 'To Russell Alberts / from
his friend / Robert Frost'.

A6.1   1924 NEW HAMPSHIRE (First English Edition)

NEW HAMPSHIRE | A POEM | WITH NOTES | AND . : | GRACE
NOTES | : . BY | ROBERT FROST | • • | [orn. of a tree] | • | LONDON |
GRANT RICHARDS LTD | ST MARTINS STREET | 1 9 2 4

Note: The collation, contents, and text content of the English edition are as in
the first edition, but the title-leaf is a cancel, having the title as given above and,
on the verso, 'PRINTED IN | THE UNITED STATES OF AMERICA'.

Paper: Paper and measurements as in the first edition. Top edge trimmed and
stained dull brown (64.brGy), other edges uncut.

Binding: Light gray (112.1.OlGy) paper-covered boards. Shelfback of light tan
(between 92.yW and 93.yGy) rough linen cloth. Covers blank. Spine lettered in
dark blue (175.v.d.gB), 'New | Hamp-|shire | Robert | Frost | Grant | Richards'.

Dust Jacket: Light yellow brown (76.l.yBr) paper impressed with a 'linen' pat-
tern, lettered overall in black. Front cover: 'NEW HAMPSHIRE | a poem with
notes and grace notes | by ROBERT FROST | with woodcuts by | J. J.
LANKES'. Spine: NEW | HAMP-|SHIRE | By | ROBERT | FROST | 6/– | net |
GRANT | RICHARDS'. Back cover blank. Front inner flap: publisher's adver-
tisement within a single rule frame for seven titles by Sturge Moore. Back inner
flap: publisher's advertisement for poetry (21 titles).

Publication: This edition consists of 150 sets of sheets of the original printing
bound up with the cancel title-leaf of Grant Richards, Ltd., London.

Barrett Copies:

592714. On the front open endpaper recto, in Frost's hand, 'See page 6 – R. F.'
On p. 6, beneath the text, Frost has written, 'Nother / footnote. / My difficulty
arises from his being / a cross between New Hampshire / Yankee and Pennsylvania Dutch and / between farmer and professor. R. F.' This note refers to the

14th line on p. 6 which is marked with 'x': 'And she has one I don't know what to call him, . . .'.
592713. In dust jacket.

A6.2   1955 NEW HAMPSHIRE (First Separate Edition)

[red-brown: J. J. Lankes woodcut of a tree with grindstone beneath] | [black] NEW HAMPSHIRE | A Poem by Robert Frost | HANOVER · NEW HAMPSHIRE | The New Dresden Press, 1955 | [red-brown: press device]

Collation: [1]⁸ [2]⁶; pp. [i–vi], [1–2] 3–19 [20–22] = 14 leaves.

Contents: pp. i–ii: blank; p. iii: 'THIS FIRST SEPARATE EDITION OF | ROBERT FROST's POEM NEW HAMPSHIRE | IS LIMITED TO 750 NUMBERED COPIES | SIGNED BY THE AUTHOR | [in holograph] Robert Frost | Copy number: [number supplied by hand]'; p. iv: blank; p. v: title-page; p. vi: 'From NEW HAMPSHIRE by Robert Frost | Copyright, 1923, by Henry Holt and Company, Inc. | Copyright, 1951, by Robert Frost. | Reprinted by permission of the publishers.'; p. 1: half-title, 'NEW HAMPSHIRE'; p. 2: blank; p. 3: first page of text with title printed in red-brown, 'NEW HAMPSHIRE'; pp. 4–19: remainder of text; pp. 20–22: blank.

Paper: White wove paper watermarked 'Arches'. Leaves measure 191 × 133 mm. Top edge trimmed, other edges uncut. Endpapers of the same stock.

Binding: Gray-brown (63.l.brGy) paper-covered boards, backed with tan crushed linen; the two sections delineated by a thick gilt rule at the juncture. Covers blank. The spine has a gray-brown paper label lettered in gilt vertically from bottom to top, 'FROST · NEW HAMPSHIRE'. The book has a protective jacket of semitransparent rough white Japanese paper.

Publication: A prospectus (see below) of the volume gives the following information: 'The present volume, the initial publication of The New Dresden Press, has been printed at The Stinehour Press of Lunenburg, Vermont, using Bulmer type and all rag, mould-made Arches paper, and hand bound in boards by Paul and Cooper in Hanover. The wood engraving of the title page is by J. J. Lankes and originally appeared in a smaller size as the tailpiece of the book *New Hampshire*. The edition is limited to seven hundred and fifty numbered copies, each signed by Mr. Frost. Copies are available at five dollars each.'

Barrett Copy:
592715. Number 110, signed by Frost.

Prospectus: A single four-leaf gathering on *Arches* paper, p. 1 reproducing the title-page of the book (verso blank), four pages of text. In gray-brown (63) wrappers of the same paper as that used on the book covers, lettered in red-brown and white on the front cover, '[red-brown] A PROSPECTUS | [white] for the first separate edition | of a poem by Robert Frost and the | initial publication of a new private press | [at lower right in red: press device, a typographic flower]'. Stitched with white thread at the center fold. Leaves measure 190 × 132 mm.

Barrett Copies:
592716, 593103, 598138 (with original order form laid in).

A7   1924 AN OLD MAN'S WINTER NIGHT (First Separate Edition)

[on a 50 mm. fold-over] Housewarming | at the | Fireside of | The | Hampshire | Bookshop | The | Fifteenth of | February | Nineteen Hundred | and | Twenty-Four | [decorative rule] | Northampton | Massachusetts

A single leaf of tan laid paper with vertical chainlines 27 mm. apart, watermarked 'U S A'. The left edge of the leaf is folded over to make a flap of 50 mm., printed on the recto as above. The leaf measurement after the fold is 244 × 172 mm.; edges trimmed (the fore-edge of the fold flap is rough-cut). The poem is printed on the recto of the full leaf, with title in caps and text in italics, signed in print beneath, '—Robert Frost'. At the foot of the leaf, *'One hundred and seventy-five copies printed by permission of Henry Holt and Company'*. Verso blank.

Publication: Printed first in *Mountain Interval* (1916). This printing for the Hampshire Bookshop of 175 copies on 15 February 1924.

Barrett Copy:
Uncatalogued.

A8   1924 SEVERAL SHORT POEMS (Only edition in this format)

[text title taken from p. 1] SEVERAL | SHORT POEMS | *By* | ROBERT FROST | [woodcut signed *'Woodcut By J.J. Lankes'* (also used as tailpiece for the limited edition of *New Hampshire,* 1923)] | THE PASTURE | [8-line poem text] | *Copyright by Henry Holt and Company* [1924]

Collation: [1]²; pp. [1–4]: 2 leaves.

Contents: p. 1: as given above; p. 2: text of two poems, 'Stopping by Woods on a Snowy Evening' and 'The Oven Bird'; p. 3: text of 'An Old Man's Winter Night' (beneath, a woodcut vignette of a tree); p. 4: text of two poems, 'The Runaway' and 'Nothing Gold Can Stay'; beneath, '[short rule] | Books by ROBERT

FROST | A BOY'S WILL NORTH O' [*sic*] BOSTON SELECTED POEMS | NEW HAMPSHIRE MOUNTAIN INTERVAL'.

Text Content: As given in the *Contents* section.

Paper: Heavy rough handmade laid paper with horizontal chainlines 32–35 mm. apart. Unwatermarked. Leaves measure 232 × 150 mm.; uncut.

Binding: Unbound.

Publication: Two thousand copies were printed in February 1924. They were intended for distribution at lectures by Robert Frost at East Coast colleges.

Barrett Copies:
592768. Inscribed on p. 1, 'Waller from Robert / 1951'.
592767. Signed on p. 1 beneath the text of 'The Pasture,' 'Robert Frost'. Inscribed beneath, 'For Vera the Collector.' Vera Harvey was Frost's niece by marriage; the daughter of Mrs. Frost's sister, Leona White Harvey.

A9   1928 SELECTED POEMS (First Edition [of expanded selection])

SELECTED | POEMS | BY | ROBERT   FROST | [Holt   device] | NEW YORK | HENRY HOLT AND COMPANY

Collation: [1–14]⁸; pp. [i–viii] ix–x, [1–2] 3–213 [214] = 112 leaves.

Contents: p. i: half-title, 'SELECTED POEMS'; p. ii: '[within a single rule frame] *By* ROBERT FROST || NORTH OF BOSTON | A BOY'S WILL | MOUNTAIN   INTERVAL | NEW   HAMPSHIRE | WEST-RUNNING BROOK || HENRY HOLT AND COMPANY | ONE PARK AVENUE NEW YORK'; p. iii: title-page; p. iv: 'COPYRIGHT, 1928, | BY | HENRY HOLT AND COMPANY | *First printing* | PRINTED IN THE | UNITED STATES OF AMERICA'; p. v: dedication, '*To* | HELEN THOMAS | IN MEMORY OF | EDWARD THOMAS'; p. vi: blank; p. vii: 'The poems included in this volume are reprinted from "A Boy's Will," "North of Boston," "Mountain Interval," and "New Hampshire." '; p. viii: blank; pp. ix–x: contents; p. 1: 'I' (section division); p. 2: blank; pp. 3–213: text; p. 214: blank. Section divisions with printed Roman numerals I–IX are at pp. 1, 7, 17, 67, 75, 111, 161, 173, and 205; versos blank.

Text Content:

The Pasture	Stopping by Woods on a
The Cow in Apple-Time	Snowy Evening
The Runaway	Fire and Ice
To Earthward	Fragmentary Blue
Nothing Gold Can Stay	Dust of Snow

An Old Man's Winter Night	In the Home Stretch
Home Burial	The Black Cottage
The Death of the Hired Man	The Axe-Helve
A Servant to Servants	The Road Not Taken
The Self-Seeker	The Oven Bird
The Hill Wife	A Vantage Point
"Out, Out—"	The Sound of the Trees
Putting in the Seed	Hyla Brook
Going for Water	My November Guest
Mowing	The Onset
The Need of Being Versed	Range-Finding
in Country Things	October
Two Look at Two	To the Thawing Wind
After Apple-Picking	A Time to Talk
Birches	The Code
The Gum-Gatherer	A Hundred Collars
The Mountain	Blueberries
The Tuft of Flowers	Brown's Descent
Mending Wall	Revelation
Good-Bye and Keep Cold	Storm-Fear
The Grindstone	Bond and Free
An Encounter	Flower-Gathering
A Hillside Thaw	Reluctance
The Wood-Pile	Into My Own
Snow	

Paper: Rough wove cream paper; endpapers of heavier, smooth wove cream paper. Leaves measure 216 × 136 mm.; edges trimmed, top edge stained green (137.d.yG).

Binding: Light gray (264.l.Gray and 265.med.Gray, in a pattern simulating laid paper) paper-covered boards. Green (145.m.G) cloth backstrip. Front cover: '[at the lower right corner, a facsimile signature stamped in gilt] Robert Frost'. Spine stamped in gilt: '[orn. rule] SELECTED | POEMS | [leaf orn.] FROST | [orn. rule] | HENRY HOLT | AND COMPANY'. Back cover blank.

Dust Jacket: Pale green (paler than 143.v.l.G) coated paper, lettered and decorated in dark green (146.d.G). Front cover: 'SELECTED POEMS | BY | ROBERT FROST | [photograph of Frost] | *Photo by Doris Ullman* | HENRY HOLT AND COMPANY | ONE PARK AVENUE NEW YORK'. Spine: 'SELECTED | POEMS | BY | ROBERT | FROST | [Holt device] | Henry Holt | and Company.' Back cover: '[within a triple rule frame; the outer rule made up of dots] MODERN POETS AND POETRY | [list of books by Frost, A. E. Housman, Carl Sandburg, Walter de la Mare, Scudder Middleton, Lew Sarett, Glen Ward Dresbach, E. V. Lucas, and Burton E. Stevenson; Holt imprint beneath]'. Front inner flap: '[within a triple rule frame, the outer rule of dots] 'SELECTED POEMS | 1928 Edition | *by* ROBERT FROST | [17-line blurb followed by the Holt device and imprint]'. Back inner flap: '[within the same triple rule] WEST-RUNNING BROOK | *by* ROBERT FROST | [32-line blurb followed by Holt device and imprint]'.

Publication: The book was published 19 November 1928 in an edition of 3,475 copies.

Barrett Copies:
592614. In dust jacket. Inscribed on the front open endpaper recto, a fair copy of 'The Secret Sits' in RF's hand; beneath, 'Robert Frost / To Russell Alberts / Cambridge October 18 1943'. The poem was printed first in *Poetry* (April 1936) as 'Ring Around' and later in *A Witness Tree* (1942).
592615.

A10   1928 WEST-RUNNING BROOK (First Edition)

WEST-RUNNING | BROOK | BY | ROBERT FROST | [Holt device] | NEW YORK | HENRY HOLT AND COMPANY

FIRST STATE (presumed)

Collation: [1–4]⁸ [5]⁴; pp. [i–vi] vii–viii, [1–4] 5–64 = 36 leaves.

Contents: p. i: half-title, 'WEST-RUNNING BROOK'; p. ii: woodcut frontispiece signed 'L' [J. J. Lankes]; p. iii: title-page; p. iv: '*Copyright, 1928, | by | Henry Holt and Company | Printed in the United States of America | The Plimpton Press, Norwood, Mass.*'; p. v: dedication, 'To E[linor]. M[iriam]. F[rost].'; p. vi: blank; pp. vii–viii: contents; pp. 1–64: text.
Sections with section-titles at:
page 1: 'I | SPRING POOLS | *From snow that melted only yesterday*'. Verso blank
   1': 'II | FIAT NOX | *Let the night be too dark for me to see | Into the future. Let what will be be.*' Verso blank
   33: 'III | WEST-RUNNING BROOK'. Verso blank
   39: 'IV | SAND DUNES'. Verso blank
   49: 'V | OVER BACK'. Verso blank
   55: 'VI | MY NATIVE SIMILE | "The sevenfold sophie of Minerve." ' Verso blank

Illustrations: Woodcut illustrations on leaves integral with the text at pp. 3, 19, 41. Versos blank.

Text Content:

Spring Pools

The Freedom of the Moon

The Rose Family

Fireflies in the Garden

Atmosphere—Inscription for a

   Garden Wall

Devotion

On Going Unnoticed

The Cocoon

A Passing Glimpse

   To Ridgley Torrence

A Peck of Gold

Acceptance

Once by the Pacific

Lodged

A Minor Bird

Bereft

Tree at My Window

The Peaceful Shepherd

The Thatch

A Winter Eden

The Flood

Acquainted with the Night

West-running Brook

Sand Dunes

Canis Major

A Soldier

Immigrants

Hannibal

The Flower Boat

The Times Table

The Investment

The Last Mowing

The Birthplace

The Door in the Dark

Dust in the Eyes

Sitting by a Bush in Broad

   Sunlight

The Armful

Riders

On Looking up by Chance at

   the Constellations

The Bear

Paper: Rough laid paper with vertical chainlines 30 mm. apart, watermarked 'De Coverly Rag Laid'. Endpapers of mottled tan wove paper, treated for the mottled effect on inner side only. Leaves measure 217 × 142 mm. Top edge trimmed and stained light green (135.l.yG); other edges rough-cut.

Binding: Dark gray-green (151.d.gy.G) paper-covered boards, backed with dark green (147.v.d.G) linen cloth. A gold paper label measuring 84 × 55 mm. set in a panel stamped on the cover. On it is printed in black a reduced version of the frontispiece woodcut. Spine stamped in gilt and lettered perpendicularly from bottom to top, '+ WEST-RUNNING BROOK + ROBERT FROST +'. Back cover blank.

Dust Jacket: Light gray (264.l.Gy) wove paper (patterned like laid paper), lettered in dark green (108.d.Ol) and decorated in deep red (41.dp.rBr). Front cover: '[two thick double red rules] | WEST-RUNNING | BROOK | [red outline of a five-pointed star] | ROBERT | FROST | [two thick double red rules]'. Spine: '[lettered perpendicularly from bottom to top between red rules extending from the front cover] WEST-RUNNING BROOK·ROBERT FROST'. Back cover: '[red rules as on front cover] A POET'S SUMMARY | OF WEST-RUNNING BROOK | [8-line quote from Joseph Auslander in the *Forum*] | [4-line notice of the de luxe edition] | OTHER WORKS BY ROBERT FROST | [5 titles] | [Holt device and imprint]'. Front inner flap: '[red rules as on front cover] |

1 A *vita* prepared by William Prescott Frost, Jr., n.p., 24 June 1872

2 'Evensong.' Unpublished poem, *ca.* 1891, in Frost's early hand

TWILIGHT

Why am I first in thy so sad regard,
O twilight gazing from I know not
  where?
I fear myself as one more than I guessed!—
Am I instead of one so very fair?—
That thou art sorrowful and I oppressed?

High in the isolating air,
Over the inattentive moon,
Two birds sail on great wings,
  And vanish soon.

(And they leave the north sky bare!)

The far-felt solitudes that harbor night,
Wake to the singing of the wood-bird's
  fright.

By invocation, O wide silentness,
Thy spirit and my spirit pass in air!
They are unmemoried consciousness,
  Nor great nor less!
And thou art here and I am everywhere!

3 *Twilight* (1894) and the Lawrence High School graduation program for 1892, containing 'Class Hymn' by Frost

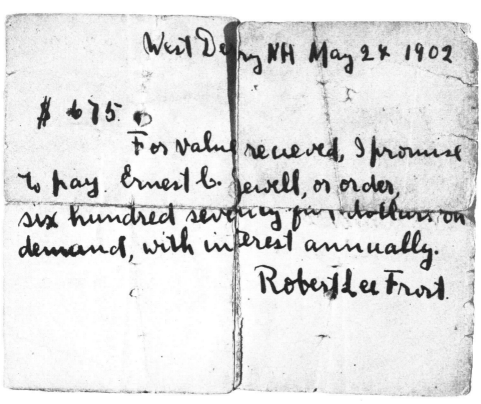

West Derry NH May 24 1902

$ 675.

For value received, I promise to pay. Ernest C. Jewell, or order, six hundred seventy-five dollars on demand, with interest annually.

Robert Lee Frost.

4 Promissory note. West Derry, N.H., 24 May 1902

Old Stick-In-The-Mud.

Irma went wagging her dress out into the big pasture And one of the fence posts away down in the low ground saw her and asked her what she was after.

Checkerberries!

Are you sure it isnt cranberries. I know where there are some of those, or were last fall.

No checkerberries!

Well I guess I can direct you to some of those. Just ahead of you.

I dont see any.

Not there; to your right to your right. Oh no no no no. Here you come here and hold this wire and I'll go and find some for you.

So Irma went and unbuttoned the wires barbed wires from him – there were three of them and he showed her how she would have to hold them to keep them just the right distance apart so that the cow couldnt get out one in her

mouth and one in each hand. She had to take a very awkward position and the wire in her mouth made it hard for her to talk.

The fence post pulled himself out of his hole and set off. He didnt seem to know as well where the checkerberries were as he thought he did, for he went zig-zagging here and there brushing the grass with his feet without finding any. once stooping to pick any. Finally he came back to Irma and said:–

I just thought what would I pick berries into if I happened to find berries.

If you happened to find berries Irma sputtered on account of the wire in her mouth. I thought you said you knew where the berries were. Pick them into your hands. But hurry up. I cant keep these wires spaced right much longer.

But I havent any hands. Perhaps I'd better go up to the house for a can.

If you do! Irma sputtered. I'll just drop everything and let the fence fall.

Dont do that. The cow will get out.

I will!— now!

5   Robert Frost's notebook. Derry, N.H., *ca.* 1906

ROBERT BRIDGES

FLYCATCHERS

SWEET pretty fledgelings, perched on the rail a row,
Expectantly happy, where ye can watch below?
Your parents a-hunting i' the meadow grasses—O
All the gay morning to feed you with flies;

Ye recall me a time sixty summers ago,
When, a young chubby chap, I sat just so,
With others on a school-form rank'd in a row,
Not less eager and hungry than you, I trow,
With intelligences agape and eyes aglow,
While an authoritative old
Stood over us and from a desk fed us with flies.

Dead flies—such as litter the library south-window,
That buzzed at the panes until they fell stiff-baked on the sill
Or are roll'd up asleep i' the blinds at sunrise,
Or wafer'd flat in a shrunken folio.

A dry biped he was, nurtured likewise
On skins and skeletons, stale from top to toe
With all manner of rubbish and all manner of lies.

THOMAS HARDY

"MY SPIRIT WILL NOT HAUNT THE MOUND"

MY spirit will not haunt the mound
    Wherein I rest,
But travel, memory-possessed,
To where my tremulous being found
    Life largest, best.

395

7 *Poetry and Drama*, I, no. 4 (Dec. 1913), 395. Frost's notes in the margins of poems by Robert Bridges and Thomas Hardy

A BOY'S WILL

INTO MY OWN

One of my wishes is that those dark trees,
So old and firm they scarcely show the breeze,
Were not, as 'twere, the merest mask of gloom,
But stretched away unto the edge of doom.

I should not be withheld but that some day
Into their vastness I should steal away,
Fearless of ever finding open land,
Or highway where the slow wheel pours the sand.

I do not see why I should e'er turn back,
Or those should not set forth upon my track
To overtake me, who should miss me here
And long to know if still I held them dear.

They would not find me changed from him them
    knew—
Only more sure of all I thought was true.

B

6 *A Boy's Will* (1913). Galley proofs with Frost's corrections

In an Art-factory.

A room like studio, badly lighted through large dim windows by a street lamp that throws a ripple pattern on the walls. Kettle is visible with water (hot thrown?) around the walls. A doorframe after the rattling of a key figure in a row. A doorsperum after the rattling of keys in thelock and Tony enters from a dark staircase leading placed by the hand. He throws down a match he burned out and lights another.

Stand. there you are till I find the gas. There is jet here — or was the last I knew. (He brings out another match searching the wall before he finds it.)

(As the gas leaps into a rising flare thereupon) Oh that won't do.

No that no improvement. Thecafe gone. Its flame is warm and twisight (He puts the gas to low twist)

She cold Tony

Shut the door then.

I'm afraid it's — and shut it. it's cool it's warm outside than in. (She shuts it)

It should be said that this play was written many years ago and has been kept ever for publication and possible promotion then when I wholly have done the as the then I intended for comparison. I have read it a few times aloud. Two or three references to public events and personages I remember date if approximately I remember reading it to few and crowds that may or when others now. It is easy to see what I have been contemptuous of all along. I moved the theme the ridiculing cut — for objectivity I suppose. I moved [borrowed] out of my works were and about and peace in Fogg's Partridge Taft Dutchess Chopin etc.

R.F.   Ripton June 22 1959

This is the only copy in my hand. May Morrison has a copy but is now copying.

Ripton Vermont USA
August 30 1948

Dear Lesley: There's an American Novel, there's American Poetry and
there's me R.F. That is according to you. And don't think I'm not
touched and impressed by these words so often repeated. If your
regard for me. I don't see how you can ever be even with me when
you really admire me as much. You have a special claim on
me. and my poetry; you typed at the age of twelve some of my
earliest manuscript going into a book. and you have come a long way
on it ever since in bookstores and editorial offices and from
the platform. You came along at just the right age to grow up
in satisfaction out of my strange career. Not everybody in the family
had the same luck. I can be very very sad for the little good
to and and Irma got out of knowing my children. Marjorie was
in the way of profiting by being an artist and child of an artist. But
she married by death. You alone are left to share my life with you
plenum in what I do and your participation in it. I stay the
same ecstasy in my belief in your ability and my patience
with you in your deliberate self preservation. You may be
... that I'm mad or at my regular letter keeper ...

... very. They delude us
tell me there's kind very something they. We found of out from
tempered under laughter. Affectionately
R.F.

THE SECRET SITS

We dance round in a ring and suppose,
But the Secret sits in the middle and knows.

The Secret of Poetry

1 Poetry is a prowess like athletics.

2 Poetry is the renewal of words so that
the language may never wear out.

3 Poetry is the dawning of an idea. It
gets its freshness from having been
caught just as it came over you.

4 Poetry is that which evaporates from
both prose and verse when translated.

5 Poetry is the Liberal Arts. The Liberal
Arts are poetry.

Each one of them turned out to be
the subject of a whole talk at a college
this spring. 1953

[495]

10 *Complete Poems* (1949), p. 495. 'The Secret of Poetry,' 13 holograph lines

FROST– | THE FULL MAN | [26-line quote from Jessie B. Rittenhouse in *Braithwaite's Anthology of Magazine Verse for 1926*] | [red rules as on front cover]'. Back inner flap: '[red rules as on front cover] | SOME DEFINITIONS | BY ROBERT FROST | [28 lines] | [red rules as on front cover]'.

Note: A later dust jacket is on one of the first edition copies in the Barrett collection. This jacket differs in the following ways: Plain gray (264–65) wove paper without the simulated chainlines. The red rules are on the front cover and spine only. The star on the front cover is 6-pointed and solid, rather than 5-pointed in red outline. Back cover: '[within a thick green rule frame] *Poetry by* ROBERT FROST | [swelling green rule] | [7 titles, including *Collected Poems,* not published until 1930, and the 1934 editions of *A Boy's Will* and *Selected Poems*] | [swelling green rule] | [Holt imprint]'. Front inner flap: $2.50 | SELECTED POEMS | THIRD EDITION | *by* | ROBERT FROST | [swelling green rule] | [15-line blurb] | [Holt imprint]'. Back inner flap: 'A BOY'S WILL | *by* | ROBERT FROST | [swelling green rule] | [13-line blurb] | $1.75 | [Holt imprint]'. This jacket was apparently incorrectly supplied to a copy of the first edition from a copy of a later imprint.

SECOND STATE (presumed)

Note: With the words, 'First Edition' on the copyright page; otherwise identical with the first state.

Publication: Clymer & Green (p. 43) state: 'The publishers of this book report that 9,400 copies . . . were printed, but it is generally believed that of these only 1,000 copies contained the words "First Edition" on the verso of the title-page.' If this assumption of proportion is correct, it seems more likely that copies without 'First Edition' were printed first and the oversight remedied only after the greater part of the edition had been distributed. The book was published on 19 November 1928 and sold for $2.50.

Barrett Copies:

592807. First state in dust jacket. On the front open endpaper recto, Frost has written a fair copy (no textual variation) of 'The Gift Outright.' It is signed and inscribed 'To Cornelius Weygand's / Disciple Russell Alberts / October 1943'.

592808. First state in dust jacket. Inscribed on the front open endpaper recto, 'For Lillian Rowell / from her friend / Robert Frost / 1929'. Lillian Rowell was the wife of the attorney Wilbur E. Rowell.

592809. First state in dust jacket. On the front open endpaper recto, Frost has written a fair copy (with no textual variation) of 'A Peck of Gold,' which appears in this book on p. 14. He has headed it 'Page Fourteen'. It is signed and further inscribed 'Another Californian recollection written / into this book for Mr. Thornton when I / visited him in Chicago on my way home / from reading it at Berkeley and Palo / Alto in 1953.'

592811. First state in later dust jacket. On the contents page (p. vii), Frost has added to the page number 5 for the first poem, 'Spring Pools,' in ink, '4 and' to indicate a fair copy of the poem he has written on p. 4 opposite the printed poem. No textual variation.

592806. Second state in the earlier dust jacket. Inscribed by Frost on the front open endpaper recto, 'For Vera— / These flowery waters and these watery flowers / from / her uncle Robert'. The quotation is from the second to last line of the first poem, 'Spring Pools' (p. 5).

453783. Second state.

592810. Second state.

A10.1   1928 WEST-RUNNING BROOK (Second Edition, Limited)

WEST-RUNNING | BROOK | BY | ROBERT   FROST | [device   of   a Greek coin with an owl and the greek letters AΘE] | NEW YORK | HENRY HOLT AND COMPANY

Collation: $[1]^4(1_1 + X_1)$ $[2-4]^4$ $[5-6]^8$ $[7]^4$; pp. $[\pi i-iv]$, $[i-iv]$ vii–viii, $[1-2]$ 3–58 $[59-62]$ = 37 leaves.
    Note: X_1 is the limitation leaf inserted with the stub following 1_3.

Contents: pp. πi–ii: blank; p. πiii: inserted limitation, '*One thousand copies of West-running Brook | have been specially printed and bound, and | have been signed by the Author. Of these, | nine hundred and eighty copies are for sale. | This copy is Number* [holograph] | Robert Frost [signature in holograph]'; p. πiv: blank; p. i: half-title, 'WEST-RUNNING BROOK'; p. ii: blank; p. iii: title-page; p. iv: '*Copyright, 1928, by Henry Holt and Company | Printed in the United States of America | D. B. Updike, The Merrymount Press, Boston*'; p. v: dedication, 'To E. M. F.'; p. vi: blank; pp. vii–viii: contents; pp. 1–58: text; pp. 59–62: blank. Section-titles with blank versos, as in the first edition, at pp. 1–2, 15–16, 29–30, 35–36, 43–44, and 49–50; unpaged, but included in the consecutive pagination.

Illustrations: Frontispiece and three woodcut illustrations printed on the same paper, but inserted or tipped in and not included in the pagination. Each is signed in pencil by the artist, J. J. Lankes. Each with a protective tissue.
Frontis.: tipped in following 1_2 (pp. i–ii)
Plate 1: inserted following 4_3 (pp. 19–20); stub following 4_1 (pp. 15–16)
Plate 2: inserted preceding 6_1 (pp. 39–40); stub following 6_8 (pp. 53–54)
Plate 3: tipped on the stub of plate 2 following 6_8 (pp. 53–54)

Text Content: As in the first edition.

Paper: Heavy white laid paper watermarked 'CRANE'S OLDE BOOK'. Vertical chainlines measuring 41 mm. apart. Endpapers of the same stock. Leaves measure 227 × 152 mm.; top edge trimmed and gilt, other edges uncut.

Binding: Decorative paper-covered boards impressed with a pattern of maple leaves in light brown (60.l.gyBr), red orange (38.d.rO) green (150.gyG), and yellow (87.m.Y), delineated in dark brown on a ground of gray (154.l.gGy). Backed with dark olive green (126.d.OlG) fine linen cloth. Covers unlettered. Spine lettered in gilt, from bottom to top, '[orn.] WEST-RUNNING BROOK : ROBERT FROST [orn.]' In a gray-green (150.gyG) paper-covered box with paper label on the spine measuring 55 × 18 mm., lettered in black, '[decorative rule] | West-|running | Brook | [orn.] | Robert | Frost | [decorative rule]'.

Publication: Though printed in the same year as the first edition by the same publisher, this edition is in an entirely different setting and format with different pagination.

Barrett Copies:
592804. On the front open endpaper recto, Frost has written a fair copy (untitled) of 'A Minor Bird' which is printed on p. 19 of the book. Signed and inscribed 'For Crosby Gaige'.
592805. On the front open endpaper recto, inscribed 'To R. V. Thornton / from / Robert Frost / with best wishes'.

A11   1929 A WAY OUT (First Separate Edition)

A Way Out | A ONE ACT PLAY | *by* | ROBERT FROST || [orn. in red brown] || *New York* | THE HARBOR PRESS | 1929

Collation: [1]⁶ [2–4]⁴; pp. [i–xiv], [1] 2–19 [20–22] = 18 leaves.

Contents: pp. i–iv: blank; p. v: half-title, 'A Way Out || [orn. appended to rule]'; p. vi: blank; p. vii: title-page; p. viii: 'COPYRIGHT 1917 BY ROBERT FROST | COPYRIGHT 1929 BY ROBERT FROST | *Applications for permission to perform this play should be addressed to* | *the author, South Shaftsbury, Vermont*'; p. ix: dedication, 'TO | ROLAND A. WOOD | WHO CREATED THE PART OF ASIE | ACADEMY OF MUSIC | NORTHAMPTON, MASS. | FEBRUARY 24, 1919 | [small outlined star]'; p. x: blank; pp. xi–xii: introduction, signed by Frost in holograph on p. xii; p. xiii: second half-title, 'A Way Out'; p. xiv: blank; pp. 1–19: text; p. 20: blank; p. 21: colophon, '*Four hundred and eighty-five copies printed* | *at the Harbor Press of which this is* | No. [number supplied in ink] | [seahorse orn.]'; p. 22: blank.

Paper: Rough white laid paper with vertical chainlines 25 mm. apart, watermarked 'MARLOWE'. Endpapers of the same stock. Leaves measure 196 × 119 mm.; edges uncut.

Binding: Pale orange (53.m.O) paper-covered boards. Backed with fine black linen cloth with double rickrack lines stamped in gilt on the cloth portions of the

front and back covers. Covers blank. The spine lettered in gilt, from bottom to top perpendicularly, 'A Way Out *by* Robert Frost'.
Publication: Frost's play *A Way Out* was first printed in the *Seven Arts*, 1, no. 4 (Feb. 1917), and reprinted in Helen Louise Cohen's *More One-Act Plays by Modern Authors* (New York: Harcourt, Brace and Co. [1927]). This separate edition was published on 29 May 1929. The book was sold for $7.50.

Barrett Copies:
592798. A review copy, unbound. Signed by Frost on p. xii, with 'Review Copy' written in place of the copy number on p. 21. Laid in is a prospectus with the title-page reproduced on the recto of the first of two integral leaves.
592799. Signed on the title-page, 'Robert Frost / to / Waller Barrett'.
592800. Inscribed on the front pastedown endpaper, 'In Libra / R. V. Thornton / per Robert Frost', beneath the bookplate of David B. Owens.
Uncatalogued. The Lawrance Thompson copy, inscribed on the front open endpaper recto, 'To Larry / from Robert / Boston 1941'.

A12   1929 THE LOVELY SHALL BE CHOOSERS (First Edition)

[within a border rule consisting of decorative horizontal rules at top and bottom; double vertical rules] THE | LOVELY SHALL | BE | CHOOSERS | [orn.] | *BY ROBERT FROST* | [Random House device] | *RANDOM HOUSE* | New York | 1929

Collation: [1]⁴; pp. [1–8] = 4 leaves.

Contents: pp. 1–2: blank; p. 3: title-page; pp. 4–5: text of poem; p. 6: colophon, 'The Poetry Quartos | *475 copies for Random House, printed in Silvermine Conn. U.S.A.* | [orn.] [P. J.] [orn.] | *Copyright, 1929, by Robert Frost*'; pp. 7–8: blank.
    Note: Initials 'P. J.' on the colophon are those of Paul Johnston who designed and printed *The Poetry Quartos*.

Paper: White laid paper with vertical chainlines 38 mm. apart. Watermarked with initials 'R H' within a decorative frame rule. Leaves measure 252 × 158 mm.; bottom edge uncut, other edges trimmed.

Binding: Brown-orange (54.brO) wrappers of heavy laid paper with vertical chainlines 37 mm. apart. Watermarked with a small eagle over a hand; beneath in diagonal script, 'Handcraft'. The leaves are stitched at the center fold with white thread. Front cover: 'THE LOVELY | SHALL BE CHOOSERS || *BY ROB-ERT FROST* || [drawing in black and orange by Paul Johnston] || *THE PO-ETRY QUARTOS* | Random House, New York, 1929'. Back cover blank.
    This pamphlet is enclosed with eleven others in a yellow (86.l.Y) fold-over wrapper of heavy laid paper with vertical chainlines 25 mm. apart and watermarked 'FABRIANO (ITALY).' All lettering in black. Front flap: 'THE POETRY

QUARTOS || *Twelve brochures, each containing a new poem by* | *an American poet; designed, printed, and made by* | Paul Johnston *and published by* Random House || CHECK LIST || MONOLOGUE FOR MOTHERS, *by Genevieve Taggard* | THE LOVELY SHALL BE CHOOSERS, *by Robert Frost* | RIGA-MAROLE, RIGAMAROLE, *by Vachel Lindsay* | THE PRODIGAL SON, *by Edwin Arlington Robinson* | ADIRONDACK CYCLE, *by Louis Untermeyer* | BODY AND STONE, *by Alfred Kreymborg* | RED ROSES FOR BRONZE, *by "H. D."* | BIRTHDAY SONNET, *by Elinor Wylie* | THE ASPIRANT, *by Theodore Dreiser* | SAGACITY, by *William Rose Benét* | PRELUDE, *by Conrad Aiken* | ROOTS, *by Witter Bynner* | The drawings on the covers and design of box cover are | by Paul Johnston || 475 copies printed in Silvermine, Connecticut, U.S.A. | Published in May, 1929'. Back cover: '|| [Random House device] ||'. Spine: '[three stars] ||| The | Poetry | Quartos | [star] | RANDOM | HOUSE | 1929 ||| [three stars]'. The twelve wrapper-enclosed pamphlets are contained in a black paper-covered box with an overall design in light olive-green (106.l.Ol). No lettering.

Publication: Designed by Paul Johnston and published in May 1929 in an edition of 475 copies by Random House. The pamphlets were sold only as a set for $10.00 the set.

Barrett Copies:
592681. The Frost pamphlet is signed on the title-page, 'Robert Frost / to / Earle Bernheimer'.

A13   1929 THE COW'S IN THE CORN (First Separate Edition)

THE COW'S IN THE CORN | *A ONE-ACT IRISH PLAY* | *IN RHYME* | *BY* | ROBERT FROST | [shamrock orn. printed in green] | THE SLIDE MOUNTAIN PRESS | *GAYLORDSVILLE* | *MCMXXIX*

Collation: [1–4]⁴; pp. [1–32] = 16 leaves.

Contents: pp. 1–2: blank pastedown endpaper; pp. 3–6: blank flyleaves; p. 7: half-title, 'THE COW'S IN THE CORN' (beneath, Frost's holograph signature); p. 8: blank; p. 9: title-page; p. 10: 'Copyright 1929 by James Raye Wells | *Printed in the U.S.A.*'; p. 11: dedication, 'To | *James and Hilda Wells*'; p. 12: blank; p. 13: '*Stage and amateur rights for this play* | *are owned and controlled by the author.* | *No public performance or reading may* | *be given without his written consent.* | *All rights reserved, including that of* | *translations into foreign languages in-* | *cluding that of the Scandinavians, the* | *Agerbaijans and the Kara-futoanei.*'; p. 14: blank; p. 15: 8-line introduction, signed in print '*R. F.*'; p. 16: blank; p. 17: 'Characters in the Play | *Mrs. O'Toole* | *Mr. O'Toole*' (an errata slip is tipped in: '*Erratum: throughout 2nd page of* | *play in O'Toole read* ' *for,*'); p. 18: blank; pp. 19–21: text; p. 22: blank; p. 23: colophon, '*The second book published by* | THE SLIDE MOUNTAIN PRESS | *Ninety-one copies printed and | bound by James & Hilda Wells | Each signed by the author | Number* [number in ink]'; p. 24–30: blank; pp. 31–32: blank terminal pastedown endpaper.

Paper: White laid paper with horizontal chainlines 27 mm. apart. The watermark '(FRANCE)' appears on one leaf only. Another watermark or countermark, because of its position at the extreme upper right corner of the leaves, cannot be made out. Endpapers (integral leaves of the first and final gatherings) are of the same stock. Leaves measure 160 × 118 mm.; edges uncut.

Binding: Decorative paper-covered flexible boards. The paper has a pattern of squares and circles in red-orange (34.v.rO), blue (179.dp.B), and yellow (84.s.Y) on a white ground. Covers blank. A white paper label on the spine lettered in black from bottom to top, *'Frost—The Cow's in the Corn'*.

Publication: Lawrance Thompson's *Selected Letters* contains a note (pp. 346–47) and three letters to James R. Wells (nos. 268, 277, and 279) that tell something of the publication of this play. The note explains that Wells, 'an attractive playboy, with money enough to engage in fine press printing,' 'established the Slide Mountain Press and talked RF into signing a flexible contract. The following letter [no. 268] reveals the various phases of their jockeying for position. In the end RF won; he permitted Wells to print and publish a limited edition of a "One-Act Irish Play" written by RF and called *The Cow's in the Corn.*' Wells sent Frost a check for $61.42 in October 1929 for his part in the publication, but Frost returned it and requested ten copies of the book instead. In September he had written to Wells, 'send the really beautifully written printed and bound books along for me to sign and so earn a maximum royalty on the retail published price' (no. 277). The play was first printed in the *Dearborn Independent,* 18 June 1927. See F9.12 for variant reading of the text contained in a letter to Lesley Frost, 5 Nov. 1918.

Barrett Copies:
592623. Beneath his signature on the half-title, RF has added 'to / William Manthey-Zorn / November 21 1936 // Now-transferred to / kindlier keeping in / the hands of Earle Bernheimer / R. F.' William Manthey-Zorn was the son of RF's friend and neighbor in Amherst, Otto Manthey-Zorn.

A14   1930 COLLECTED POEMS (Limited Edition)

ROBERT FROST | COLLECTED | POEMS | NEW YORK | RANDOM HOUSE | 1930

Collation: [1]⁴ [2–23]⁸ [24]⁴; pp. [i–viii], [1–4] 5–349 [350–360] = 184 leaves.

Contents: pp. i–ii: blank; p. iii: half-title, 'COLLECTED POEMS | [in Frost's hand] Robert Frost'; p. iv: blank; p. v: title-page; p. vi: 'Copyright 1930 by Henry

Holt and Company, Inc. | Manufactured in the United States of America'; p. vii:
'COLLECTED POEMS | A BOY'S WILL | NORTH OF BOSTON | MOUN-
TAIN INTERVAL | NEW HAMPSHIRE | WEST-RUNNING BROOK'; p.
viii: blank; p. 1: *'The Pasture'* (8-line poem); p. 2: blank; p. 3: section-title, 'A
BOY'S WILL'; p. 4: blank; pp. 5–349: text; p. 350: blank; p. 351: 'TABLE OF
CONTENTS'; pp. 352–357: contents; p. 358: '[Random House device] | The
edition of this book is limited to | one thousand numbered copies | Printed at
The Spiral Press·New York | for Random House | Completed in September
1930 | This copy is number | [number in ink]. Section-titles with blank versos at
pp. 45 ('NORTH OF BOSTON'), 129 ('MOUNTAIN INTERVAL'), 197
('NEW HAMPSHIRE'), and 301 ('WEST-RUNNING BROOK').

Text Content: In this collection two poems are printed for the first time, 'The
Last Word of a Bluebird' (listed with the poems from *Mountain Interval*) and
'What Fifty Said' (listed with the poems from *West-Running Brook*). Three
poems have been dropped from *A Boy's Will*: 'Asking for Roses,' 'In Equal
Sacrifice,' and 'Spoils of the Dead.' A new poem, 'In Hardwood Groves' (printed
first in the *Dearborn Independent,* 18 Dec. 1926, as 'The Same Leaves'), has been
added to the poems from *A Boy's Will.* 'Locked Out' (printed first in *The Forge,*
Feb. 1917) has been added to *Mountain Interval;* and two poems, 'The Lovely
Shall Be Choosers' (printed first in *The Poetry Quartos,* 1929) and 'The Egg and
the Machine' (printed first in *The Second American Caravan,* New York, 1928,
as 'The Walker'), have been added to the poems from *West-Running Brook*. All
poems in the first editions of *North of Boston* and *New Hampshire* are included.
'The Pasture,' which was first printed as introductory to *North of Boston,* is not
listed in the table of contents but appears here as introductory to the entire volume.

Paper: White laid paper with vertical chainlines 28 mm. apart. Watermarked,
'HOLLAND' and with the Spiral Press triskelion device. Leaves measure 237 ×
155 mm.; top edge trimmed and gilt, other edges uncut. Endpapers of the same
stock, but with chainlines running horizontally.

Binding: Light tan heavy linen cloth, beveled edges. Front and back covers blank.
A brown leather label on the spine, 49 × 31 mm., lettered in gilt within a gilt
rule frame, 'ROBERT | FROST | [orn.] | COLLECTED | POEMS'.

Publication: The 1,000 copies of the limited edition were published four weeks in
advance of the trade edition, which was set from plates made from the limited
edition type, as was the English edition.

In 1966 Joseph Blumenthal supplied a commentary to a Pierpont Morgan Library exhibition catalogue, *The Spiral Press through Four Decades* (New York
1966), in which he wrote in detail about the printing of the 1930 *Collected Poems:*
'Early in 1929, when Random House was still active in the publication of press
books, they made arrangements with Frost's publisher, Henry Holt and Company, to prepare joint publication of the first collected edition of Frost's poems.
Random House would issue a signed, limited edition of one thousand copies and

the plates would then be turned over to Holt for their manufacturing printer to use in running the trade edition. . . . The manuscript consisted of previously printed pages with a few scattered corrections written in, plus a few hitherto un-published poems. There would be approximately 350 printed pages when com-pleted. I planned it for setting by hand in Lutetia type, then a recently issued face of great distinction by the eminent Dutch type designer, Jan van Krimpen. . . . Paper for the book was ordered from the Pannecook Mill in Holland with a Spiral watermark. It was a fine, tough, laid sheet, mouldmade. No ink we could find would lay adequately on that sheet without dampening, and dampening could not even be considered in machine printing. After weeks of experimenting with new inks made for us, we finally arrived at a satisfactory combination of tackiness, dullness, depth of black, and printability. We named it "Frost Black" and still use it. . . . The *Collected Poems* was finally ready for press, printed and bound. Only one error was ever found, to my knowledge. On page 128 "faces" became "laces" because a plate was damaged and the letter incorrectly replaced.'

Barrett Copies:

592549. Signed by Frost on p. iii.

592550. Signed by Frost on p. iii. Four lines of a poem not represented in the verse collected by Frost for publication. Inscribed and signed for Russell Alberts on the open endpaper recto, 'If those stars shining there by name / Are vast as men of science claim / All anyone like me can say / Is they must be as far away / As those same men of science claim / They shine with such a little ray'. These lines do not occur in any poem in RF's collected works; nor does a word check reveal their source in Edward Connery Lathem's *A Concordance to the Poetry of Robert Frost* (New York: Holt Information Systems, 1971).

A14.1   1930 COLLECTED POEMS (Trade Edition)

COLLECTED POEMS | OF ROBERT FROST | [red-brown vignette woodcut] | [black] NEW YORK | HENRY HOLT AND COMPANY

FIRST IMPRESSION FROM PLATES OF THE LIMITED EDITION TYPE

Collation: [1–22]⁸ [23]⁶; pp. [i–xii], [1–4] 5–349 [350–352] = 182 leaves.

Contents: pp. i–ii: blank; p. iii: title-page; p. iv: '*First Trade Edition* | Copyright 1930 by Henry Holt and Company, Inc. | Manufactured in the United States of America'; p. v: 'CONTENTS' section-title; pp. vi–xi: contents; p. xii: blank; p. 1: '*The Pasture*' (8-line poem); p. 2: blank; p. 3: section-title, 'A BOY'S WILL'; p. 4: blank; pp. 5–349: text; pp. 350–352: blank. Section-titles with blank versos at pp. 45, 129, 197, and 301.

Illustration: Photographic portrait of RF, signed 'Doris Ulmann,' is tipped in preceding the title-page. Facsimile signature, 'Robert Frost', beneath.

Text Content: As in the limited edition.

Paper: White wove paper watermarked 'WARREN'S | OLDE STYLE'. Leaves measure 218 × 146 mm. Top edge trimmed and stained red-brown, fore-edge uncut, bottom edge rough-cut. Endpapers of heavier white wove paper.

Binding: Light orange-brown (57.l.Br) medium linen cloth. Front cover stamped in gilt, '[within a thick-thin border rule] COLLECTED POEMS | OF ROBERT FROST'. Spine stamped in gilt, '[thick-thin rule] COLLECTED | POEMS | OF | ROBERT | FROST | [orn.] | HENRY HOLT | AND COMPANY | [thin-thick rule]'. Back cover blank.

Dust Jacket: Light yellow-brown (76.l.yBr) laid paper with vertical chainlines 21 mm. apart. Watermarked '[quasi-blackletter] Canterbury | [in a diamond-shaped rule] D | Laid'. Front cover: '[9 orange (51.dp.O) rules] | [brown (56.dp.Br)] ROBERT FROST | [10 orange rules] | [brown] COLLECTED | POEMS | [10 orange rules] | [Holt device in brown] | [brown] HENRY HOLT AND COMPANY | [10 orange rules]'. Spine: orange (51) rules carried over from front cover, lettering in brown (56), '[rules] | ROBERT | FROST | [rules] | COLLECTED | POEMS | [rules] | HENRY HOLT | AND COMPANY | [rules]'. Back cover: an advertisement for Holt publications, 'MODERN POETS AND POETRY | [titles of works by Frost, A. E. Housman, Carl Sandburg, Scudder Middleton, Lew Sarett, Glenn Ward Dresbach; verse anthologies edited by E. V. Lucas and Burton E. Stevenson] | [Holt imprint]'. Front inner flap lettered in brown, '$5.00 | COLLECTED POEMS | OF ROBERT FROST | [11-line blurb]'. Back inner flap lettered in brown, 'FROST — | THE FULL MAN | [25-line blurb from an article by Jessie B. Rittenhouse in *Braithwaite's Anthology of Magazine Verse for 1926*]'.

Publication: The trade edition was printed from plates made from the limited edition type and issued in an edition of 3,870 copies having a new title-page and with the contents removed from the back to the front.

Barrett Copies:

592551. Inscribed on the front open endpaper recto, 'To Vera from her Uncle R. F.'

592552. Inscribed on the front open endpaper recto to Russell Alberts, signed and dated November 1944, 'It may have been at two o'clock / That under me a point of rock / Developed in the grass and fern / And as I lay afraid to turn / Or so much as uncross my feet / Lest having wasted precious heat / I never should again be warmed, / The largest firedrop ever formed / From two stars having coalesced / Went streaking molten down the west.' These are lines 18–27 of 'An Unstamped Letter in Our Rural Letter Box,' first printed as the Christmas card for 1944. Variant reading, line 21: And as I woke afraid to turn] 1st ed.; And as I lay afraid to turn] MS.

Uncatalogued. The Lawrance Thompson copy, with biographical notes in Thompson's hand throughout the text.

Textual Note: The texts of certain poems as they appear in the *Collected Poems* differ from the original texts in the first editions of *A Boy's Will, North of Boston*,

Mountain Interval, New Hampshire, and *West-Running Brook.* For a full account of these changes, see Frederick B. Adams, Jr.'s article in the *Colophon,* NS2, no. 3 (Summer 1936), 470–77.

A14.2   1930 COLLECTED POEMS (First English Edition)

COLLECTED POEMS | OF ROBERT FROST | [red brown: J. J. Lankes' vignette, as in the American trade edition] | [black] LONGMANS, GREEN AND CO. | LONDON · NEW YORK · TORONTO | 1930

Collation: [1–22]⁸ [23]⁶; pp. [i–xii], [1–4] 5–349 [350–352] = 182 leaves.

Contents, Text Content: As in the American trade edition.

Illustration: The Doris Ulmann portrait preceding the title-page and faced with a protective tissue. Signed in facsimile, 'Robert Frost'.

Paper: White wove paper watermarked 'WARREN'S | OLDE STYLE'. Leaves measure 216 × 145 mm. Top edge trimmed and stained red-brown, fore-edge rough-cut, bottom edge trimmed. Endpapers of a heavier wove white paper.

Binding: Light brown (57.l.Br) linen cloth. Front and back cover blank. Spine stamped in gilt, 'COLLECTED | POEMS | OF | ROBERT | FROST | [orn.] | LONGMANS'.

Dust Jacket: White wove paper, internally marbled. Printed in brown overall. Front cover: '*Collected Poems of* | ROBERT FROST | [J. J. Lankes' vignette as on title page] | [2-line blurb from the *London Mercury*] | [2-line blurb from the *Spectator*]'. Spine: '||| *Collected* | *Poems   of* | ROBERT | FROST | [orn.] | [publisher's device] | *LONGMANS* |||'. Back cover (at bottom edge): '*Made in Great Britain*'. Front inner flap (at lower right corner): '15 / – | NET'. Back inner flap blank.

Publication: One thousand sets of the American sheets bound in England with a new title-page were published by Longmans, Green and Co.

Barrett Copy:
592553. In dust jacket.

A15   1931 TWO LETTERS FROM ROBERT FROST (First Edition)

ROBERT FROST | ˙·˙ | TWO LETTERS WRITTEN ON | HIS UN-DERGRADUATE DAYS | AT DARTMOUTH COLLEGE | IN 1892 | HANOVER | THE PRINTER'S DEVIL PRESS | 1931

Collation: [1]¹² ; pp. [1–24] = 12 leaves.

Contents: pp. 1–2: blank; p. 3: title-page; p. 4–6: blank; p. 7: 'NOTE | Acknowledgement is made to Mr. H. | G. Rugg, Assistant Librarian at Dart-|mouth College, for his kind permission | to print these letters.' pp. 8–10: blank; pp. 11–13: Letter I; p. 14: blank; pp. 15–16: Letter II; pp. 17–18: blank; p. 19: 'Ten copies of these letters have been | printed from hand-set type by | Frank B. Cornell in June. | [printer's device (circle enclosing a printer's devil holding the letters 'P' and 'D')] | Copy No. [number supplied in ink]'; pp. 20–24: blank.

Paper: White wove coated paper. Leaves measure 190 × 127 mm., edges trimmed.

Binding: Blackish green (151.d.gyG) heavy wove paper wrappers, patterned as with lighter gray green vertical chainlines. Stapled at the center fold. A white paper label measuring 47 × 65 mm. printed in black: '[within a thick-thin frame rule] TWO LETTERS | FROM | ROBERT FROST'.

Publication: The Printer's Devil Press was the first name of the press established in the Baker Library at Dartmouth in 1930. In 1932 it became The Arts Press, and in 1934, The Baker Library Press. As The Baker Library Press it printed *Three Poems* (1935; cf. A18). Letter I appears in its entirety as no. 112 (pp. 166–68) in Thompson's *Selected Letters*. Harold G. Rugg was Librarian of Dartmouth College.

Barrett Copies:

592788. Inscribed on blank p. 1, 'Again I see and sign these letters / and the confession of college inadequacy / they seem to make. / Robert Frost / Cambridge 1944 / For Russell Alberts / and now / for R. V. Thornton / Dec 4 1935'. Signed also on the title-page, 'Robert Frost'.

592677. A proof sheet of Letter I only. Single fold of two leaves. At the top of the first printed page, Frost has written, 'I never saw this before but remember / having written the letters. R. F.'

A16   1932 THE AUGUSTAN BOOKS OF POETRY (First Edition of this selection)

[cover-title] [within an elaborate decorative border] *THE AUGUSTAN BOOKS   OF | POETRY || ROBERT | FROST || LONDON: ERNEST BENN LTD. | BOUVERIE HOUSE, FLEET STREET*

Collation: [1]¹⁶; pp. [i–ii] iii–iv, 5–30 [31–32] = 16 leaves.

Contents: p. i: cover title; p. ii: advt., 'BENN'S | AUGUSTAN BOOKS OF POETRY | *New Titles for* 1932 | [12 titles]'; p. iii: biographical sketch in italics of Robert Frost; p. iv: contents; pp. 5–30: text; p. 31: 'BIBLIOGRAPHY | Col-lected Poems, 1930. *Longmans*, London. | Collected Poems, 1930. *Henry Holt*, New York City. | PRINTED IN GREAT BRITAIN BY | BILLING AND SONS LTD., GUILDFORD'; p. 32: advt., 'BENN'S | AUGUSTAN BOOKS OF POETRY | [109 listings]'.

Text Content:

The Runaway	The Road Not Taken
The Onset	My November Guest
Storm Fear	To Earthward
Stopping by Woods on a Snowy Evening	Reluctance
An Old Man's Winter Night	Nothing Gold Can Stay
Dust of Snow	Tree at My Window
The Need of Being Versed in Country Things	Acquainted with the Night
The Tuft of Flowers	Once by the Pacific
Mending Wall	The Peaceful Shepherd
Two Look at Two	A Soldier
Birches	Fireflies in the Garden
The Death of the Hired Man	Spring Pools

Paper: White wove paper measuring 219 × 134 mm.; edges trimmed. Stitched at the center fold.

Bindings:
Binding A: Self-wrapper with title-page as front cover.
Binding B: Dull red (43.m.rBr) simulated linen paper pasted over the original self-wrapper with a panel cut in the front cover exposing only 'ROBERT FROST' of the cover-title lettering.

Barrett Copies:
592570. Binding A.
590981. Binding B. Inscribed on the front cover, 'Robert Frost to Russell Alberts'.

A17   1933 THE LONE STRIKER (First Edition)

[cover title; lettering in red, decoration in black] THE LONE STRIKER | [drawing of a man standing on a hill, signed 'WAD' (W. A. Dwiggins), within a triple border rule] | *ROBERT FROST*

Collation: [1]⁴; pp. [1–8] = 4 leaves.

Contents: pp. 1–2: blank; pp. 3–5: text, subscribed in print on p. 5, 'ROBERT FROST | *South Shaftsbury, Vermont*.'; pp. 6–8: blank.

Paper: Cream laid paper with vertical chainlines 25 mm. apart. No visible watermark. Leaves measure 187 ×122 mm.; edges trimmed.

Binding: Light pink-tinted tan (33.brPk) laid paper with vertical chainlines 23 mm. apart. Watermarked '(AMERICA)'. The front cover is lettered and decorated as above. Back cover printed in black: 'NUMBER EIGHT of *THE BOR- ZOI CHAP BOOKS* | Published by Alfred A. Knopf, 730 Fifth Avenue, New |

York. Designs by W. A. Dwiggins. Printed at the | Plimpton Press.' The leaves are stitched at the center fold with white silk thread knotted at the spine. The preliminary and terminal blank leaves serve as underwrappers over which the flaps of the paper wrapper fold at the fore-edges. On the front inner wrapper, lettered from bottom to top, 'COPYRIGHT 1935, BY ROBERT FROST'. Enclosed in an envelope of the same paper.

Publication: Printed in an edition of 2,000 copies and sold for $.25 the copy.

Barrett Copy:
592679. Signed on p. 3, 'Robert Frost / 1940'. Original envelope.
Uncatalogued. The Lawrance Thompson copy, signed on p. 2, 'To Larry from R. F.' Original envelope.

A18   1935 THREE POEMS (First Edition)

[within a gray-blue (186.gyB) thick-thin rule frame] THREE POEMS | ROBERT   FROST | BAKER   LIBRARY   PRESS | HANOVER,   N.H. [1935]

Collation: [1]⁶; pp. [1–12] = 6 leaves

Contents: pp. 1–2: blank; p. 3: title-page; p. 4: '*Copyright, 1935* | *The Daniel Oliver Associates* | *of Dartmouth College* | *Hanover, New Hampshire.*'; p. 5–8: text; p. 9: blank; p. 10: colophon and limitation notice, '*The* | *three poems* | *printed in this* | *brochure have never* | *before been published in book* | *form. They are now reprinted by the* | *Daniel Oliver Associates of Dartmouth College* | *with the kind permission of the author. The edition, no* | *copies of which are for sale, is limited to one* | *hundred twenty-five copies, hand set* | *in Caslon Oldstyle, &* printed* | *on Worthy Hand and* | *Arrows. This copy* | *is Number* | [number supplied in ink]'; pp. 11–12: blank.

Text Content:
The Quest of the Orchis
Warning
Caesar's Lost Transport Ships

Paper: Cream laid paper with vertical chainlines 37 mm. apart; watermark of a hand holding four arrows, lettering beneath: 'WORTHY'. Leaves measure 253 × 190 mm.; top edge trimmed, other edges uncut.

Binding: Light blue (181.l.B) heavy laid paper wrappers with horizontal chainlines 27 mm. apart; watermarked 'Georgian'. Stitched at the center fold with light blue flax string. On the front cover is a cream paper label measuring 50 × 89 mm. and lettered in black within a gray-blue thick-thin rule frame: 'THREE POEMS | ROBERT FROST'. Back cover blank.

Publication: 'The Quest of the Orchis' was printed first in *The Independent* (27 June 1901) and later included in *A Witness Tree* (1942) with the title, 'The Quest of the Purple-Fringed'. 'Warning' was printed in *The Independent* (9 Sept. 1897) and 'Caesar's Lost Transport Ships,' in *The Independent* (14 Jan 1897). Neither poem has been included in later collected works.

Barrett Copy:
592782. On the title-page, beneath the title, RF has written, 'with notes for / Earle Bernheimer'. He has supplied numbers '1', '2', and '3' above the title of each poem. On blank p. 12, he has written, 'Notes / 1 Only three or four times have I come on such a / dazzling stand of the Purple Fringed; the last time / was in July 1937 on the side of Stratton Mountain / in Vermont. / 2 My refrains with the repetition of "forget" was in / print before I could have seen Kipling's. / 3 One of two Caesarean poems I wrote in the / Lawrence High School. Caesar's Commen/taries is still one of the books I get most / imaginative about. Darwin's Voyage of / the Beagle is another. / R. F.'

A19   1935 THE GOLD HESPERIDEE (First Separate Edition)

The | Gold Hesperidee | By | ROBERT FROST

FIRST STATE

Collation: [1]⁶; pp. [i–ii], [1–4] 5–8 [9–10] = 6 leaves.

Contents: pp. i–ii: blank; p. 1: title-page; p. 2: limitation, '*Copy number* [12 mm. space]. | *THE BIBLIOPHILE PRESS* | *Cortland, N.Y.* | *A*'; p. 3: publisher's foreword (11 lines); p. 4: blank; pp. 5–8: text (a vignette of a man jumping on his hat precedes the text on p. 5); pp. 9–10: blank.

   Note: All copies of the first state have the reading on p. 7, second line from the bottom, ' 'Twas Sunday, and Square Hale was dressed for meeting.' According to the publisher's statement, 67 of the 500 copies printed were rubber-stamped 'English' on p. 2 under the words 'Copy number' (see *Publication* note).

Paper: White wove paper. Leaves measure 162 × 114 mm., edges trimmed.

Bindings:
Binding A: Tan (79.l.gyBr) heavy crushed wove paper wrappers measuring 186 × 123 mm. Front cover printed in black, '[within a thick rule frame] The Gold Hesperidee. | [vignette of a top-hatted man standing under an apple tree] | Robert Frost.' Back cover blank. Stitched at the center fold with light brown cotton string.
Binding B: Occurs only on the second state. See the *Binding* note of the second state.
Binding C: Pale yellow (89.p.Y) heavy crushed wove paper wrappers measuring

186 × 123 mm. Lettering and decoration as on binding A. Stitched at the center fold with the same light brown string.

SECOND STATE

Collation: As in the first state.

Contents: As in the first state, but with the verso of the second leaf (the limitation notice, p. 2) reset and a correction made on its conjugate leaf recto (p. 7). p. 2: '*Limited to 200 copies* | *Copy number* [number supplied by hand in blue or red ink] | *THE BIBLIOPHILE PRESS* | *Cortland, N.Y.* | *B*'. p. 7: the second line from the bottom in the first state has been split to make two lines, ' 'Twas Sunday, and Square Hale was dressed | for meeting.'
   Note: In addition to these alterations, the numbering at the foot of pp. 5–8 has been moved approximately 10 mm. to the left to justify to the center width of the larger page size.

Paper: As in the first state, but with leaves measuring 183 × 127 mm.; edges trimmed.

Binding:
Binding B: Light yellow (87.m.Y) heavy crushed (heavier than bindings A and C) wove paper wrappers measuring 208 × 139 mm. Printed on the front cover as on bindings A and C. Stitched at the center fold with a heavier red-brown string.

Publication: The poem was printed first in *Farm and Fireside* (Sept. 1921) and collected in *A Further Range* (1936). Variant readings in this version:
line 8: And turned from] AFR; To turn from] FF and GH
  24: growing] AFR; blowing] FF and GH
  28: codlin] AFR; codlin'] FF and GH. [Cf. Thompson, *Selected Letters*, no. 290, p. 370: '*Codlin* should be in your dictionary. It is a form still in use among apple men. . . . Codlin is to codling as leggin is to legging. . . . *Codlin'* would look funny in any book of mine. I haven't dropped a g that way in a lifetime of writing.']
  Robert Frost inscribed a copy of this edition at Agnes Scott College with the statement, 'One of my boys here at Amherst made this book. . . .' Clymer & Green (pp. 67–68) give an account of the publication history based on correspondence or an interview with the publisher; however, they refer throughout to the two states as two 'editions.' For the sake of clarity, their information is here rephrased. Five hundred copies of the first state were printed, but the publisher withdrew the entire edition when the clumsily long seventeenth line on p. 7 was noticed. No copies were numbered although 37 copies had been distributed beyond recall according to his records. He then reset p. 7 and the limitation statement on p. 2 and printed 203 copies of this second state on a larger page size and bound in heavier, larger paper wrappers; some sewn with fine black silk and some with heavy brownish-yellow silk. Nine copies were imperfect and were de-

stroyed, and about 184 were issued after they had been numbered by hand in blue and red ink. Copies of the corrected second state were soon exhausted, and the publisher decided to make use of some of the countermanded first state copies to meet demand. In about 67 of these, under the words 'Copy number' on p. 2, the word 'English' was rubber-stamped. The publisher stated to Clymer & Green that 'the remaining 400 or so copies of this first printing would be destroyed, but whether they actually have been [*i.e.,* in 1936] or not it is impossible at this time to say.'

Earle W. Newton is identified as owner and operator of The Bibliophile Press in a review of the book printed in the *Amherst Graduates' Quarterly* (Nov. 1935), which pointed out, 'The limited edition of 200 copies was sold out two days after publication.' This unexpected popularity of the pamphlet is probably what decided Newton to save some of the rejected first state copies from destruction and sell them.

Barrett Copies:
592651. First state, binding A.
592652. First state, binding A. Inscribed on the recto of the preliminary blank, 'To Russell [Alberts] / from R. F. / May 1944'.
593062. First state (rubber-stamp), binding A.
593063. First state (rubber-stamp), binding C. Signed on the front cover, 'Robert Frost / for / Russell Alberts' and on the title-page, 'Robert Frost'.
592647. Second state, binding B. Number 144. Signed on the recto of the preliminary blank leaf, 'Robert Frost / to / Russell Alberts'.

A20   1936 FROM SNOW TO SNOW (First Edition)

FROM SNOW TO SNOW | *by* ROBERT FROST | [swelling rule] | STORM FEAR   *January* | A WINTER EDEN   *February* | TO THE THAWING WIND   *March* | BLUE-BUTTERFLY DAY   *April* | SPRING POOLS   *May* | THE TUFT OF FLOWERS   *June* | THE MOUNTAIN   *July* | THE OVEN BIRD   *August* | THE COW IN APPLE TIME   *September* | THE ROAD NOT TAKEN   *October* | GOODBYE AND KEEP COLD   *November* | STOPPING BY WOODS | ON A SNOWY EVENING   *December* | [swelling rule] | HENRY HOLT & COMPANY • NEW YORK

Collation: [1]¹⁰; pp. [1–4] 5–20 = 10 leaves.

Contents: p. 1: half-title, 'FROM SNOW TO SNOW'; p. 2: facsimile of the poem 'Stopping by Woods on a Snowy Evening' in Frost's holograph; p. 3: title-page; p. 4: 'COPYRIGHT 1936 BY HENRY HOLT AND COMPANY, INC., NEW YORK | PRINTED IN THE UNITED STATES OF AMERICA'; pp. 5–20: text.

Text Content: As listed on the title-page.

 Note: Three hundred copies of this edition have a single conjugate fold of two leaves tipped in preceding the half-title, having the contents: p. 1: '*The Hampshire Bookshop* | *1916 – 1936* | *TWENTIETH ANNIVERSARY WEEK* | Robert Frost | Guest of Honor | on the evening of | *April 16, 1936*'; p. 2: blank; p. 3: an 18-line letter in Frost's hand to Miss Dodd (proprieter of the Hampshire Bookshop) reproduced in facsimile; p. 4: blank. The insert is on unwatermarked white laid paper with vertical chainlines 28 mm. apart. Leaves measure 199 × 128 mm.

Paper: White laid paper with vertical chainlines 23 mm. apart. Watermarked 'CHAMPLAIN | TEXT'. Leaves measure 202 × 130 mm.; edges trimmed.

Bindings:

Binding A: A single 4to fold of heavy light-tan mottled paper wrappers. Printed in gray-blue (186.gyB) on the front cover: '[Within a triple border rule] FROM | SNOW | TO | SNOW | BY ROBERT FROST'. Stapled at the center fold. Back cover blank.

Binding B: Rough tan (60.l.gyBr) linen cloth. Lettered in dark brown on the front cover: 'FROM SNOW TO SNOW | [oval dot] | ROBERT FROST'. Back cover and spine blank. Stitched at the center fold. This binding also has endpapers of the same mottled paper as binding A.

Publication: See *Publication* note for A20.1.

A20.1   1936 FROM SNOW TO SNOW

SECOND PRINTING FROM THE FIRST EDITION PLATES

Collation: [1–3]⁴; pp. [πi–ii], [1–4] 5–20 [21–22] = 12 leaves.

Note: The contents and text content are as in the first edition, and this printing was from the original plates, but gathered in fours with blank flyleaves at front and back (pp. πi–ii, pp. 21–22).

Paper: White laid paper with vertical chainlines 24 mm. apart. Watermarked 'WARREN'S | OLDE STYLE'. Leaves measure 196 × 126 mm.; edges trimmed. Endpapers of heavy white wove paper.

Binding: Fine green (150.gyG) linen cloth. Stamped in silver on the front cover: '[Two stars on a diagonal] | FROM SNOW | TO SNOW | [large dot] | ROBERT FROST | [two stars on a diagonal]'. Back cover and spine blank.

Dust Jacket: Heavy white paper printed in green (147.v.d.G) overall. Front cover: 'ROBERT FROST | [triple rule] | From Snow to Snow | [triple rule] | [woodcut vignette, signed 'L' (J. J. Lankes), of a winter scene] | Mr. Frost's own selection of his most ap-|propriate poem for each month of the year.' Back cover and spine blank. Front inner flap: '[Within a triple border rule frame] COL-

LECTED POEMS | OF ROBERT FROST | [21-line blurb by Mark Van Doren in the *American Scholar*]'. Back inner flap: '[Within a triple border rule frame] SELECTED POEMS | THIRD EDITION | BY ROBERT FROST | [10-line advertising blurb with the Henry Holt imprint beneath]'.

Publication: The first edition of this pamphlet was printed for the Annual Convention of the Department of Superintendence of the National Education Association in St. Louis, Mo., and was distributed on that occasion in late February 1936. In April 300 copies of the pamphlet were used as a keepsake for the twentieth-anniversary dinner of the Hampshire Bookshop, Northampton, Massachusetts, with an insert (described above) tipped in. On 19 November 1936 about 1,200 sets of the sheets remaining from the first printing were bound up in light brown cloth (binding B) and placed on public sale at $.75 the copy by Holt. Holt issued a new printing of 3,000 copies bound in green cloth which was placed on sale 1 December 1936. This was followed by another printing of 1,200 copies on 24 December 1936.

Barrett Copies:
592640. First edition, binding A. Signed on the front cover, 'Robert Frost / Amherst 1937'. With the original envelope, printed in gray on the front cover, '[within a triple rule frame] FROM SNOW TO SNOW | − BY − | ROBERT FROST | [orn.] | WITH THE COMPLIMENTS OF | HENRY HOLT AND COMPANY'.
592637. First edition (insert), binding A.
592635. First edition (insert), binding A. Signed on p. 1 of the insert, 'Robert Frost'.
592638. First edition, binding B (first published edition).
592636. Second printing.
Uncatalogued. First edition, binding A. The Lawrance Thompson copy, inscribed on p. 1, 'To Lawrance Thompson / the friendly best / of / Robert Frost'. Original envelope with a panel printed in gray in the upper left corner, '[within a triple rule] FROM SNOW TO SNOW | − BY − | ROBERT FROST | [orn.] | WITH THE COMPLIMENTS OF | HENRY HOLT AND COMPANY'.

A21   1936 A FURTHER RANGE (Limited Edition)

A | FURTHER | RANGE | BY | ROBERT | FROST | [dull red (16)] *Book Six* | [black: swelling rule] | HENRY HOLT AND COMPANY | NEW YORK

Collation: [1–14]⁴; pp. [i–iv], [1–12] 13–102 [103–108] = 56 leaves.

Contents: pp. i–ii: blank pastedown endpaper; pp. iii–iv: blank open endpaper; p. 1: limitation notice, 'A FURTHER RANGE | *Eight hundred and three copies*

| of this book were especially printed and | bound, and signed by the author |
[RF's hand] Robert Frost | *This copy is number* | [number inserted ink]'; p. 2:
blank; p. 3: title-page; p. 4: '*Copyright, 1936, by Robert Frost* | *Printed in the
United States of America*'; p. 5: 'To E[linor]. F[rost]. | [5-line dedication]'; p. 6:
7-line note in italics on previous publication of poems; pp. 7–10: contents; p. 11:
section-title, 'TAKEN DOUBLY'; p. 12: blank; pp. 13–102: text; p. 103: blank;
p. 104: '[Spiral device] | Printed at The Spiral Press: New York | Completed in
May · 1936'; pp. 105–108: blank terminal open and pastedown endpapers. Section-
titles with blank versos at pp. 45 ('TAKEN SINGLY'), 67 ('TEN MILLS'), 73
('THE OUTLANDS'), 83 ('BUILD SOIL'), and 99 ('AFTERTHOUGHTS').

Text Content:

A Lone Striker

Two Tramps in Mud Time

The White-tailed Hornet

A Blue Ribbon at Amesbury

A Drumlin Woodchuck

The Gold Hesperidee

In Time of Cloudburst

A Roadside Stand

Departmental

The Old Barn at the Bottom
  of the Fogs

On the Heart's Beginning to
  Cloud the Mind

The Figure in the Doorway

At Woodward's Gardens

A Record Stride

Lost in Heaven

Desert Places

Leaves Compared with Flowers

A Leaf Treader

On Taking from the Top to
  Broaden the Base

They Were Welcome to Their
  Belief

The Strong Are Saying Nothing

The Master Speed

Moon Compasses

Neither Out Far nor In Deep

Voice Ways

Design

On a Bird Singing in Its Sleep

After-flakes

Clear and Colder

Unharvested

There Are Roughly Zones

A Trial Run

Not Quite Social

Provide, Provide

Precaution

The Span of Life

The Wrights' Biplane

Assertive

Evil Tendencies Cancel

Pertinax

Waspish

One Guess

The Hardship of Accounting

Not All There

In Divés' Dive

The Vindictives—The Andes

The Bearer of Evil Tidings—The Himalayas

Iris by Night—The Malverns

Build Soil

To a Thinker

A Missive Missile

Paper: Fine white wove paper watermarked 'C P' within a double rule frame.
Leaves measure 238 × 158 mm. Top edge trimmed and stained dark brown,
other edges uncut. Endpapers of the same stock.

Binding: Coarse tan linen cloth threaded with red-brown. Front and back covers
blank. Spine: on a brown morocco label, stamped in gilt within a single gilt rule,

lettered from bottom to top, 'ROBERT FROST · A FURTHER RANGE'. In a green (150.gyG) paper-covered board box, no lettering. Newton McKeon notes a gray-brown (61.gyBr) box with limitation number in holograph at the spine.

Note: The limited edition was printed from type which was later plated (with certain alterations) to produce the trade edition. See *Publication* note following the trade edition entry.

Barrett Copies:

592641. On the limitation page (p. 1), instead of signing in the space supplied, Frost has written, 'this one is [signed by the author] / her Uncle Robert / for / Hilda [Hilda Harvey, daughter of Mrs. Frost's sister, Leona White Harvey]'.

592642. Lacking the box.

Uncatalogued. The Lawrance Thompson copy. Inscribed on the limitation page (p. 1) with the third stanza (lines 9–12) of 'Not Quite Social,' which is printed on p. 65 of the book. Signed beneath, 'R. F. / To L. T.'

Other uncatalogued material from the Lawrance Thompson collection:

1. Early trial proofs of 14 poems for the limited edition of *A Further Range*. Twenty-two unpaged leaves printed on rectos only; cream laid paper with horizontal chainlines 30 mm. apart, watermarked '[a pair of scales within a circle surmounted by a St. Andrew's cross at the top of an ascending line] / Utopian'. The 14 poems represented are: 'A Lone Striker,' 'Departmental,' 'Unharvested,' 'Voice-Ways,' 'To a Thinker [with the title here, 'To a Thinker in Office'],' 'The Master Speed [here, 'Master Speed'],' 'Desert Places,' 'Two Tramps in Mud Time,' 'Moon Compasses,' 'Not Quite Social,' 'The Bearer of Evil Tidings,' 'Neither Out Far nor In Deep.' 'A Missive Missile,' 'After-flakes.' These proofs differ from the later proofs (A21.1) and from the published editions; most particularly, the poem 'Unharvested,' which appears here in a variant reading printed nowhere else. This seems to be an experimental version following the original printing in *Saturday Review of Literature* (10 Nov. 1934) and preceding the final version printed in the book on p. 62. Full textual collation will be supplied below for this poem and other variants among the proofs and printed editions.

2. Trial page proofs of all poems for the limited edition of *A Further Range*. Eighty-two leaves printed on rectos only; white wove paper. The first 4 leaves are contents with all poems represented. Contents leaves 1, 2, and 3 are in the setting that appears in the published edition, but differently numbered. The fourth leaf (which, in the first edition is the listing for the fifth section, 'BUILD SOIL,' followed by the sixth section, 'AFTERTHOUGHT') has the single section heading 'THERE IS AN AEON LIMIT SET', and the first poem listed is 'A Missive Missile'. The poem 'To a Thinker' is listed here with the title 'Our Darkest Concern (Very much as delivered at Amherst, June 1935)'. The proof text leaves have the printed pagination 9–86. The section-titles are not present. Other variants supplied below. Tipped to the first leaf is a typed note by Lawrance Thompson, 'PAGE PROOFS OF *A FURTHER RANGE*. / These sheets, given to me by Harry Scherman, / President of Book-

of-the-Month Club, were the / sheets sent to Scherman by Henry Holt & Co. / The editors read these sheets and decided to issue *A Further Range* as a "book-of-the-month" / for June, 1936. Thus the author and the / publisher were assured that at least 50,000 copies would be sold.'

3. A publisher's dummy in dull green cloth, black morocco label on the spine, lettering stamped in gilt, 'NEW POEMS *by* ROBERT FROST'. This was an early rejected title for *A Further Range.* Thirty-two leaves of white laid paper with vertical chainlines 27 mm. apart; watermarked 'STRATHMORE PERMANENT', countermark 'U.S.A.' The book is in five gatherings of 4 and 8 (the preliminary and terminal gatherings in 4). The first three leaves only contain printed matter:

Leaf 1 recto: title-page, '[within a triple border rule consisting of an ornamental leaf-rule in green, two single rules in black] [black] NEW POEMS | BY ROBERT FROST | [Holt device in green] | [black] HENRY HOLT & COMPANY | NEW YORK · 1936'

2 verso: lines 1–22 of 'Two Tramps in Mud Time'

3 recto: lines 23–45 of 'Two Tramps in Mud Time'

On leaves 4 recto and 5 recto, Robert Frost has inscribed the last 27 lines of the poem and signed beneath, 'Robert Frost / For Lawrance Thompson'. Line 71 of the RF holograph version has a variant reading: 'Is the work ever really done' for 'Is the deed ever really done'.

At front is tipped a broadside prospectus of *A Further Range,* announcing publication on 20 April of both limited and trade editions. The dedication of the book is quoted with a variant reading from the published version, 'To E. F., for what it may mean to her that beyond the White Mountains were the Green, yes, and beyond both. This was published with the 'yes, and' deleted. The book was not published until May 1936.

4. Another trial binding (covers only) in dark red cloth; gray morocco label on the spine, lettering stamped in gilt, 'NEW POEMS *by* ROBERT FROST'.

In the apparatus that follows, text is keyed to the limited edition, and the following abbreviations are used for the texts compared: 1st, limited edition; T, trade edition; P1, proof 1 (14 poems only); P2, proof 2 (complete text); D, dummy ('Two Tramps in Mud Time' only). The poem 'Unharvested' will be given separate treatment below.

page 13 ('A Lone Striker') : lines 1–26] 1st,T,P2(p. 9); lines 1–27] P1

13: line space after line 16] 1st,T; no line space] P1,P2

14: lines 27–53]1st,T; lines 27–54] P1; lines 28–56] P2(p. 10)

14: line spaces after lines 35, 49] 1st,T; no line spaces] P1,P2(p. 10)

15: lines 54–62] 1st,T; lines 55–62] P1; lines 57–62] P2(p. 11)

15, line 62: Come get him –] 1st,T; Come get him:] P1,P2

16 ('Two Tramps in Mud Time') : lines 1–24] 1st,T,P1; lines 1–25 with no space between lines 24 and 25] P2(p. 12); lines 1–22] D(p. 26)

16: line 24 unsplit] 1st,P1,P2; line 24 split] T

17: lines 25–50] 1st,T; lines 25–49] P1; lines 26–51] P2(p. 13); lines 23–45] D

18: lines 51–72] 1st,T; lines 50–72] P1; lines 52–72] P2(p. 14)

20 ('The White-Tailed Hornet'): lines 27–54] 1st,P2(p. 16); lines 27–52] T
20: lines 33 and 40 unsplit] 1st,P2; lines 33 and 40 split] T
21: lines 55–70] 1st,P2(p. 17); lines 53–70] T
28 ('The Gold Hesperidee'): lines 25–50] 1st,P2(p. 24); lines 25–49] T
28: line 41 unsplit] 1st,P2; line 41 split] T
29: lines 51–58] 1st,P2; lines 50–58] T
32 ('A Roadside Stand'): lines 1–26] 1st,P2(p. 28); lines 1–25] T
32: line 5 unsplit] 1st,P2; line 5 split] T
33: lines 27–51] 1st,P2; lines 26–51] T
33: lines 26 and 43 unsplit] 1st,P2; lines 26 and 43 split] T
50 ('A Leaf Treader'): Setting of 1st and P2(p. 44) measures 105 mm. in
    width. Setting of T measures 90 mm. in width. Lines of each setting are
    differently split.
56 ('Neither Out Far nor In Deep'), line 9: The land may vary more;]
    1st,T,P2(p. 50); Some say the land has more;] P1
63 ('There Are Roughly Zones'): no split lines] 1st,P2(p. 57); lines 3, 6, 12, 18,
    19 split] T
71: title printed 'In Divés' Dive'] 1st,T; title printed 'In Dives' Dive'] P2(p.
    63)
79–80 ('The Bearer of Evil Tidings'): lines 1–22, lines 23–44] 1st,T,P2(p.68);
    lines 1–20, lines 21–44] P1
96–97 ('To A Thinker'): lines 1–27, lines 28–36] 1st,T,P2(pp. 85–86, with the
    title listed in the contents, 'Our Darkest Concern'; correctly titled in text);
    lines 1–26, lines 27–36] P1 (with the title 'To a Thinker in Office')

UNHARVESTED
Saturday Review of Literature (10 Nov. 1934). First version, printed with the
title, 'Ungathered Apples':

> A scent of ripeness from over a wall.
> There, sure enough, stood an apple tree
> Of all but its trivial foliage free
> And breathing light as a lady's fan.
> And there there had been an apple fall
> As complete as the apple had given man.
> The ground was one circle of solid red.
> May something go always unharvested,
>
> Much, much stays out of our stated plan—
> Apples or something forgotten and left
> To smelling their sweetness would be no theft.

Uncorrected trial proof, leaf 6:

> A scent of ripeness from over a wall
> And sure enough there was an appletree
> Of all but its trivial foliage free
> It was breathing light as a lady's fan.

> But there there had been an apple fall
> As complete as the apple had given man.
> The ground was one circle of solid red.
> May something go always unharvested!
> May much stay out of our stated plan
> Apples or something forgotten and left
> So smelling their sweetness would be no theft.

Limited edition, trade edition, and the page proofs of the limited edition (p. 56); the final version:

> A scent of ripeness from over a wall.
> And come to leave the routine road
> And look for what had made me stall,
> There sure enough was an apple tree
> That had eased itself of its summer load,
> And of all but its trivial foliage free,
> Now breathed as light as a lady's fan.
> For there there had been an apple fall
> As complete as the apple had given man.
> The ground was one circle of solid red.
>
> May something go always unharvested!
> May much stay out of our stated plan,
> Apples or something forgotten and left,
> So smelling their sweetness would be no theft.

A21.1   1936 A FURTHER RANGE (Trade Edition)

BOOK SIX | [swelling rule] | A | FURTHER | RANGE | BY | ROBERT |
FROST | [swelling rule] | HENRY HOLT AND COMPANY | NEW
YORK

*FIRST IMPRESSION FROM PLATES OF THE LIMITED EDITION
TYPE*

Collation: [1–5]⁸ [6]⁴ [7]⁸; pp. [i–ii], [1–12] 13–102 = 52 leaves.

Contents: pp. i–ii: blank; p. 1: half-title, 'A FURTHER RANGE'; p. 2: blank;
p. 3: title-page; p. 4: '*First Printing | Copyright, 1936 by Robert Frost | Printed
in the United States of America*'; p. 5: 'To E. F. | [5-line dedication]'; p. 6: 7-line
note on previous publication of poems (in italics); pp. 7–10: contents; p. 11:
section-title, 'TAKEN DOUBLY'; p. 12: blank; pp. 13–102: text. Section-titles
with blank versos as in the limited edition at pp. 45, 67, 73, 83, and 99.

Text Content: As in the limited edition.

Paper: Cream laid paper with vertical chainlines 21 mm. apart. Unwatermarked. Leaves measure 216 × 139 mm. Top edge trimmed and stained dull red (16.d.R); other edges uncut. Endpapers of heavy white wove paper of a mottled pattern.

Binding: Red (16) rough linen cloth. Stamped in gilt on the front cover, '[within a triple (thick-thin-thin) rule frame] A | FURTHER | RANGE | [star] | ROB-ERT | FROST'. Stamped in gilt on the spine (reading from bottom to top), 'A FURTHER RANGE [star] ROBERT FROST'. Back cover blank. Covers measure 222 × 144 mm. (Note varying dimensions of book club edition.)

Dust Jacket: Smooth cream wove paper. Front cover lettered in cream on a dull red (16) panel within eight dull red (16) border rules, 'A | FURTHER | RANGE | BY | ROBERT | FROST'. Spine lettered in dull red (16), reading from bottom to top, 'A FURTHER RANGE BY ROBERT FROST'. Back cover lettered in dull red (16), '[within four dull red rules] *Poetry by* ROBERT FROST | [8 titles with prices] | [Holt imprint]'. Front inner flap lettered in dull red within triple red rules, 'COLLECTED POEMS | OF ROBERT FROST | [21-line blurb by Mark Van Doren in the *American Scholar*]'. Back inner flap lettered in red within triple red rules, 'SELECTED POEMS | THIRD EDI-TION | BY ROBERT FROST | [10-line advertisement with Holt imprint beneath]'.

Note: There was a second impression of 6,000 copies. See *Publication* note.

THIRD IMPRESSION FROM THE TRADE EDITION PLATES
(Book-of-the-Month Club Edition)

Title as in the Trade Edition

Collation: [1–5]⁸ [6]⁴ [7]⁸; pp. [1–12] 13–102 [103–104] = 52 leaves.

Contents: As in the trade edition, but with the blank preliminary leaf no longer present and with the addition of a blank leaf following the final page of text. The words 'First Printing' are not present on p. 4. The page numbers on pp. 16, 21, 25, 29, 36, 40, 44, 48, 53, 56, 61, and 64 are in a different type-font from the corresponding page numbers in the trade edition. Damage to these plates occurred in transportation and new types were supplied.

Paper: As in the trade edition, but with leaves measuring 219 ×143 mm.

Binding: As in the trade edition, but with a slightly smoother cloth. Covers measure 225 × 149 mm. (larger than the trade edition binding).

Dust Jacket: As in the trade edition.

Note: The trade edition and the book club edition contain alterations on 10 pages effected in the plates made from the limited edition type. On these pages lines were split for plating to make a smaller page possible: pp. 16, 20, 27, 28, 32, 33, 50, 53, 63, 89.

Publication and Bibliographical Definition: The publishing history of this title presents unusual bibliographical problems that are dealt with specifically in Fredson Bowers' *Principles of Bibliographical Description* (New York, 1949, pp. 390–91). The arrangement used in the foregoing descriptions follows his suggested order, and Professor Bowers' analysis is this: 'A difficulty which fortunately does not often occur is exemplified by Robert Frost's *A Further Range* (1936). According to Frost's bibliographer [Clymer & Green], the publisher gave the following account of the books: "My First is five times my Limited (oversubscribed); my Second is half again as large as my First; my Third is Book-of-the-Month Club for June; my Whole is just short of 70,000." From this statement they deduce that the Limited Edition was 803 copies (as stated in the edition), the first trade impression 4000, the second 6000, and Book-of-the-Month 59,000, totalling 69,800. The Limited Edition was printed from type, but when the type was later plated to produce the trade edition, the type-page was narrowed so that various long lines were turned over without affecting, however, the original imposition of the type-pages. Strictly speaking, the type itself—being the true first edition—is not disturbed by printing and subsequent plating, and technically the first impression from the plates was the actual second impression of the parent first edition. But if the Limited Edition is removed to the place of a subsidiary edition, then the impressions of the trade edition can be listed in their correct order; and the book is most easily handled by listing the Limited Edition (from type), followed by the Trade Edition, first and second impressions (plates of 'Limited Edition' type), and then the Book-of-the-Month Club Edition as a subedition with the note that it was composed of the third impression from the Trade Edition plates.'

Both limited and trade editions were intended for simultaneous publication on 30 May 1936. The limited edition actually preceded the trade by nine days and is, technically, the true first edition both bibliographically and chronologically.

Barrett Copies:

592644. Trade edition, first impression. Inscribed on the front open endpaper recto, 'Robert Frost / Pittsfield / Sign of the Open Book / (Store kept by / my daughter / Lesley Frost)'. Inscribed on the blank front flyleaf recto are lines 9–16 of the poem on p. 63 of the book, 'There Are Roughly Zones,' signed 'Robert Frost / For R. V. Thornton / December 16 1953 Chicago.' There is a variant reading in line 14 of the holograph version: That though there is no fixed line between wrong and right] AFR; That though there is no fixed line between right and wrong] MS.

592645. Trade edition, first impression. Inscribed on the front open endpaper recto, 'For Vera / from / her Uncle Robert / May 1936'.

592643. Third impression (Book-of-the-Month Club edition).

A21.2   1937 A FURTHER RANGE (First English Edition)

BOOK   SIX | A   FURTHER   RANGE | *by* | ROBERT   FROST | [publisher's device] | JONATHAN CAPE | THIRTY BEDFORD SQUARE | LONDON

Collation: [A]⁸ B–F⁸; pp. [1–4] 5–94 [95–96] = 48 leaves.

Contents: p. 1: half-title, 'A FURTHER RANGE'; p. 2: '*By the same author* | NORTH OF BOSTON | A BOY'S WILL | MOUNTAIN INTERVAL | NEW HAMPSHIRE | WEST-RUNNING BROOK | SELECTED POEMS'; p. 3: title-page; p. 4: 'FIRST IMPRESSION 1937 | JONATHAN CAPE LTD. 30 BEDFORD SQUARE, LONDON | AND 91 WELLINGTON STREET WEST, TORONTO | PRINTED IN GREAT BRITAIN IN THE CITY OF OXFORD | AT THE ALDEN PRESS | PAPER MADE BY GROSVENOR, CHATER & CO., LTD. | BOUND BY A. W. BAIN & CO., LTD.'; pp. 5–7: contents; p. 8: blank; p. 9: dedication (as in previous editions); p. 10: 7-line notice in italics of previous publication of poems; p. 11: section-title, 'TAKEN DOUBLY'; p. 12: blank; pp. 13–94: text; pp. 95–96: blank. Section-titles with blank versos at pp. 41, 63, 69, 77, and 91.

Text Content: As in all other editions.

Paper: Smooth wove white paper watermarked 'BASINGWERK PARCHMENT'. Leaves measure 201 × 142 mm. Top edge trimmed, fore-edge uncut, bottom edge rough-cut. Endpapers of rougher cream wove paper.

Binding: Fine blue (182.m.B) linen cloth. Covers plain. Spine stamped in gilt, 'A | FURTHER | RANGE | ROBERT | FROST | [publisher's device]'.

Dust Jacket: Heavy wove paper. Front cover with a blue (168.brill.gB) ground lettered   in   white,   'A | FURTHER | RANGE | new | poems   by | ROBERT | FROST'. Back cover with a white ground lettered in blue (168) and black, '[black] SELECTED POEMS | [blue] ROBERT | FROST | [black] with introductory essays by | W. H. AUDEN | C. DAY LEWIS | PAUL ENGLE | EDWIN MUIR | 5s. net | JONATHAN CAPE THIRTY BEDFORD SQUARE LONDON'. Inner flaps plain white.

Barrett Copy:
592646. Inscribed on the front open endpaper recto, 'To Russell Alberts / from / Robert Frost / Cambridge'.

A22   1936 SELECTED POEMS (First Edition of expanded selection)

SELECTED POEMS | *by* | ROBERT FROST | *Chosen by the Author* | *With* | *Introductory Essays* | *by* | W. H. AUDEN | C. DAY LEWIS | PAUL ENGLE | *and* | EDWIN MUIR | [publisher's device] | JONATHAN CAPE | THIRTY BEDFORD SQUARE | LONDON

Collation: [A]⁸ B–O⁸; pp. [1–4] 5–221 [222–224] = 112 leaves.

Contents: p. 1: half-title, 'SELECTED POEMS'; p. 2: *'By the same author* | [7 titles; the last, *A Further Range,* '(To be published early in 1937)'] p. 3: title-page; p. 4: 'FIRST PUBLISHED 1936 | JONATHAN CAPE LTD. 30 BED-FORD SQUARE, LONDON | AND 91 WELLINGTON STREET WEST, TORONTO | PRINTED IN GREAT BRITAIN IN THE CITY OF OX-FORD | AT THE ALDEN PRESS | PAPER MADE BY JOHN DICKINSON & CO., LTD. | BOUND BY A. W. BAIN & CO., LTD.'; pp. 5–8: contents; p. 9: 'INTRODUCTORY ESSAYS | by | W. H. AUDEN | C. DAY LEWIS | PAUL ENGLE | EDWIN MUIR'; p. 10: blank; pp. 11–35: introductory essays; p. 36: blank; p. 37: section-title, 'I'; p. 38: blank; pp. 39–221: text; pp. 222–224: blank. Section-titles with blank versos at pp. 43, 51, 57, 97, 103, 133, 141, 173, 183, and 215.

Text Content:

Introductory Essays	"Out, Out—"
The Pasture	Putting in the Seed
The Cow in Apple-Time	Going for Water
The Runaway	Mowing
To Earthward	The Need of Being Versed in
Stopping by Woods on a Snowy Evening	Country Things
Fire and Ice	Two Look at Two
Spring Pools	After Apple-Picking
Dust of Snow	Birches
Acquainted with the Night	The Gum-Gatherer
Once by the Pacific	The Mountain
Tree at My Window	The Tuft of Flowers
A Soldier	Mending Wall
An Old Man's Winter Night	Good-Bye and Keep Cold
Home Burial	The Grindstone
The Death of the Hired Man	The Bear
A Servant to Servants	The Wood-Pile
The Self-Seeker	The Armful
The Hill Wife	A Brook in the City

A Peck of Gold	October
On Looking Up by Chance at	To the Thawing Wind
the Constellations	A Time to Talk
Canis Major	The Code
Snow	A Hundred Collars
The Black Cottage	The Witch of Coös
The Axe-Helve	Blueberries
West-running Brook	Brown's Descent
The Road Not Taken	Revelation
The Oven Bird	Storm-Fear
Hyla Brook	Flower-Gathering
My November Guest	Reluctance
The Onset	Into My Own
Range-Finding	

Paper: White wove paper measuring 200 × 132 mm. Top edge trimmed and stained dark blue, fore-edge trimmed, bottom edge uncut. Endpapers of cream wove paper.

Binding: Blue (178.s.B) fine linen cloth. Front and back covers blank. Spine stamped in gilt, 'SELECTED | POEMS | ROBERT | FROST | [publisher's device]'.

Dust Jacket: White wove paper, internally marbled, printed in red-orange (36.dp.rO) and black, '[red] SELECTED | POEMS | [black] ROBERT FROST | *Chosen by the author* | *with* | *Introductory Essays by* | W. H. AUDEN | C. DAY LEWIS | PAUL ENGLE | *and* | EDWIN MUIR'. Spine, '[black] SE-LECTED | POEMS | *by* | [red] ROBERT | FROST | [black] *Chosen* | *by the* | *Author* | *With* | *Introductory* | *Essays* | *by* | W. H. | AUDEN | C. DAY | LEWIS | PAUL | ENGLE | EDWIN | MUIR | [red] [publisher's device]'. Front inner flap lettered in black, 'SELECTED POEMS | [18-line blurb] | \5s. net'. Back inner flap blank.

Publication: This edition was published on 13 November 1936. The arrangement is new, and it is the first book of Frost's to contain material by others.

Barrett Copies:
592566. Inscribed on the open endpaper recto, 'To Vera from her Uncle Rob / May 1937'.
592567. Inscribed on the open endpaper recto with a fair copy of the final stanza of 'Canis Major' which appears at p. 139 of this edition. Signed 'Robert Frost / To Russell Alberts / Cambridge 1944'.

A23   1939 COLLECTED POEMS (First Edition)

COLLECTED | POEMS   OF | ROBERT   FROST | 1939 | [red-brown: wood-engraved vignette of a house, by J. J. Lankes] | [black] NEW YORK | HENRY HOLT AND COMPANY

Collation: π_1 [1–27]^8 [28]^{10}; pp. [πi–ii], [i–xvi], [1–4] 5–436 = 227 leaves.

Contents: pp. πi–ii: blank (recto signed in holograph, 'Robert Frost'); p. i: title-page; p. ii: 'COPYRIGHT, 1930, 1939, BY HENRY HOLT AND COMPANY, INC. | COPYRIGHT, 1936, BY ROBERT FROST | First Printing | PRINTED IN THE UNITED STATES OF AMERICA'; pp. iii–vi: RF's preface, '*The Figure a Poem Makes*', subscribed and dated in print on p. vi, 'R. F. | *Boston, January 11, 1939*.'; p. vii: contents section-title; p. viii–xv: contents; p. xvi: blank; pp. 1–436: text.
   Note: Contents pp. vii–xii and text pp. 1–349 are apparently printed from the plates of the 1930 edition of *Collected Poems*. Contents pp. xiii–xv are in a new setting intended to match the preceding contents pages and comprise the contents listing for *A Further Range*. Text pp. 351–436, the text of *A Further Range*, are similarly in new imitative setting appended to the earlier one.

Illustration: A photographic portrait of RF, by Doris Ulmann, tipped in facing the title-page. Printed on white wove paper slightly heavier than the text paper.

Text Content: RF's introduction, 'The Figure a Poem Makes,' is printed here for the first time. The collection contains all the poems included in the first editions of *North of Boston, New Hampshire,* and *A Further Range.* The poems from *A Boy's Will, Mountain Interval,* and *West-running Brook* are those included in the 1930 *Collected Poems* with the additions and deletions from the first editions that occurred in that collection.

Paper: White wove paper; unwatermarked. Leaves measure 215 × 145 mm. Top edge trimmed and stained red-brown, fore-edge uncut, bottom edge rough-cut. Endpapers of heavier smooth white wove paper.

Binding: Beige medium linen cloth. Within a red-brown panel (69 × 118 mm.) on the front cover, a gilt-stamped version of J. J. Lankes' title-page vignette of a house. Spine: '[oak leaf orn. in red-brown and gilt] | [lettered in gilt within a red-brown panel 58 mm. in height] COLLECTED | POEMS | OF | ROBERT FROST | [oak leaf orn. in red-brown and gilt] | [red-brown] HENRY HOLT | AND COMPANY'. Back cover blank.

Dust Jacket: Red-brown (40.s.rBr) coated paper. Front cover: '[Lankes' wood-engraving of a house in black and white] | [white] COLLECTED | POEMS OF | ROBERT | FROST | 1939'. Spine '[lettered in white reading from top to

bottom] COLLECTED POEMS OF | ROBERT FROST − 1939 − | [horizon-
tal] HOLT'. Back cover identical to the front. Front inner flap (black lettering
on cream ground): '$5.00 | COLLECTED POEMS | *by* | ROBERT FROST |
[27-line blurb] | [Holt imprint]'. Back inner flap (black on cream): 'THE PO-
ETRY OF ROBERT FROST: | [statements by Louis Untermeyer, Louise
Townsend Nicholl, William Rose Benét, and James Norman Hall] | [Holt im-
print]'.

Publication: According to information supplied in a letter from William Sloane,
manager of the Holt trade department, to George F. Whicher, dated 9 February
1939, 3,750 copies were printed on 25 January 1939, and the book was published
on 16 February.

Barrett Copies:
592554. Signed by RF on the blank preliminary leaf recto.
592555. Inscribed on p. vi, beneath the preface, 'Robert Frost / to / R. V. Thornton / Chicago December 16 1953'.
Uncatalogued. The Lawrance Thompson copy, inscribed on the front open endpaper recto, 'To Larry, the whole thing again / for him to take entirely / new
view of after his days / at Key West trying to pacify / my purturbéd [*sic*] spirit.
/ R. F. / But was it not written years ago / If I shed such a darkness / . . . . . .
/ How swarthy I must be [lines 6 and 10 of 'After-flakes']. / Petals I may have
once pursued / Leaves are all my darker mood [lines 19, 20 of 'Leaves Compared
with Flowers']'. Both poems were included in *A Further Range* (1936).
Uncatalogued. A Lawrance Thompson copy. The Halcyon House edition, March
1939. Inscribed with a fair copy of 'On the Ascent [*i.e.*, 'Time Out'; printed first
in the *Virginia Quarterly* (1942), collected in *A Witness Tree* (1942)]'. Dated
1939 and signed beneath, 'Robert Frost / For Lawrence [*sic*] Thompson'.

A24   1939 A CONSIDERABLE SPECK (First Separate Edition)

A | CONSIDERABLE | SPECK | [fly orn.] | ROBERT FROST

A single folio gathering, measuring 387 × 295 mm., uncut, on cream wove paper
watermarked 'HAND MADE'; countermark 'U S A'. pp. [1–4].

Contents: p. 1: cover title, as above; p. 2: blank; p. 3: (within a border rule made
up of fly ornaments like the single ornament on p. 1) text of the poem with a
large initial 'A' in light brown; p. 4: blank.

Publication: Laid in is a small broadside, 216 × 139 mm., '[quasi-blackletter]
The Colonial Society | of Massachusetts ||| [standard font] This poem was written
and delivered by Robert Frost | at the Annual Dinner on November twenty-first,
1939. | It has been printed by Mr. Dard Hunter, Jr. from the first | font of type
that he has cut and cast himself, and is one | of his first pieces of printing. It is

on hand-made paper, | made by him and his father, an authority on paper, with | whom he is associated at the Dard Hunter Paper Museum | at Massachusetts Institute of Technology. | Augustus P. Loring, Jr. | *Recording Secretary*.' According to a note of Earle Bernheimer also laid in, this is one of less than 100 copies printed. The poem was first printed in the *Atlantic Monthly* (July 1939).

Barrett Copy:
595826. Inscribed beneath the poem on p. 3, 'Robert Frost / to Earle Bernheimer / Feb. 21 1941'.

A25   1942 A WITNESS TREE (Limited Edition)

A WITNESS TREE | BY | ROBERT FROST | HENRY HOLT & COMPANY • NEW YORK | 1942

Collation: [1]¹⁰ [2–5]⁸ [6]¹⁰; pp. [i–viii], [1–8] 9–91 [92–96] = 52 leaves.

Contents: pp. i–iv: blank; p. v: half-title and limitation notice, 'A WITNESS TREE | *This edition has been limited to* | *seven hundred and thirty-five copies* | *and signed by the author* | [holograph] Robert Frost | *This copy is number* [number inserted ink]'; pp. vi–vii: blank; p. viii: frontis. portrait; p. 1: title-page; p. 2: '*Copyright, 1942, by Robert Frost* | *Printed in the United States of America*'; p. 3: dedication, 'TO K[athleen]. M[orrison]. | FOR HER PART IN IT'; p. 4: blank; pp. 5–7: contents; p. 8: blank; p. 9: two introductory poems, 'Beech' and 'Sycamore,' in italics; p. 10: blank; p. 11: section-title, 'ONE OR TWO'; p. 12: blank; pp. 13–91: text; p. 92: '[Spiral Press device] | THE SPIRAL PRESS | NEW YORK'; pp. 93–96: blank. Section-titles with blank versos at pp. 39 ('TWO OR MORE'), 53 ('TIME OUT'), 65 ('QUANTULA'), 77 ('OVER BACK').

Illustration: The frontispiece portrait of RF by Enit Kaufman, so signed, is on the verso of the fourth leaf of the first gathering. Printed in red-brown.

Text Content:

Beech	Song Be the Same
Sycamore	The Subverted Flower
The Silken Tent	Wilful Homing
All Revelation	A Cloud Shadow
Happiness Makes Up in Height for What It Lacks in Length	The Quest of the Purple-Fringed
	The Discovery of the Madeiras
Come In	The Gift Outright
I Could Give All to Time	Triple Bronze
Carpe Diem	Our Hold on the Planet
The Wind and the Rain	To a Young Wretch (Boethian)
The Most of It	The Lesson for Today
Never Again Would Birds'	Time Out

To a Moth Seen in Winter
A Considerable Speck (Microscopic)
The Lost Follower
November
The Rabbit Hunter
A Loose Mountain (Telescopic)
It Is Almost the Year Two
    Thousand
In a Poem
On Our Sympathy with the
    Under Dog
A Question
Boeotian

The Secret Sits
An Equalizer
A Semi-Revolution
Assurance
An Answer
Trespass
A Nature Note
Of the Stones of the Place
Not of School Age
A Serious Step Lightly Taken
The Literate Farmer and
    the Planet Venus

Paper: Cream laid paper with vertical chainlines 24 mm. apart. Watermarked 'Linweave Text [letter 'L' superimposed on letter 'T']'; countermark, 'Made in U S A'. Leaves measure 238 × 159 mm. Top edge trimmed, fore-edge uncut, bottom edge rough-cut. Endpapers of the same stock.

Binding: Gray-green (150.gyG) decorative paper-covered boards with an overall design of leaves, dots, and dashes. Shelfback of dark gray-green (151.d.gyG) linen cloth. A gilt rule runs vertically and delineates the juncture between cloth and paper. Spine stamped in gilt with lettering from bottom to top, '[within a single-rule frame] A WITNESS TREE BY ROBERT FROST'. Back cover unlettered.

Publication: Published 23 April 1942 in an edition of 735 copies, price $7.50.

Barrett Copy:
592816. Inscribed on the front open endpaper recto, 'To R. V. Thornton / from / Robert Frost'.

A25.1   1942 A WITNESS TREE (Trade Edition)

A | WITNESS | TREE | BY | ROBERT | FROST | HENRY HOLT AND COMPANY | NEW YORK

FIRST IMPRESSION FROM THE PLATES OF THE LIMITED EDITION TYPE

Collation: [1–6]⁸; pp. [i–v], [1–8] 9–91 [92] = 48 leaves.

Contents: pp. 1–2: blank; p. 3: half-title, 'A WITNESS TREE'; p. iv: blank; p. 1: title-page; p. 2: 'FIRST PRINTING | *Copyright, 1942, by Robert Frost* | *Printed in the United States of America*'; p. 3: dedication, TO K[athleen]. M[orrison]. | FOR HER PART IN IT'; p. 4: blank; pp. 5–7: contents; p. 8:

blank; p. 9: two introductory poems, 'Beech' and 'Sycamore,' in italics; p. 10: blank; p. 11: section-title, 'ONE OR TWO'; p. 12: blank; pp. 13–91: text; p. 92: blank. Section-titles with blank versos at pp. 39 ('TWO OR MORE'), 53 ('TIME OUT'), 65 ('QUANTULA'), 77 ('OVER BACK').

Illustration: Crayon drawing in black of RF by Enit Kaufman, unsigned, on slightly heavier paper, tipped in preceding the title-page.

Text Content: As in the limited edition.

Paper: White wove fibrous paper. Leaves measure 215 × 142 mm. Top edge trimmed and stained dark green, fore-edge uncut, bottom edge rough-cut. End-papers of heavy wove light orange-yellow (70.l.OY) paper.

Binding: Greenish blue (173.m.gB) linen cloth; the fabric pattern highly visible. The front cover stamped in gilt, '[within a frame of 6 rules] A | WITNESS | TREE | [5-pointed star] | ROBERT | FROST'. The spine gilt-stamped and lettered from top to bottom, 'A WITNESS TREE [5-pointed star] ROBERT FROST'. Back cover blank.

Dust Jacket: Wove paper. Covers and spine with a beige (79.l.gy.yBr) ground. On the front cover is a wash drawing of a tree in black, gray, and red-brown, signed 'Alan Haemer'. Above the drawing, printed in red, 'ROBERT FROST'. Imposed on the drawing in white, 'A | WITNESS | TREE' and beneath, in red, 'NEW POEMS'. The spine is lettered from top to bottom, '[red] *Robert Frost* | [white] A WITNESS TREE | [red] *Holt*'. Back cover blank. The flaps are white printed in black. Front flap: '$2.00 | A WITNESS TREE | *New Poems by* | ROBERT FROST | [27-line blurb] | *Jacket Design by Alan Haemer* | [Holt imprint in 3 lines]'. Back flap: 'ROBERT FROST | [14-line blurb] | [the Enit Kaufman drawing of RF in black]'.

Publication: Eighty-five hundred copies published 6 April 1942.

Barrett Copies:
592818. Inscribed on the front open endpaper recto, 'For Vera / from her Uncle / Rob / April 1942'. A prospectus for *A Witness Tree* is laid in.
592817. Inscribed on the front open endpaper recto, 'Ring around a Rosy / We dance round in a ring and suppose / But the Secret sits in the middle and knows / Robert Frost / For Roy Virgil Thornton. / 1953'. The poem appears in *A Witness Tree* on p. 71 with the title 'The Secret Sits'. In this copy is an advance notice slip with the Holt imprint announcing the price as $2.50 and publication date as 12 August 1942. This information is contradicted by the fact that the book was published on 6 April 1942 at $2.00.

Related Barrett Copies:
592815. Two variant salesman's dummies: one in unlettered red cloth with the correct state of the dust jacket; the other in unlettered brown cloth with a trial state of the dust jacket on which only the front cover and spine are printed in more muted colors, the front inner flap blank save for the color register marks.

Back cover and back inner flap are of plain butcher-paper supplied to complete the mock-up jacket. Both copies are inscribed on the title-page, 'Robert Frost / to / Earle Bernheimer'. The text consists of a trial title-page (which has lettering as in the first edition, but with a publisher's device in red-brown between the title and imprint), trial table of contents, two pages of the poem 'The Lesson for Today,' and the poem 'Wilful Homing.' The verso of the title-page is as in the first edition. The headline on the first of the two contents pages is, '*CONTENTS*' ('TABLE OF CONTENTS' in the first edition); pagination is simulated opposite each title with '00.' Listing is not included for the frontispiece portrait and the two introductory poems, 'Beech' and 'Sycamore,' preceding the first section, 'ONE OR TWO.' The section, 'QUANTULA,' is entirely omitted. Variant poem titles: 'A Silken Tent' for 'The Silken Tent,' 'Willful Homing' for 'Wilful Homing,' 'The Cloud Shadow' for 'A Cloud Shadow,' 'The Discovery of the Madeira Islands' for 'The Discovery of the Madeiras,' 'For the Fall of Nineteen Thirty Eight' for 'November,' 'The Loose Mountain' for 'A Loose Mountain (Telescopic),' 'It Is Nearly the Year Two Thousand' for 'It Is Almost the Year Two Thousand.' The title head-line for the first poem is in italics, '*The Lesson for Today*' (caps in the first edition). In line 15 of the poem, the Latin quotation is not italicized, as in the first edition. The title of the second poem is given as '*Willful* [sic] *Homing*'. The text and title changes indicate that these dummies preceded the trial copy listed below.

592813. A trial printing bound in plain gray cloth, inscribed on the open end-paper recto, 'Robert Frost / to / Earle Bernheimer / New York / May 9 1942'. White wove paper with the watermark 'WARREN'S | OLDE STYLE'. Text printed on rectos only of 87 leaves. The half-title and frontispiece portrait are not present; the 'Table of Contents' pages are in trial setting with pagination that corresponds to this text but differs after p. 68 from the first edition pagination and arrangement of poems in that 'Boeotian' and 'The Secret Sits' (here without title) appear together on p. 69 (in the first edition, they are on pp. 70 and 71 respectively with titles) and 'Assurance,' 'A Question,' and 'An Answer'—none with titles—are together on p. 72 (in the first edition, they are on pp. 74, 75, and 69, each with title). The poem 'The Lesson For Today' (pp. 46–52) is in a setting with one more line to the page and nine lines on p. 52 (13 lines in the first edition). In many of the poems, capital initials of the lines are not evenly justified to the left margin as they are in the first edition. This volume, though 235 mm. tall (as opposed to 221 mm. in the first edition), has the correct first dust jacket. There are no textual variations.

492820. A braille edition of *A Witness Tree*. Title: 'A WITNESS TREE | *By* ROBERT FROST || Embossed in One Volume || COPYRIGHT, 1942, BY | ROBERT FROST | Reprinted | By permission of the Author and Publishers | HENRY HOLT AND COMPANY | NEW YORK || *Printed for the* | LIBRARY OF CONGRESS | WASHINGTON, D.C. | 1942 | CLOVERNOOK PRINTING HOUSE FOR THE BLIND | MT. HEALTHY, OHIO'. Printed title-page (verso blank), 32 leaves of braille, one blank leaf. Blank boards with cloth backstrip. A paper label in braille on the front cover; the spine lettered, 'A WITNESS TREE Frost'. Stapled at the center fold.

593072 and 596349. Two prospectuses for *A Witness Tree,* announcing publication day as April 23. A single folded sheet of four pages; J. J. Lankes' woodcut of a tree on p. 1, Enit Kaufman's portrait of RF on p. 2. On p. 4: 'The number of copies in the special edition will be absolutely limited to orders received by March 23, 1942.'

A25.2   1943   A WITNESS TREE (First English Edition)

A WITNESS TREE | *by* | ROBERT FROST | [publisher's device] | JON-ATHAN CAPE | THIRTY BEDFORD SQUARE | LONDON.

Collation: [A]⁸ B-D⁸; pp. [i–iv], [1–4] 5–57 [58–60] = 64 leaves.

Contents: pp. i–iv: blank (pp. i–ii as pastedown endpaper; pp. iii–iv, open end-paper); p. 1: half-title and dedication, 'A WITNESS TREE | *To* | *K. M.* | *for her part in it*'; p. 2: '*By the Same Author* | [8 titles in caps]'; p. 3: title-page; p. 4: 'FIRST PUBLISHED 1943 | JONATHAN CAPE LTD. 30 BEDFORD SQUARE, LONDON | AND 91 WELLINGTON STREET WEST, TO-RONTO | [swelling rule] | PRINTED IN GREAT BRITAIN IN THE CITY OF OXFORD | AT THE ALDEN PRESS | PAPER BY SPALDING & HODGE LTD. | BOUND BY A. W. BAIN & CO. LTD.'; pp. 5–7: contents; pp. 8–57: text (section-titles as headlines on pp. 8, 27, 36, 45, and 48); pp. 58–60: blank (pp. 59–60 as pastedown endpaper).

Illustration: The Enit Kaufman portrait in dark gray tipped in facing the title-page. On white wove paper slightly heavier than the text.

Text Content: As in earlier editions.

Paper: White wove paper. Leaves measure 201 × 141 mm. Top edge trimmed and stained blue, fore-edge uncut, bottom edge rough-cut.

Binding: Blue (182.m.B) linen cloth. Covers blank; spine lettered in gilt from bottom to top, 'A WITNESS TREE = ROBERT FROST'.

Dust Jacket: Heavy wove paper. Front cover: black ground with a design of a tree in shallow intaglio in white, greenish blue (173.m.gB), and black; lettering on a ribbon incorporated in the design, '[black] A | WITNESS | TREE | [beneath the tree in white] Robert Frost | [signed in the lower right corner in greenish blue] TISDALL'. Spine in greenish blue unlettered. The back cover: white ground with a scallop of black extending the height of the right margin, '[greenish blue] COLLECTED POEMS | by ROBERT FROST | [black] [19-line blurb by William Rose Benét; 4-line blurb by Louis Untermeyer] | 18s. net'. Front inner flap: 'A WITNESS TREE | [26-line blurb]' | [diagonal] 5s. net'. Back inner flap: 'BRITAIN | [design of earth with a microphone] | CALLS THE WORLD | [29-line for B.B.C. broadcast] | FROM LONDON COMES | THE VOICE OF BRITAIN | . . . THE VOICE OF FREEDOM'.

Barrett Copies:
592819. Inscribed on p. iii, 'Robert Frost / to / Russell Alberts / in friendship'.

A26   1943 COME IN (First Edition)

[red-brown] COME IN | AND OTHER POEMS | [black] *by* | ROBERT FROST | Selection, | biographical introduction, | and commentary by | LOUIS UNTERMEYER | [red-brown] ILLUSTRATED BY | JOHN O'HARA COSGRAVE II | [black] HENRY HOLT *and* COMPANY

Collation: [1]^8(1_1 + X^2) [2–11]^8 [12]^4 [13]^8; [i–vi] vii–x, [1–2] 3–192 [193–194]: 102 leaves.
     Note: The frontis. and title-leaf are conjugates (X^2) on heavier paper tipped in between $1_{1\text{-}2}$. They have implied pagination, iii–vi.

Contents: p. i: half-title, 'COME IN | *And Other Poems*'; p. ii: blank; p. iii: blank; p. iv: frontispiece; p. v: title-page; p. vi: 'COPYRIGHT, 1943, | BY | HENRY HOLT AND COMPANY, INC. | The poems quoted in this volume are from *A Boy's Will*, | *North of Boston, Mountain Inverval, New Hampshire*, | *West-Running Brook, A Further Range, and A Witness | Tree*. No part of this book may be reproduced in | any form, by mimeograph or any other means, without | permission from the publisher. | *first printing* | PRINTED IN THE | UNITED STATES OF AMERICA'; pp. vii–x: contents; p. 1: second half-title (as the first); p. 2: blank; pp. 3–16: 'AN INTRODUCTION', signed in print on p. 16, 'LOUIS UNTERMEYER'; pp. 17–192: text; p. 193: wood-engraved illustration by John O'Hara Cosgrave II; p. 194: blank.

Illustrations: Frontispiece on heavy white wove paper; a reproduction in colors of a watercolor by John O'Hara Cosgrave II of birch trees. Black and white wood-engraved vignettes and part-page illustrations throughout the text.

Text Content:
I. Introduction by Louis Untermeyer
    The Pasture
II. The Code and Other Stories
    The Tuft of Flowers
    Blueberries
    Home Burial
    The Witch of Coös
    Paul's Wife
    Ghost House
    At Woodward's Gardens
    The Vindictives
    Wild Grapes

    The Code
III. The Hired Man and Other People
    Birches
    Mowing
    Mending Wall
    The Mountain
    Brown's Descent, or The
        Willy-Nilly Slide
    The Vanishing Red
    To the Thawing Wind
    A Lone Striker
    Two Tramps in Mud Time

Love and a Question
An Old Man's Winter Night
The Gum-Gatherer
The Investment
The Figure in the Doorway
To a Young Wretch
The Wood-Pile
The Death of the Hired Man

IV. Stopping by Woods and Other
      Places
Hyla Brook
The Flower Boat
The Census-Taker
A Brook in the City
Evening in a Sugar Orchard
The Onset
Spring Pools
In a Disused Graveyard
Sand Dunes
The Birthplace
For Once, Then, Something
A Serious Step Lightly Taken
Tree at My Window
Sitting by a Bush in Broad
   Sunlight
Stopping by Woods on a Snowy
   Evening

V. The Runaway and Other Animals
The Oven Bird
Our Singing Strength
A Minor Bird
Never Again Would Birds'
   Song Be the Same
A Blue Ribbon at Amesbury
A Drumlin Woodchuck
A White-tailed Hornet
Waspish

Departmental
Fireflies in the Garden
Design
Canis Major
Two Look at Two
The Cow in Apple Time
The Runaway

VI. Country Things and Other
      Things
The Road Not Taken
The Need of Being Versed in
   Country Things
The Sound of Trees
In Hardwood Groves
Nothing Gold Can Stay
After Apple-Picking
The Grindstone
The Kitchen Chimney
Gathering Leaves
A Leaf Treader
A Hillside Thaw
On a Tree Fallen across the
   Road
A Passing Glimpse
Dust of Snow
Fire and Ice
Riders
The Master Speed
The Gift Outright
A Considerable Speck
The Silken Tent
Good-Bye and Keep Cold
A Prayer in Spring
Into My Own
Come In

VII. An Afterword
Choose Something Like a Star

Paper: Cream wove paper. Leaves measure 211 × 137 mm. Edges trimmed, top edge stained red-brown. Pictorial endpapers printed in colors; a watercolor, signed 'J. O'H. Cosgrave II', on the free endpaper recto and the note 'Mount Kearsage | from Flaghole | Andover N.H | '42' on the pastedown at lower left. Reverse on the terminal endpapers.

Binding: Cream glazed linen cloth. On the front cover is a vignette of a farmhouse stamped in red-brown. Spine: '[red-brown] ROBERT | FROST | COME |

IN | AND | OTHER | POEMS | [vignette of a farmhouse with smoking chimney] | HOLT'. Back cover blank.

Dust Jacket: Heavy white wove paper printed in colors. Front cover: '[within a double-rule border in black] [red-brown] ROBERT | FROST | [black] COME IN | AND OTHER POEMS | [the frontispiece watercolor of birches by J. O. Cosgrave II, reproduced in colors] | [black] WITH COMMENTARY BY | [red-brown] LOUIS UNTERMEYER'. Spine: '||| [red-brown] ROBERT | FROST | [black] COME | IN | AND | OTHER | POEMS | [detail of the Cosgrave cover illustration in colors] | [black] HOLT |||'. Back cover: a pale blue (171.v.l.gB) panel bordered on three sides by the white of the jacket paper. Front inner flap: '[black] $2.50 | COME IN | by ROBERT FROST | *Selected, and with a commentary | and biographical introduction,* | *by* LOUIS UNTERMEYER | [31-line blurb] | [Holt imprint]'. Back inner flap: '[black] OUR MEN WANT | BOOKS | SEND ALL YOU CAN SPARE | [vignette of an eagle with books] | [21 lines of mailing instructions and a mailing label]'.

Publication: Published 5 April 1943. An enlargement of this volume with additional material by Louis Untermeyer was published by Holt with the title *The Road Not Taken* in 1951 (Barrett 592758).

Barrett Copies:
595425. Galley proof sheets of the first edition, without illustrations. On the blank verso of the final galley, RF has written, 'Robert Frost to Earle Bernheimer.' Above, in another hand, 'Galley Proof of / "Come In" / by / Robert Frost. / Rec'd. 3/24/43. (Book not issued yet.) / (Pub. date — 4/5/43. / Introduction / by / Louis Untermeyer'.
592620. Inscribed on the front free endpaper, 'To Vera / from her / Uncle Rob / April 2 1944'.
592621. Another copy.
598924. A copy of the 'Armed Services Edition,' inscribed on p. i, 'Robert Frost's / signature for / Russell Alberts / December 25 1944'. Oblong format 98 × 140 mm., pp. i–ii, 1–156. Leaves of cheap pulp cream paper, stapled at the center fold. Heavy paper wrappers cut flush with the leaves.

A26.1   1944 COME IN (First English Edition)

COME IN | *AND OTHER POEMS* | by | ROBERT FROST | [publisher's device] | *Selected, with a biographical | introduction and commentary, by* | LOUIS UNTERMEYER | JONATHAN CAPE | THIRTY BEDFORD SQUARE | LONDON

Collation: [A]⁸ B–I⁸ K⁸; pp. [πi–iv], [1–4] 5–151 [152–156] = 80 leaves.

Contents: pp. πi–ii: pastedown blank endpaper; pp. πiii–iv: free blank endpaper; p. 1: half-title, 'COME IN | *and other poems*'; p. 2: '*by the same author* | [9 titles in caps]'; p. 3: title-page; p. 4: 'FIRST PUBLISHED 1944 | JONATHAN

CAPE LTD. 30 BEDFORD SQUARE, LONDON | AND 91 WELLINGTON STREET WEST, TORONTO | ['BOOK | PRODUCTION | WAR ECON-OMY | STANDARD' within the device of an open book surmounted by a lion] | THIS BOOK IS PRODUCED IN COM-|PLETE CONFORMITY WITH THE | AUTHORIZED ECONOMY STANDARDS | PRINTED IN GREAT BRITAIN IN THE CITY OF OXFORD | AT THE ALDEN PRESS | PAPER BY SPALDING & HODGE LTD. | BOUND BY A. W. BAIN & CO. LTD.'; pp. 5–7: contents; p. 8: blank; pp. 9–19: introduction signed in print 'Louis Untermeyer | [beneath on p. 19, the title-poem]'; pp. 20–151: text; p. 152: blank; pp. 153–154: terminal free blank endpaper; pp. 155–156: terminal pastedown blank endpaper.

Text Content: As in the first edition.

Paper: Cheap white wove paper. Leaves measure 192 × 125 mm.; top and fore-edge trimmed, bottom edge rough-cut. Top edge stained dark blue. Endpapers integral with the first and final gatherings.

Binding: Blue (182.m.B) fine linen cloth, covers blank. Spine stamped in gilt and lettered from bottom to top, '[horizontal: publisher's device] | COME IN = ROBERT FROST'.

Dust Jacket: Cream wove paper with a green (145.m.G) ground on the front cover and spine with white lettering. Front cover: 'COME IN | *poems by* | ROBERT FROST | [2 fern fronds in green on a white patch] | *selected by* | LOUIS UNTERMEYER | *with a commentary* | *and biographical* | *introduction*'. Spine: '[lettered from bottom to top] COME IN * poems by * ROBERT FROST'. Back cover blank. Front inner flap: '[lettered in black] COME IN | [27-line blurb]'. Back inner flap: '[black] *This message is addressed to readers outside Great Britain* | ['THE VOICE | OF | BRITAIN' against a world map] | [28-line blurb]'. To conserve paper during wartime, sheets of unused printed dust jackets were sometimes reversed and the jacket for another book printed on the blank side. The Barrett copy of the English edition of *Come In* has the front cover, spine, and front inner flap of Friedrich Sieburg's *Germany: My Country* printed on the inside of the dust jacket.

Barrett Copies:
592622. With dust jacket as described above.

A27   1945 A MASQUE OF REASON (Limited Edition)

A MASQUE | OF REASON | [red-brown] BY | [black] ROBERT | FROST | [red-brown] [Holt device] | [black] HENRY HOLT AND COMPANY | NEW YORK

Collation: [1–5]⁴; pp. [i–iv], [1–6] 7–30 [31–36] = 20 leaves.

Contents: pp. i–iv: blank; p. 1: '*This edition has been | limited to eight hundred numbered copies | and here signed by the author* | [holograph] Robert Frost |

This copy is number | [arabic number inserted ink]; p. 2: blank; p. 3: title-page; p. 4: '*Copyright,* 1945, *by Robert Frost* | *Printed in the* | *United States of America*'; p. 5: half-title, 'A MASQUE OF REASON'; p. 6: blank; pp. 7–30: text (printed in black and red-brown); pp. 31–32: blank; p. 33: 'Printed at The Spiral Press · New York | February 1945'; pp. 34–35: blank.

Paper: White laid paper with horizontal chainlines 37 mm. apart. No visible watermark. Leaves measure 254 × 180 mm. Top edge trimmed, other edges uncut. Endpapers of the same stock.

Binding: Light brown (61.gyBr) paper-covered boards, backed with tan (76.l.yBr) linen cloth. On the front cover in the upper right corner is a dark brown stamped panel, lettered in gilt-stamp, '[within a gilt-stamped rule] A | MASQUE | OF | REASON | BY | ROBERT | FROST'. Spine stamped with gilt within a gilt-ruled dark brown panel, reading from bottom to top, 'A MASQUE OF REASON BY ROBERT FROST'. Back cover blank. In a black board slipcase.

Publication: Eight hundred copies printed by The Spiral Press, 8 February 1945.

Barrett Copies:
592686. Number 328, signed. Also, inscribed on the open endpaper recto, 'To Vera [Harvey] / from her / Uncle Rob / March 26 1945 / Cambridge'.
592685. Number 30, signed.
599542. Page proofs of the limited edition with a few editorial corrections of spelling and punctuation. Cased with a set of broadsheet proofs of the trade edition and galley proofs of the trade edition with an earlier trial setting of the preliminaries. On the half-title (p. 1), RF has written (referring to a cross ornament), 'Let's not use crosses for / ornaments. R. F. / How about some little Christmas trees / or some little birds.' There are eleven corrections in his hand in the galley text. Most are for spelling and punctuation; however, on p. 3, line 7, he changes 'Lovelace' to 'Waller'. On p. 21, line 7, he changes 'Conversationalists' to 'Conversationists' and on p. 23, line 13, the phrase 'rich and rare' is changed to 'sisal hemp'.

A27.1 1945 MASQUE OF REASON (Trade Edition)

A MASQUE | OF REASON | BY | ROBERT FROST | HENRY HOLT AND COMPANY | NEW YORK

Collation: [1–4]^{4}; pp. [i–vi], 1–23 [24–26] = 16 leaves.

Contents: p. i: half-title, 'A MASQUE OF REASON'; p. ii: blank; p. iii: title-page; p. iv: 'COPYRIGHT 1945 BY ROBERT FROST | *First Printing* | PRINTED IN THE UNITED STATES OF AMERICA'; p. v: second half-title, A MASQUE OF REASON'; p. vi: blank; pp. 1–23: text; pp. 24–26: blank.

Paper: Rough cream wove paper. Leaves measure 212 × 141 mm. Top and bottom edges trimmed, fore-edge rough-cut. Endpapers of heavier beige wove paper.
Binding: Dark blue (183.d.B) fine linen cloth. Covers blank. Spine stamped in gilt from top to bottom, 'ROBERT FROST · A MASQUE OF REASON · HOLT'.

Dust jacket: Wove paper. The front cover and spine have a pictorial ground representing bushes and small plants against a blue-green space dominated by a fireball of orange, yellow, purple, and white. Lettering on the front cover in black quasi-blackletter, '𝕽𝕺𝕭𝕰𝕽𝕿 𝕱𝕽𝕺𝕾𝕿 | A | 𝕸𝖆𝖘𝖖𝖚𝖊 | OF | 𝕽𝖊𝖆𝖘𝖔𝖓'. Signed in yellow, 'Palacias'. Spine lettered in black quasi-blackletter, 'A 𝕸𝖆𝖘𝖖𝖚𝖊 OF 𝕽𝖊𝖆𝖘𝖔𝖓 𝕽𝕺𝕭𝕰𝕽𝕿 𝕱𝕽𝕺𝕾𝕿 [white] HOLT'. Back cover with white ground and a photographic portrait of Frost, lettered beneath in black, 'ROBERT FROST.' Front inner flap, black lettering on white, '$2.00 | A MASQUE | OF REASON | *by* | ROBERT FROST | [28-line blurb] | (*Continued on back flap*)'. Back flap, '(*Continued from front flap*) | [10-line blurb] | [leaf orn.] | BOOKS BY | ROBERT FROST | [11 titles] | [leaf orn.] | [Holt imprint]'.

Publication: Fifteen thousand were published 26 March 1945. Priced at $2.00.

Barrett Copies:
708935. Laid in is a review slip listing the price as $2.00 and the date of publication as 26 March.
592688. Inscribed on the front open endpaper, 'To R. V. Thornton / from / Robert Frost'.
592689. Inscribed on the front open endpaper, 'To Vera / from her / Uncle Rob / March 26 1945'. Beneath in pencil, 'My book / Vera Harvey'.

A28   1946 THE COURAGE TO BE NEW (First Edition)

[The Courage to Be New by Robert Frost]

Broadside printing on a sheet of heavy wove cream paper, measuring 182 × 126 mm.; edges trimmed, bottom edge uncut.

Contents: '[dark gray-blue vignette of an eagle and stars] | [black] ORRIS C. MANNING MEMORIAL | RIPTON · VERMONT · 28 JULY | 1946 | [first two stanzas of 'The Courage to Be New'] | ROBERT FROST | [dark gray-blue] DECORATION BY THOREAU MACDONALD'.

Publication: Printed for the dedication services of Orris C. Manning Memorial Park, Ripton, Vermont, 28 July 1946. The poem was collected in *Steeple Bush* (1947) with two added stanzas under the title 'The Courage to Be New.'

Barrett Copy:
592742. This copy is signed 'Robert Frost / to / R. V. Thornton'. With it is the original outline sketch for the broadside in pencil, signed 'Robert Frost', and a first trial proof printed in black with printer's notes in red pencil, also signed by Frost.

A29   1946 THE POEMS OF ROBERT FROST (First Edition of This Selection)

THE POEMS | OF | ROBERT FROST | *With an Introductory Essay* | "THE CONSTANT SYMBOL" | *by the Author* | [Modern Library device] || THE MODERN LIBRARY • NEW YORK ||

Collation: [1–15]¹⁶; pp. [i–iv] v–xiii [xiv] xv–xxiv, [1–2] 3–445 [446–456] = 240 leaves.

Contents: p. i: half-title, 'THE MODERN LIBRARY | *OF THE WORLD'S BEST BOOKS* | [swelling rule] | THE POEMS OF | ROBERT FROST | [swelling rule] | [6-line blurb in italics advertising Modern Library books]; p. ii: blank; p. iii: title-page; p. iv: 'COPYRIGHT, 1930, 1939, BY HENRY HOLT & CO., INC. | COPYRIGHT, 1936, 1942, BY ROBERT FROST | COPYRIGHT, 1946, BY RANDOM HOUSE, INC. | FIRST *Modern Library* EDITION, 1946 | [Random House device forming top rule of an otherwise single-rule frame containing:] | *Random House* IS THE PUBLISHER OF | THE MODERN LIBRARY | BENNETT A. CERF · DONALD S. KLOPFER · ROBERT K. HAAS | Manufactured in the United States of America | Printed by Parkway Printing Company Bound by H. Wolff'; pp. v–xiii: contents; p. xiv: blank; pp. xv–xxiv: introductory essay, 'The Constant Symbol,' with the poem 'To the Right Person' on p. xxiv; subscribed 'ROBERT FROST | July, 1946'; p. 1: section-title, '*A Boy's Will*'; p. 2: blank; pp. 3–436: text; pp. 437–445: index of first lines; p. 446: blank; pp. 447–454: list of Modern Library titles; pp. 455–456: blank. Section-titles with blank versos at pp. 33 ('NORTH OF BOSTON'), 115 ('MOUNTAIN INTERVAL'), 177 ('NEW HAMPSHIRE'), 261 ('WEST-RUNNING BROOK'), 307 ('A FURTHER RANGE'), 381 ('A WITNESS TREE').

Text Content: This collection contains all poems published in previous collected works with the exception of 42 which RF chose to exclude:

A Late Walk	In Hardwood Groves
Wind and Window Flower	My Butterfly
In a Vale	The Wood-Pile
A Dream Pang	The Self-Seeker
The Trial by Existence	The Exposed Nest
Pan with Us	A Patch of Old Snow

In the Home Stretch
Meeting and Passing
A Girl's Garden
Locked Out
Maple
Place for a Third
The Pauper Witch of Grafton
A Fountain, a Bottle, a Donkey's
  Ears and Some Books
I Will Sing You One-O
In a Disused Graveyard
A Boundless Moment
Evening in a Sugar Orchard
The Valley's Singing Day
A Hillside Thaw
The Lockless Door

The Rose Family
The Cocoon
The Thatch
The Door in the Dark
The Armful
The Old Barn at the Bottom of the Fogs
On Taking from the Top to Broaden
  the Base
After-flakes
Clear and Colder
To a Thinker
The Subverted Flower
The Discovery of the Madeiras
In a Poem
An Equalizer
Not of School Age

In the contents section of this edition, the poem 'Willful Homing' is incorrectly listed as 'Wilful Homecoming', which is partially corrected to 'Wilful Homing' on p. 395. The spelling 'wilful' was used in the first edition of *A Witness Tree,* but changed in the 1949 *Complete Poems* to 'willful'.

Paper: White wove paper. Leaves measure 177 × 122 mm.; edges trimmed, top edge stained dark green. Endpapers of wove paper printed on the facing pastedown and open endpaper recto with the Modern Library devices in gray and white.

Binding: Blue-green (164.m.bG) very fine linen cloth. Front cover: at the upper center, a single gilt rule frame 88 × 53 mm.; within this, a black cloth panel bordered with a gilt rule 42 × 31 mm., lettered in gilt, 'THE POEMS | OF | ROBERT | FROST'. On the lower right, within the larger gilt rule frame is the Modern Library device in gilt stamp. Spine: '[gilt-stamped Modern Library device] | [on a black cloth panel within a single gilt rule frame, lettered in gilt:] THE | POEMS | OF | ROBERT | FROST | [orn.] | MODERN | LIBRARY'. Back cover blank.

Dust Jacket: Light gray laid paper with horizontal chainlines 20 mm. apart; lettering in red-brown (41.dp.rBr) and black. Front cover: '[red-brown] THE | POEMS | OF | ROBERT | FROST | [black] *With an Introductory Essay* | "THE CONSTANT SYMBOL" | *by the Author* | [red-brown thick-thin rule] | [black] A MODERN LIBRARY BOOK'. Spine: '[black] ROBERT | FROST | [red-brown: Modern Library device] | [within a red-brown rule frame, lettered vertically from top to bottom in black] *The Poems of* ROBERT FROST | [horizontal, in black] 242 | MODERN | LIBRARY'. Back cover and flaps are ads for Modern Library books. On the front inner flap is a 16-line blurb for this edition. On the inside of the jacket is a complete list of titles available in Modern Library editions.

Publication: RF made this selection of his published poems. The essay 'The Constant Symbol' appears in print here for the first time. The poem 'To the Right Person' was printed first in the *Atlantic Monthly* (Oct. 1946).

Barrett Copy:
592558.

A30   1947 STEEPLE BUSH (Limited Edition)

STEEPLE BUSH | BY ROBERT FROST | HENRY HOLT AND COM-PANY | NEW YORK 1947 [extending the length of the title-page is a drawing of a weed in yellow-gray, by Loren MacIver]

Collation: [1–5]⁸; pp. [i–xii], [1–2] 3–63 [64–68] = 40 leaves.

Contents: pp. i–ii: blank; p. iii: 'THIS EDITION OF STEEPLE BUSH | HAS BEEN LIMITED TO | SEVEN HUNDRED FIFTY-ONE COPIES | HERE SIGNED BY THE AUTHOR | [holograph] Robert Frost | THIS IS COPY NUMBER | [number in ink]'; p. iv: blank; p. v: title-page; p. vi: 'FIRST PRINTING | COPYRIGHT 1947 BY HENRY HOLT AND COMPANY · INC | PRINTED IN THE UNITED STATES OF AMERICA'; p. vii: dedication, 'FOR | PRESCOTT · JOHN · ELINOR · LESLEY LEE | ROBIN AND HAROLD'; p. viii: blank; pp. ix–xi: contents; p. xii: blank; p. 1: half-title, 'STEEPLE BUSH'; p. 2: blank; pp. 3–62: text; p. 63: '*Notes*'; p. 64: blank; p. 65: '[Spiral Press device] | PRINTED AT THE SPIRAL PRESS · NEW YORK | DECORATION BY LOREN MacIVER'; pp. 66–68: blank. Section-titles with blank versos at pp. 15, 23, 33, 49.

Text Content:

A Young Birch
Something for Hope
One Step Backward Taken
Directive
Too Anxious for Rivers
An Unstamped Letter in Our
    Rural Letter Box
To an Ancient
The Night Light
Were I in Trouble
Bravado
On Making Certain Anything
    Has Happened
In the Long Night
A Mood Apart

The Fear of God
The Fear of Man
A Steeple on the House
Innate Helium
The Courage to Be New
Iota Subscript
The Middleness of the Road
Astrometaphysical
Skeptic
Two Leading Lights
A Rogers Group
On Being Idolized
A Wish to Comply
A Cliff Dwelling
It Bids Pretty Fair

Beyond Words
A Case for Jefferson
Lucretius versus the Lake Poets
Haec Fabula Docet
Etherealizing
Why Wait for Science
Any Size We Please
An Importer

The Planners
No Holy Wars for Them
Bursting Rapture
U.S. 1946 King's X
The Ingenuities of Debt
The Broken Drought
To the Right Person

Paper: White wove paper watermarked 'Old Stratford'. Leaves measure 234 × 156 mm. Top and bottom edges trimmed, fore-edge uncut. Endpapers of the same stock.

Binding: Gray-green (150.gyG) paper-covered boards backed with tan linen cloth. On the front cover is Loren MacIver's title-page design repeated in gilt-stamp. Spine: '[stamped in gilt within a gilt-ruled black panel; lettered from bottom to top] ROBERT FROST · STEEPLE BUSH'. Back cover blank. In a plain, unlettered slipcase covered with the gray-green paper used for the binding.

Publication: Published in April 1947 by The Spiral Press in an edition of 751 copies.

Barrett Copy:
592773. Number 168. Inscribed on the open endpaper recto, 'To Vera [Harvey] from her Uncle Robert / 1947'.

A30.1   1947 STEEPLE BUSH (Trade Edition)

STEEPLE BUSH | BY | ROBERT FROST | [Holt device] | NEW YORK | HENRY HOLT AND COMPANY

FIRST IMPRESSION FROM THE LIMITED EDITION PLATES

Collation: [1–5]⁸; pp. [i–xii], [1–2] 3–62 [63–68] = 40 leaves.

Contents: pp. i–ii: blank; p. iii: half-title, 'STEEPLE BUSH'; p. iv: blank; p. v: title-page; p. vi: 'COPYRIGHT 1947 BY HENRY HOLT AND COMPANY · INC | PRINTED IN THE UNITED STATES OF AMERICA'; p. vii: dedication, 'FOR | PRESCOTT · JOHN · ELINOR · LESLEY LEE | ROBIN AND HAROLD'; p. viii: blank; pp. ix–xi: contents; p. xii: blank; p. 1: second half-title; p. 2: blank; pp. 3–62: text; p. 63: '*Notes*'; pp. 64–68: blank. Section-titles with blank versos at pp. 15, 23, 33, 49.

Text Content: As in the limited edition.

Paper: White laid paper with vertical chainlines 24 mm. apart. Watermarked 'Hamilton | Andorra'. Leaves measure 212 × 140 mm. Edges trimmed. End-papers of heavier white wove paper.

Binding: Light blue green (163.l.bG) fine linen cloth. Covers blank. Spine lettered in gilt from top to bottom, '[within a gilt-ruled black panel] STEEPLE BUSH · ROBERT FROST | [at the foot, printed horizontally in black] Holt'.

Dust Jacket: Heavy, light-gray paper, printed overall in dull reddish-purple (duller than 259.d.pR). Front cover, '[within a border rule that consists of thin-thick rule at top, thick-thin rule at bottom, and single rules at the sides] STEEPLE BUSH | [vignette of a fence, weeds, and a house in the background] | Robert Frost'. Spine: '[thin-thick rule] | [lettering from top to bottom] STEEPLE BUSH Robert Frost | [horizontal lettering] HOLT | [thick-thin rule]'. Back cover: '*Books of poetry by ROBERT FROST | published by Henry Holt and Company . . .* | [12 titles, including *A Masque of Mercy*, noted as 'In preparation'] | [Holt imprint]'. Front inner flap: '$2.50 | SB | *Steeple | Bush* | by | Robert Frost | [20-line blurb] | (*Continued on back flap*)' Back inner flap: '(*Continued from front flap*) | [12-line blurb] | *About the author* . . . | [14-line blurb] | [Holt imprint] | [in the lower left corner, printed diagonally beneath a dotted line] STEEPLE BUSH | ROBERT FROST | HENRY HOLT | AND CO.'

Publication: Seventy-six hundred copies published 17 April 1947. Priced at $2.50.

Barrett Copies:
592775. Inscribed on the front open endpaper, 'To Russell Alberts / from his friend / Robert Frost / 1948'.
592776.

A31   1947 A MASQUE OF MERCY (Limited Edition)

A | MASQUE OF | MERCY | [dark blue-green] BY | [black] ROBERT | FROST | [dark blue-green: Holt device] | [black] HENRY HOLT AND COMPANY | NEW YORK

Collation: [1–4]⁴ [5]⁶ [6]⁴; pp. [i–ii], [1–6] 7–46 [47–50] = 26 leaves.

Contents: pp. i–ii: blank; p. 1: 'THIS EDITION OF A MASQUE OF MERCY | HAS BEEN LIMITED TO | SEVEN HUNDRED FIFTY-ONE COPIES | HERE SIGNED BY THE AUTHOR | [holograph] Robert Frost | THIS COPY IS NUMBER | [number in ink]'; p. 2: blank; p. 3: title-page; p. 4: '*Copyright, 1947, by | Henry Holt and Company, Inc. | Printed in the | United States of America*'; p. 5: 'A MASQUE OF MERCY | CHARACTERS | MY BROTHER'S KEEPER | JESSE BEL, HIS WIFE | PAUL, A DOCTOR | JONAS DOVE, A FUGITIVE'; p. 6: blank; pp. 7–46: text (printed in black and dark blue-green); p. 47: blank; p. 48: '[Spiral Press device in dark blue-green] | [black] Printed at The Spiral Press · New York | September 1947'; pp. 49–50: blank.

Paper: White laid paper with horizontal chainlines 26 mm. apart. No visible watermark. Leaves measure 253 × 179 mm. Edges trimmed. Endpapers of the same stock, but with chainlines running vertically.

Binding: Beige (91.d.gyY) paper-covered boards with vertical chainlines 25 mm. apart. Backed with dark blue (187.d.gyB) linen cloth. On the front cover in the upper right corner is a black-stamped panel, lettered in gilt-stamp, '[within a gilt-stamped rule frame] A | MASQUE | OF | MERCY | BY | ROBERT | FROST'. A vertical gilt rule delineates the juncture between cloth and paper. Spine stamped with gilt within a gilt-ruled black panel, reading from bottom to top, 'A MASQUE OF MERCY BY ROBERT FROST'. Back cover blank, but with the vertical gilt rule as on the front cover. In a plain, unlettered slipcase of the same beige paper.

Publication: The Spiral Press printed 751 copies in September 1947. Priced at $7.50.

Barrett Copy:
592682. Number 33, signed by Frost.

A31.1   1947 A MASQUE OF MERCY (Trade Edition)

𝕬 𝕸𝖆𝖘𝖖𝖚𝖊 | 𝕺𝖋 𝕸𝖊𝖗𝖈𝖞 | BY | ROBERT FROST | HENRY HOLT AND COMPANY | NEW YORK

Collation: [1–3]⁸; pp. [i–vi], 1–39 [40–42] = 24 leaves.

Contents: p. i: half-title, 'A MASQUE OF MERCY'; p. ii: blank; p. iii: title-page; p. iv: 'COPYRIGHT, 1947, BY HENRY HOLT AND COMPANY, INC. | *First printing* | PRINTED IN THE UNITED STATES OF AMERICA'; p. v: 'CHARACTERS | *My Brother's Keeper* | *Jesse Bel, his wife* | *Paul, a doctor* | *Jonas Dove, a fugitive*'; p. vi: blank; pp. 1–39: text; pp. 40–42: blank.

Paper: White wove paper. Leaves measure 212 × 143 mm.; edges trimmed. Endpapers of heavier wove stock.

Binding: Light blue (182.m.B) fine linen cloth. Covers blank. Spine gilt-stamped reading from top to bottom, 'ROBERT FROST · A MASQUE OF MERCY · HOLT'.

Dust Jacket: Heavy wove paper watermarked 'Hamilton | Kilmory'. Front cover coated with greenish blue (168.brill.gB), lettered in white, 'A | MASQUE | OF | MERCY | Robert Frost'. Spine also with white lettering on green-blue (168),

'Frost | [lettered from top to bottom] A MASQUE OF MERCY | [horizontal] Holt'. Back cover with black lettering on white ground, '*The poetry of ROBERT FROST* | [12 titles listed] | [Holt imprint]'. Front inner flap (black lettering on white): '$2.50 | MOM | A MASQUE OF | MERCY | ROBERT FROST | [30-line blurb] | *Henry Holt and Company*'. Back inner flap (black lettering on white): 'A MASQUE OF | REASON | ROBERT FROST | [26-line blurb] | $2.00 | Ltd. Ed. $7.50 | *Henry Holt and Company* | [in the lower left corner printed diagonally beneath a dotted line] MASQUE OF MERCY | ROBERT FROST | HENRY HOLT | AND CO.'

Publication: Seventy-five hundred copies printed 12 September 1947. Priced at $2.50. Printed in the *Atlantic Monthly* (Nov. 1947).

Barrett Copies:
592683. Inscribed on the open endpaper recto, 'No, everything I say is said in scorn / Some people want you not to understand them. / But I want you to understand me wrong / Robert Frost / quoting someone else. / For R. V. Thornton.' The quotation is a speech of 'My Brother's Keeper' in the play, p. 25, lines 5–7.
592684. Inscribed on the open endpaper, 'To Vera from R. F. / with affection.'

A32   1947 A SEMI-REVOLUTION (First Separate Edition)

[red] TWO POEMS | [black] ON | [red] REVOLUTION | [black] A SEMI-REVOLUTION | *by Robert Frost* | • • | A TOTAL REVOLU-TION | AN ANSWER FOR ROBERT FROST | *by Oscar Williams* | [orn.] | Printed at the | BOOKBUILDERS WORKSHOP | 90 Beacon Street, Boston | 1947

Collation: [1]²; pp. [1–4] = 2 leaves.

Contents: p. 1: title-page; p. 2: the Frost poem with red initial and arabic '1' above title; p. 3: the Williams poem with red initial and arabic '2' above the title; p. 4: '[at the foot] Designed and printed by Charles Butcher as a class project.'

Paper: Cream wove paper with leaves measuring 145 × 111 mm.; edges trimmed. Pasted to the cover at the center fold.

Binding: Pale gray-green laid paper with horizontal chainlines 35 mm. apart. A small section of a large watermark visible in the corner of the front cover. On the front cover is a cream paper label (48 × 68 mm.) printed in red, '[within a border rule] *Two Poems* | *on* | *Revolution*.'

Publication: Responding to our inquiry, Charles Butcher kindly furnished the following information: 'There were 25 "good" copies and about 7 "seconds" printed. . . . Oscar Williams told me that Frost was not happy about the booklet. . . . The original distribution was to poet friends, most of whom I knew through my brother-in-law, Richard G. Eberhart. The original list of recipients included John Ciardi, Robert Frost, Oscar Williams, Richard Eberhart, Jack Sweeney, Robert Lowell, Dylan Thomas and others. . . . The printing of Frost's poem was not a first printing [first in *A Witness Tree,* 1942] and was done without his permission (no copies were for public sale). The poems were copied from Oscar Williams' anthology.'

Butcher was learning printing when he undertook this project at the Merrymount Press, Boston, in 1947. He subsequently worked as a printing designer for the Lincoln & Smith Press and later established The Wazygoose Press as a hobby.

Barrett Copy:
592789. Signed on p. 3, beneath the poem, 'Oscar Williams'.

A33   1947 A SERMON (First Edition)

A SERMON BY Robert Frost | SPOKEN ON THE FIRST DAY OF | THE FEAST OF TABERNACLES AT | THE ROCKDALE AVENUE TEMPLE | CINCINNATI · OHIO · THURSDAY | MORNING · OCTOBER · 10 · 1946

Collation: [1]¹⁰; pp. [1–20] = 10 leaves.

Contents: pp. 1–4: blank; p. 5: title-page; p. 6: 'COPYRIGHT 1947 BY VICTOR E. REICHERT | CINCINNATI · OHIO'; p. 7: three paragraphs explaining the occasion of the sermon; p. 8: blank; pp. 9–14: text; pp. 15–16: blank; p. 17: '*Five hundred copies of this Sermon have been | printed for Dr. Victor E. Reichert in October, 1947 | at The Spiral Press · New York*'; pp. 18–20: blank.

Note: On p. 14, line 2, 'That's His worry'. The word 'worry' has been overscored in black ink and 'mercy' written above it.

Paper: Cream laid paper with horizontal chainlines approximately 28 mm. apart. Watermark of a castle. Leaves measure 226 × 129 mm.; edges trimmed.

Binding: Gray-red (between 19.gyR and 20.d.gyR) wove paper wrappers cut flush with the leaves and folded over pp. 1–2 and 19–20. A gray paper label, 14 × 69 mm., is pasted in a slightly larger blind-stamped panel on the front cover, '[within a dark gray frame rule and lettered in dark gray] SERMON BY ROBERT FROST'. Stapled at the center fold.

Publication: Five hundred copies printed for Dr. Victor E. Reichert by The Spiral Press to commemorate Frost's unplanned address to the congregation of the Rockdale Avenue Temple in Cincinnati, of which Reichert was the Rabbi. From the note on p. 7, 'a recording was made while Robert Frost spoke from the pulpit. William S. Clark II and Victor E. Reichert prepared this text on the basis of the recording.' RF did not authorize this publication.

Barrett Copy:
592766.

A34   1948 A MASQUE OF REASON (First English Edition)

A   MASQUE   OF | REASON | by | ROBERT   FROST | *containing* | A Masque of Reason   A Masque of Mercy | (Two New England Biblicals) | together with | Steeple Bush and other Poems | [publisher's device] | But Mishna is strong wine | LONGFELLOW | It was the wanton gospeller | Hawthorne | JONATHAN   CAPE | THIRTY   BEDFORD   SQUARE | LONDON

Collation: [A]⁸ B–H⁸; pp. [i–iv], [1–2] 3–119 [120–124] = 64 leaves.

Contents: pp. i–ii: blank; p. iii: half-title, 'A MASQUE OF REASON'; p. iv: '*By the same author* | [4 titles]'; p. 1: title-page; p. 2: 'FIRST PUBLISHED 1948 | Dewey Classification | 811.5 | PRINTED IN GREAT BRITAIN IN THE CITY OF OXFORD | AT THE ALDEN PRESS | BOUND BY A. W. BAIN & CO. LTD., LONDON'; pp. 3–4: contents; pp. 5–7: introduction by Robert Frost (unsigned); p. 8: blank; p. 9: section-title, 'A MASQUE OF REASON'; p. 10: blank; pp. 11–28: text of *A Masque of Reason;* p. 29: section-title, 'A MASQUE OF MERCY'; p. 30: blank; pp. 31–59: text of *A Masque of Mercy;* p. 60: blank; p. 61: section-title, 'STEEPLE BUSH'; p. 62: blank; pp. 63–118: text of *Steeple Bush;* p. 119: 'NOTES'; pp. 120–122: blank free endpaper; pp. 123–124: blank pastedown endpaper.

Text Content: Texts of *A Masque of Reason* and *A Masque of Mercy;* text of *Steeple Bush* as in the first edition.

Paper: White wove coated paper with the watermark 'BASINGWERK PARCH-MENT'. Leaves measure 198 × 134 mm. Edges trimmed; top edge stained dark blue. Front endpapers of a rougher white wove stock. The terminal endpapers are the last two leaves of the final H gathering.

Binding: Bright deep blue (179.d.B) linen cloth. Covers blank. Spine stamped in silver from bottom to top, '[Publisher's device at the foot] A MASQUE OF REASON ══ ROBERT FROST'.

Dust Jacket: Heavy white wove paper. Front cover: '[quasi-blackletter in red-brown] A | Masque of | Reason | [gray-blue] by Robert Frost | [black] author of A Witness Tree, | Come In and other poems'. On the left, printed in black and gray-blue, is a line of six comedy/tragedy masks. Spine, lettered from bottom to top, '[black] [publisher's device] [red-brown] A MASQUE OF REASON [gray-blue] ROBERT | FROST'. Back cover: '[black] The works of | [gray-blue] ROBERT FROST | [3-line swash in gray-blue] | [black] [7 titles, including those in this volume]'. Front inner flap: 'A MASQUE OF REASON | [19-line blurb] | With an Introduction by the author. | DEWEY CLASSIFICATION | 811.5 | [printed diagonally in the lower right corner] 7s.6d. net'. Back inner flap: '[gray-blue] NOW | AND | THEN | [black] *A Journal of* | *Books and Personalities* | *issued from time to time* | *from* | *Thirty Bedford Square* | [24-line blurb] | [publisher's imprint]'.

Barrett Copies:

592687. Inscribed on the front open endpaper recto, 'Robert Frost / to / R. V. Thornton / December 16 1953 / Chicago / 77 West Washington St.'

592690. Inscribed on the front open endpaper recto, 'To Earle as a straight gift, this one of / six the first received copies from England / is given under my hand on the twenty / fourth of November nineteen hundred / and forty-eight / Robert Frost who wrote it all / without benefit of ghosts.' On the front inner flap, beneath the printed line 'With an Introduction by the author.', Frost has written, 'The ink used to inscribe this book / is guaranteed indelible.—The author.' In addition, beneath the endpaper inscription, Frost has made the note, 'Erratum: line 3 page 59 / " [Erratum:] " [line] 20 " [page] 65 [*i.e.,* 63].' On p. 59 (which is the last page of text of *A Masque of Mercy*), the last word of line 3 is printed 'arrange'. Frost has overscored this and written above it 'assuage'. This is a typographical error in the English edition; the word appears as 'assuage' in all other editions. On p. 63, in the poem 'A Young Birch' (first published as the 1946 Christmas card and collected in *Steeple Bush,* 1947), line 20 reads, 'When you were sick in bed or out of town.' Frost has overscored 'sick in bed' and written above it 'reading books'. This is a change that Frost apparently decided upon in 1948, for the printed phrase in all appearances of the poem until *Complete Poems of Robert Frost* (Holt, 1949) is 'sick in bed'. It is 'reading books' in the *Complete Poems* and all subsequent printings.

A35 1949 COMPLETE POEMS OF ROBERT FROST (Limited Edition)

COMPLETE | POEMS | OF | ROBERT | FROST | 1949 || HENRY HOLT AND COMPANY | NEW YORK

Collation: [1–42]⁸; pp. [πi–iv], [i–iv] v–xxi [xxii], 1–642 [643–646] = 336 leaves.

Contents: pp. πi–iv: blank; p. i: limitation notice, 'This edition has been limited to five | hundred copies and signed by the author | [holograph] Robert Frost | This copy is number | [number inserted ink]; p. ii: blank; p. iii: title-page; p.

iv: '*Copyright, 1930, 1939, 1943, 1947, 1949, by | Henry Holt and Company, Inc.* |
Copyright, 1936, 1942, 1945, 1948, by Robert Frost | DESIGNED BY MAURICE
SERLE KAPLAN | PRINTED IN THE UNITED STATES OF AMERICA
| *First Printing*'; pp. v–viii: introduction by Frost, 'THE FIGURE A POEM
MAKES', signed in print 'R. F.'; pp. ix–xxi: contents; p. xxii: blank; pp. 1–642:
text; pp. 643–646: blank.

Illustration: A photographic portrait of Robert Frost, signed *'Photograph by
Clara E. Sipprell',* on smooth white wove parchment paper. Tipped in facing the
title-page; recto blank, photograph verso.

Text Content: In addition to RF's introduction, 'The Figure a Poem Makes'
(printed first in *Collected Poems,* 1939), this collection contains everything included in the 1930 and 1939 collections as well as all the poems from *Steeple Bush*
(1947), the texts of *A Masque of Reason* and *A Masque of Mercy,* and three
poems previously printed elsewhere: 'Choose Something Like a Star' (printed
first in *Come In,* 1943; later collected as 'Take Something Like a Star'), 'Closed
for Good' (the 1948 Christmas poem), and 'From Plane to Plane' (printed first
in *What's New* [North Chicago, Ill.: Abbott Laboratories, Dec. 1948]).

Paper: Heavy white wove paper. Leaves measure 235 × 154 mm. Edges trimmed;
top edge stained blue-green. Endpapers of blue-green (164.m.bG) wove paper.

Binding: Beige heavy linen cloth. Facsimile signature stamped in blue-green on
the front cover, 'Robert Frost'. Spine: '[within a blue-green stamped panel bor-
dered by a single blue-green rule; lettering in gilt] COMPLETE | POEMS |
OF | ROBERT | FROST | 1949 | [blue-green] HENRY HOLT | AND COM-
PANY'. Back cover blank. In a plain, unlettered blue-green paper-covered slipcase.

Publication: Published in April 1949. Reissued in two volumes by The Limited
Editions Club in September 1950.

Barrett Copies:
592560. Number 114. On the second blank flyleaf recto is a fair copy, untitled, of
'Auspex' (printed in *In the Clearing,* 1962, and published for the first time in
Elizabeth Shepley Sergeant's *Robert Frost, The Trial by Existence,* 1960). Variant
readings are as follows:
line 1: California] ITC; Californian] TBE,MS
   3: And measured,] ITC; And measured] TBE,MS
   4: in all its] ITC; in all his] TBE,MS
   7: I was rejected by the royal bird] ITC; I'd been rejected by the royal bird]
     TBE; I was rejected by Jove's royal bird] MS
   8: Ganymede] ITC, TBE; Ganemede] MS
   9: Not find a barkeep unto Jove in me?] ITC; Not find a barkeep to the gods
     in me?] TBE; Not fine a bartender to Jove in me?] MS
   10: I have remained resentful to this day] ITC; I have resented ever since that
     day] TBE,MS

12: That there was anything I couldn't be.] ITC,TBE; There was a single
  thing I couldn't be.]
Beneath the poem, Frost has signed his name and added, 'This is December 16
1953 and I am with Mr / Thornton in Chicago on my way home / from San
Francisco where I got so / reminiscent of childhood days out there / that I may
never stop talking about them. / The poem is my memory. R. F.'

   This manuscript version differs from that in Barrett 705115 (Frost's own copy
of the trade edition of *Complete Poems 1949* [see A35.1] only in line 10, which,
in that version, is, 'I have remained resentful to this day'.

592559. Galley proofs. Includes 336 galley leaves corrected and inscribed 'Robert
Frost / to / R V Thornton' on the first galley. There are 82 holograph corrections, primarily of punctuation and spelling.

A35.1   1949 COMPLETE POEMS OF ROBERT FROST 1949 (Trade Edition)

COMPLETE | POEMS | OF | ROBERT | FROST | 1949 || HENRY
HOLT AND COMPANY | NEW YORK

Collation: [1–21]¹⁶; pp. [πi–iv], [i–iv] v–xxi [xxii], 1–642 [643–646] = 336 leaves.

Contents: pp. πi–iv: blank; p. i: half-title, 'COMPLETE | POEMS | OF | ROB-
ERT | FROST'; p. ii: blank; p. iii: title-page; p. iv: '*Copyright, 1930, 1939, 1943,
1947, 1949, by* | *Henry Holt and Company, Inc.* | *Copyright, 1936, 1942, 1945, 1948,
by Robert Frost* | DESIGNED BY MAURICE SERLE KAPLAN | PRINTED
IN THE UNITED STATES OF AMERICA | *First Printing*'; pp. v–viii: intro-
duction by Robert Frost, 'THE FIGURE A POEM MAKES', signed 'R. F.' on
p. viii; pp. ix–xxi: contents; p. xxii: blank; pp. 1–642: text; pp. 643–646: blank.

Illustration: A photographic portrait of Robert Frost, signed '*Photograph by
Clara E. Sipprell*', on white wove paper heavier than the text paper. Tipped in
facing the title-page; recto blank, photograph verso.

Text Content: As in the limited edition.

Paper: White wove paper. Leaves measure 212 × 140 mm. Edges trimmed, top
edge stained dark green. Endpapers of heavier white wove paper.

Binding: Blue-green (164.m.bG) linen cloth. Facsimile gilt-stamped signature,
'Robert Frost', on the front cover. Spine gilt-stamped, '|| COMPLETE | POEMS
| OF | ROBERT | FROST | *1949* || HENRY HOLT | AND COMPANY'. Back
cover blank.

Dust Jacket: Coated wove cloth. Front cover and spine with a yellow-green
(120.m.YG) ground, lettered in white. Front cover: 'Complete Poems | of ROB-

ERT | FROST | [vignette in black and white of a man plowing, by John King] | 1949'. Spine, reading from top to bottom, 'Complete Poems of ROBERT FROST 1949 | [horizontal] Holt'. Back cover printed in black on a white ground, 'The poetry of ROBERT FROST || [11 titles with prices] | [Holt imprint]'. Front inner flap (black printing on white): $6.00 | CPRF | Complete Poems of | Robert Frost, 1949 | [24-line blurb] | *Frontispiece by Clara E. Sipprell* | *Jacket Design by John King* | [Holt imprint]'. Back inner flap (black printed on white): 'What others have said: | [4 blurbs by James Norman Hall, Louise Townsend Nicholl, William Rose Benét, and Louis Untermeyer] | [Holt imprint]'.

Publication: Published 11 May 1949 in an edition of 7,325 copies.

Barrett Copies:
592562. Inscribed beneath the frontispiece portrait, 'Robert Frost / to his friend / R. V. Thornton'.
592561. Rebound in full red crushed oasis, gilt-stamped floriated border within a single gilt rule. In the center of the front cover is an inlaid oval portrait miniature of Robert Frost, painted on ivory in colors by Stanley Hardy of Bath, England. The miniature is under glass and bordered by a gilt-stamped ornamental frame. Gilt-stamped dentelles, signed at the foot, 'BOUND BY BAYNTUN OF BATH, ENGLAND | FOR KROCH'S & BRENTANO'S – CHICAGO'. The spine has five raised bands; the first, fourth, fifth, and sixth panels with floriated gilt-stamping. The second panel, 'COMPLETE | POEMS'; third panel, 'ROBERT | FROST', and at the foot, '1949'. Back cover gilt-stamped as the front, but without the center decoration. All edges trimmed and gilt; marbled endpapers. Inscribed on the first flyleaf recto, 'To R. V. Thornton / for making so much more of me / than I deserved / Robert Frost / Chicago / Nov. 13 1955 / Reminding me of great days / in England that set all this / in motion. / R. F.'
705115. *Robert Frost's Copy*. A later printing, lacking the note *'First Printing'* on p. iv. On the title-page Frost has written, 'This is the copy I read from at all / my places this fall and early winter of 1951* / R. / I tried to keep within the covers of this Complete Poems by writing any new / ones on the flyleaves. R. F.* / *And again this fall and early winter of 1952 / And again this spring of 1953'. On the open endpaper recto and the rectos of the preliminary flyleaves is a fair copy of 'A Cabin in the Clearing' which contains numerous variant readings from the first edition 1951 Christmas card:
line 24: So do they also ask philosophers] F; So do they often ask philosophers] MS

30–41: first edition:

> If the day ever comes when they know *who*
> They are, they may know better where they are,
> But who they are is too much to believe—
> Either for them or the onlooking world,
> They are too sudden to be credible,

Listen, they murmur talking in the dark
On what should be their daylong theme continued.
Putting the lamp out has not put their thought out.
Let us pretend the dew drops from the eaves
Are you and I eavesdropping on their unrest—
A mist and smoke eavesdropping on a haze—
And see if we can tell the bass from the soprano.

30–41: MS:

If the day comes when they know *who*
They are they will know better where they are.
They are too sudden to be credible
Either to themselves or to the onlooking world.

Listen they murmur talking in the dark.
Putting the lamp out has not put their thought out
Let us pretend the dew drops from the eaves
Are you and I eaves dropping on their questions
A smoke and mist eaves dropping on a haze
To try to tell the base from the soprano.

In the manuscript, the names of the speakers in the dialogue, 'Mist' and 'Smoke,' are not included as they are in the first edition and later printings.

On the blank recto of the inserted frontispiece portrait, Frost has written, 'For Subjects of Talks / There a[re] Roughly Zones Kenyon / Whose worths unknown although / its height be taken Oberlin / Lost Followers Yale / What begins more ethereal than / substantial in lyric ends more / substantial than ethereal in epic / Gainesville'. On p. ix, above the 'CONTENTS' headline, Frost has inserted 'A Cabin in the Clearing', and on p. xvi of the contents, after the listing of 'Iris by Night' at p. 418, 'Percheron Horse 420'. On p. xix, following the listing of 'In the Long Night' at p. 533, Frost has inserted, 'The Bad Island 534'. On p. 31, above the poem title ('The Tuft of Flowers'), Frost has written, 'This was the first one ever read in public. I didn't read / it myself but sat by and heard someone read it for me.' On p. 199, above the poem title ('New Hampshire'), Frost has written, 'Wrote this all one night and never / looked back'. On p. 247 (above the title, 'Two Witches'), 'In the name of the Demons / Hasmodat Acteus Megalestus Ormenus / Wiens Nicon Mimon and Zeper*'; and at the foot of the page, '*Taken from a leaden tablet found near Rylon / where a witch was buried at the crossroads before my time'. At the foot of p. 257 (the end of the poem 'An Empty Threat'), 'Does No One at All But Me / Ever feel this way in the least?' (used as the title of the 1952 Christmas poem). At the foot of p. 312, Frost has written a fair copy of 'Auspex' (printed in *In the Clearing*, 1962; first published in E. S. Sergeant's *RF, The Trial by Existence*, 1960), but titled here 'Auspices' and differing textually:
line 1: California] ITC; Californian] TBE,MS
  3: And measured,] ITC; And measured] TBE,MS

4: in all its] ITC; inall his] TBE,MS

7: I was rejected by the royal bird] ITC; I'd been rejected by the royal bird]
   TBE; I was rejected by Jove's royal bird] MS

8: Ganymede] ITC,TBE; Ganemede] MS

9: Not find a barkeep unto Jove in me?] ITC; Not find a barkeep to the gods
   in me?] TBE; No[t] find a bartender unto Jove in me?] MS

10: I have remained resentful to this day] ITC,MS; I have resented ever since
    that day] TBE

12: That there was anything] ITC,TBE; There was a single thing] MS

Beneath the holograph poem, 'R. F. / This is another memory of those events of
/ seventy years ago.' At the foot of p. 319 (under the poem 'The Peaceful Shepherd'), 'Would hate to make a system / of off-rhyme. But one now / and then
for the roughness of / handcraft—'. On pp. 351 and 353 (which are the section
titles for *A Further Range* and 'Taken Doubly') is a fair copy of 'The Bad Island
—Easter' (first printed in *In the Clearing,* 1962), here titled, 'The Bad Island—
Easter So called because It Hasn't Risen / (On a head from Easter Island in the
portico of the British Museum)'. There are a few minor variant punctuations
and two misspellings, 'primative' for 'primitive' and 'isle' for 'aisle'; only one
variant reading, in line 57: What heights of altrur—] F; Whatever altrur—] MS.
On p. 359, in the third from the last printed line of 'Two Tramps in Mud Time,'
Frost has corrected the line, 'And the work is play for mortal stakes,' to read,
'And the work is play-for-mortal-stakes*'; beneath, '*Should be printed with hyphens / to make all one word of it.' Nowhere (at least nowhere in the Barrett
collection) are the hyphens used in the printed versions of the poem. On p. 372,
Frost has asterisked the word 'Formic' in line 22 ('Then word goes forth in
Formic:') of the poem 'Departmental'; on p. 373, he has written, '*That acid
language'. On p. 415, at the end of the poem ('The Vindictives'), 'Someone
wrote a long letter to ask me / for thesis purposes which side I was on / in all
this.' On p. 420 (blank verso of section-title, 'Build Soil') is a fair copy of 'The
Draft Horse' (first printed in *In the Clearing,* 1962), here listed in Frost's hand
on p. xvi of the contents as 'Percheron Horse'. The manuscript version has only
one variant reading in line 3: Behind too heavy a horse] F; Behind a great
Percheron horse] MS. However, the manuscript does not contain the third
stanza of the poem. Beneath, 'This belongs with The Lockless Door / and was
written at about the same time'. 'The Lockless Door' was published in *New
Hampshire,* indicating that 'The Draft Horse' was written about 1923. On p.
467, above the title ('The Gift Outright'), 'My complete history of the Revolution'. In the long blank space on p. 495 beneath the two-line poem 'The Secret
Sits,' Frost has written, 'The Secret of Poetry / 1 Poetry is a prowess like athletics. / 2 Poetry is the renewal of words so that the language may never wear
out. / 3 Poetry is the dawning of an idea. It / gets its freshness from having
been / caught just as it came over you. / 4 Poetry is that which evaporates from /
both prose and verse when translated. / 5 Poetry is the Liberal Arts. The Liberal
/ Arts are poetry. / Each one of these turned out to be / the subject of a whole
talk at a college / this spring. 1953'. On blank pp. 534 and 535 is another fair

copy of 'The Bad Island—Easter' with the same misspellings as the version on pp. 351 and 353, but with the reading of line 57 changed to 'What heights of altrur—' and the third and fourth from the last lines of the printed version combined to make one line, 'Into a belief in being a thief'. On p. 559 (section-title, 'Editorials'), in Frost's holograph, 'Aries Taurus / Gemini Cancer / Ask in chorus / Whats the answer.' On p. 576, line 4 from the bottom of the page (in 'Closed for Good'), 'Beneath the brush of snow.', Frost has overscored the word 'brush' and written in the margin 'spread'. The word appears as 'spread' in the printed version in *In the Clearing* (1962). In the 1948 Christmas card first edition, it is 'brush'. On the rectos of the two terminal flyleaves and the terminal open and pastedown endpapers is a fair copy of 'America Is Hard to See' (collected in *In the Clearing;* first printed in *Atlantic Monthly,* June 1951, as 'And All We Call American'). This holograph version is titled 'For Columbus Day'. Variant readings:

line 6: to a cruise] ITC,MS; for a cruise] A
  12: in his venture.] ITC,MS; in his future.] A
  20: mariner, Da Gama,] ITC; mariner Da Gama] A,MS
  23: And with] ITC; But with] A,MS
  27: Da Gama's] ITC,A; da Gama's] MS
  31: Valladolid.] ITC; them in madrid.] A,MS
  33: my chance] ITC; my way] A,MS
  42: but still] ITC,A; yet still] MS
  48: for his.] ITC; as his] A,MS
  52: a strait,] ITC; a strait] A; a straight] MS
  53: river mouth] ITC,A; rivermouth] MS
  54: North . . . South.] ITC; north . . . south.] A,MS
  55: navy, I predict,] ITC; navy I predict] A,MS
  64: outside—] ITC,A; outside] MS
  69: tractor-plow . . . motor-drill.] ITC,A; tractor plow . . . motor drill.] MS
  70: will,] ITC; will] A,MS
  71: quake,] ITC; quake] A,MS
  73: rude;] ITC; rude:] A; rude] MS
  78: fortune-hunting] ITC,A; fortune hunting] MS

Note: For additional historical information concerning this copy see Thompson's *Selected Letters* (p. 554, no. 429).

Uncatalogued. The Lawrance Thompson copy, inscribed on the open endpaper recto, 'To Larry / from the same old Robert / Princeton / April 13 1956 / Night after one of our / great times together'. On one of the front flyleaves, RF has inscribed a fair copy of 'Away!'; signed beneath, 'Robert Frost / Written out for Larry / on Nov 11 1958 at Princeton'. There are many penciled notes in the text in Thompson's hand.

Uncatalogued. Another Lawrance Thompson copy. The eleventh printing December 1960. Inscribed on the front open endpaper recto, 'To Larry / for his companionship / further in our travels and confidences / than we ever went be-

fore / Robert / Home in New York after Jerusalem / Athens and London
March 27 1961 / At the Westbury.'

A35.2   1951 COMPLETE POEMS OF ROBERT FROST (First English Edition)

Complete | POEMS | *of* | ROBERT FROST | [publisher's device] | *LON-DON* | JONATHAN CAPE 30 BEDFORD SQUARE

Collation: [A]⁸ B–Z, AA–HH⁸; pp. [1–4] 5–494 [495–496] = 248 leaves.

Contents: p. 1: half-title, 'COMPLETE POEMS OF ROBERT FROST'; p. 2: blank; p. 3: title-page; p. 4: \ FIRST PUBLISHED 1951 | Dewey Classification | 811.5 | PRINTED IN GREAT BRITAIN IN THE CITY OF OXFORD | AT THE ALDEN PRESS | BOUND BY A. W. BAIN & CO. LTD., LONDON'; pp. 5–16: contents; pp. 17–20: Frost's introduction, 'THE FIGURE A POEM MAKES', signed in print with initials, 'R. F.', on p. 20; pp. 21–494: text; pp. 495–496: blank.

Text Content: As in the American limited and trade editions.

Paper: White wove paper. Leaves measure 198 × 132 mm. Edges trimmed, top edge stained green. Endpapers of heavier white wove paper.

Binding: Blue-green (bluer than 160.s.bG) fine linen cloth. Covers blank. Spine stamped in gilt, 'COMPLETE | POEMS | OF | ROBERT | FROST | [publisher's device]'.

Dust Jacket: Against a stylized decorative ground of black, gray, orange, and white, lettered in black, 'The Complete | POEMS | of | Robert Frost'. Spine with a similar ground, lettered from bottom to top in black, '[horizontal] [publisher's device] | Robert The | Complete Poems Frost'. Back cover blank, white. Front inner flap (printed black on white): 'THE COMPLETE POEMS OF ROBERT | FROST | [19-line blurb] | DEWEY CLASSIFICATION | 811.5 | [printed diagonally in the lower right corner] 18s. net'. Back inner flap blank, white.

Barrett Copies:
592565. An uncorrected proof copy in cream paper wrappers, lettered in black. Front cover: 'COMPLETE POEMS | OF ROBERT FROST | [Jonathan Cape device] | Uncorrected Proof'. Spine, reading from bottom to top: 'COMPLETE POEMS OF ROBERT FROST'. Back cover: '[at the foot] The Alden Press (Oxford) Ltd. | Oxford'. With a variant title-page, 'COMPLETE POEMS | OF ROBERT FROST | [publisher's device] | JONATHAN CAPE | THIRTY BEDFORD SQUARE | LONDON'. The copyright page has the note 'FIRST PUBLISHED 1950'; otherwise, the book is textually identical to the English edition.

At front, tipped in at the inside front cover, is a printed sheet announcing *Complete Poems of Robert Frost* on Jonathan Cape's winter list for 1950 and priced at 15s.

592608. First English edition in dust jacket.

Uncatalogued. The Lawrance Thompson copy. Third impression, 1956. Inscribed on the front open endpaper recto with lines 219–36 of 'Kitty Hawk'; signed beneath, 'Robert Frost / To Lawrance Thompson / as it was talked to him in England / May 26–June 21 1957'. This version has two variant readings from the final version printed in *In the Clearing* (1962): line 229 has 'Of the soul's misgiving' for 'Of a great misgiving'. Line 234 is deleted, and the line 'Both of which are matter' is supplied for lines 234–35, '(Don't forget the latter / Is but further matter)'.

A36   1951 HARD NOT TO BE KING (First Separate Edition)

[Brown-orange (54.brO)] Hard not to be King | [black] BY ROBERT FROST | [crown orn.] House of Books, Ltd. | NEW YORK, 1951

Collation: [1–3]⁴; pp. [1–24] = 12 leaves.

Contents: pp. 1–2: blank; p. 3: 'THIS FIRST EDITION IS LIMITED TO | THREE HUNDRED NUMBERED COPIES | SIGNED BY THE AUTHOR | [holograph] Robert Frost | THIS IS NUMBER [supplied in ink]; p. 4: blank; p. 5: title-page; p. 6: 'COPYRIGHT 1951 | BY ROBERT FROST'; p. p. 7: '[crown orn.] How hard it is | to keep from being king | When it's in you | and in the situation'; p. 8: blank; pp. 9–22: text; p. 23: blank; p. 24: 'THIS IS NUMBER ELEVEN OF | THE CROWN OCTAVOS | PUBLISHED BY THE HOUSE OF BOOKS, LTD. | 2 West 56 STREET, NEW YORK | AND MADE BY PETER BEILENSON | MOUNT VERNON, NEW YORK'.

Paper: Cream laid paper with vertical chainlines 21 mm. apart. Leaves measure 190 × 127 mm.; edges trimmed. Endpapers of the same stock.

Binding: Deep blue (179.dp.B) fine linen cloth. Front cover stamped in gilt, 'HARD | NOT | TO BE | KING | [crown orn.] | Robert | Frost'. Spine stamped in gilt reading from bottom to top, 'HARD NOT TO BE KING · FROST'. Back cover blank.

Publication: Three hundred copies were printed for The House of Books, Ltd. by Peter Beilenson, Mount Vernon, N.Y. The book was priced at $3.50, and first copies were sent out by the House of Books on 25 June 1951. The poem was also printed in the *Proceedings of the American Academy of Arts and Letters and the National Institute of Arts and Letters,* 2nd ser., no. 1 (1951), with the title 'How Hard It Is to Keep from Being King When It's in You and in the Situation.' The Academy *Proceedings* preceded the separate publication by a few days.

Barrett Copy:
592658.

A37   1954 AFORESAID (First Edition)

[blue-green] AFORESAID | [black] BY | ROBERT FROST | [blue-green] leaf orn.] | [black] *Plus uno maneat perenne saeclo* | HENRY HOLT AND COMPANY | NEW YORK

Collation: π_1 [1–8]^8; pp. [i–vi] vii–xiii [xiv], [1–2] 3–114 [115–116] = 65 leaves.

Contents: p. i: 'The publication of this volume coincides | with the celebration of the author's | eightieth birthday | [holograph] Robert Frost | *This edition has been limited* | *to six hundred and fifty numbered copies,* | *of which five hundred are for sale.* | *This copy is number* [number inserted ink]'; p. ii: blank; p. iii: half-title, 'AFORESAID'; p. iv: blank; p. v: title-page; p. vi: '[copyright notices in italics (3 lines)] All rights reserved, including the right to reproduce | this book or portions thereof in any form. | Library of Congress Catalog Card Number: 54–8021 | Printed in the United States of America'; pp. vi–x: 'THE PRE-REQUISITES', a foreword by Robert Frost, unsigned; pp. xi–xiii: contents; p. xiv: blank; p. 1: second half-title; p. 2: blank; pp. 3–114: text; p. 115: blank; p. 116: '[at the foot] Manufactured by Quinn & Boden Company, Inc., Rahway, New Jersey'.

Illustration: Photographic portrait of Frost on white coated paper tipped in facing the title-page.

Text Content:

The Silken Tent	The Witch of Coös
My November Guest	Home Burial
The Tuft of Flowers	An Old Man's Winter Night
Reluctance	Hyla Brook
Desert Places	The Oven Bird
To Earthward	Stopping by Woods on a
Once by the Pacific	Snowy Evening
A Soldier	The Onset
The Gift Outright	Love and a Question
The Death of the Hired Man	Looking for a Sunset Bird in Winter
The Mountain	For Once, Then, Something
The Wood-Pile	Spring Pools
Birches	Tree at My Window

Acquainted with the Night
Directive
The Lovely Shall Be Choosers
West-running Brook
Paul's Wife
Two Tramps in Mud Time
The White-tailed Hornet
The Investment
Provide, Provide
A Drumlin Woodchuck
In Time of Cloudburst
On Looking Up by Chance at
  the Constellations
Sitting by a Bush in Broad
  Sunlight
Design
The Secret Sits
Precaution
Bravado
The Hardship of Accounting
Departmental
A Considerable Speck
Etherealizing

Why Wait for Science
All Revelation
Happinness Makes up in Height
  for What It Lacks in Length
Come In
Never Again Would Birds' Song
  Be the Same
Carpe Diem
A Young Birch
The Last Word of a Bluebird
The Night Light
A Mood Apart
Iota Subscript
The Courage to Be New
The Lost Follower
The Most of It
The Road Not Taken
Dust of Snow
A Winter Eden
Choose Something Like a Star
Closed for Good
The Need of Being Versed in
  Country Things

Paper: Cream wove paper. Leaves measure 235 × 152 mm., edges trimmed. End-papers of blue-green (slightly darker than 149.p.G) laid paper with vertical chain-lines 20 mm. apart, watermarked 'TWEEDWEAVE'.

Binding: Gray-green linen cloth (weave pattern clearly visible as green and white threads). A dark green (146.d.G) panel, 71 × 83 mm., stamped on the front cover, lettering gilt-stamped within a single gilt rule frame, 'AFORESAID | [leaf orn.] | Robert Frost'. Spine, with gilt-stamped lettering reading perpendicu-larly from top to bottom, '[within a dark green panel with a gilt rule] AFORE-SAID [leaf orn.] Robert Frost | [horizontal within a dark green panel] HOLT'. Back cover blank. In a board slipcase covered with blue-green (+149) paper (the same stock as the endpapers); a white paper label on the spine, lettered in blue-green within a blue-green rule frame, reading perpendicularly from top to bottom, 'Aforesaid [leaf orn.] *Robert Frost* || [horizontal] *Holt*'.

Publication: Published on 26 March 1954 as a 'birthday' book in honor of RF's eightieth birthday in a limited edition of 650 copies. The selection was made by RF, and he wrote a reminiscence, 'The Prerequisites,' as a preface.

Barrett Copies:
592573. Number 69. Above the limitation notice on p. 1, RF has written, 'To Hilda and Vera [Harvey] / from their Uncle Robert'.
592574. Number 356.
592575. Number 13.

A38   1955 ROBERT FROST SELECTED POEMS (First Edition of this selection)

ROBERT FROST | SELECTED POEMS | [swelling rule] | WITH AN INTRODUCTION BY | C. DAY LEWIS | PENGUIN BOOKS

Collation: [A]¹⁶ B–D¹⁶ E⁸ F–I¹⁶ [$1 also signed 'R. F.' in lower inner margin; B–D only, $2 signed]; pp. [1–4] 5–259 [260–272] = 136 leaves.

Contents: p. 1: half-title, 'THE PENGUIN POETS | D 27 | ROBERT FROST | [Penguin device]; p. 2: blank; p. 3: title-page; p. 4: 'Penguin Books Ltd, Harmondsworth, Middlesex | AUSTRALIA: Penguin Books Pty Ltd, 762 Whitehorse Road, | Mitcham, Victoria | SOUTH AFRICA: Penguin Books (S. A.) Pty Ltd, Gibraltar House | Regent Road, Sea Point, Cape Town | [very short rule] | This selection first published | in Penguin Books 1955 | Made and printed in Great Britain | by The Whitefriars Press Ltd | London and Tonbridge'; pp. 5–11: contents; p. 12: blank; pp. 13–17: introduction by C. Day Lewis, subscribed with the date *'January 1955'* on p. 17; p. 18: blank; pp. 19–253: text; p. 254: blank; pp. 255–260: index of first lines; p. 261: section-title of a catalogue of Penguin books; 5 short lines of text in italics surmounted by the Penguin device; p. 262: blank; pp. 263–272: ads for Penguin books.

Text Content: In this selection, all previously collected poems are included with the following exceptions, excluded by RF:

A Late Walk	Pea Brush
Stars	An Encounter
Wind and Window Flower	The Bonfire
Flower Gathering	A Girl's Garden
Rose Pogonias	The Exposed Nest
Waiting	Brown's Descent
In a Vale	The Vanishing Red
A Dream Pang	The Census-Taker
The Vantage Point	Wild Grapes
Pan With Us	The Pauper Witch of Grafton
My Butterfly	A Fountain, a Bottle, a Donkey's
The Generations of Men	Ears and Some Books
The Housekeeper	In a Disused Graveyard
Good Hours	Blue-Butterfly Day
Christmas Trees	Not to Keep
A Patch of Old Snow	A Brook in the City
In the Home Stretch	A Boundless Moment
Meeting and Passing	Evening in a Sugar Orchard
Bond and Free	Gathering Leaves

The Valley's Singing Day
A Hillside Thaw
Plowmen
The Gold Hesperidee
A Roadside Stand
The Old Barn at the Bottom of the
  Fogs
Lost in Heaven
  Broaden the Base
On Taking from the Top to
  Belief
They Were Welcome to Their
The Master Speed
Moon Compasses
After-flakes
Clear and Colder
Unharvested
Assertive
To a Thinker
Beech
Sycamore
I Could Give All to Time
The Most of It
A Cloud Shadow
The Quest of the Purple-Fringed
The Discovery of the Madeiras
To a Young Wretch (Boethian)
Time Out
To a Moth Seen in Winter
November
The Rabbit Hunter
In a Poem
On Our Sympathy with the Under
  Dog
A Question
An Equalizer
A Semi-Revolution
Trespass
A Nature Note

Of the Stones of the Place
Not of School Age
The Literate Farmer and the Planet
  Venus
Too Anxious for Rivers
Our Singing Strength
The Lockless Door
The Freedom of the Moon
The Rose Family
Atmosphere
Devotion
The Cocoon
Acceptance
The Thatch
Canis Major
The Flower Boat
The Times Table
The Last Mowing
The Door in the Dark
Dust in the Eyes
The Armful
What Fifty Said
An Unstamped Letter in Our Rural
  Letter Box
Were I in Trouble
In the Long Night
The Fear of God
The Fear of Man
Innate Helium
Astrometaphysical
Skeptic
Two Leading Lights
A Rogers Group
A Wish to Comply
A Cliff Dwelling
Any Size We Please
Bursting Rapture
U.S. 1946 King's X
The Ingenuities of Debt

Paper: Cream wove paper. Leaves measure 180 × 110 mm.; edges trimmed, covers cut flush with the leaves.

Binding: Heavy wove paper wrappers with an overall pattern of two stylized black ornaments arranged alternately in rows against a ground of light tan dotted with white. On the front cover is a white panel with a triple thin-thick-thin tan rule inside the border. Within the rule: '[black] *Robert* | *Frost* | [tan star orn.] | [black] SELECTED BY HIMSELF | AND WITH AN INTRO- DUCTION | BY C. DAY LEWIS | [Penguin device in tan] | [black] THE PENGUIN | POETS | 3|6'. Spine lettered in black with rules in tan on a panel of white '[thin-thick-thin rule] D27 || [lettered vertically from bottom to top] Robert Frost || [horizontal] D27 | [thin-thick-thin rule]'. Back cover without lettering.

Publication: This collection of poems, though a common trade edition in modest commercial format, is of consequence in that it is a truly 'selected' volume dis- tinct from cheap reprint texts. RF made this selection of 185 of his published poems.

Barrett Copy:
592569.
Uncatalogued. The Lawrance Thompson copy, inscribed on the half-title, 'Larry from Robert / The Connaught / London England / May 21 / 1957'.

A39   1959 YOU COME TOO (First Edition)

YOU COME TOO | FAVORITE POEMS FOR YOUNG READERS | ROBERT FROST | [vignette wood-engraving of birches] | *With wood en- gravings by* THOMAS W. NASON | [swelling rule] | HENRY HOLT AND COMPANY • NEW YORK

Collation: [1]⁴ [2–6]⁸ [7]⁴; pp. [1–5] 6–94 [95–96] = 48 leaves.

Contents: p. 1: half-title, 'YOU COME TOO'; p. 2: blank; p. 3: title-page; p. 4: '[copyright and all rights reserved notices; 5 lines] | [swelling rule] | IN CAN- ADA, GEORGE J. MCLEOD, LTD. | *Printed in the United States of America* | *Library of Congress Catalog Card Number*: 59–12940 | 92941–1619 F I R S T E D I T I O N'; p. 5: dedication, 'TO BELLE MOODIE FROST | WHO KNEW AS A TEACHER | THAT NO POETRY WAS GOOD FOR | CHILDREN THAT WASN'T EQUALLY | GOOD FOR THEIR ELDERS'; pp. 6–10: foreword, signed in print 'HYDE COX | *Crow Island* | *Manchester, Massachusetts*'; pp. 11–12: contents; p. 13: section-title, ' "*I'm going out . . .*" | [wood-engraved vignette]'; pp. 14–92: text; pp. 93–94: index of titles. Section- titles; each with a vignette wood-engraving:
page 23: ' "*The woods are lovely,* | *dark and deep . . .*" '
   33: ' "*I often see flowers . . .*" '
   39: ' "*He has dust in his eyes* | *and a fan for a wing . . .*" '
   53: ' "*I was one of the children told . . .*" '
   61: ' "*Men work together . . .*" '
   77: ' "*We love the things* | *we love . . .*" '
   83: ' "*I took the one* | *less traveled by . . .*" '

Illustration: Woodcut-engravings in black and white, by Thomas W. Nason, in the text.

Text Content:

The Pasture	The Exposed Nest
Good Hours	The Oven Bird
Going for Water	A Nature Note
Blueberries	A Minor Bird
Looking for a Sunset Bird in Winter	A Peck of Gold
Acquainted with the Night	The Last Word of a Bluebird
A Hillside Thaw	Not of School Age
Good-by and Keep Cold	The Birthplace
Stopping by Woods on a Snowy Evening	A Girl's Garden
Come In	The Tuft of Flowers
A Patch of Old Snow	Mending Wall
Christmas Trees	A Time to Talk
Birches	Brown's Descent
A Young Birch	The Death of the Hired Man
A Passing Glimpse	Fire and Ice
The Last Mowing	Hyla Brook
Pea Brush	Tree at My Window
The Telephone	Dust of Snow
The Rose Family	The Freedom of the Moon
One Guess	The Kitchen Chimney
Fireflies in the Garden	The Road Not Taken
Blue-Butterfly Day	Gathering Leaves
Departmental	A Record Stride
A Drumlin Woodchuck	After Apple-Picking
The Runaway	Two Tramps in Mud Time
The Cow in Apple Time	

Paper: White wove paper. Leaves measure 209 × 139 mm.; edges trimmed. End-papers of heavy light gray wove paper.

Binding: Yellow-orange (71.m.OY) linen cloth. A vignette of a bird on a fence post is stamped in the lower right corner of the front cover in black. Spine lettered from top to bottom, '[black] YOU COME TOO [red-brown: acorn orn.] [black] BY ROBERT FROST | [horizontal] HOLT'. Back cover blank.

Dust Jacket: Beige laid paper with vertical chainlines 21 mm. apart. Watermarked 'Hamilton | Kilmory'. Front cover lettered in black, 'YOU COME TOO | FAVORITE POEMS FOR YOUNG READERS | ROBERT FROST | *With wood engravings by* | THOMAS W. NASON | [wood engraving of birches in light gray, by Thomas W. Nason] | HENRY HOLT AND COMPANY · NEW YORK'. Spine lettered in black from top to bottom, 'YOU COME TOO *by* ROBERT FROST [portion of the front cover wood engraving in gray] | [horizontal] HOLT'. Back cover, '[reproduction of a photographic portrait of Frost] | © KARSH, OTTAWA | ROBERT FROST [overlapping portion of front cover wood-engraving in gray]'. Front inner flap, '$3.00 | Y C T | You Come Too | *Favorite Poems for Young Readers* | Robert Frost | *With wood engravings by Thomas W. Nason* | [swelling rule] | People keep saying it's not good | To learn things by heart, | But pretty things well said — | It's nice to have them in your head. | ROBERT FROST* | [21-line blurb, including the poem, 'The Pasture'] | [2 footnotes beneath designated with asterisk and dagger; the first refers to the Frost poem transcribed above: 'Copyright © March 31, 1959, *Look.*']. Back flap, '[22-line biographical blurb on Frost] | [swelling rule] | [Holt imprint]'.

Publication: In this selection, the poem 'Blueberries' has the first 27 lines only of 105. Frost was angry about this and referred to it as 'not a full basket.'

Barrett Copies:

592821.
Uncatalogued. The Lawrance Thompson copy, inscribed on the front open endpaper recto, 'To Larry Thompson / who will not be / surprised by anything / I say about our great / friend / Hyde Cox / Crow Island / October 12, 1959'. Beside the reference to 'our great friend,' RF has signed his initials. Cox wrote the foreword for the book.

A40   1961 DEDICATION (First Separate Edition)

DEDICATION | THE GIFT OUTRIGHT | THE INAUGURAL ADDRESS | [olive-brown: woodcut of an eagle holding shield, arrows, and olive branch] | [black] WASHINGTON, D.C. | JANUARY THE TWENTIETH | 1961

Collation: [1–3]⁴; pp. [1–24] = 12 leaves.

Contents: pp. 1–2: blank; p. 3: title-page; p. 4: 'PRINTED FOR FRIENDS OF | THE SPIRAL PRESS · NEW YORK | [swelling rule] | "DEDICATION" | COPYRIGHT © 1961 BY ROBERT FROST | "THE GIFT OUTRIGHT" | FROM *A Witness Tree*, COPYRIGHT 1942 BY ROBERT FROST'; p. 5: 'DEDICATION · THE GIFT OUTRIGHT | [red] BY ROBERT FROST | [black] PRESENTED ON THE STEPS OF THE | NATION'S CAPITOL IN WASHINGTON, D.C. | AS PART OF THE INAUGURAL CEREMONIES | JANUARY THE TWENTIETH · 1961'; p. 6: blank; pp. 7–9: text of 'Dedication'; p. 10: blank; p. 11: text of 'The Gift Outright'; p. 12: blank; p. 13: 'THE INAUGURAL ADDRESS OF | [red] JOHN FITZGERALD KENNEDY | [black] FOLLOWING HIS OATH OF OFFICE | AS THE THIRTY-FIFTH PRESIDENT OF | THE UNITED STATES OF AMERICA ON | JANUARY THE TWENTIETH · 1961 | [gray: the presidential spread eagle-emblem]'; p. 14: blank; pp. 15–19: text of the inaugural address; p. 20: blank; p.

21: '[olive-brown: Spiral Press device] [black] This book has been made to cele-
brate an historic event. | The edition consists of five hundred copies set in Emerson
type | and printed at The Spiral Press, New York in March of 1961. The |
presidential eagle was cut in wood by Fritz Kredel especially for | this publication.
Typography by Joseph Blumenthal. | This copy is number [number inserted in
ink]'; pp. 22–24: blank.

Note: The first 250 copies have the variant reading on p. 4: 'PRINTED FOR
FRIENDS OF | HOLT, RINEHART AND WINSTON. . . .'

Paper: White laid Strathmore paper with vertical chainlines 24 mm. apart; unwatermarked. Leaves measure 295 × 191 mm. Top edge trimmed, fore-edge uncut, bottom edge rough-cut. Endpapers of the same stock.

Binding: Very light brown-gray (lighter than 63.l.brGy) paper over boards. On
the front cover, printed in brown-gray (64.brGy), is the seal of the President of
the United States, engraved in wood by Fritz Kredel and printed from the block.
Spine lettered from top to bottom: '[red: 5-pointed star in outline] [gray-brown]
JANUARY THE TWENTIETH · 1961 [red: star]'. Back cover blank.

Publication: Five hundred copies printed by The Spiral Press in March 1961 for
friends of Holt, Rinehart and Winston and of The Spiral Press. Numbers 1–250
were for Holt; 251–500 for Spiral. A pamphlet edition from the same type was
later printed for Holt as a keepsake for the dinner RF was given by President
Kennedy's cabinet. The new poem, 'Dedication,' was printed first in newspapers
immediately following the presidential inauguration on 20 January 1961 with various titles. It was collected in *In the Clearing* (1962) with the title, 'For John F.
Kennedy His Inauguration,' substantially altered. 'The Gift Outright' was printed
first in the *Virginia Quarterly Review* (Spring 1942) and collected in *A Witness
Tree* (1942).

Barrett copy:
592650. Number 382 ('friends of Spiral Press').

A41   1962 IN THE CLEARING (Limited Edition)

IN THE | CLEARING | BY | ROBERT | FROST | [beige: Holt device] |
[black: swelling rule] | HOLT, RINEHART AND WINSTON | NEW
YORK

Collation: [1–5]⁸ [6]⁶ [7]⁸; pp. [i–ii], [1–12] 13–101 [102–106] = 54 leaves.

Contents: p. i: half-title, 'IN THE CLEARING BY ROBERT FROST'; p. ii:
blank; p. 1: 'THIS EDITION OF | IN THE CLEARING | HAS BEEN LIM-
ITED TO | FIFTEEN HUNDRED NUMBERED COPIES | AND SIGNED
BY THE AUTHOR | [holograph] Robert Frost | THIS COPY IS NUMBER |

[inserted in ink]'; p. 2: blank; p. 3: title-page; p. 4: '*Copyright 1942, 1948, 1950, 1951, 1952, 1953, 1954, 1955, 1956, 1958* | *by Robert Frost* | *Copyright* © *1959, 1960, 1961, 1962 by Robert Frost* | [all rights reserved notice (2 lines)] | Published simultaneously in Canada by Holt, Rinehart and Winston of | Canada, Limited. | *Library of Congress Catalog Card Number 62-11578* | Note: "The Gift Outright" (page 31), which concludes "For John F. Kennedy His | Inauguration," and which Mr. Frost read at the Inaugural ceremonies, January 20, | 1961, in Washington, D.C., was first published in *A Witness Tree, 1942.* | 82941–2012 | PRINTED IN THE UNITED STATES OF AMERICA'; p. 5: 'DEDICA-TION | [swelling rule] | *Letters in prose to* | *Louis Untermeyer, Sidney Cox, and John Bartlett* | *for them to dispose of as they please;* | *these to you in verse for keeps*'; p. 6: blank; p. 7: lines 219–224 and 246–257 of 'Kitty Hawk' in italics (called 'But God's Own Descent' in the contents); p. 8: blank; pp. 9–10: contents; p. 11: second half-title, 'IN THE CLEARING | *"And wait to watch the water clear, I may."* '; p. 12: blank; pp. 13–101: text; p. 102: blank; p. 103: '[Spiral Press device] | THE SPIRAL PRESS · NEW YORK | MARCH · 1962'; pp. 104–106: blank.

Text Content:

But God's Own Descent
Pod of the Milkweed
Away!
A Cabin in the Clearing
Closed for Good
America Is Hard to See
One More Brevity
Escapist—Never
For John F. Kennedy His Inauguration
Accidentally on Purpose
A Never Naught Song
Version
A Concept of Self-Conceived
Forgive, O Lord
Kitty Hawk
Auspex
The Draft Horse
Ends
Peril of Hope
Questioning Faces
Does No One at All Ever Feel This Way in the Least?
The Bad Island—Easter
Our Doom to Bloom
The Objection to Being Stepped On
A-Wishing Well
How Hard It Is to Keep from Being King When It's in You and in the Situation
Lines Written in Dejection on the Eve of Great Success
The Milky Way Is a Cowpath
Some Science Fiction
Quandry
A Reflex
In a Glass of Cider
From Iron
Four-Room Shack Aspiring High
But Outer Space
On Being Chosen Poet of Vermont
We Vainly Wrestle with the Blind Belief
It Takes All Sorts of In and Outdoor Schooling
In Winter in the Woods Alone

Paper: White laid paper with vertical chainlines 30 mm. apart. No watermarks. Leaves measure 242 × 158 mm.; edges trimmed. Endpapers of the same stock.

Binding: Light brown linen cloth (weave pattern clearly visible as dark brown and white threads). Covers blank. Spine with the lettering stamped in gilt, reading perpendicularly from top to bottom, within a black-stamped panel with a gilt boarder, 'ROBERT FROST · IN THE CLEARING'. In a board slipcase covered with black paper.

Publication: Fifteen hundred copies printed by The Spiral Press, March 1962.

Barrett Copies:
592661. Number 101.
597624. Number 124.
597280. Number 122.
Uncatalogued. The Lawrance Thompson copy, number 19. Inscribed on the front open endpaper recto, 'Larry from Robert / Two Israelites / (latter day)'. RF refers to the trip that he and Lawrance Thompson took together to Israel and Greece in March 1961.

A41.1   1962 IN THE CLEARING (Trade Edition)

IN THE | CLEARING | BY | ROBERT | FROST | [Holt device] | [swelling rule] | HOLT, RINEHART AND WINSTON | NEW YORK

FIRST IMPRESSION FROM PLATES OF THE LIMITED EDITION TYPE

Collation: [1–4]⁸ [5]⁴ [6–7]⁸; pp. [1–12] 13–101 [102–104] = 52 leaves.

Contents: p. 1: half-title, 'IN THE CLEARING BY ROBERT FROST'; p. 2: blank; p. 3: title-page; p. 4: '[copyright notice; 3 lines in italics as in the limited edition] | [all rights reserved notice (2 lines) as in ltd. ed.] | [simultaneous Canadian publication notice (2 lines) as in ltd. ed.] | FIRST EDITION | *Library of Congress Catalog Card Number: 62–11578* | [3-line note on 'The Gift Outright' as in ltd. ed.] | *82941–1912* | *Printed in the United States of America*'; p. 5: dedication as in the limited edition; p. 6: blank; p. 7: lines 219–224 and 246–257 of 'Kitty Hawk' in italics (called 'But God's Own Descent' in the contents); p. 8: blank; pp. 9–10: contents; p. 11: second half-title, 'IN THE CLEARING | *"And wait to watch the water clear, I may."* '; p. 12: blank; pp. 13–101: text; pp. 102–104: blank.

Text Content: As in the limited edition.

Paper: White wove paper. Leaves measure 227 × 151 mm.; edges trimmed. Endpapers of heavy cream-gray wove stock.

Binding: Slate-gray medium linen (visible weave) cloth. Covers blank. Spine stamped in silver, lettering from top to bottom, 'ROBERT FROST [diagonal slash in silver] IN THE CLEARING *Holt · Rinehart · Winston*'.

Dust Jacket: Coated paper with a black ground on the front cover and spine; white on the back cover and flaps. The front cover is dominated by a black and white photographic portrait of RF in profile by David H. Rhinelander; lettered at top, '[white] ROBERT FROST | [red] IN THE CLEARING'. Spine lettered from top to bottom: '[white] ROBERT FROST [diagonal slash] [red] IN THE CLEARING [white] *Holt · Rinehart · Winston*'. Back cover lettered in black: 'ALSO AVAILABLE | THE COMPLETE POEMS | OF ROBERT FROST | including *A Boy's Will, North of Boston,* | *West-Running Brook, A Further Range,* | *A Witness Tree, Steeple Bush,* and | *A Masque of Mercy* | YOU COME TOO | a collection of favorite Frost poems | especially selected for | young readers | HOLT, RINEHART AND WINSTON.' Front inner flap, lettered in black: '$4.00 | ITC | IN THE CLEARING | *New Poems by* | ROBERT FROST | [20-line blurb] | *(continued on back flap)* | Jacket photograph by David H. Rhinelander'. Back inner flap: '*(continued from front flap)* | [25-line continued blurb] | [Holt imprint]'.

Publication: Published on RF's birthday, 26 March 1962.

Barrett Copies:
592662.
Uncatalogued. The Lawrance Thompson copy, inscribed on the front open end-paper recto, 'Larry from Robert / furthering friendship in Florida / when this first arrived in Mid-March / 1962 / Pencil Pines / South Miami'. This is apparently an advance copy sent to RF in Florida by Holt.

A41.2   1962 IN THE CLEARING (First English Edition)

IN THE | CLEARING | BY | ROBERT | FROST | [Holt device] | [swelling rule] | HOLT, RINEHART AND WINSTON | LONDON

Collation: [1]^8 2^8 [3]^8 4–5^8 6^4 7^8; pp. [1–6] 7–101 [102–104] = 52 leaves.

Contents: p. 1: half-title, 'IN THE CLEARING BY ROBERT FROST'; p. 2: blank; p. 3: title-page; p. 4: 'FIRST PUBLISHED IN GREAT BRITAIN 1962 | [copyright and all rights reserved notices as in American editions] | [note on 'The Gift Outright' as in American editions] | 82941-1912 | *Printed by offset in Great Britain by* | *William Clowes and Sons, Limited, London and Beccles*'; pp. 5–6: contents; pp. 7–10: 'INTRODUCTION | by | ROBERT GRAVES', signed in print on p. 10, 'ROBERT GRAVES | Deyá | Majorca, | Spain. | *June 1962*'; p. 11: second half-title, 'IN THE CLEARING | *"And wait to watch the water clear, I may."* '; p. 12: blank; pp. 13–101: text; pp. 102–104: blank.

Text Content: As in the American editions, but with the introduction by Robert Graves.

Paper: White wove paper. Leaves measure 229 × 152 mm.; edges trimmed. End-papers of heavy white 'linen-weave' stock.

Binding: Slate-gray linen cloth (visible weave) of a slightly coarser texture than the American trade edition.

Barrett Copy:
592663.

A42   1969 ONE FAVORED ACORN (First Separate Edition)

[cover-title] [within a red-brown rule-frame] [black] ONE | FAVORED | ACORN | BY | ROBERT | FROST

Collation: [1]⁸; pp. [1–16] = 8 leaves.

Contents: pp. 1–4: blank; p. 5: 'ONE FAVORED ACORN | BY ROBERT FROST | This booklet has been printed for | Middlebury College in celebration of | the dedication of the Robert Frost | cabin and land in Ripton, Vermont | on July the twelfth, 1969'; p. 6: 'Copyright © 1967 by the | Estate of Robert Frost'; p. 7: wood-engraving in gray-brown of a fence post by J. J. Lankes; pp. 8–9: text of poem; p. 10: blank; p. 11: [Spiral Press device] | FOUR HUNDRED COPIES PRINTED AT | THE SPIRAL PRESS · NEW YORK'; pp. 12–16: blank.

Paper: White laid paper with vertical chainlines 25 mm. apart. No watermark. Leaves measure 177 × 112 mm.; edges trimmed.

Binding: Heavy yellow-brown (74.s.yBr) paper wrapper, folded at the fore-edges over the preliminary and terminal blank leaves. Stitched with white thread at the center fold. Lettered on the front cover as above.

Publication: The booklet was printed for distribution to invited guests at a luncheon given by Middlebury College on the occasion of the dedication of the Homer Noble Farm, including the cabin, as a national historic landmark. The poem had been printed first in a Holt, Rinehart and Winston publication, *Frost: The Poet and His Poetry,* by David A. Sohn and Richard Tyre (New York and Toronto, 1967; pp. 26–27).

Barrett Copy:
Uncatalogued. The Lawrance Thompson copy.

B   Christmas Cards

B1   1929 CHRISTMAS TREES (First Separate Edition)

[within a border rule of 6-pointed stars printed in blue-green] CHRIST-MAS TREES | *A poem by Robert Frost* | *Sent to you* | *with holiday greetings* | *from* | NORMA & HERSCHEL | BRICKELL [three others as listed below]

Collation: [1]⁸; pp. [1–16] = 8 leaves.

Contents: pp. 1–4: blank; p. 5: title-page; p. 6: blank; pp. 7–10: text; p. 11: '[small green tree orn.] *Printed with the gracious permission* | *of Mr. Robert Frost, at The Spiral Press*.'; pp. 12–16: blank.

Paper: Cream wove paper. Leaves measure 140 × 110 mm.; top and bottom edges trimmed, fore-edge uncut.

Binding: Silver-coated paper wrappers flush with the leaves and folded over pp. 1–2 and 15–16. Front cover printed in black '[thick-thin rule extending perpendicularly from top to bottom] CHRISTMAS TREES'. Back cover and spine blank. Leaves stitched at the center fold.

Publication: The Spiral Press printed 275 copies with four varying names on the title-page:
  Leonard Blizard (50)
  Ann and Joseph Blumenthal (75)
  Norma and Herschel Brickell (100)
  Henry Holt and Company (50)
The poem had been printed first in *Mountain Interval* (1916) and again in *An Annual of New Poetry* (London, 1917). In 1937 Henry Holt and Company printed another separate edition as a Christmas greeting (Barrett 594733, inscribed 'For R. V. T. | from R. F.').

Joseph Blumenthal's own recollection of this first Christmas card is printetd in *The Spiral Press through Four Decades* (New York: The Pierpont Morgan Library, 1966) : 'while the book [*Collected Poems*, 1930] was in work, it occurred to me that his poem "Christmas Trees" would make a most appropriate holiday greeting booklet for my wife and myself. Frost's publishers gave permission.

Through foolish and unpardonable diffidence, I failed to ask Mr. Frost, whom I had not yet met, if he wished copies for himself. Later he chided me for this and charged me with the responsibility of getting back a half dozen booklets for himself and his family. . . . It was the beginning of the tradition of the Frost Christmas cards which was to continue until 1962.'

Barrett Copy:
594734. The 'Norma and Herschel Brickell' copy only, inscribed on p. 3, 'To Earle Bernheimer / from / Robert Frost'.

B2   1934 TWO TRAMPS IN MUD-TIME (First Separate Edition)

[within a border rule of brick-red stars, lettering in black] TWO TRAMPS IN MUD-TIME | A NEW POEM | BY ROBERT FROST | [red star] | SENT WITH | HOLIDAY GREETINGS | FROM | ELINOR & ROBERT FROST [or other names as listed below] | CHRISTMAS • 1934

Collation: [1]⁶; pp. [1–12] = 6 leaves.

Contents: pp. 1–2: blank; p. 3: title-page; p. 4: 'Copyright 1934 by Robert Frost'; p. 5–9: text of poem (at p. 9, 'Printed by The Spiral Press • New York'); pp. 10–12: blank.

Paper: Cream wove paper, watermarked '[star] ARAK [star] | W & A'. Leaves measure 161 × 115 mm.; top and bottom edges trimmed, fore-edge uncut.

Binding: A single quarto fold of light brown (58.m.Br; but see note below) laid paper with horizontal chainlines 37 mm. apart. Covers blank. Leaves stitched at the center fold with white thread.
    Note: The copy with 'Elinor & Robert Frost' on the title-page has a light brown cover. Other copies examined have red-brown (43.m.rBr) covers.

Publication: The Spiral Press printed 775 copies with six varying names on the title-page:
    Elinor & Robert Frost (as above) (200)
    Leonard Blizard (25)
    Ann and Joseph Blumenthal (125)
    Henry Holt & Company (200)
    The Melchers of Montclair (175)
    Mr. and Mrs. Richard Thornton (50)
The poem had been printed first in the *Saturday Review of Literature* (6 Oct. 1934); later collected in *A Further Range* (1936).

Barrett Copies:
594797. Four copies representing all but 'Holt' and 'Thornton'.
Those inscribed:

Elinor & Robert Frost. Inscribed on the title-page, 'Robert [Frost] to Robert
[Hillyer]'. Robert Hillyer, the American poet, brought Frost to Harvard in
1935 and remained a lifelong friend.

Ann and Joseph Blumenthal. Inscribed on the title-page, 'To Russell Alberts
from Robert Frost'.

The Melchers of Montclair. Signed on the title-page, 'Robert Frost'.

B3   1935 NEITHER OUT FAR NOR IN DEEP (First Separate Edition)

[within a border rule of yellow stars] *Neither Out Far Nor in Deep* | A
POEM BY ROBERT FROST | WOODCUT BY J. J. LANKES | [yellow
star] | *Sent with Holiday Greetings* | *at Christmas 1935 from* | ELINOR &
ROBERT FROST

Collation: [1]⁸; pp. [1–16] = 8 leaves.

Contents: pp. 1–4: blank; p. 5: title-page; p. 6: blank; p. 7: half-title, 'NEITHER
OUT FAR NOR IN DEEP | [woodcut of ocean beach by J. J. Lankes]'; pp. 8–9:
text; p. 10: '*Printed at The Spiral Press* | [yellow star] | *Copyright 1935 by Robert
Frost* | [yellow star] | *Courtesy of The Yale Review*'; pp. 11–16: blank.

Paper: Heavy wove white paper. Leaves measure 131 × 104 mm.; edges trimmed.
Watermarked 'Worthy Signature'.

Binding: Japanese *Kikone* paper flush with the leaves and folded over pp. 1–2 and
15–16. Both covers blank. Stitched at the center fold.

Publication: The Spiral Press printed 1,235 copies with eight varying names on
the title-page:
    Elinor & Robert Frost (as above) (450)
    Leonard W. Blizard (25)
    Ann & Joseph Blumenthal (175)
    Edee B. & Julius J. Lankes (100)
    Henry Holt & Company (200)
    From J. J. Lankes (60)
    The Melchers of Montclair (175)
    Mr. & Mrs. Richard Thornton (50)
Printed first in the *Yale Review* (March 1934) and later collected in *A Further
Range* (1936).

Barrett Copies:
594748. Four copies:
    Elinor & Robert Frost. Inscribed 'To Vera from her uncle' in Frost's hand on
        the title-page.

Elinor & Robert Frost. With the original envelope addressed in Frost's hand to Mr. & Mrs. Wilbur E. Rowell.

The Melchers of Montclair.

Mr. & Mrs. Richard Thornton. Inscribed 'To E[arle]. J. B[ernheimer]. from R[obert]. F[rost].' on the title-page.

594749. Fives copies:

Henry Holt & Company. Inscribed 'To E. J. B. from R. F.'

Ann & Joseph Blumenthal.

Edee B. & Julius J. Lankes.

From J. J. Lankes. Signed 'Robert Frost' on the first blank leaf.

Leonard W. Blizard.

B4 1936 EVERYBODY'S SANITY (First Separate Edition)

[cover title] Everybody's | Sanity | by | ROBERT | FROST | *Christmas greetings for 1936 from | Grant, Helen, & Anna Victoria Dahlstrom | Los Angeles, California*

Collation: [1]⁴; pp. 1–6 [7–8] = 4 leaves.

Contents: pp. 1–6: text; pp. 7–8: blank.

Paper: Very rough cream laid paper with vertical chainlines 51 mm. apart. Watermarked 'JOHN HENRY NASH | [dog]'. Leaves measure 161 × 112 mm. Top edge-rough-cut, other edges uncut.

Binding: Yellow-green (103.d.gY) heavy rough wove paper wrappers watermarked 'LOMBARDIA | [dragon within a shield] | ITALY | [backward swastika in a single rule frame]'. Lettering in black as transcribed above. Stitched with white thread at the center fold.

Publication: Information on the printing of this pamphlet comes from Grant Dahlstrom by way of John S. Van E. Kohn, who received a letter from Dahlstrom, owner and operator of The Castle Press, Pasadena, since 1943. On 28 January 1972, he wrote, '*Everybody's Sanity* is the title I gave to Robert Frost's letter to the . . . [Amherst] students who put on some sort of a celebration of Frost's sixtieth birthday when I cribbed it from a New York Times report. I asked his permission but he didn't reply until about a year later. I used it as a Christmas greeting and there were a hundred or so printed. All but ten or fifteen were mailed to friends and family. The paper used came from a demonstration of making paper by hand in the Los Angeles County Museum [in 1931] by Hugh and Peter King who had come here after the closing down of the Dard Hunter mill in Connecticut and were seeking financial backing for a like operation on the Pacific coast. I set the type by hand and had it printed by the Adcraft Press in Los Angeles and I folded & sewed them myself.' 'At the time of printing . . .

0

 tore

I was employed in the commercial printing department of the Down Town Shopping News . . . where I had the press work done.'

Dahlstrom used other paper for some copies. John Kohn reports two copies examined with the text paper watermarked 'Van Gelder Zonen'.

Jacob Zeitlin of Zeitlin & Ver Brugge, Los Angeles, has corroborated this information and added to it: 'He [Dahlstrom] printed it on an albion hand press and there were 100 to 150 copies in all. The paper bearing the John Henry Nash watermark was produced in 1931 by Hugh King and his brother, Peter, in a demonstration project set up in the basement of the Los Angeles County Museum. They borrowed a deckle from John Henry Nash which contained his watermark. Dahlstrom supplemented this paper with some sheets of Van Gelder. The covers were printed on several different coloured papers.

'Grant Dahlstrom is one of our outstanding Southern California printers. He comes from Ogden, Utah, where he was born about 1902. He got his training from Porter Garnett at the Laboratory Press in Pittsburgh . . . at Carnegie Institute of Technology. He came to Los Angeles about 1928 and was typographer for Bruce McAllister and the Mayer's Co. For the last twenty years he has operated his own shop under the name of the Castle Press in Pasadena. . . . His books have been exhibited in nearly every year's selection of the Rounce & Coffin Western Books.'

Information concerning previous and later publication is generously supplied by Robert Frost's bibliographer, Newton McKeon: It was published first as RF's letter to the *Amherst Student* (25 March 1935), in which the penultimate paragraph has the phrase 'everybody's sanity' used as Dahlstrom's title. It was reprinted in the *New York Times,* where Dahlstrom saw it. The Dahlstrom Christmas booklet, according to McKeon, 'alters the original considerably not only by excision, but by substituting phrases not in the original printed version, by paragraphing arbitrarily, by running sentences together, punctuating ad lib, employing caps for l.c. and vice versa.' Versions are reprinted in Sergeant's *Trial by Existence,* Thompson's *Selected Letters* and *The Years of Triumph,* and Lathem's *Selected Prose.*

Barrett Copy:

594739. Inscribed on p. 1 by Frost, 'It is for this I suppose I am / reckoned anti Platonist. / R. F.'

B5   1937 TO A YOUNG WRETCH (First Separate Edition)

ROBERT FROST · TO A YOUNG WRETCH | [woodcut by J. J. Lankes of evergreens in a snowy nocturnal landscape in dark blue (188.blackish B), gray-blue (186.gyB), and white, signed 'L']

Collation: [1]¹⁰; pp. [1–20] = 10 leaves (oblong format).

Contents: pp. 1–4: blank; p. 5: 'With Holiday Greetings | from Elinor and Robert Frost | December · 1937'; p. 6: blank; p. 7: title-page; p. 8: '*Copyright* 1937 *by*

Robert Frost · Amherst · Massachusetts'; pp. 9–12: text of poem; p. 13: 'Wood-cuts by J. J. Lankes · Printed at The Spiral Press, New York'; pp. 14–20: blank.

Paper: White laid paper with horizontal chainlines 27 mm. apart., watermarked '[quasi-blackletter] Vidal[——]' and a shield containing a scroll and a balloon(?), surmounted by a crown. Leaves measure 71 × 127 mm. (oblong format). All edges trimmed.

Binding: Gold Japanese paper wrappers flush with the leaves and pasted at the flaps to pp. 2 and 19. Printed in dark blue (188) on the front cover, '[within a thin-thick rule frame] TO A YOUNG WRETCH'. Back cover has a decorative ornament in dark blue (188) of a holly branch. Stitched at the center fold.

Publication: The Spiral Press printed 820 copies with seven varying names:
   Elinor and Robert Frost (as above) (275)
   Leonard W. Blizard (25)
   Ann and Joseph Blumenthal (170)
   Edee and J. J. Lankes (50)
   J. J. Lankes (100)
   The Melchers · Montclair / Marguerite and Fred (150)
   Nina and Richard Thornton (50)
Printed also in the *Saturday Review of Literature* (Dec. 25, 1937). Collected in *A Witness Tree* (1942).

Barrett Copies:
592792. Eight copies, representing all the names (two with 'Elinor and Robert Frost'). Those with Frost inscriptions:
   Elinor and Robert Frost. Inscribed on p. 5, 'To Vera / from R. F.'
   Nina and Richard Thornton. Inscribed on p. 5, 'Robert Frost / for Earle Bern-heimer.
   The Melchers. Inscribed on p. 3, 'Robert Frost / For Earle Bernheimer'.
   Leonard W. Blizard. Inscribed on p. 5, 'Robert Frost / For Earle Bernheimer'.
   Edee and J. J. Lankes. Signed on p. 3, 'R. F.—4'.
   J. J. Lankes. Signed on p. 3, 'R. F.—5'.

B6   1938 CARPE DIEM (First Separate Edition)

[Carpe Diem by Robert Frost]

Collation: [1]⁴; pp. [1–8] = 4 leaves.

Contents: p. 1: '[within a red triple rule frame] HOLIDAY | GREETINGS | FROM | ROBERT FROST | 1938'; pp. 2–3: blank; pp. 4–5: text, with the title on p. 4, 'CARPE DIEM | BY | ROBERT FROST'; pp. 6–8: blank.
   Note: A copy has been seen with a blue triple rule frame on p. 1.

Paper: A single quarto fold of gray-white (effect created by small blue threads in white paper) laid paper with horizontal chainlines 24 mm. apart. Leaves measure 158 × 113 mm. Paper watermarked '[——]WEAVE MILANO'. Enclosed in an envelope of the same paper.

Publication: The Spiral Press printed 230 copies with three varying names on p. 1:
   Robert Frost (as above) (150)
   Henry Holt & Company (30)
   T. J. Wilson (50)
Printed first in the *Atlantic Monthly* (Sept. 1938). Collected in *A Witness Tree* (1942).

Barrett Copies:
594731. The 'Holt' copy with blue triple rule at p. 1. Inscribed on p. 5, 'Robert Frost / to / R. V. Thornton'.
594732. Three copies, representing all names; all with red triple rules at p. 1.

B7   1939 TRIPLE PLATE (First Edition)

TRIPLE PLATE | BY ROBERT FROST | [white star outlined in gray within three white circles outlined in gray]

Collation: [1]¹⁰; pp. [1–20] = 10 leaves (oblong format).

Contents: pp. 1–4: blank; p. 5: 'Holiday Greetings · December 1939 | from | ROBERT FROST'; p. 6: blank; p. 7: title-page; p. 8: blank; pp. 9–11: text of poem; p. 12: blank; p. 13: '*Decorations by Fritz Eichenberg* | [gray star] | *Printed at The Spiral Press* | [gray star] | *Copyright*, 1939, *by Robert Frost*'; pp. 14–20: blank.

Paper: Cream laid paper with horizontal chainlines 28 mm. apart. An elaborate pictorial watermark of a snow-covered house with the word 'Winterbourne' rising as smoke from the chimney; countermark, 'MADE IN ENGLAND'. Leaves measure 95 × 115 mm. Edges trimmed.

Binding: Heavy dark blue (201.d.pB) wove paper wrappers flush with the leaves and pasted at the flaps to pp. 2 and 19. Pictorial design by Fritz Eichenberg in white extending over both covers: a small figure standing on a hill at lower right of the front cover, looking up at a star-filled night sky; a large bright star at upper left of the front cover. Covers unlettered. Stitched with white thread at the center fold.

Publication: The Spiral Press printed 1,825 copies with eight varying names:
   Robert Frost (as above) (450)
   Leonard W. Blizard (25)

Ann & Joseph Blumenthal (150)
Fritz Eichenberg (25)
Henry Holt and Company (900)
The Melchers of Montclair / Marguerite and Fred (200)
Helen Olson (50)
William Sloane (25)
Collected in *A Witness Tree* (1942) with the title 'Triple Bronze.'

Barrett Copies:
594796. Nine copies, representing all eight names (two with 'Robert Frost').
Those with Frost inscriptions:
   Robert Frost. Signed on p. 3, 'Robert Frost'.
   Robert Frost. Signed on p. 5, 'To Vera from RF'.
   Fritz Eichenberg. Signed on p. 5, 'Robert Frost / For Earle Bernheimer'.
   The Melchers. Signed on p. 3, 'R. L. F. / 1939–40'.
   Helen Olson. Signed on p. 5, 'Robert Frost'.

B8   1940 OUR HOLD ON THE PLANET (First Edition)

OUR HOLD ON THE PLANET | [flower orn.] | By ROBERT FROST

Collation: [1]⁶; pp. [1–12] = 6 leaves.

Contents: pp. 1–2: blank; p. 3: 'Christmas Greetings | *from* | ROBERT FROST | 1940'; p. 4: blank; p. 5: title-page; p. 6: 'Copyright, 1940 | by | ROBERT FROST'; pp. 7–11: text of poem; p. 12: blank.
   Note: Three variant names:
   Robert Frost (as above, 250)
   Henry Holt and Company (600)
   Marguerite and Fred Melcher (125)

Paper: Cream laid paper with vertical chainlines 30 mm. apart. Watermarked 'albion laid [eagle holding a capital letter 'A']'. Leaves measure 90 × 118 mm. Fore-edge uncut, other edges trimmed. Oblong format.

Binding: Light green (136.m.yG) heavy wove paper wrappers, lettered on the front cover in quasi-blackletter in dark green (146.d.G), 'Our hold on the Planet'. Front cover decorated with sixteen silver stars. Back cover blank. The wrapper is made up of a single quarto fold uncut at the fore- and bottom edges. Stitched at the center fold with white thread.

Publication: An edition of 975 copies printed. Collected in *A Witness Tree* (1942).

Barrett Copies:
594792. Four copies, representing all three names (two with 'Robert Frost').
Those with Frost inscriptions only are listed:

Robert Frost. Signed on p. 1, 'Robert Frost'.
Robert Frost. Inscribed on p. 1, 'To Vera from Uncle Rob'.

B9   1941 I COULD GIVE ALL TO TIME (First Separate Edition)

[I Could Give All to Time by Robert Frost]

Collation: [1]⁴; pp. [1–8] = 4 leaves.

Contents: p. 1: '[woodcut in dark green and red brown of trees in a winter land-scape, signed 'J'] | J. J. Lankes'; pp. 2–3: blank; p. 4: 'CHRISTMAS GREET-INGS | *from* | ROBERT FROST | 1941'; p. 5: 'I COULD GIVE ALL TO TIME | By ROBERT FROST | [15-line poem] | *Copyright 1941 by Robert Frost*'; pp. 6–8: blank.
   Note: Three variant names:
  Robert Frost (as above, 150)
  Henry Holt and Company (770)
  Marguerite and Fred Melcher (180)

Paper: A single quarto fold of white wove paper with the watermark of an eagle holding a capital letter 'A' (Albion). Leaves measure 163 × 123 mm. The text is printed in dark green. With an envelope of the same paper.

Publication: One thousand copies printed. The poem was printed first in the *Yale Review* (Autumn 1941) and collected in *A Witness Tree* (1942).

Barrett Copies:
594745. Four copies, representing all three names (two with 'Robert Frost'). Those with Frost inscriptions only listed below:
   Robert Frost. Inscribed on p. 1, 'Hilda and Vera from their Uncle'. With the
     original envelope addressed in Frost's hand.
   Robert Frost. Signed on p. 5, 'Robert Frost'.

B10   1942 THE GIFT OUTRIGHT (First Separate Edition)

[The Gift Outright by Robert Frost]

Collation: [1]⁴; pp. [1–8] = 4 leaves.

Contents: p. 1: [drawing printed in black of a winter landscape; tree in fore-ground, church and houses in background, signed 'J. O'H. Cosgrave II'. Sky and trees colored by hand in blue and red] | *Hand colored from an original by J. O'Hara Cosgrave II*'; pp. 2–3: blank; p. 4: 'CHRISTMAS GREETINGS |

FROM | ROBERT FROST | 1 9 4 2'; p. 5: 'THE GIFT OUTRIGHT | By ROBERT FROST | [holly leaf orn.] | [16-line poem] | *Coypright, 1942, by Robert Frost*'; pp. 6–8: blank.

 Note: Three variant names:
 Robert Frost (as above, 150)
 Henry Holt and Company (1,000)
 Marguerite and Fred Melcher (100)

Papers: A single quarto fold of white wove paper watermarked 'Leonard' with the countermark of an eagle holding a capital 'A'. Leaves measure 165 × 124 mm.

Publication: An edition of 1250 copies printed. Printed first in the *Virginia Quarterly Review* (Spring 1942). Collected in *A Witness Tree* (1942).

Barrett Copies:
594743. Three copies, representing all names. Those with Frost inscriptions only listed:
 Marguerite and Fred Melcher. Signed on p. 5, 'Robert Frost'.
 Robert Frost. Inscribed on p. 5, 'Robert Frost / to / Waller Barrett'. Also, Frost has underlined the words 'Massachusetts' and 'Virginia' in line 4 of the poem.

B11   1943 THE GUARDEEN (First Edition)

[The Guardeen, fragment of an unpublished play by Robert Frost]

Collation: [1]²; pp. [1–4] = 2 leaves.

Contents: p. 1: 'The pages, here reproduced from the | original manuscript of the first draft of | an unpublished play by Robert Frost, | are printed in an edition of 96 copies by | the Ward Ritchie Press, Los Angeles, | California, for Earle J. Bernheimer. | This is copy number | [number in ink]. | *Christmas, 1943*'; pp. 2–3: the facsimile, printed in black on an orange-yellow (72.d.OY) panel measuring 210 × 305 mm. (comprises the entire panel centered on the inner pages of the two conjugate leaves); p. 4: blank.

Paper: White wove paper. Leaves measure 279 × 203 mm. Top and fore-edges trimmed, bottom edge uncut.

Binding: Pale yellow-orange (73.p.OY) wove wrappers measuring 292 × 211 mm.; edges trimmed (fore-edge of front cover only uncut). Front cover lettered in deep orange, 'Season's Greetings | for the year 1943 from | Earle J. Bernheimer'. Stitched at the center fold.

Publication: The Ward Ritchie Press, Los Angeles, printed 96 copies privately for Earle J. Bernheimer. The play has never been published, and the fragment in facsimile here has never been reprinted. The original manuscript in two versions is in the Barrett collection (E27).

Barrett Copy:

594744.
Uncatalogued. The Lawrance Thompson copy. Inscribed on p. 1, 'For Larry Thompson— / To mark a most happy / meeting that made him / "My November Guest", / Earle Bernheimer. / —"But oh, the agitated heart, / Till some one finds us really out." ' Lines 3–4 of 'Revelation,' printed first in *A Boy's Will* (1913).

B12   1944 TWO LEADING LIGHTS (First Edition)

[Two Leading Lights, a poem by Robert Frost]

Collation: [1]²; pp. [1–4] = 2 leaves.

Contents: p. 1: facsimile of telegram from Kathleen Morrison to Earle Bernheimer, printed in black on light yellow-brown (87.m.Y). Message reads, 'ROBERT SUGGESTS YOU USE POEM MAILED TO YOU YESTERDAY FOR | CHRISTMAS CARD IF YOU LIKE IT'; p. 2: blank; p. 3: the facsimile of the poem, printed in black on a light yellow-brown (87.m.Y) panel measuring 229 × 146 mm.; p. 4: 'This heretofore unpublished poem by | Robert Frost is limited to 52 copies, | printed by the Ward Ritchie Press, | Los Angeles, California, for | Earle J. Bernheimer. | This is copy number [number in ink] | [small 8-pointed star orn.] | *Christmas*, 1944 | E. J. Bernheimer.'

Paper: White laid paper with vertical chainlines 39 mm. apart. Watermarked '[hand grasping 4 arrows] | WORTHY'. Leaves measure 279 × 206 mm. Top edge trimmed, other edges uncut.

Binding: Pale yellow-orange (73.p.OY) wove wrappers measuring 293 ×216 mm.; edges trimmed (fore-edge of front cover only uncut). Front cover lettered in deep orange, 'Season's Greetings | for the year 1944 from | Earle J. Bernheimer'. Stitched at the center fold.

Publication: The Ward Ritchie Press, Los Angeles, printed 52 copies privately for Earle J. Bernheimer. The poem was sent to Bernheimer by RF on 5 December 1944 for the purpose. Later printed in *Steeple Bush* (1947).

Barrett Copies: Two copies laid in with manuscript of poem:
Number One, further inscribed in Bernheimer's hand, 'Rec'd. from printer on 12/27/44.' on p. 4.
Number Ten. Also inscribed 'To R. V. Thornton / from / R. F.' Laid in are

proofs of the cover text and the limitation page with Bernheimer's corrections and approval notes on each. These accompany the single white wove paper leaf on which RF has written the poem in ink. The facsimile was taken from this leaf, which measures 227 × 146 mm.

B13   1944 AN UNSTAMPED LETTER IN OUR RURAL LETTER BOX (First Edition)

[dark brown] An Unstamped Letter | in Our | Rural Letter Box | BY | ROBERT FROST | [vignette woodcut of a mailbox]

Collation: [1]¹⁰; pp. [1–20] = 10 leaves.

Contents: pp. 1–4: blank; p. 5: 'THIS NEW POEM | IS SENT TO YOU | WITH HOLIDAY GOODWILL | FROM | ROBERT FROST | DECEMBER 1944'; p. 6: blank; p. 7: title-page; p. 8: blank; pp. 9–12: text of poem; p. 13: '*Woodcut by Thomas W. Nason* | [star] | *Printed at The Spiral Press* | [star] | *Copyright* 1944 *by Robert Frost*'; pp. 14–20: blank. Text printed in brown.

Paper: Cream laid paper with chainlines 28 mm. apart, watermarked with a castle like the paper used for *On Making Certain Anything Has Happened* (1945), which has the countermark 'CAPULETI'. Leaves measure 134 × 98 mm., edges trimmed.

Binding: Brick red (43.m.rBr) rough wove paper wrappers flush with the leaves. A cream paper label, 18 × 60 mm., on the front cover, printed in brown, '[within a single-rule frame] AN UNSTAMPED LETTER IN | OUR RURAL LET-TER BOX'. Wrapper flaps fold over pp. 1–2 and 19–20. Stitched with white thread at the center fold.

Publication: The Spiral Press printed 2,050 copies with six varying names:
    Robert Frost (as above) (300)
    Ann & Joseph Blumenthal (200)
    Henry Holt and Company (1,250)
    Marguerite and Fred Melcher (100)
    Margaret & Thomas W. Nason (100)
    William Sloane (100)
Collected in *Steeple Bush* (1947).

Barrett Copies:
594801. Seven copies, representing all six names (two with 'Robert Frost'). Those with Frost inscriptions:
    Robert Frost. Inscribed on p. 3, 'For Vera from Uncle Rob'.
    Robert Frost. Signed on p. 3, 'Robert Frost / Ripton Vermont'.
    Margaret and Thomas W. Nason. Inscribed on p. 1, 'R. A. from R. F.'

B14   1945 ON MAKING CERTAIN ANYTHING HAS HAPPENED
(First Edition)

ON | MAKING | CERTAIN | ANYTHING | HAS | HAPPENED |
[yellow-brown] [a compass chart, a compass instrument and a star] | BY
ROBERT FROST

Collation: [1]⁸; pp. [1–16] = 8 leaves.

Contents: pp. 1–4: blank; p. 5: '[yellow-brown: a falling star] | This new poem |
comes to you with | Holiday Greetings | from | Robert Frost | December 1945';
p. 6: '*Copyright* | 1945 | *by Robert Frost*'; p. 7: title-page; pp. 8–9: text of poem;
p. 10: blank; p. 11: 'Decorations by Armin Landeck | [yellow-orange star] |
Printed at The Spiral Press'; pp. 12–16: blank.

Paper: Cream laid paper with vertical chainlines 27 mm. apart. Watermarked
'[castle] | CAPULETI'. Leaves measure 136 × 97 mm. Edges trimmed.

Binding: Heavy wove paper wrappers coated with dark slate gray (192.d.bGy)
on the outer side. Decorated in white on both covers with an astronomical chart
of the constellations. Front cover: lettered in yellow-brown on a white panel
bordered by a yellow-brown rule, 'ON MAKING CERTAIN | ANYTHING
HAS HAPPENED'. Wrappers flush with the leaves and folded over pp. 1–2
and 15–16. Stapled at the center fold.

Publication: The Spiral Press printed 2,600 copies with eight varying names:
    Robert Frost (as above) (300)
    Siri Andrews (250)
    Ann & Joseph Blumenthal (200)
    Joseph A. Brandt (250)
    Henry Holt and Company (1,050)
    Beatrice & Armin Landeck (100)
    Marguerite & Fred Melcher (150)
    William Sloane (300)
Collected in *Steeple Bush* (1947).

Barrett Copies:
594787. Eight copies, representing all eight names. Those copies with Frost inscriptions:
    Robert Frost. Inscribed on p. 7, 'Robert Frost / to / Waller Barrett'.
    Joseph A. Brandt. Signed on p. 3, 'Robert Frost'.
    William Sloane. Signed on p. 3, 'Robert Frost'.
    Siri Andrews. Signed on p. 3, 'Robert Frost'.

B15   1946 A YOUNG BIRCH (First Edition)

A YOUNG BIRCH | [gray: woodcut of four birches] | ROBERT FROST

Collation: [1]⁸; pp. [1–16] = 8 leaves.

Contents: pp. 1–4: blank; p. 5: 'This new poem brings you | Holiday Greetings from | Robert Frost | December 1946 | [vignette of rock and flowers in gray and yellow-green]'; p. 6: '[gray] *Copyright* | 1946 | *by Robert Frost*'; p. 7: title-page; pp. 8–9: text of poem; p. 10: blank; p. 11: 'Decorations by Joseph Low | [gray: Spiral Press device] | Printed at The Spiral Press'; pp. 12–16: blank.

Paper: White laid paper with chainlines 26 mm. apart. Watermarked 'UN-BLEACHED | ARNOLD'. Leaves measure 138 × 114 mm. Fore-edge uncut, top and bottom edges trimmed.

Binding: Wrappers of the same stock, flush with the leaves and folded over pp. 1–2 and 15–16. Woodcut of birches on front cover extending to back cover and flaps, in gray and tan. Stapled at the center fold.

Publication: The Spiral Press printed 3,445 copies. The discrepancy of 250 copies between the total number and the numbers of variant name copies is accounted for by 25 sets with all names represented made up for Robert Frost. In 1946 and from 1949 on, 25 or 30 sets were sent to Frost.
Ten varying names:
  Robert Frost (as above) (300)
  Siri Andrews (500)
  Joseph A. Brandt (250)
  Ann & Joseph Blumenthal (225)
  Joe Duffy (240)
  Alfred C. Edwards (50)
  Henry Holt & Company (1,160)
  Denver Lindley (150)
  Ruth & Joseph Low (150)
  Marguerite & Fred Melcher (170)

Barrett Copies:
594800. Eleven copies, representing all ten names (two with 'Robert Frost'). Those with Frost inscriptions:
  Robert Frost. Inscribed on p. 3, 'Vera from Uncle Rob'. With the original envelope.
  Robert Frost. Signed on p. 5, 'Robert Frost'.

B16   1947 ONE STEP BACKWARD TAKEN (First Separate Edition)

[red] ONE STEP BACKWARD TAKEN | [black] BY ROBERT FROST

Collation: [1]⁶; pp. [1–12] = 6 leaves.

Contents: p. 1: cover-title; p. 2: blank; p. 3: '[black] *This poem brings you* |
[red] HOLIDAY GREETINGS | [black] *from* | [red] ROBERT FROST';
p. 4: '[gray] *Copyright* 1947 *by Henry Holt and Company, Inc.*'; p. 5: title-page;
pp. 6–7: text; p. 8: blank; p. 9: 'THE SPIRAL PRESS · NEW YORK'; pp. 10–11:
blank; p. 12: back cover, repeating the cover-title.

Paper: White wove paper; leaves measure 124 × 98 mm., edges trimmed.

Binding: Of the same paper as the text and comprising pp. 1 and 12 as above.
Front cover: '[red] ONE STEP BACKWARD TAKEN | [thick (4 mm.)
gray-brown rule extending the width of the cover] | [red] BY ROBERT
FROST'. The back cover repeats the front. Stapled at the center fold.

Publication: The Spiral Press printed 3,050 copies with ten varying names:
    Robert Frost (as above) (350)
    Ann & Joseph Blumenthal (250)
    Siri Andrews (150)
    Mr. & Mrs. Joseph A. Brandt (400)
    Sallye & Joe Brandt (150)
    Joseph A. Duffy (200)
    Alfred C. Edwards (50)
    Henry Holt & Company (1,200)
    Denver Lindley (150)
    Marguerite & Fred Melcher (150)
Printed first in the *Book Collector's Packet* (Jan. 1946). Collected in *Steeple Bush*
(1947).

Barrett Copies:
594791. Ten copies representing all ten names.

B17   1947 THE FALLS (First separate edition)

[The Falls by Robert Frost]

Collation: [1]²; pp. [1–4] = 2 leaves.

Contents: p. 1: '*The Falls* appeared in 1894 in a thin volume | of poetry, by
Robert Frost, titled *Twilight*. Two copies were printed, privately, for him. |

Later, he destroyed one copy. With the Au-|thor's friendly and gracious per-mission the|poem is shown, in facsimile, on the following|page. It is the only printing of *The Falls* other|than in *Twilight*, 1894.|Limited to 60 num-bered copies.|Copy|[numbered by hand]|THE WARD RITCHIE PRESS · LOS ANGELES|*Printed for Earle J. Bernheimer'*; p. 2: blank; p. 3: the facsimile of the original printing in *Twilight*, within a broken rule frame; p. 4: blank.

Paper: White laid paper with vertical chainlines 25 mm. apart. Leaves measure 203 × 140 mm.; edges trimmed.

Binding: Pale yellow-orange (73.p.OY) wove paper wrappers, measuring 216 × 146 mm.; top and fore-edges trimmed, bottom edge uncut. Front cover lettered in bright orange, 'Season's Greetings|from|Earle J. Bernheimer|CHRISTMAS|1947'. Stitched at the center fold.

Publication: Printed first in *Twilight* (1894) and reprinted here separately in facsimile for the first and only time. Sixty copies privately printed for Earle J. Bernheimer by the Ward Ritchie Press, Los Angeles.

Barrett Copy:
594740. Number 45.

B18   1948 ON THE INFLATION OF THE CURRENCY 1919 (First Edition)

[On the Inflation of the Currency 1919]

Collation: [1]²; pp. 1–4 = 2 leaves.

Contents: p. 1: 'Limited to 60 numbered copies.|Copy [number in ink]| Privately printed for Earle J. Bernheimer—1948.'; p. 2: 10-line printed letter to Bernheimer, dated 'November 24th, 1948' and signed in facsimile holograph, 'Ever yours|Robert Frost'; p. 3: facsimile holograph fair copy of the poem within a single-rule frame; p. 4: blank.

Paper: White wove paper. Leaves measure 203 × 140 mm.; edges trimmed.

Binding: Pale yellow-orange (73.p.OY) heavy wove paper wrappers measuring 216 × 145 mm.; top and fore-edge trimmed, bottom edge uncut. Front cover lettered in red-orange, 'Season's Greetings|from|Earle J. Bernheimer|CHRIST-MAS|1948'. Back cover blank. Stitched at the center fold with heavy yellow cord, terminating in a 100 mm. fringed tassel.

Publication: The letter from Robert Frost to Bernheimer printed on p. 2 gives the most immediate information about the poem, 'The one about the currency

would be all right, I guess. It has never been published though it came near
being years ago when it was brand new. I offered Carl Van Doren the choice
between it and something else and he took the something else, I think "The
Pauper Witch of Grafton". If you date the currency one it will show how history
repeats itself in very short cycles and that will be amusing.' Carl Van Doren was
literary editor of *The Nation* in which 'The Pauper Witch of Grafton' was first
printed 13 April 1921. 'On the Inflation of the Currency' has never been reprinted or collected. The original manuscript from which the facsimile was
made is in the Barrett Collection (E11).

Barrett Copy:
594741. Number 41.

B19   1948 CLOSED FOR GOOD (First Edition)

[black] CLOSED FOR GOOD | [dark brown: wood-engraving of a fence
gate and tree, by Thomas W. Nason] | BY ROBERT FROST

Collation: [1]⁸; pp. [1–16] = 8 leaves.

Contents: pp. 1–4: blank; p. 5: 'This new poem brings | Holiday Greetings
from | Robert Frost | [brown: vignette of acorns and leaves] | [black] December
1948'; p. 6: blank; p. 7: title-page; p. 8: '*Copyright* 1948 *by Robert Frost*'; pp.
9–11: text of poem; p. 12: 'Wood Engravings | by Thomas W. Nason | [brown:
Spiral Press device] | [black] Printed at | The Spiral Press, New York'; pp.
13–16: blank.

Paper: Thick white wove paper with a partially visible watermark in quasi-
blackletter, 'Marars(?)'. Leaves measure 133 × 98 mm. Edges trimmed.

Binding: Gray-green (155.gGy) laid paper wrappers with vertical chainlines
26 mm. apart. No visible watermarks. Flush with the leaves, flaps folded over pp.
1–2 and 15–16. Script lettering in white at the foot of the front cover, 'Closed
For | Good'. Stapled at the center fold.

Publication: The Spiral Press printed 2,275 with eight varying names:
  Robert Frost (as above) (375)
  Ann & Joseph Blumenthal (275)
  Alfred C. Edwards (75)
  Doris Flowers (75)
  Glenn Gosling (75)
  Henry Holt and Company (1,050)
  Marguerite & Fred Melcher (175)
  Margaret & Tom Nason (175)

Collected in *Complete Poems of Robert Frost* (1949) and later included in *In the Clearing* (1962).

Barrett Copies:
594735. Eight copies representing all names. The 'Robert Frost' copy is inscribed on the title-page, 'David Page / Robert Frost'.

B20   1948 GREECE (First Separate Edition)

[cover title]   GREECE | ROBERT   FROST | [orn.] | BLACK   ROSE PRESS | CHICAGO

Collation: [1]⁴; pp. [1–8] = 4 leaves.
  Note: A single quarto fold, unopened at the top edge fold.

Contents: p. 1: title-page; pp. 2–4: blank; p. 5: text of poem, 'Greece'; pp. 6–7: blank; p. 8: 'THIS poem, which appeared in the *Boston | Evening Transcript* on April 30, 1897, was | one of Robert Frost's earliest published | poems. Forty-seven copies of this edition | have been printed for Christmas distribution | to friends of the BLACK ROSE PRESS. | 1948 | This is copy number [number in ink]'.

Paper: Cream laid paper with vertical chainlines 26 mm. apart. Watermarked 'Made in U.S.A.' in script. Leaves measure 178 × 124 mm. Fore-edge of the first two leaves of the quarto fold are uncut, top edges unopened, other edges trimmed. Unbound. In an envelope of similar laid paper with the watermark '. . . nweave Fox'.

Publication: The poem was inspired by Turkey's declaration of war against Greece on 17 April 1897. It was printed in the *Boston Evening Transcript* of 30 April 1897 by Charles Hurd, literary editor of the *Transcript* and a friend of RF (see Thompson, *The Early Years,* pp. 539–40). This first separate edition was the only publication printed under the name Black Rose Press. The press was owned by Richard H. Templeton who, with Lester Sprunger, the typographer, operated The Phoenix Press from 1937 to 1963. The Black Rose press-work was done by Philip Reed in Chicago. Templeton had been a student of RF's at Amherst in 1928 and wanted to print 'The Middletown Murder' in 1947, but could not gain RF's approval. A letter received from Templeton on 16 August 1972 generously supplies us with the information about the publication of 'Greece': 'Frustrated in my first attempt, I decided in 1948 to proceed with an idea without his permission. I had spent several years getting copies of all uncollected poems of Frost. In the quest of these, I had learned of the appearance of "Greece" in the *Boston Evening Transcript*. I obtained a photostat of page 6 of the April 30, 1897 issue. . . . Forty-seven copies were printed; however as I recall it, I sent only twenty-four copies as a Christmas greeting in 1948. The recipients were friends of mine who were printers like Elmer Adler and a few librarians. I then . . . sent copy number 26 to the . . . Library of Congress. . . . Just prior to doing this, I learned that Frost had an idea that I had done something without his permission so I sent him a copy. I then asked my good friend Howie Schmitt to see if he could prevail upon Frost to inscribe a copy for me' RF inscribed the copy, 'Robert Frost / to / Richard H. Templeton * / June 5 1951 / *For digging it out of the past'. Templeton goes on to say, 'The remaining copies I reserved for libraries having Frost collections. I refused to sell any copies. . . .'

Barrett Copy:
Uncatalogued. The Lawrance Thompson copy.

B21   1949 ON A TREE FALLEN ACROSS THE ROAD (First Separate Edition)

ON A TREE FALLEN ACROSS THE ROAD | (TO HEAR US TALK) | BY ROBERT FROST

Collation: [1]⁸; pp. [1–16] = 8 leaves (oblong format).

Contents: pp. 1–2: blank; p. 3: 'ROBERT FROST'S SELECTION | FOR CHRISTMAS 1949'; p. 4: 'COPYRIGHT | *Complete Poems of Robert Frost* | 1949'; p. 5: title-page; pp. 6–9: text of poem; p. 10: blank; p. 11: 'THE SPIRAL PRESS · NEW YORK'; pp. 12–16: blank. Printed in gray.

Paper: White wove paper watermarked 'CURTIS RAG'. Leaves measure 76 × 121 mm. Edges trimmed.

Binding: Pale blue (closest to 185.p.B) laid paper wrappers with chainlines 27 mm. apart. Watermarked 'FABRIANO (ITALY)'. Wrappers flush with the leaves, flaps folded over pp. 1–2 and 15–16. Printed in red on the front cover, '*Holiday Greetings* FROM ROBERT FROST | DECEMBER · 1949'. There are fourteen varying names on the front cover as listed below.

Publication: The Spiral Press printed 3,060 copies, including 25 extra sets for Robert Frost (350 copies) and 50 copies with the name space left blank for Lesley Frost. Fourteen names:
   Robert Frost (as above) (225)
   Ann & Joseph Blumenthal (325)
   William E. Buckley (125)
   Alfred C. Edwards (75)
   Doris Flowers (150)
   Lesley Frost (60)

Lesley & Robert Frost (65)
Glenn Gosling (75)
Henry Holt & Company (935)
Marjorie & Gilbert Loveland (125)
Robert H. MacMurphey (125)
Marguerite & Fred Melcher (175)
Edgar T. Rigg (125)
Gwen & Ed Rigg (75)

Printed first in *Farm and Fireside* (Oct. 1921). Collected in *New Hampshire* (1923).

Barrett Copies:
594750. Fourteen copies representing all names. The 'Robert Frost' copy is inscribed on the front cover, 'The full set for Mr. R. V. Thornton / from Robert Frost'.

B22   1950 DOOM TO BLOOM (First Edition)

DOOM TO BLOOM | BY ROBERT FROST | [gray: woodcut of a re-clining female figure holding a book, by Fritz Eichenberg]

Collation: [1]⁸; pp. [1–16] = 8 leaves (oblong format).

Contents: pp. 1–2: blank; p. 3: '*With this new poem* | [red] ROBERT FROST [black] *sends you* | *Holiday Greetings and good wishes* | [red] DECEMBER 1950'; p. 4: blank; p. 5: title-page; p. 6: '*Copyright 1950 by Robert Frost*'; pp. 7–10: text of poem in italics; pp. 11–12: blank; p. 13: 'Wood-engravings by Fritz Eichenberg | [red: Spiral Press device] | [black] Printed at The Spiral Press · New York'; pp. 14–16: blank.
   Note: The 'Robert Frost' copies are the only ones with this setting of p. 3. All other variants have the reading, '*With this new poem by Robert Frost* | [varying names in red] | [black] *sends you Holiday Greetings and good wishes* | [red] DECEMBER 1950'.

Paper: White wove paper, unwatermarked. Leaves measure 79 × 118 mm. Edges trimmed.

Binding: Wove paper wrappers coated on the exposed side with red-orange (38.d.rO) and cut flush with the leaves. A design of blown flowers in white extending to both covers. Flaps folded over pp. 1–2 and 15–16. Stapled at the center fold.

Publication: The Spiral Press printed 3,750 copies, included 25 sets for Frost (400 copies). Sixteen names:
   Robert Frost (as above) (425)

Theodore Amussen (125)
Ann & Joseph Blumenthal (325)
William E. Buckley (125)
Alfred C. Edwards (75)
Eleanor and Al Edwards (75)
Margaret & Fritz Eichenberg (225)
Lesley Frost (125)
Lesley and Robert Frost (125)
Henry Holt and Company (1,050)
Marjorie and Gilbert Loveland (100)
Robert H. MacMurphey (125)
Marguerite and Fred Melcher (175)
Edgar T. Rigg (125)
Gwen and Ed Rigg (75)
Mr. and Mrs. Edgar T. Rigg (75)
Collected in *In the Clearing* (1962) with the title 'Our Doom to Bloom.'

Barrett Copies:

594738. Seventeen copies representing all names (two 'Robert Frost' copies). Those inscribed by Frost:

Robert Frost. Inscribed on p. 3, 'To R. V. Thornton owner of Twilight / Robert Frost'.
Robert Frost. Inscribed on p. 3, 'To the Barretts / Robert Frost'.
Robert H. MacMurphey. Inscribed on p. 3, 'To Waller [Barrett]'.

B23   1951 A CABIN IN THE CLEARING (First Edition)

A CABIN IN THE CLEARING | BY ROBERT FROST | [gray: vignette of a cabin in trees]

Collation: [1]⁸; pp. [1–16] = 8 leaves.

Contents: pp. 1–2: blank; p. 3: 'At Christmas 1951 a new poem | comes to you with Holiday Greetings | from Robert Frost | [blue-gray: a vignette of withered tree stump]'; p. 4: blank; p. 5: title-page; p. 6: '[gray] *Copyright* 1951 *by Robert Frost*'; pp. 7–10: text of the poem, which is a dialogue between 'Smoke' and 'Mist,' has all the 'Mist' lines printed in gray-blue and the 'Smoke' lines in gray. The final 2-line summation on p. 10 is in black; p. 11: '[gray] *Decorations by Leo Manso* | [gray-blue star] | *Printed at The Spiral Press, New York*'; pp. 12–16: blank.
    Note: The 'Robert Frost' copies only have this setting of p. 3. All other variants have the reading, 'A new poem by Robert Frost | comes to you with Holiday

Greetings | from [varying names] | at Christmas 1951 | [tree stump vignette]'.

Paper: White wove paper watermarked 'CURTIS RAG'. Leaves measure 146 ×
118 mm. Edges trimmed.

Binding: Wove paper wrappers coated on the exposed side with gray-blue (between 185 and 186) and cut flush with the leaves; flaps folded over pp. 1–2 and
15–16. On the front cover, '[white: a 5-pointed star] | A CABIN IN THE
CLEARING | [dark gray: a line of smoke rising behind the title]'. Stapled at the
center fold.

Publication: The Spiral Press printed 3,750 copies, including 25 extra sets for
Frost (350 copies). Fourteen names:
  Robert Frost (as above) (475)
  Theodore Amussen (150)
  Ann & Joseph Blumenthal (375)
  William E. Buckley (150)
  Alden H. Clark (75)
  Alfred C. Edwards (100)
  Eleanor & Alfred Edwards (100)
  Lesley Frost (150)
  Henry Holt and Company (1,325)
  Marguerite & Fred Melcher (175)
  Edgar T. Rigg (100)
  Mr. & Mrs. Edgar T. Rigg (75)
  Gwen and Ed Rigg (75)
  Ben Wright (75)
Collected in *In the Clearing* (1962).

Barrett Copies:
594716. Fifteen copies representing all names (two 'Lesley Frost' copies).
Those inscribed:
  Robert Frost. After his printed name on p. 3, Frost has written, 'or to be more
    exact / Robert Lee Frost / This is Number 2 of this imprint / Number 1
    went as of obligation to Joseph Blumenthal who / printed it. Since you are /
    interested in such details.' (Inscribed for C. Waller Barrett).
  Lesley Frost. On p. 3, Lesley Frost has written above the printed text, 'For
    Hilda and Vera' and beneath, 'with my love, and best for 1952. / Lesley'.
This set is enclosed in a white paper wrapper on which Frost has written, 'Mr.
Thornton / the complete set / of 14 vols for 1951 / as an illustration / from /
Robert Frost'.
Uncatalogued. The Lawrance Thompson copy, inscribed on p. 3, 'Larry and
Jan / [printed text: At Christmas 1951 a new poem] / by an old pen / [printed
text: comes to you with Holiday Greetings] / the most Riptonian / [printed
text: from Robert Frost] at Ripton still / glowing with the time you / gave him
in the madding / crowd'.

B24   1952 DOES NO ONE BUT ME AT ALL EVER FEEL THIS
WAY IN THE LEAST (First Edition)

DOES NO ONE BUT ME | AT ALL | EVER FEEL THIS WAY | IN
THE LEAST | [moss-green swelling rule] | BY ROBERT FROST

Collation: [1]⁸; pp. [1–16] = 8 leaves.

Contents: pp. 1–2: blank; p. 3: 'A new poem again brings you | Holiday Greet-
ings from Robert Frost | at Christmas 1952'; p. 4: lithograph of ocean waves in
black, white and moss-green, by Howard Cook; p. 5: title-page; p. 6: '[pale
green] *Copyright* 1952 *by Robert Frost*'; pp. 7–10: text of poem. On p. 9 is a
half-page lithograph in black, white, and moss-green of sea birds on rocks; p. 11:
'DRAWINGS BY HOWARD COOK | [gray-green: Spiral Press device] |
Printed at The Sprial Press · New York'; pp. 12–16: blank.

   Note: The 'Robert Frost' copies only have this setting of p. 3. All other variants
have the reading, 'A new poem by Robert Frost | again brings you Holiday
Greetings | from [varying names] | at Christmas 1952'.

Paper: White laid paper with vertical chainlines 26 mm. apart. Watermarked
'CURTIS RAG'. Leaves measure 141 × 118 mm. Edges trimmed.

Binding: Beige (79.l.gy.yBr) laid paper wrappers with horizontal chainlines 27
mm. apart. No visible watermarks. Wrappers cut flush with leaves and flaps
folded over pp. 1–2 and 15–16. Both covers have an overall design in dark green
of an underwater scene with six fishes and marine plants. Stapled at the center
fold.

   Note: A variant light blue-gray (between 185 and 186) laid paper with the
design printed in dark red occurs on the 'Ann and Joseph Blumenthal' and
'Barbara and Howard Cook' copies.

Publication: The Spiral Press printed 3,875 copies, including 25 sets for Frost
(350 copies). Fourteen varying names:
   Robert Frost (as above) (475)
   Theodore Amussen (200)
   Lesley Frost Ballantine and Joseph W. Ballantine (225)
   Ann & Joseph Blumenthal (375)
   William E. Buckley (150)
   Alden Clark (50)
   Barbara & Howard Cook (175)
   Alfred C. Edwards (100)
   Eleanor & Al [Edwards] (75)
   Henry Holt & Company (1,300)

Marguerite & Fred Melcher (175)
Edgar T. Rigg (100)
Gwen & Ed [Rigg] (50)
Mr. & Mrs. Edgar T. Rigg (75)
Collected in *In the Clearing* (1962).

Barrett Copies:
594737. Fourteen copies representing all names. With them is a paper folder inscribed, '14 vols—Complete Set 1952 / for Mr. Thornton / from / Robert Frost'.

B25   1953 ONE MORE BREVITY (First Edition)

[red] One More Brevity [black] A NEW POEM BY | ROBERT FROST. IT COMES TO YOU | WITH WARM HOLIDAY GREETINGS | AT CHRISTMAS [red] 1953 [black] FROM | ROBERT FROST | [gray: a calligraphic line-drawing of a Christmas tree superimposed on the last two lines]

Collation: [1]^8; pp. [1–16] = 8 leaves.

Contents: pp. 1–4: blank; p. 5: title-page; p. 6: '*Copyright* 1953 *by Robert Frost*'; pp. 7–11: text of poem; p. 12: blank; p. 13: '*Decorations by Philip Grushkin* | [gray: Spiral Press device] | *Printed at The Spiral Press · New York*'; pp. 14–16: blank.

Paper: White wove paper watermarked 'CURTIS RAG'. Leaves measure 169 × 112 mm. Edges trimmed.

Binding: Yellow-cream (like 90.gyY) heavy laid paper wrappers with vertical chainlines 26 mm. apart. No visible watermarks. Flush with the leaves; flaps folded over pp. 1–2 and 15–16. On the front cover, 'ONE MORE BREVITY [two rough-drawn line-drawings of 5-pointed stars; a red star superimposed on a gray]'. Back cover blank. Stapled at the center fold.

Publication: The Spiral Press printed 4,501 copies, including 25 sets for Frost (375 copies). Fourteen varying names:
  Robert Frost (as above) (587)
  Lesley Frost Ballantine and Joseph W. Ballantine (304)
  Ann & Joseph Blumenthal (425)
  William E. Buckley (209)
  Alden Clark (80)
  Alfred C. Edwards (134)
  Eleanor and Al [Edwards] (112)
  Henry Holt and Company (1,575)

I. Robert Kriendler (75)
Marguerite and Fred Melcher (175)
William Raney (130)
Edgar T. Rigg (80)
Mr. & Mrs. Edgar T. Rigg (80)
Gwen and Ed [Rigg] (80)
Ben Wright (80)
Collected in *In the Clearing* (1962).

Barrett Copies:
594789. Fourteen copies representing all names.

B26   1954 FROM A MILKWEED POD (First Edition)

FROM A MILKWEED POD | BY ROBERT FROST | [wood-engraving of a milkweed plant in dark olive-green, by Thomas W. Nason]

Collation: [1]⁸; pp. [1–16] = 8 leaves.

Contents: pp. 1–2: blank; p. 3: 'A new poem at Christmas 1954 | again comes to you with greetings | for the holidays from | Robert Frost'; p. 4: blank; p. 5: title-page; p. 6: '[dark olive-green] *Copyright* 1954 *by Robert Frost*'; pp. 7–11: text of poem preceded on p. 7 by a headpiece vignette of six butterflies printed in gray; p. 12: blank; p. 13: '[dark olive-green] *Wood engravings by Thomas W. Nason* | [Spiral Press device] | *Printed at The Spiral Press, New York*'; pp. 14–16: blank.
   Note: The 'Robert Frost' copies are the only ones with this setting of p. 3. All other variants have the reading, 'A new poem by Robert Frost | at Christmas 1954 again comes | to you with warm greetings for | the holidays from | [varying names]'.

Paper: White laid paper with vertical chainlines 27 mm. apart. Watermarked 'Old Stratford'. Leaves measure 146 × 117 mm. Edges trimmed.

Binding: Olive-gray (110.gyOl) laid paper wrappers with horizontal chainlines 27 mm. apart. Watermarked 'CANSON & MONTGOLFIER FRANCE' and 'INGRES'. Wrappers flush with the leaves with flaps folded over pp. 1–2 and 15–16. On the front cover, '[dark brown] from a | Milkweed | Pod | [wood-engraving of a milkweed pod and escaping seeds in dark brown and white, by Thomas Nason]'. Stapled at the center fold.

Publication: The Spiral Press printed 5,076 copies, including 25 sets for Frost (425 copies). Eighteen varying names:
  Robert Frost (as above) (598)
  Lesley Frost and Joseph W. Ballantine (266)

Ann & Joseph Blumenthal (400)
William E. Buckley (200)
Marjory and Howard Cady (112)
Howard Cady (111)
Alden Clark (32)
Al Edwards (136)
Eleanor and Al [Edwards] (106)
Lesley Lee Francis (31)
Henry Holt & Company (1,767)
Marguerite & Fred Melcher (154)
Margaret & Tom Nason (223)
Edgar T. Rigg (104)
Gwen and Ed Rigg (50)
Mr. & Mrs. Edgar T. Rigg (55)
Ben Wright (52)
The Ben Wrights (254)
Collected in *In the Clearing* (1962).

Barrett Copies:
594742. Nineteen copies representing all names (two copies of 'Al Edwards').

B27   1955 SOME SCIENCE FICTION (First Edition)

Some Science | Fiction | by | Robert Frost | [gray: a 5-sphered molecular structure]

Collation: [1]⁸; pp. [1–16] = 8 leaves.

Contents: pp. 1–2: blank; p. 3: 'This new poem carries with it | the warmest holiday greetings | [red] AT CHRISTMAS 1955 | and the best of wishes for the | New Year from | Robert Frost'; p. 4: blank; p. 5: title-page; p. 6: 'Copyright 1955 by Robert Frost'; pp. 7–10: text of poem; pp. 11–12: blank; p. 13: '*Printed at the Spiral Press, New York* | [gray: Spiral Press device] | *With decorations by Philip Grushkin*'; pp. 14–16: blank.
    Note: There were 75 copies in which no name was printed on p. 3. These were the copies made up for Elinor Wilber (see below).

Paper: White laid paper with vertical chainlines 27 mm. apart, watermarked 'Old Stratford'. Leaves measure 130 × 93 mm. Edges trimmed.

Binding: Wrappers of the same stock flush with the leaves. On the front cover, lettered in black against a pattern of intersecting orange, green and red ellipses and stylized red, orange, and green stars, 'SOME SCIENCE FICTION'. Back cover: a green 'star' formed of three slashes, a red 'star' formed of four orange slashes, and a red-orange 'star' of three orange slashes and two red. Wrapper flaps folded over pp. 1–2 and 15–16. Stapled at the center fold.

Note: The 'Ann & Joseph Blumenthal' copies are on white wove paper with no visible watermark. The binding of these copies is gray laid paper wrapped with horizontal chainlines 25 mm. apart; flush with the leaves and having the same cover printing.

Publication: The Spiral Press printed 5,650 copies, including 25 sets of 16 variants only (375 copies) for Frost (the special sets for Frost did not include copies with his name, all of which were sent to his secretary, Kathleen Morrison, for mailing). Seventeen variants:

> Robert Frost (as above) (575)
> Lesley Frost and Joseph W. Ballantine (275)
> Ann & Joseph Blumenthal (475)
> William E. Buckley (250)
> Howard Cady (125)
> Alden Clark (50)
> Al Edwards (150)
> Eleanor and Al Edwards (125)
> Henry Holt and Company (2,000)
> Mr. & Mrs. J. Patrick Lannan (375)
> Marguerite & Fred Melcher (175)
> Gwen and Ed Rigg (75)
> Edgar T. Rigg (125)
> Mr. & Mrs. Edgar T. Rigg (75)
> [Elinor Wilber (name left blank)] (75)
> Ben Wright (75)
> The Ben Wrights (275)

Collected in *In the Clearing* (1962) with an additional quatrain.

Barrett Copies:

592764. Thirteen copies representing thirteen of the names. Wrapped in a paper slip on which Frost has written, 'For R. V. Thornton / one poem in seventeen / volumes by / Robert Frost'.

592793. Five copies representing the other four names of which two are the 'Ann & Joseph Blumenthal' variant binding.

B28   1956 KITTY HAWK (First Edition)

[red brown] Kitty Hawk | [black] 1894 | by Robert Frost | [gray: woodcut of waves, by Antonio Frasconi]

Collation: [1]¹⁰; pp. [1–20] = 10 leaves.

Contents: pp. 1–2: blank; p. 3: 'CHRISTMAS 1956 | and this new poem | bring you the warmest | greetings for the holidays | and the new year from | ROBERT

FROST [name imposed on a geometric bright yellow sun]'; p. 4: blank; p. 5: title-page; p. 6: 'COPYRIGHT 1956 BY ROBERT FROST'; pp. 7–14: text of poem; p. 15: 'Woodcuts by Antonio Frasconi | [red: Spiral Press device] | [black] Printed at The Spiral Press, New York'; pp. 16–20: blank.

Paper: White laid paper with vertical chainlines 26 mm. apart. Watermarked 'Old Stratford' and 'U.S.A.' Leaves measure 151 × 78 mm. Edges trimmed.

Binding: Wrappers of the same stock, flush with the leaves. Flaps folded over pp. 1–2 and 19–20. On the front cover, '[red-brown] Kitty | Hawk' imposed on a woodcut map, by Antonio Frasconi, which extends over both covers; executed in pale yellow, red-brown, dark gray, blue-gray, and white. Most copies stapled at the center fold; however, the 'Ann & Joseph Blumenthal' copy is stitched at the center fold with white thread.

Publication: The Spiral Press printed 7,000 copies, including 25 sets for Frost (525 copies). Twenty-one varying names:
  Robert Frost (as above) (600)
  Lesley Frost and Joseph W. Ballantine (250)
  Ann & Joseph Blumenthal (400)
  William E. Buckley (250)
  Howard Cady (100)
  Alden Clark (25)
  Al Edwards (125)
  Eleanor and Al Edwards (100)
  Lesley Lee Francis (50)
  Leona & Antonio Frasconi (150)
  Lillian Frost (50)
  Phyllis and William Prescott Frost (100)
  Henry Holt and Company (2,950)
  Mr. & Mrs. J. Patrick Lannan (600)
  Marguerite and Fred Melcher (150)
  Edgar T. Rigg (100)
  Mr. & Mrs. Edgar T. Rigg (50)
  Gwen and Ed Rigg (50)
  Elinor and Malcolm Wilber (75)
  Ben Wright (50)
  The Ben Wrights (50)
After this first appearance, Robert Frost revised the poem 'Kitty Hawk' three times. The second version, much altered and expanded to 432 lines, was printed in the *Atlantic Monthly* (Nov. 1957). This version also appeared in *Anthology of Magazine Verse for 1958* (1959) containing a few typographical errors of spelling and punctuation. A new poem of 64 lines with the title 'The Great Event is Science. The Great Misgiving, The Fear of God, is That the Meaning of it Shall be Lost' was printed in the *Saturday Review* (21 March 1959). This poem contained 33 lines excerpted from the second version. The final version, having 471 lines, provided the central theme for Frost's last book, *In the Clearing* (1962). It

incorporates the 64-line poem in its entirety, discards sections of version two, and contains further text written for this version.

Barrett Copies:
594746. Twenty-three copies representing all names (two copies each of 'Robert Frost' and 'Lesley Frost and Joseph W. Ballantine'). One of the 'Lesley Frost and Joseph W. Ballantine' copies is inscribed on p. 3, 'To / Hilda and Vera / from / Lesley'.

B29   1957 MY OBJECTION TO BEING STEPPED ON (First Edition)

MY | OBJECTION | TO BEING | STEPPED ON | [olive green: swelling rule] | A | NEW POEM | BY | ROBERT FROST

Collation: [1]^8; pp. [1–16] = 8 leaves.

Contents: pp. 1–2: blank; p. 3: '[red-orange floral orn. (on 9 variants); olive-green 8-pointed star (on 12 variants)] At Christmas 1957 | this poem brings you | the warmest Holiday | greetings and good wishes | from | Robert Frost'; p. 4: blank; p. 5: title-page; pp. 6–7: Woodcut engraving in dark brown by Leonard Baskin of weeds and thistles, extending over both pages; pp. 8–9: text of poem; p. 10: 'COPYRIGHT 1957 BY ROBERT FROST'; p. 11: 'Wood engravings by Leonard Baskin | [dark brown: Spiral Press device] | Printed at The Spiral Press, New York'; pp. 12–16: blank.

Paper: White wove paper watermarked 'UNBLEACHED ARNOLD'. Leaves measure 133 × 90 mm. Edges trimmed.

Binding: Wrappers of the same stock, flush with the leaves with flaps folded over pp. 1–2 and 15–16. On the front cover is a wood engraving of a thistle olive-green by Leonard Baskin with 'MY | OBJECTION | TO' to the left of the stem and 'BEING | STEPPED | ON' to the right (lettering in black). On the back cover is the same engraving in black without lettering. Stapled at the center fold.

Publication: The Spiral Press printed 8,290 copies, including 25 sets for Frost (525 copies). Nine varying names with a floral ornament on p. 3:
Robert Frost (as above) (650)
Lesley Frost and Joseph W. Ballantine (300)
Esther and Leonard Baskin (100)
Ann & Joseph Blumenthal (400)
Lesley Lee Francis (75)
Lillian Frost (70)
Phyllis and William Prescott Frost (125)
Marguerite and Fred Melcher (175)
Elinor and Malcolm Wilbur [*sic*] (95)

Twelve varying names with an 8-pointed star:
  William E. Buckley (285)
  Helen and Alden Clark (120)
  Al Edwards (200)
  Eleanor and Al Edwards (125)
  Henry Holt and Company (3,675)
  Mr. and Mrs. J. Patrick Lannan (650)
  Edgar T. Rigg (125)
  Mr. and Mrs. Edgar T. Rigg (70)
  Gwen and Ed Rigg (70)
  Harry Shaw (95)
  Ben Wright (70)
  The Ben Wrights (290)
Collected in *In the Clearing* (1962) with the title 'The Objection to Being Stepped On'.

Barrett Copies:
594747. Twenty-two copies representing all names (two copies with 'Robert Frost'). Copy inscribed:
  Robert Frost. Signed on p. 3. On the title-page, Frost has scored through the title word 'MY' and written above it, 'THE'.

B30   1958 AWAY! (First Edition)

AWAY! | BY | ROBERT FROST | [deep red: wood-engraving of a fallow hillside field, by Stefan Martin]

Collation: [1]⁸; pp. [1–16] = 8 leaves.

Contents: pp. 1–2: blank; p. 3: '[yellow-green: vignette of an evergreen tree] [black] Greetings for | [red] CHRISTMAS 1958 | [black] and best wishes for the new | year come to you with this | new poem, from | Robert Frost'; p. 4: blank; p. 5: title-page; p. 6: 'COPYRIGHT 1958 BY ROBERT FROST'; pp. 7–9: text of poem; p. 10: blank; p. 11: 'Wood engravings by Stefan Martin | [dark red: Spiral Press device] | Printed at The Spiral Press, New York'; pp. 12–16: blank.

Paper: White laid paper with vertical chainlines 27 mm. apart. No visible water-marks. Leaves measure 133 × 98 mm. Edges trimmed.

Binding: Buff laid paper wrappers with chainlines 27 mm. apart. No visible watermarks. (Note: In five copies examined, the chainlines ran horizontally; in seventeen, vertically.) Wrappers flush with leaves, flaps folded over pp. 1–2 and 15–16. On the front cover, '[gray] Away!' Extending over front and back covers and front inner flap is a wood-engraving in dark olive green of a village, by Stefan Martin. Most copies stapled at the center fold; however, two copies ('Ann & Joseph Blumenthal' and 'Patricia and Stefan Martin') are stitched with white thread.

Publication: The Spiral Press printed 9,155 copies, including 30 sets for Frost (660 copies). Twenty-two varying names:
 Robert Frost (as above) (660)
 Lesley Frost Ballantine and Joseph W. Ballantine (360)
 Ann & Joseph Blumenthal (410)
 Leda & Stanley Burnshaw (85)
 Helen & Alden Clark (35)
 Al Edwards (185)
 Eleanor and Al Edwards (110)
 Lesley Lee Francis (85)
 Lillian Frost (85)
 Phyllis & William Prescott Frost (110)
 Henry Holt and Company (4,550)
 Mr. and Mrs. J. Patrick Lannan (460)
 Patricia and Stefan Martin (135)
 Marguerite and Fred Melcher (160)
 Edgar T. Rigg (170)
 Mr. & Mrs. Edgar T. Rigg (60)
 Gwen and Ed Rigg (60)
 Craig T. Senft (135)
 Harry Shaw (210)
 Elinor and Malcolm Wilbur [*sic*] (110)
 Ben Wright (60)
 The Ben Wrights (260)
Collected in *In the Clearing* (1962).

Barrett Copies:
594714. Twenty-two copies representing all names.

B31 1959 A-WISHING WELL (First Edition)

[yellow brown] A-Wishing Well [black] by Robert Frost

Collation: [1]⁸; pp. [1–16] = 8 leaves.

Contents: pp. 1–2: blank; p. 3: title-page; p. 4: 'Copyright © *1959 by Robert Frost*'; p. 5: '[yellow brown: vignette wood-engraving of a branch of leaves] [black] AT CHRISTMAS 1959 | THIS NEW POEM BRINGS YOU | WARM HOLIDAY GREETINGS AND | THE BEST OF WISHES FOR THE | NEW YEAR FROM | ROBERT FROST'; p. 6: blank; pp. 7–11: text of poem with three wood-engraved vignettes: p. 7 (a star printed in yellow-brown), p. 8 (a flying crane with rocket in beak; a new moon: printed in gray), p. 11 (Noah's ark on Mt. Ararat printed in yellow-brown); p. 12: blank; p. 13: 'Wood engravings by Thomas W. Nason | [yellow-brown: Spiral Press device] | Printed at the Spiral Press, New York'; pp. 14–16: blank.

Paper: White wove paper watermarked 'CURTIS RAG'. Leaves measure 146 × 98 mm. Edges trimmed.

Binding: White soft wove paper wrappers cut flush with leaves. Flaps folded over pp. 1–2 and 15–16. On the front cover: '[black] A-WISHING WELL' and a pictorial wood-engraved design in yellow-brown of a clay pipe with circles rising as smoke to an anthropomorphic sun; the earth as a planet behind. Stapled at the center fold.

Publication: The Spiral Press printed 10,760 copies, including 30 sets for Frost (600 copies). Twenty varying names:
　Robert Frost (as above) (670)
　Lesley Frost Ballantine and Joseph W. Ballantine (370)
　Ann & Joseph Blumenthal (445)
　Walter I. Bradbury (210)
　Leda and Stanley Burnshaw (100)
　Helen and Alden Clark (100)
　Al Edwards (185)
　Eleanor and Al Edwards (105)
　Lesley Lee Francis (75)
　Frank Forsberg (50)
　Lillian Frost (75)
　Phyllis & William Prescott Frost (100)
　Henry Holt and Company (6,870)
　Marguerite & Fred Melcher (160)
　Margaret and Tom Nason (160)
　Edgar T. Rigg (210)
　Mr. and Mrs. Edgar T. Rigg (50)
　Gwen and Ed Rigg (50)
　Craig T. Senft (100)
　Elinor and Malcolm Wilber (75)
Collected in *In the Clearing* (1962).

Barrett Copies:
594798. Two copies (the 'Robert Frost' and 'Al Edwards' variants only).
Uncatalogued. The Lawrance Thompson set. A complete set of 20 variants.

B32   1960 ACCIDENTALLY ON PURPOSE (First Edition)

[red] ACCIDENTALLY ON PURPOSE | [black] BY ROBERT FROST

Collation: [1]⁸; pp. [1–16] = 8 leaves (oblong format).

Contents: pp. 1–2: blank; p. 3: 'GREETINGS AT [red] Christmas 1960 | [black] AND HOLIDAY GOOD WISHES COME TO | YOU WITH THIS NEW POEM, FROM | ROBERT FROST'; p. 4: blank; p. 5: title-page; p. 6: 'Copyright © 1960 by Robert Frost'; pp. 7–12: text of poem; p. 13: blank; p. 14: 'THE SPIRAL PRESS [red: press device] NEW YORK'; pp. 15–16: blank.

Paper: White wove paper watermarked 'CURTIS RAG'. Leaves measure 77 × 125 mm. Edges trimmed.

Binding: White Chinese rice paper wrappers with long, black threads imbedded in the paper for a decorative effect. Wrappers flush with the leaves and flaps folded over pp. 1–2 and 15–16. On the front cover, 'ACCIDENTALLY ON PURPOSE | [a thick red rule extending the width of the cover]'. The back cover repeats the front. Stapled at the center fold in all copies but one: the 'Ann & Joseph Blumenthal' copy is stitched with white thread at the center fold.

Publication: The Spiral Press printed 10,600 copies, including 30 sets for Frost (600 copies). Twenty varying names:
    Robert Frost (as above) (700)
    Lesley Frost Ballantine and Joseph W. Ballantine (350)
    Ann & Joseph Blumenthal (450)
    Walter I. Bradbury (200)
    Leda and Stanley Burnshaw (75)
    Helen and Alden Clark (100)
    Frederic S. Cushing (300)
    Al Edwards (175)
    Eleanor and Al Edwards (100)
    Frank Forsberg (50)
    Lesley Lee Francis (75)
    Lillian Frost (100)
    Phyllis & William Prescott Frost (100)
    Holt, Rinehart, Winston, Inc. (6,600)
    Marguerite and Fred Melcher (150)
    Edgar T. Rigg (200)
    Mr. & Mrs. Edgar T. Rigg (50)
    Gwen and Ed Rigg (50)
    Craig T. Senft (75)
    Elinor and Malcolm Wilber (100)
Collected in *In the Clearing* (1962).

Barrett Copies:
591791. Twenty-two copies representing all twenty names (two copies each of 'Robert Frost' and 'Al Edwards').

B33   1961 THE WOOD-PILE (First Separate Edition)

THE | WOOD- | PILE | BY ROBERT FROST [brown: to the right of the first three lines, a wood-engraving of trees and a wood-pile]

Collation: [1]⁸; pp. [1–16] = 8 leaves.

Contents: pp. 1–2: blank; p. 3: '[brown: wood-engraving of a chickadee facing the first two lines] [black] GREETINGS AT | CHRISTMAS [red] 1961 | [black] AND BEST WISHES FOR THE | COMING YEAR FROM | [red] ROBERT FROST'; p. 4: blank; p. 5: title-page; p. 6: 'This poem has been re-printed from | COMPLETE POEMS OF ROBERT FROST | copyright 1930, 1939 by Holt, Rinehart & Winston, Inc.'; pp. 7–9: text of poem, preceded on p. 7 by a wood-engraved head-piece printed in brown of a tree stump and axe; p. 10: blank; p. 11: 'Wood engravings by Thomas W. Nason | [red: Spiral Press device] | [black] Printed at The Spiral Press, New York'; pp. 12–16: blank.

Paper: White laid paper with vertical chainlines 26 mm. apart. Watermarked 'CURTIS RAG'. Leaves measure 145 × 113 mm. Edges trimmed.
    Note: The 'Ann & Joseph Blumenthal' and 'Margaret & Tom Nason' copies are on soft white wove paper (see also *Binding* note).

Binding: Wrappers of the same stock, flush with the leaves, flaps folded over pp. 1–2 and 15–16. On the front cover, a wood engraving of bare trees in a winter landscape (trees in black and white, the background sky in light gray); lettered on the lower left, 'THE WOOD-PILE | [red] BY ROBERT FROST'. Stapled at the center fold.
    Note: The Blumenthal and Nason copies are bound in the same soft white wove paper as the text and stitched at the center fold with white thread.

Publication: The Spiral Press printed 15,060 copies, including 30 sets for Frost (630 copies). Twenty-one names:
    Robert Frost (as above) (700)
    Lesley Frost Ballantine and Joseph W. Ballantine (375)
    Ann & Joseph Blumenthal (620)
    Leda & Stanley Burnshaw (75)
    Helen and Alden Clark (100)
    Frederic S. Cushing (300)
    Al Edwards (175)
    Eleanor and Al Edwards (100)
    Frank Forsberg (75)

Lillian Frost (100)
Phyllis and William Prescott Frost (100)
Holt, Rinehart & Winston (10,265)
Holt, Rinehart & Winston, Robert H. Kelsey—F. Howard Clark (400)
Marguerite & Fred Melcher (150)
Margaret & Tom Nason (220)
Edgar T. Rigg (200)
Mr. & Mrs. Edgar T. Rigg (50)
Gwen and Ed Rigg (50)
Craig T. Senft (125)
Elinor & Malcolm Wilber (100)
Lesley & Stanislav Zimic (150)

Published first in *North of Boston* (1914); included in all subsequent editions of complete or collected poems.

Barrett Copies:

594799. Twenty-three copies representing all names (two each of 'Blumenthal' and 'Edwards').

B34   1962 THE PROPHETS REALLY PROPHESY AS MYSTICS THE COMMENTATORS MERELY BY STATISTICS (First Separate Edition)

[black] The Prophets Really Prophesy | as Mystics [brown] The Commen-tators | Merely by Statistics | [black] *A new poem by* ROBERT FROST

Collation: [1]⁸; pp. [1–16] = 8 leaves.

Contents: pp. 1–2: blank; p. 3: '[red 5-pointed star] | [black] GREETINGS | [red] CHRISTMAS | [black] 1962 | FROM ROBERT FROST'; p. 4: blank; p. 5: title-page; p. 6: 'Copyright © 1962 by Robert Frost'; pp. 7–9: text of poem; p. 10: blank; p. 11: 'THE SPIRAL PRESS [device] NEW YORK'; pp. 12–16: blank.

Paper: White laid paper with vertical chainlines 30 mm. apart. No visible water-marks. Leaves measure 145 × 114 mm. Edges trimmed.

Binding: White laid paper wrappers (chainlines 27 mm. apart), flush with the leaves. Wrapper flaps folded over pp. 1–2 and 15–16. The chainlines run hori-zontally in most copies; however, four copies examined have vertical chainlines. Lettered on the front cover, '[brown] THE PROPHETS | REALLY | PROPH-ESY AS | MYSTICS | [gray] THE COMMEN-|TATORS | MERELY BY | STATISTICS'. Back cover blank. Most copies have a double staple at the center fold. The 'Ann & Joseph Blumenthal' copies are stitched with white thread.

Publication: The Spiral Press printed 17,055 copies, including 30 sets for Frost (630 copies). Twenty-one names:
  Robert Frost (as above) (800)
  Lesley Frost Ballantine and Joseph W. Ballantine (375)
  Ann & Joseph Blumenthal (500)
  Leda and Stanley Burnshaw (100)
  Marjory and Howard Cady (100)
  Helen and Alden Clark (125)
  Frederic S. Cushing (100)
  Al Edwards (175)
  Eleanor and Al Edwards (100)
  Frank Forsberg (75)
  Lillian Frost (100)
  Phyllis and William P. Frost (100)
  Holt, Rinehart and Winston (12,500)
  Holt, Rinehart and Winston, Robert H. Kelsey · F. Howard Clark (500)
  Marguerite and Fred Melcher (150)
  Edgar T. Rigg (200)
  Mr. and Mrs. Edgar T. Rigg (50)
  Gwen and Ed Rigg (50)
  Craig T. Senft (75)
  Elinor and Malcolm Wilber (100)
  Lesley and Stanislav Zimic (150)
First printed in *Poetry,* 101 (Oct.–Nov. 1962).

Barrett Copies:
594795. Twenty-four copies representing all names (two each of 'Robert Frost', 'Ann & Joseph Blumenthal' and 'Lesley Frost Ballantine . . .'). Those inscribed:
  Lesley Frost Ballantine and Joseph W. Ballantine. Signed 'Lesley' on p. 3.

B35   1962 THE CONSTANT SYMBOL (First Separate Edition)

THE | CONSTANT | SYMBOL | BY | ROBERT FROST | [swelling red rule] | [black] WITH CHRISTMAS GREETINGS | FROM | CORNE-LIA & WALLER BARRETT | [red] 1962

Collation: [1]¹⁰; pp. [1–20] = 10 leaves.

Contents: pp. 1–2: blank; p. 3: ' *"Strongly spent | is synonymous with kept."* | ROBERT FROST'; p. 4: frontispiece; p. 5: title-page; p. 6: blank; p. 7: '[red] FOREWORD | [black: 22-line text] | C[lifton]. W[aller]. B[arrett].'; p. 8: '[at the foot] THE CONSTANT SYMBOL was first published in 1946. The text of this | first separate edition is reproduced from that publication. The facsimile is the | first page of the original holograph manuscript in the Barrett Library of American | Literature at the University of Virginia.'; pp. 9–15: text (on p. 15 is the poem 'To the Right Person,' signed beneath in print, 'ROBERT FROST | July, 1946'); p. 16: blank; p. 17: '[at the foot] THE SPIRAL PRESS · NEW YORK'; pp. 18–20: blank.

Illustration and Facsimile: On p. 4 is a frontispiece photographic portrait of Robert Frost, signed beneath in facsimile holograph, 'To Cornelia and Waller from Robert'. Stitched in at the center fold and comprising two conjugate leaves is the facsimile manuscript reproduced on verso leaf 1 and recto leaf 2 which together form a single page of manuscript with lines running from bottom to top. The facsimile is on white wove paper, watermarked 'Strathmore | BAY PATH BOLD | 50 o/o COTTON FIBER USA'.

Paper: Cream-white wove paper watermarked 'CURTIS RAG'. Leaves measure 235 × 158 mm.; edges trimmed.

Binding: Cream laid paper wrappers with vertical chainlines 27 mm. apart. Cut flush with the leaves and folded over pp. 1–2 and 19–20. Front cover: '[red swelling rule] | [black] T H E C O N S T A N T S Y M B O L | [red swelling rule]'. Back cover blank. Stitched at the center fold with white thread.

Publication: The Spiral Press printed 500 copies privately for Mr. and Mrs. Clifton Waller Barrett. 'The Constant Symbol' had been printed first as the introductory essay in 1946 Modern Library edition of Frost's poems. The poem 'To the Right Person' was first printed in the *Atlantic Monthly* (Oct. 1946).

Barrett Copy:
594736.

C First Appearances of Poetry in Books and Periodicals

C1   1892. CLASS HYMN. *Order of Exercises for the Forty-First Anniversary of the Lawrence High School* [Lawrence, Mass.], 1 July 1892. Robert Frost also gave the valedictory address, listed nineteenth on the programme as 'Original declamation . . . "A Monument to Afterthought Unveiled"'. The poem was later printed in the *High School Bulletin* (Lawrence, Mass.), 13, no. 10 (June 1892), 10, and in the Report of the Superintendent of Schools to the School Committee, 1892. The music for the hymn was written by Elinor Frost's mother.

C2   1901. THE QUEST OF THE ORCHIS. *The Independent* (New York), 53, no. 2743 (27 June 1901), 1494. AWT 1942 (as 'The Quest of the Purple-Fringed'). Barrett 592752. Inscribed 'To Russell Alberts from R. L. Frost 1946'.

C3   1906. THE TRIAL BY EXISTENCE. *The Independent* (New York), 61, no. 3019 (11 Oct. 1906), 876. ABW 1913. Barrett 594613.

C4   1907. THE LOST FAITH. *Derry News* (West Derry, N.H.), 27, no. 16 (1 March 1907), 1. Barrett 592780.

C5   1907. A LINE-STORM SONG. *New England Magazine* (Boston), 37, no. 2 (Oct. 1907), 204. ABW 1913. Barrett 592678. Signed 'Robert Frost' on p. 204.

C6   1910. A LATE WALK. *Pinkerton Critic* (Derry, N.H.), 7, no. 2 (Oct. 1910), 7. ABW 1913. Barrett 592672.

C7   1913. THE FEAR. *Poetry and Drama* (London), 1, no. 4 (Dec. 1913), 406–9. NOB 1914. Barrett 592631. See C8 for an account of Robert Frost's notes and annotations in this volume.

C8   1913. A HUNDRED COLLARS. *Poetry and Drama* (London), 1, no. 4 (Dec. 1913), 409–13. NOB 1914. Barrett 592631. Frost's contemporary holograph notes:

page 395: in the margin of Robert Bridges' 'Flycatchers': 'I heard this great man / in a brave theory of rhythm / at lunch at the Vienna Café not / long since. He holds that our syllables / are to be treated in verse as having / quantity of many shades. That is to say / they are quarter third and fifth / notes as the case may be. Who knows / not that nor acts upon it is no poet. / Well here we have him acting upon / it, we are to presume. Poor old man. He is past seventy. It is the fashion / to play up to him. He still seems / capable of the emotion of disgust / Mind you he has done good things.'

395: in the margin of Thomas Hardy's 'My Spirit Will Not Haunt the Mound': 'Hardy is almost ne[ver?] / in a public place where / he is not heard. They say [he is?] / like a little old stone-mason. [This?] / is not the best poem he ever [wrote?]. / He is an excellent poet and t[he?] / greatest living novelist here. [Elinor?] / and I saw a terrible little curtain raiser (hair-raiser would be better) [of?] / the Three Travellers that he made. One traveller after another comes in out / of a storm to a feast in a cottage. The first is a convicted sheep stealer / escaped from jail where he was to have been hanged next morning. The second / is the hangman on his way to the jail to hang him. He sits with the convict on / the same bench and sings him a hanging song. He gets his rope out of a / bag— But I believe it is all in a short story somewhere. You may have read it.'

396: in the margin of Walter de La Mare's 'The Enchanted Hill': 'This seems ineffectual. / But the author is the one man / we are all agreed to praise here. / His "The Listeners" is the best / poem since the century came in. / He is hardly of the fashion, which / makes it the stranger that he is / so much honored. Earns his / living by reading manuscripts / for a publisher.'

398: in the margin of Francis MacNamara's 'The Lost Soul': 'I never heard of the / author of this essay / in the Browningesque.'

400: Frost has marked two lines and written in the margin: 'This is in the fashion. / See some of the poems / following.'

402: in margin of Rupert Brooke's 'The Funeral of Youth: Threnody': 'This boy I have met once. / He is near you now, in Calif. [*note: Rupert Brooke was in California in 1913*] / [He?] effects a metaphysical / [——] and would be /[the?] later John Donne.'

403: margin of the Rupert Brooke poem: 'You see what he's / trying to revive.'

404: margin of Rupert Brooke's poem, 'He Wonders Whether to Praise Or to Blame Her': 'We know this hardly / treated girl, oh very well. / Her beauty is her red hair. / Her cleverness is in painting. /

She has a picture in the New / English exhibition. Her mother / has written a volume of verse / in which he gets his. Very / funny. No one will die.'

405: margin of Brooke's 'The Way That Lovers Use': 'Wow!'

416: margin of John Alford's 'Revolt: An Ode': 'This boy has taken a / dislike to me on account of / a review in which he suffered / in comparison with me. / Here we get down to someone / who just can't write poetry.'

417: margin of Alford's 'Vision': 'Ever thus will young / poets write about themselves.'

418–19: margins of three poems: 'In the fashion', 'More so', 'Rather so'

421: margin of W. H. Davies' 'The Bird of Paradise': 'Davies is lovely. Tramped / in America till he lost a leg under / a freight car. Came home and sold / his own ballads on penny sheets till / they gave him a pension to take him off / the streets. Has done some good things / in unconscious art. Said he to me, / "I remember you were there the other night. / I spoke to you didn't I? But I was awful. / After you went I went out of the restaurant / a minute for one more drink and I / never found my way back." '

427: margin of Sherard Vines' 'To the River-Villager': 'Not bad'

428: margin of Frances Cornford's 'The Old Witch in the Copse': 'Suppose I were to say the only / good lines in the magazine are / the ones I have marked here.' Frost has marked four lines with these comments, 'Way to say it', 'This too', 'Lovely fancy', 'And this'.

429: margin of Harold Monro's 'Children of Love': 'The gloomy spirit that edits / this. No one can laugh when he / is looking. His taste in literature / is first for the theological and after / that for anything that has the bite / of sin. He got up a penny sheet of / Blake to sell in the slums and you ought to have seen the risky / selections he made. But dear me / everybody is writing with one foot / in the red-light district.'

442: end of play text, signed in print 'DUNSANY': 'Only lords sign thus'

485–88: article, 'American Poetry,' by John Alford. Above the title: 'This is what makes it impossible that I would live long / under a criss-cross flag. Me for the three colors the bluebird wears.' Foot of p. 485: 'This cub doesn't know how to find his way / around among American writers. No one he mentions / is thought anything of on the other side—no one of recent date. / Emerson is so American, so original, especially in form, / I'll bet you five he couldn't read him if he tried. / Whitman and Poe are stomach-ache.' Margin of p. 486: 'Not that I weep for these [referring to several minor American poets].' Margin p. 487: 'This is true. But / one gets tired of / hearing it.' and 'The magazine / has had a row / with Ezra [Pound]. This / is olive branch. / Monro needs him / in his business.'

Note: Internal evidence in the notes—especially in those concerning Rupert Brooke—prove that these annotations made by Frost for his friend John T. Bartlett were contemporary and could not have been written later than early 1914. The notes are published as letter 69 in *Selected Letters*.

C9   1916. IN THE HOME STRETCH. *Century Magazine* (New York), 'Outdoor number,' 92, no. 3 (July 1916), 383–91. MI 1916. Barrett 592665. Signed 'Robert Frost 1916–1939'.

C10   1916. SNOW. *Poetry*, 9, no. 11 (Nov. 1916), 63–72. MI 1916. Barrett 592763.

C11   1916. AN ENCOUNTER. *Atlantic Monthly*, 118, no. 5 (Nov. 1916), 612. MI 1916. Barrett 592629.

C12   1916. THE BONFIRE. *Seven Arts* (New York), 1, no. 1 (Nov. 1916), 25–28. MI 1916. Barrett 592597. Signed 'Robert Frost 1916–1939'.

C13   1917. NOT TO KEEP. *Yale Review*, 6, no. 2 (Jan. 1917), 25. NH 1923. Barrett 592736. Also printed in *War Poems* (New Haven, 1919), p. 14. Barrett 592735.

C14   1921. THE AIM WAS SONG. *Measure* (New York), no. 1 (March 1921), p. 22. NH 1923. Barrett 592581. Inscribed 'Robert Frost to Russell Alberts' on p. 22.

C15   1921. PAUL'S WIFE. *Century Magazine* (New York), 103, no. 1 (Nov. 1921), 83–99. NH 1923. Barrett 594606. Inscribed 'One of the longer pieces I read oftenest aloud Robert Frost'.

C16   1921. THE RETURN OF THE PILGRIMS. *In* George Pierce Baker, *The Pilgrim Spirit* (Boston, 1921), pp. 134–35. WRB 1928 (fourth stanza only as 'Immigrants').
Barrett 592746. First issue with 'Brewster' in line 8, p. 74. Gray printed wrappers. Inscribed 'Robert Frost to Earle Bernheimer'.
Also: Barrett 594611. Second issue with erratum slip on p. 74. Gray cloth, dust jacket. Inscribed 'Robert Frost to Earle Bernheimer'.
Barrett 592747. Second issue with erratum slip. Gray cloth, dust jacket.
Barrett 592612. Third issue with 'THE' on p. 55 misspelled 'THP'. Gray cloth, dust jacket. Inscribed 'Robert Frost to Earle Bernheimer'.
Barrett 592748. Third issue. Gray printed wrappers.

C17   1923. THE STAR-SPLITTER. *Century Magazine* (New York), 106, no. 5 (Sept. 1923), [681–85]. Decorations by J. J. Lankes. NH 1923. Barrett 594607. Inscribed 'and let's give J. J. Lankes credit for the pictures. R. F.'

C18   1923. A FOUNTAIN, A BOTTLE, A DONKEY'S EARS, AND SOME BOOKS. *The Bookman* (New York), 58, no. 2 (Oct. 1923), 121–24. NH 1923. Barrett 592633. Signed 'Robert Frost' on p. 121.

C19   1924. LODGED. *New Republic,* 37, no. 479 (6 Feb. 1924), 281. WRB 1928. Barrett 595499. Signed 'Robert Frost 1940'.

C20   1926. THE PASSING GLIMPSE. *New Republic,* 46, no. 594 (21 April 1926), 275. WRB 1928 (as 'A Passing Glimpse'). Barrett 595733. Inscribed 'This was in the years when Ridgely Torrence was poetry editor of The New Republic and the editor I liked best to publish with. Robert Frost'.

C21   1927. A WINTER EDEN. *New Republic,* 49, no. 632 (12 Jan. 1927), 215. WRB 1928. Barrett 592634.

C22   1927. BEREFT; THE COCOON; THE TIMES TABLE. *New Republic,* 49, no. 636 (9 Feb. 1927), 327. WRB 1928. Barrett 595428.

C23   1928. ACQUAINTED WITH THE NIGHT. *Virginia Quarterly Review,* 4, no. 4 (Oct. 1928), [541]. WRB 1928. Barrett 593066.

C24   1928. THE MIDDLETOWN MURDER. *Saturday Review of Literature,* 5, no. 12 (13 Oct. 1928). Barrett 595828.

C25   1928. THE WALKER. *The Second American Caravan* (New York, 1928), p. 70. *Collected Poems,* 1930 (as 'The Egg and the Machine'). Barrett 592794. Signed 'Robert Frost' on p. 70.

C26   1934. DESERT PLACES. *American Mercury* (Camden, N.J.), 31, no. 124 (April 1934), 464. AFR 1936. Barrett 711186.

C27   1934. CLEAR AND COLDER. *Direction* (Peoria, Ill.), 1, no. 1 (Autumn 1934), 31. AFR 1936. Barrett 592617.

C28   1935. GOOD RELIEF. Lesley Frost (ed.), *Come Christmas* (New York, 1935), pp. 4–5. Frontis. facsimile of MS. Barrett 592655, 592654 (inscribed on recto of the first facsimile leaf, 'Robert Frost').

C29   1936. THE WHITE-TAILED HORNET OR DOUBTS ABOUT AN INSTINCT. *Yale Review,* 25, no. 3 (April 1936), 459–61. AFR 1936 (as 'The White-Tailed Hornet'). Barrett 592812.

C30   1936. A BLUE RIBBON AT AMESBURY. *Atlantic Monthly,* 157, no. 4 (April 1936), 420–21. AFR 1936. Barrett 592585.

C31 1936. AT WOODWARD'S GARDENS; TEN MILLS. *Poetry,* 48, no. 1 (April 1936), 1–5. AFR 1936. Barrett 592616.

C32 1936. THE STRONG ARE SAYING NOTHING. *American Mercury* (Camden, N.J.), 38, no. 149 (May 1936), 58. Barrett 711187.

C33 1936. A RECORD STRIDE. *Atlantic Monthly,* 157, no. 5 (May 1936), 593. AFR 1936. Barrett 592756.

C34 1936. A ROADSIDE STAND; A DRUMLIN WOODCHUCK; A TRIAL RUN. *Atlantic Monthly,* 157, no. 6 (June 1936), [669]–70. AFR 1936. Barrett 592759.

C35 1936. THE LOST FOLLOWER. *Boston Herald Harvard Tercentenary* (13 September 1936), p. 8. AWT 1942. Barrett 595837.

C36 1937. 'Unless I call it a pewter tray . . . [first line]'. Charles Jay Connick, *Adventures in Light and Color* (New York, 1937), p. 92. Design for 'Birches' on p. 90. Barrett 595426. Inscribed on p. 92, 'First and only printing of these lines I ever saw R. F.' and 'To Russell from R. F.'

C37 1938. GEODE. *Yale Review,* 27, no. 3 (Spring 1938), [482]. AWT 1942 (as 'All Revelation'). Barrett 592649.

C38 1938. CARPE DIEM; HAPPINESS MAKES UP IN HEIGHT FOR WHAT IT LACKS IN LENGTH. *Atlantic Monthly,* 162, no. 3 (Sept. 1938), [316]. AWT 1942. Barrett 592607.

C39 1938. A NATURE NOTE ON WHIPPOORWILLS. *Coolidge Hill Gazette* (Cambridge, Mass.), (Dec. 1938), p. 3. AWT 1942 (as 'A Nature Note'). Barrett 592704.

C40 1939. JOHN L. SULLIVAN ENTERS HEAVEN. Louis Untermeyer, *From Another World* (New York, 1939), pp. 141–42. Barrett 592666. Inscribed on p. 206 beneath the chapter title, 'I suppose this means me — R. Frost'. Also inscribed by Untermeyer, 'for Earle Bernheimer that demon collector—of everything except Vermouth.' Louis Untermeyer'. A letter from Untermeyer to Earle Bernheimer is laid in which reads in part, 'Robert must have been pulling your leg about "not remembering" the parody of Vachel Lindsay ("John L. Sullivan Enters Heaven") part of which I incorporated in FROM ANOTHER WORLD. He often spoke about it jestingly and, since there was no chance of his including it in any of his collected poems, I put at least part of it into print. I say "part" because the poem itself is longer than my printed version. I have the original before me at the moment. It consists of several small pages written in R. F.'s characteristic hand. It is dated February 18th (1918) and is part of a longer letter. Robert appended a typical Frostian postscript: "This can only be read successfully by its author. You can read it yourself from the book for merely the price of the book: one dollar. You can hear the author read it himself for one hundred dollars. It is worth the difference." ' (See E9.)

C41   1940. TRESPASS. *American Prefaces* (University of Iowa, Iowa City), 5, no. 9 (June 1940). AWT 1942. Barrett 595839.

C42   1941. COME IN. *Atlantic Monthly*, 167, no. 2 (March 1941), [145]. AWT 1942. Barrett 592669.

C43   1941. THE LITERATE FARMER AND THE PLANET VENUS. *Atlantic Monthly*, 167, no. 3 (March 1941), [284]–87. AWT 1942. Barrett 592747.

C44   1941. I COULD GIVE ALL TO TIME. *Yale Review*, 31, no. 1 (Sept. 1941), [24]. AWT 1942. Barrett 592660. Inscribed on p. 24, 'Robert Frost to Russell Alberts'.

C45   1942. TIME OUT; TO A MOTH SEEN IN WINTER; THE GIFT OUTRIGHT. *Virginia Quarterly Review*, 18, no. 2 (Spring 1942), [240–42]. AWT 1942. Barrett 592783. Inscribed 'Robert Frost to Russell Alberts'.

C46   1944. IN THE LONG NIGHT. *Dartmouth in Portrait* (Hanover, N.H., 1944), p. 3. SB 1947. Barrett 595424.

C47   1946. THE NIGHT LIGHT; WERE I IN TROUBLE WITH NIGHT TONIGHT; BRAVERY. *Yale Review*, 36, no. 1 (Sept. 1946), [37]. SB 1947 (as 'The Night Light,' 'Were I in Trouble,' and 'Bravado'). Barrett 592717. Inscribed 'Robert Frost to Russell Alberts 1946'.

C48   1946. DIRECTIVE; THE MIDDLENESS OF THE ROAD; ASTROMETAPHYSICAL. *Virginia Quarterly Review*, 22, no. 1 (Winter 1946), 1–4. SB 1947. Barrett 592627. Inscribed 'To Russell Alberts my first signature to them in print Robert Frost'.

C49   1954. THE BAD ISLAND—EASTER. *London Times Literary Supplement,* special number (17 Sept. 1954), p. xviii. Barrett 595836.

C50   1959. SOMEWHAT DIETARY. *Massachusetts Review* (Amherst) 1, no. 1 (Oct. 1959), 24 and facsimile holograph frontispiece. Barrett 592771.

C51   1961. PERIL OF HOPE. *Agnes Scott News* (Agnes Scott College, Decatur, Ga.), 46, no. 11 (8 Feb. 1961), facsimile holograph p. 1. Barrett 592744.

D First Appearances of Prose in Books and Periodicals

D1   1917. A WAY OUT. *Seven Arts* (New York), 1, no. 4 (Feb. 1917), 347–62. Barrett 592796. Inscribed 'From the author an available editor of the magazine in those distant days R. F. August 16 1943'.

D2   1924. [Preface.] *Memoirs of the Notorious Stephen Burroughs of New Hampshire, with a preface by Robert Frost* (New York: MacVeagh, The Dial Press, 1924), pp. v–viii. Barrett 592602.

D3   1925. [Introduction.] *The Arts Anthology, Dartmouth Verse 1925* (Portland, Maine: The Mosher Press, 1925), pp. vii–ix. 500 copies. Barrett 592624, 595230.

D4   1928. POET—ONE OF THE TRUEST. *Percy Mackaye: A Symposium on His Fiftieth Birthday, 1925* (Hanover, N.H.: Dartmouth Press, 1928), p. 21. Barrett 592751.

D5   1930. 'I owe a debt to Wilfred Davison . . . [first line]'. *Wilfred Davison Memorial Library* ([Middlebury, Vt.] Bread Loaf, 21 Jan. 1930), pp. [5–6]. Barrett 592571. Inscribed 'Robert Frost' on p. 6. Barrett 592572. Also published as *Bread Loaf Folder* (Bread Loaf School of English, Middlebury, Vt.), no. 8 (1930).

D6   1931. EDUCATION BY POETRY—A MEDITATIVE MONO-LOGUE. *Amherst Graduates Quarterly,* no. 78 (Feb. 1931), pp. [75]–85. Barrett 592628.

   Note: 'Education by Poetry' was an address given by RF to the Amherst Alumni Council, 15 November 1930. This printing represents the address in its entirety. Later in 1931 a short excerpt with the title *The Four Beliefs* was printed in an edition of 250 copies by Ray Nash at the Graphic Arts Workshop, Dartmouth College, Hanover, N.H., consisting of two unbound cognate leaves with a woodcut vignette of a tree with four apples by J. J. Lankes on p. 1. Barrett 592634, 592928. The first signed on p. 3 beneath the text, 'Robert Frost'.

D7   1935. [Introduction.] *In* Edwin Arlington Robinson, *King Jasper* (New York: Macmillan, 1935), pp. v–xv. The Lawrance Thompson copy, inscribed 'Dear Larry / What we like is griefs (don't we?) / and we like them Robinsonianly profound. / R. F.'

D8   1936. [Introduction.] *In* Sarah Norcliffe Cleghorn, *Threescore; the Autobiography of Sarah N. Cleghorn* (New York: Smith and Haas, 1936), pp. ix–xii. Barrett 592619.

D9   1938. [Letter to Amy Lowell.] *Harvard Alumni Bulletin* (Cambridge, Mass.), 40, no. 14 (Jan. 1938), 446, facsimile holograph. Barrett 592676. Inscribed 'January 6 1939 Robert Frost for Earle Bernheimer'.

D10   1939. [Preface.] *Bread Loaf Anthology* (Middlebury, Vt.: Middlebury College Press, 1939), pp. xix–xx. Barrett 592599. Bookplate of Vera Harvey.

D11   1941. TO MARK A. De W. HOWE. *In* Mark Anthony De Wolfe Howe, *A Venture in Remembrance* (Boston, 1941), pp. 120–21. Barrett 592786.

D12   1948. SPEAKING OF LOYALTY. *Amherst Graduates Quarterly* (Concord, N.H.), 37, no. 4 (Aug. 1948), 271–76. Barrett 592770. Inscribed 'To Earle from Robert Ripton 1948'.

D13   1953. [Introduction.] *In* Helen Harness Flanders and Marguerite Olney, *Ballads Migrant in New England* . . . (New York: Farrar, Straus and Young, [1953]), Barrett 592632.

D14   1956. A TALK FOR STUDENTS BY ROBERT FROST. *An Extemporaneous Talk at the Twenty-eighth Annual Commencement of Sarah Lawrence College, Bronxville, New York, June 7, 1956. Distributed by The Fund for the Republic* . . . , pp. 3–14. Barrett 592778.

D15   1957. [Introduction.] *In* Donald Hall, Robert Pack, and Louis Simpson (eds.), *New Poets of England and America* (New York: Meridian Books, 1957). Barrett 592656.

D16   1959. ON EMERSON. *Daedalus* (Cambridge, Mass.), Fall 1959, pp. 712–18. Barrett 592737.

D17   1962. PLAYFUL TALK. *American Academy of Arts and Letters,* 2nd ser., no. 12 (1962), pp. 180–89. Talk given for the 'Dinner meeting of the Institute, April 11, 1961.' Barrett 592750.

D   ADDENDUM

THE FARM-POULTRY SEMI-MONTHLY (Boston, Mass.), 14, nos. 1–24 (1 Jan. 1903–15 Dec. 1903); 15, nos. 1–24 (1 Jan. 1904–15 Dec. 1904). 48

numbers bound in two folio volumes, red cloth, backed with red calf. Spines lettered in gilt-stamp, '/// FARM / POULTRY ////// VOL. 14 [15] ///'.

Article contributions by Robert Frost:

Vol. 14, no. 9 (1 May 1903), 221–22. 'A Just Judge,' signed 'R. L. F.' Reprinted from the *Eastern Poultryman*

Vol. 14, no. 14 (15 July 1903), 301–2. 'The Question of a Feather,' signed 'R. S. F. [*sic*]'

Vol. 14, no. 16 (15 Aug. 1903), 334–35. 'Old Welch Goes to the Show,' signed 'R. L. F.'

Vol. 14, no. 17 (1 Sept. 1903), 352–53. 'The Original and Only,' signed 'R. L. F.'

Vol. 14, no. 24 (15 Dec. 1903), 481–82. 'Three Phases of the Poultry Industry,' signed 'R. L. Frost'. In the third section of this article, subtitled 'A Typical Small Breeder,' RF made reference to geese roosting in trees. The blunder was noticed by many experienced poultrymen and in the number for 15 January 1904, a letter to the editor by H. R. White inquired to know what kind of geese 'Mr. R. L. Frost' meant; 'I . . . have been among geese all my life time, and I can never remember seeing a goose in a tree.' The editor's note beneath and the letter are captioned 'It's "Up To" Mr. Frost'. The note promises an explanation from RF in a forthcoming number. In the 15 February number, RF retaliated in a letter to the editor under the heading 'Mr. Frost Explains'. In the letter he compounds the error and reveals his belief that geese require coops. The editor's note beneath corrects him publicly by stating 'Mr. Frost seems not to be aware of the fact that geese generally remain out of doors by choice practically all the time.' In the 1 March number is printed a letter to the editor signed 'John A. Hall', but actually written by RF with the permission of Hall, a prominent poultryman whose geese RF had described as roosting in trees in the original damaging article. RF manufactures a lame pardon for himself in the carefully homespun words attributed to Hall, 'I don't know how Mr. Frost made that mistake, for of course he knows better. . . . The records in your paper ought to show what they did in Lawrence this year; but I notice they don't. So Mr. Frost was pretty near right about my geese.' This ended the controversy, but it rather took the heart out of RF as a contributor to *Farm-Poultry*.

Vol. 15, no. 3 (1 Feb. 1904), 54. 'The Cockerel Buying Habit,' signed 'R. L. F.'

Vol. 15, no. 5 (1 March 1904), 110. 'The Same Thing Over and Over,' signed 'R. L. F.'

Vol. 15, no. 7 (1 April 1904), 169. 'The Universal Chicken Feed,' signed 'R. F. L. [*sic*].

One further article (not present in this collection) was printed in the number for 15 December 1905, 'Dalkins' Little Indulgence — A Christmas Story.' All of the articles have been published, with bibliographical data, in *Robert Frost: Farm-Poultryman* (1963), edited by Lawrance Thompson and Edward Connery Lathem. An account of the 'geese in a tree' episode is given there and also in *The Early Years,* pp. 286–89.

Barrett Copy:

Uncatalogued. The Lawrance Thompson set.

Part II

Manuscripts and Letters

E   Manuscripts

E1   1891–1900. AMSs [signed with initial 'R.']. 'Evensong'. N.p., n.d. [*ca.* 1891]. Unpublished. 8-line poem written in pencil on one side of a leaf of white laid paper, vertical chainlines, watermarked 'Damsk | [flower orn.] | Linene'. Leaf measures 200 × 122 mm.; edges trimmed. The title is written on the verso in pencil. The MS is in RF's early hand:

> Came the wind last
> When the dew was strown?
> Someone has passed
> That the stars are down:
> Out of the sunset,
> Into the twilight,
> Someone has passed
> That the stars are down.

E2   1891–1900. AMSs. 'Caesar's Lost Galleys'; fragment of an unpublished poem on verso. [Lawrence, Mass., Spring 1891.] 2 pp. in pencil on 1 leaf of cream laid paper, horizontal chainlines, watermarked 'BUNKER HILL | S. W. Co.', lined in pale blue. Leaf measures 254 × 199 mm., edges trimmed. 'Caesar's Lost Galleys' is initialed 'r'. The untitled fragment on the verso is signed 'R. L. Frost'. In RF's early hand.

'Caesar's Lost Galleys' was printed in *The Independent* (14 Jan. 1897) as 'Caesar's Lost Transport Ships.' It was reprinted in *Three Poems* (Hanover, N.H.: Baker Library, 1935). Variant readings in the MS are keyed to the later text:

line 5: a voice] TP; one voice] MS

   7: we had sad thoughts] TP; we had no thought] MS

Frost had discarded two final lines which are lightly overscored in pencil. He supplied in their place the lines in the printed version. The discarded lines are: 'And those of Ocean who attended heard / And overhead the windborne albatross.'

The unpublished poem fragment on the verso:

> (Where only some first cautious ghost might be.)
> Over the level plain the wind considered it,
> Wasted defenseless, and it raised the sand
> And artfully directed it, and said
> That there was time—years numberless, *the years!*
> Far off from that lorn city where the gold
> Was sunken and the houses still, against
> The east, into the growing night, assembled,
> Marching on, there was the [?drum] & host that went
> Slow and diminishing, far, far, forever.

Beneath, in RF's hand, 'I see that by mistake this last was copied upon / a piece of paper the reverse of which contains the first / draft of some lines on the lost galleys of Caesar's / which disappeared on the stormy passage of the channel / when he first sought Britain. I have lined them / in so that you may be able to read them if possible'.

E3   1891–1900. AMSs [signed with initial 'R.']. 'My Old Uncle'. N.p., n.d. 1 p. written in brown ink on the recto of a leaf of thin white wove paper, edges trimmed to 196 × 117 mm. Unpublished:

My Old Uncle

> My old uncle is long and narrow,
> And when he starts to rise
> after his after dinner nap,
> I think to myself
> He may do it this once more,
> But this is the last time.
> He lets one leg slip off the lounge
> And fall to the floor.
> But still he lies
> And looks to God through the ceiling.
> The next thing is to get to his outside elbow
> And so to a sitting posture,
> And so to his feet.
> I avert my eyes for him till he does it.
> Once I said with concern
> "What is it, uncle,

Pain or just weakness?
Can't we do anything for it?
He said "It's Specific Gravity."
"Do you mean by that that it's grave?"
"No not as bad as that yet, child;
But it's the Grave coming on."
Then I knew that when he said gravity
He didn't mean seriousness.
Old age may not be kittenish,
But it is not necessarily serious.

E4   1891–1900. AMS. 'The Road that Lost its Reason' (poem fragment).
N.p., n.d. Written in blue ink, light blue ink, and pencil on a leaf of white
wove, blue-lined paper torn from a notebook. Leaf measures 250 × 195
mm.; edges trimmed, but torn. Unpublished:

The Road that Lost its Reason

He was standing armed in the wood road
In the deer hunting season
Like a shivering outpost sentinel.
And I thought maybe he could tell
If the road had a reason.

No, the maple was not its reason
Running sugar in its veins,
Nor the spruce that comes logging down
End on like a ram against the town
With a [. . .] wheel in chains

[. . .] farm to go
[. . .] shelf
[. . .] how far
[. . .] water bar
[. . .] once himself

[. . .] path for a horse in the middle
[. . .] a couple of tracks for a cart
[. . .] couple of tracks and a path make a start
[. . .]

The bracketed ellipses are sections of the poem torn away. A similarity will be noted between line 3 of this poem and line 2 of 'Any Size We Please': 'Like a half-mad outpost sentinal'.

At the upper right corner in pencil is a drawing titled, 'Great Square of Pegasus'. In the right margin RF has written in pencil, 'Inability to like the world you / made your bed with is like / coldness in married women'. And beneath, in light blue ink, 'Union Station / Play Out of How the / World Scored Twice Off / Joan of Arc'. Lower down, in dark blue ink, 'A couple of bags of grain made a load / Of that and a heavy heart'.

E5   1902. ADs. Promissory note. West Derry, N.H., 24 May 1902. 1 p. in brown ink on a single leaf of wove paper measuring 101 × 123 mm. With the rare signature 'Robert Lee Frost'.

'$675 / For value received, I promise / to pay Ernest C. Jewell, on order, / six hundred seventy five dollars on / demand, with interest annually. / Robert Lee Frost.'

Ernest C. Jewell was a schoolmate of Frost's at Lawrence High School. They became friends when Jewell was editor of the *High School Bulletin*. In 1902 Jewell visited the Frosts in Derry and agreed to loan RF an amount sufficient to get him started in the chicken and egg business. The business was not a success, and Lawrance Thompson concludes that Jewell did not recover the full amount of the principal on his loan. Cf. Thompson, *The Early Years*, pp. 94–95, 197, 280–81, 507–8, 552–53 (the note is printed on p. 552).

E6   1906. AMSS. Robert Frost's notebook. [Derry, N.H., *ca.* 1906.] 44 pp. written in pencil and ink on 32 leaves of white wove paper, loose in an oblong half red calf notebook cover. Leaves measure 211 × 130 mm., more or less.

Forty pages contain 17 unpublished stories that Robert Frost wrote for his children, Carol, Lesley, Irma, and Marjorie. The children and a family dog, Schneider, figure as characters in most of the stories. On the versos of the first three 'story' leaves is a comic poem in 10 stanzas of 4, 5, and 6 lines (printed in Thompson, *The Early Years*, pp. 337–38); an exaggerated account of the New Hampshire winter with marginal commentary which parodies the style of Coleridge's 'Rime of the Ancient Mariner.'

On the recto of one leaf is a poem written in ink, 'The Message the Crow Gave me for Lesley one Morning Lately When I went to the Well'. Beneath the 22-line poem, Frost has signed later in blue ink, 'R. F.', and added, 'This appears to be the very first of this'. The poem was collected in *Mountain Interval* (1916) with the title 'The Last Word of a Bluebird.' The MS contains several minor differences in punctuation and spelling and one textual variation in line 2: In a low voice said, "Oh,] MI; In the dooryard said "Oh] MS.

Three pages written in pencil and ink on two leaves contain lists of ideas, jotted thoughts, titles, and random notes. One 16-line paragraph is concerned with greatness in history of aviators in relation to the greatness of Columbus's achievement, 'Why is he [Columbus] immortal then? . . . because he had the faith so few are capable of. The faith in an idea. Not for him to feel his way round Africa to Ind. He launched out in space with the supreme confidence of reason. Great in his confidence, great in his justification. The nearest him among the aviators and the only ones near him are the Wright brothers.' (printed, *The Early Years*, p. 332).

At the top of the first of these three pages is a later note in blue ink, 'This is as old as Derry days / you can see from it where one idea started / R. F. 1951'. This note seems to refer to the paragraph written in 1906, 'He came out of the . . . mist and contemplated / the terms and accepted them. They were then / as they are now: A little more pleasure than pain. / Pain greater in length and breadth but exceeded by pleasure in height. One more pleasure than pain / by actual count—the pleasure of being / alive.' (printed, *The Early Years*, pp. 331–32).

Lawrance Thompson gives an account of this notebook in *The Early Years*, pp. 302–3.

E7   1912. AMSs. 'The Lure of the West'. Written in blue ink on rectos of two leaves of cheap tan wove paper measuring 223 × 152 mm.; edges trimmed.

The comic poem was printed in Margaret B. Anderson's *Robert Frost and John Bartlett* (1963), pp. 29–30. It was inspired by stories of life in British Columbia written to Frost by the Bartletts, who had moved to Vancouver. Frost was very much tempted by the notion of moving his own family to Vancouver. Part of the third stanza reads:

> My friends in Vancouver are bright,
> But I'll tell them they'd better beware:
> If they sing me much more to that air
> I'll take the train west overnight,
> And ask them to lend me the fare.
> I'm a dangerous man to excite.

E8   1912. AMSs, with ANs included. 'A Heart in Charge' [*i.e.,* 'In Equal Sacrifice']. Note to John Bartlett, [Plymouth, N.H., *ca.* 1912]: ' "Of right," I say. But, of course, not without thinking twice. Something also depends on the cause. But why say it again? I flatter myself it is all said with the proper enigmatical reserve in the poem. R. F.'. On two long leaves of white laid paper measuring 277 × 153 mm.

The poem was printed first in *A Boy's Will* with the title 'In Equal Sacrifice.' Variant readings:

line 1: Thus of old] ABW; Hear what of old] MS

  6: By which we see and] ABW; By this and that we] MS

  8: and love's] ABW; At loyalty or love's] MS

  19: the heart he has] ABW; whose heart he may have] MS

  23: With only strength of the fighting arm,] ABW; And ringed around with certain death,] MS

  24: For one more battle passage yet,] ABW; With but one stroke remaining yet,] MS

  27: Only a signal deed to do] ABW; Only a momentary help] MS

  28: And a last sounding word to say.] ABW; For closing mightily the fray.] MS

  29: The heart he wore in a golden chain] ABW; The royal heart by a gold chain] MS

  30: He swung] ABW; He whirled] MS

  31: crying "Heart or death!"] ABW; irresistably] MS

  32: And fighting over it perished fain.] ABW; And standing over it there was slain.] MS

  38: Scorning greatly not to demand] ABW; A desperate charge and a final stand;] MS

  39: In equal sacrifice with his] ABW; And so may die, his trust forgiven] MS

  40: The heart he bore to] ABW; Far, far, far from the] MS

Thompson, *The Early Years,* pp. 577–78, has a note on the poem and on this manuscript in particular.

E9   1918. AMSs. 'John L. Sullivan Enters Heaven'. 4 leaves, yellow wove paper, measuring 203 × 127 mm. Written in brown ink on rectos only, numbered 1–4, signed on p. 4 'R. F.' with the postscript 'This can only be read successfully / by the author. You can read it yourself / from the book for the price of the book / one dollar. You can hear the author / read it for one hundred dollars. It / is worth the difference.' On p. 1, under the title, 'To be said to the tune of "Heaven overarches / you and me".'

The poem is in seven stanzas of which the first through the fourth and the seventh were printed in Louis Untermeyer's *From Another World* (New York, 1939; pp. 141–42). It was never reprinted, nor have the fifth and sixth stanzas ever been printed. Its composition was occasioned by Vachel Lindsay at a meeting with Untermeyer, Frost, and Sara Teasdale. Lindsay proposed that each poet write a poem around one specific theme. The theme he suggested in all seriousness was John L. Sullivan, the American heavyweight champion boxer. Untermeyer describes the result: 'It was Robert Frost who made the most surprising comment, a comment that was both criticism and burlesque. In a letter of February, 1918, which contained neither warning nor explanation, I received the following from Robert. It has never before appeared in print [the poem follows].'

A letter from Untermeyer to Earle Bernheimer, dated 19 August 1942, is laid in with the manuscript. It reads in part, 'I am enclosing herewith the four yellow sheets which contain the only existing copy of Robert Frost's only parody. The details, as you recall, are contained in my chapter on Vachel Lindsay in my autobiographical FROM ANOTHER WORLD.'

E10   1920. AMSs. IN AN ART FACTORY (unpublished play). N.p., n.d. (*ca.* 1920) Written in black and blue ink on the rectos of 23 of 34 leaves (some additions on versos) of a notebook with flexible red-brown heavy coated paper covers, black paper backstrip. Leaves of white wove paper ruled in light blue, measuring 208 × 171 mm. (leaves cut flush with covers). On the first recto, in 1951, Frost wrote an account of the composition: 'It should be said that this play was / written many years ago and has been kept / over for publication and possible presentation when I should have done one or two others / I intended for its companions. I have read / it a few times aloud. Two or three / references to public events and personages / date it approximately. I remember / reading it to Jean and Louis Untermeyer / when it was new. It is easy to see what / I have been antagonized by all along. / I moved the theme off into another art / for objectivity I suppose. I made Campbell / out of my talks with and about such people / as Faggi, Partridge, Taft, Du Chene, Chapin / etc. / R. F. / Ripton June 22 1951 / This is the only copy in my hand. Kay / Morrison has a copy in her typing.'

The play is in one act with a cast of two: Tony, a young sculptor, and Blanch, his sweetheart and model. To interpret the action and the dialogue is to commit the sin dealt with in the play: interference with the work of an artist by the unartistic and uninitiated. One of Tony's lines states the case, 'An artist wants a public. The more public the better. But he lives in resent-

ment toward their ways of mistaking him. He resents coarsening to them.'
Tony defines one of the public as 'one who doesn't know the right thing to
say to an artist. . . . The only person who ever said the right thing about
any art of mine—I put the words into his mouth to say it with. Sometimes
I put the wrong things in out of perversity to flagellate myself.' Tony's self-
flagellation results from what he believes to be the prostitution of his art.
He is one of several unknown artists who produce sculptures in an 'art factory' operated by an agent-entrepreneur, Campbell, who sometimes adds
'finishing touches' to the pieces to make them more salable before he markets them. Tony wants a public, but he cannot bear to have his work re-
touched in order to gain one. He restores his integrity and asserts his identity
as an artist by first mutilating and then destroying his most recent creation
before it can be 'Campbellized'; that is, not made insipid, but beautiful in
'a kind of specialized beauty that we find isolated where any fool can see it
in youth and health . . . in jewelry and fashion and in Cambell's sculpture.' 'Campbell can see only the beautiful—where I see, well, the defective,
the tragic.'

This play is Frost's statement of the dichotomy between an artist's need
to work unhindered and his need for recognition which can come only at
the risk of hindrance.

In Thompson, *Selected Letters* (To James R. Wells, no. 268, pp. 347–49),
Frost refers to *In an Art-Factory,* 'That is about one of my sculptor friends
[Aroldo du Chêne]', and offers it to Wells for publication.

E11   1921. AMS. 'On the Inflation of the Currency—1919'. N.p., n.d. [*ca.*
1921]. Written in black ink on one side of a single leaf of white wove, blue-
lined paper; torn from a notebook and measuring 212 × 172 mm., edges
trimmed.

The poem has been printed only as a facsimile (made from this copy)
Christmas keepsake by Earle J. Bernheimer in 1948 (see B18). On the
facsimile, a signature was supplied beneath the poem which does not occur
on the MS. The poem has never been reprinted or collected.

E12   1923. AMS [in the hand of Elinor Frost and signed by Frost].
'Stopping By Woods on a Snowy Evening' (final quatrain only) N.p., n.d.
[*ca.* 1923]. 4 lines and signature on one side of clipped leaf of blue wove
paper, measuring 97 × 140 mm.

Printed first in the *New Republic* (7 March 1923); collected in *New
Hampshire* (1923).

E13   1925. AMS. 'Unnoticed, Nature's Neglect' ['On Going Unnoticed'].
N.p., n.d. [*ca.* 1925]. 1 p. written in black ink on one side of a single leaf
of wove, blue-lined paper measuring 252 × 197 mm. (torn from a notebook).

   Printed first in the *Saturday Review of Literature* (28 March 1925) with
the title 'Unnoticed'; later collected in *West-Running Brook* (1928), titled
'On Going Unnoticed.' The MS contains two variant readings:
line 2: on high.] 1st, WRB; so high.] MS
   6: That seems] 1st; That is] WRB, MS

E14   1925. AMS. 'The Peaceful Shepherd'. N.p., n.d. [*ca.* 1925]. Written
in black ink on the recto of a leaf of wove white paper, ruled in blue (removed from a notebook), measuring 252 × 198 mm.; edges trimmed.

   Printed first in *New York Herald Tribune Books* (22 March 1925) and
collected in *West-Running Brook* (1928). Variant reading:
line 6: I think] MS, 1st; I fear] WRB

E15   1926. AMSs. 'Sand Dunes'. Written in brown ink on the recto of the
advertisement leaf removed from a copy of *New Hampshire* (1923). Signed
beneath and dated 'December 1926'.

   Printed first in *New Republic* (13 December 1926); later collected in
West-Running Brook (1928). No variant readings.

E16   1926. AMS. 'Once by the Pacific'; 'The Pans' (unpublished). N.p.,
n.d. [*ca.* 1926]. Two poems written in blue ink on both sides of a single
leaf of white wove, blue-lined paper torn from a notebook. Leaf measures
250 × 195 mm.; edges trimmed.

   'Once by the Pacific' was printed first in the *New Republic* (29 Dec. 1926)
and collected in *West-Running Brook* (1928). The MS text conforms to the
first printing with 'sand' for 'shore' in line 8.
   'The Pans' text:

The Pans

The voice on Patmos speaking bade me "Shut your eyes!"
I shut them once for all and lo am blind.
"Hold out your hand, it said, for the surprise."
I held it out relaxed and stood resigned.

"A penny for your thoughts" Not overmuch.
The less the better from the Greeks, I said.
I waited cringing for the coming touch.
For fear the penny might be molten lead.

And when it came I flinched, I drew away.
And clang! Clang-clang! Clang-clang! down through the night
It was a trust. The great scales of assay.
I was to have been Justice on a height,

Was to have had the gift of being just.
The scale-pans crashed and clanged. It was a trust.

E17   1929. AMSs. 'Good Relief'. [*ca.* 1929.] 1 p. in brown ink on the recto of a leaf of heavy white wove paper measuring 329 × 156 mm., edges trimmed. Mounted on a larger piece of cardboard and apparently removed from a frame; the holograph surface is slightly light-struck, leaving a white margin where the mat covered the paper.

The poem was begun in Beaconsfield, England, in 1912 (cf. Thompson, *The Early Years,* pp. 430–31, 593) and was never collected by RF. It was printed first in *Come Christmas* (New York, 1929), edited by Lesley Frost, and the frontispiece for that book was a facsimile made from this manuscript. Lawrance Thompson printed the poem again in *The Early Years* (1966, pp. 430–31). The manuscript conforms with the printed texts.

E18   1933. AMSS. 'A Stone Missive' ['A Missive Missile']; 'The Truth of It' ['They Were Welcome to Their Belief']; 'Two Tramps in Mud-Time'; 'A Record Stride'. [*ca.* 1933] Four of fifty-one poems collected in *A Further Range* (1936). Written in black and blue ink on the rectos of 6 of 7 leaves of cream laid paper with vertical chainlines 26 mm. apart, watermarked 'Vidalon'. Leaves measure 257 × 165 mm., edges rough-cut. The poem 'A Record Stride' is on the rectos of 2½ leaves of white wove, blue-lined paper torn from a notebook and laid in. Leaves measure 213 × 166 mm. The whole contained in a binding of decorative paper-covered boards. On the front cover, in Frost's hand, '[at top] 1 9 3 3 / [at bottom] R F'.

'A Stone Missive'. First in the *Yale Review* (Autumn 1934) as 'A Missive Missile'. line 1: Some son of] 1st; Someone in] AFR, MS. line 37: in some-one's] 1st, MS; in some men's] AFR. line 41: ocher-written] 1st, AFR; ocre-written] MS

'The Truth of It'. First in *Scribner's Magazine* (Aug. 1934) as "They Were

Welcome to Their Belief'. line 4: The over-confident pair.] 1st; The over-important pair.] AFR; It was neither one of the pair.] MS. The MS ver-version has an extra stanza between the third and fourth: 'And the only measure to take / (As he early understood) / That of trying to lie awake, / Could have done no possible good.'

'Two Tramps in Mud-Time'. First in the *Saturday Review of Literature* (6 Oct. 1934). line 2: splitting] 1st, AFR; chipping] MS. line 9: beech] 1st, MS; oak] AFR. Line 26: And fronts the] 1st, MS; And turns to the] AFR. line 37: Be glad of water, but don't forget] 1st, AFR; But though all seems water, we can't forget] MS. Lines 49–64 are not present in the MS. Above the last stanza, on the final MS leaf, is a quatrain: 'There was but once one day / When you could have said that word / And have been perfectly heard / And then you were swept away.'

'A Record Stride'. First in *Atlantic Monthly* (May 1936). No variant readings

E19   1934. AMSs. 'Neither Out Far Nor in Deep' (first, third, and fourth stanzas only). N.p. n.d. [*ca.* 1934]. 1 page written in purple ink on one side of a single leaf of laid paper measuring 216 × 134 mm.; edges trimmed.

Printed first in the *Yale Review* (Spring 1934), used as the Christmas poem for 1935, and collected in *A Further Range* (1936). The MS text conforms to the first printing in line 9, with the difference of one word: 'Some say the land is more,' for 'Some say the land has more,'. At bottom is a pencil note in another hand, 'This copy of one of his favorite / poems was made by Robert Frost / for Louis Dodge.'

E20   1936. AMSs. 'Fire and Ice'. N.p., n.d. [*ca.* 1936.] 1 page written in black ink on the recto of the first leaf of a double fold; integral leaf blank. Leaves measure 163 × 131 mm.; edges trimmed. Signed beneath 'Robert Frost'. A fair copy.

Printed first in *Harper's Magazine* (July 1920); collected in *New Hampshire* (1923).

E21   1936. AMSs., with ANs. included. 'The Lost Follower'. Note to 'Mr. Linscott'; Amherst, Mass., 28 June 1936, beneath the signed poem: 'This is the poem I promised Mr. [George] Schreiber for his Portraits. I trust I am not too late. It's the last touches on these things that take time. I always go to press with hesitation. Make Mr. Schreiber forgive me.' On 2 leaves (recto) of white bond paper.

The poem was printed first in the *Boston Herald* (13 Sept. 1936); later in *Portraits and Self-Portraits* (Boston, 1936), edited by George Schreiber. Collected in *A Witness Tree* (1942). Variant readings:

line 6: they] 1st, MS; we] AWT

   7: Not] 1st, MS; No] AWT

   9: less] 1st; loss] AWT, MS

  10: an] 1st, MS; the] AWT

  11: Youth] 1st, MS; Some] AWT

  25: With him] 1st, MS; With such] AWT

  26: in playful moments] 1st, MS; in a playful moment] AWT

  30: and] 1st, MS; or] AWT

  36: (as yet unbrought to earth)] 1st, AWT; As yet unbrought to earth] MS

E22   1938. AMSs. 'Geode'. Undated [*ca.* 1938], though Frost has signed beneath the poem in a different ink, 'Robert Frost', and added an inscription 'For Earle Bernheimer / On his visit at Ripton / August 17 1939'. 1 page written in blue ink on one side of a single leaf of white wove 3-holed loose-leaf paper, measuring 242 × 152 mm.; edges trimmed. Verso blank.

Printed first in the *Yale Review* (Spring 1938); later collected in *A Witness Tree* (1942) with the title 'All Revelation.' The MS text follows that of the first printing in all except line 9, which reads as in *A Witness Tree*, 'A moment' rather than 'One moment'.

E23   1938. AMSs. 'A Nature Note'. N.p., n.d. [*ca.* 1938]. Inscribed later in different ink at the foot 'To R. V. Thornton / from / R. F.' 1 page written in black ink on one side of a single leaf of white wove 3-holed loose-leaf paper, measuring 240 × 152 mm., edges trimmed.

Printed first in the *Coolidge Hill Gazette* (Dec. 1938) as 'A Nature Note on Whippoorwills'; later collected in *A Witness Tree* (1942). The first three MS stanzas conform to text in AWT; however, the final stanza follows the reading of the first printing with lines 14 and 15 transposed. Frost has supplied numbers 1–4 following the four lines indicating the correct (or AWT) sequence of the lines: 1, 3, 2, 4. In the margin: 'Notice order of lines', in his hand.

E24   1940. AMSs. 'To a Moth Seen in Winter'. N.p., n.d. [*ca.* 1940]. Written in black ink on the rectos of two white wove leaves of 3-holed loose-leaf paper, measuring 241 × 152 mm.; edges trimmed. Signed at the end with initials 'R. F.' with the note 'For Russell's collection'. In another ink, beneath the poem, Frost has written 'circa 1900'.

Printed first in the *Virginia Quarterly Review* (Spring 1942); collected in *A Witness Tree* (1942). This is an earlier version with variant readings:

line 5: those marks] 1st, AWT; these marks,] MS

    10: But stay and hear me out. I surely think] 1st, AWT; But whither away so soon. Surely I think] MS

    14: And what I pity in you is something human,] 1st, AWT; And I, I pity in you something human] MS

E25   1940. AMSs. ['Our Hold on the Planet'.] [Ripton, Vt.] 26 October 1940. Written in blue ink on one side of a leaf of white wove paper removed from a 3-ring looseleaf notebook, 242 × 152 mm. Subscribed 'Robert Frost / to / Elsie [Elizabeth Shepley] Sergeant / October 26 1940'. An early draft differing substantially from the printed versions.

Printed first as the Christmas card for 1940; collected in *A Witness Tree* (1942). Variant readings:

line 3: It didn't blow a gale and] 1st, MS; And blow a gale. It didn't]AWT

    6: It didn't, because] 1st; It didn't because] MS; And just because] AWT

    11: We may doubt the just proportion of good and ill.] 1st; good to ill.] AWT; *omit*] MS

    12: against us. But] 1st, AWT; against us but] MS

    14: Including human nature, in peace and war,] 1st, AWT; For all our proven sorrow and grounded fear] MS

    15: It must be just] 1st, MS; And it must be] AWT

    16: at the very least,] 1st, AWT; more good than ill] MS

    17: The number of people alive has been steadily more. [used as line 13] 1st; Or our number living wouldn't be steadily more,] AWT; For the fate (whatever it is) we are out to fulfill] MS

    18: Or our hold on the planet wouldn't have so increased.] 1st; Our hold] AWT; Or else we wouldn't have been so increasingly here.] MS

E26   1940. AMSs. ['I Could Give All to Time'.] [Ripton, Vt.] 26 October 1940. Written in blue ink on one side of a leaf of white wove paper removed from a 3-ring looseleaf notebook, 152 × 242 mm. Subscribed 'Robert Frost to Elsie [Elizabeth Shepley] Sergeant / 26 October 1940'. An early version of the poem.

Printed first in the *Yale Review* (Autumn 1941); collected in *A Witness Tree* (1942). Variant readings:

line 4: overjoyed] 1st, AWT; glad or sad] MS
 6: inland] 1st, AWT; mountain] MS
 7: eddies] 1st, AWT; water] MS
 11: Time] 1st, AWT; change] MS
 12: have thought. But why] 1st; have held. But why] AWT; have cherished. Why] MS
 13: forbidden] 1st, AWT; forbid] MS

E27 1941. AMSs. THE GUARDEEN (unpublished play). Written in
ink on the rectos of 52 leaves (many notes, additions, and corrections on
versos) of a red and black cloth-bound notebook, lettered in gilt on the
spine '|||RECORD||||27/R|150||'. Leaves of white woven paper
ruled in light blue, measuring 207 × 173 mm. Pages numbered 1–72, 83–114,
147–152. The hiatus between pp. 72 and 83 is filled by a single inserted
gathering of sixteen leaves of white unlined paper measuring 204 × 142
mm., stitched in with white string. This insert supplies a replacement for
the excised portion of text. It is written on 12 pages of rectos with notes and
corrections on some versos. Pages 115–46, which contained Frost holograph
visible on stubs, have been excised; pp. 147–52 are blank. On p. 2, Frost has
written 'First Version / for Earle Bernheimer / January 12 1942 / from /
Robert Frost'.

SECOND VERSION

AMSs. (unpublished). Written in ink on the rectos of 52 leaves (some
notes, additions, and corrections on versos) of a second notebook as described above. A revision of the first version, but with numerous changes
and corrections in the present text. On p. 2, Frost has written 'Second Version / for Earle Bernheimer / from his friend / Robert Frost / Cambridge
Mass Jan 12 1942'.

 The text consists of one act in five scenes. In précis, the story as far as it
goes is of a young graduate student who is prevailed upon to rent a cabin
in a depressed back-mountain community of New Hampshire at the suggestion of a professor who comes from the area and is related to most of its
inhabitants. The professor hopes that the student will find the country people interesting and will assist him in a sociological research project. The
owner of the cabin, a wily down-easter, has an ulterior motive in securing
the young man's services as 'guardeen' of the cabin's treasure—a barrel of

prime hard cider—which is the quarry of the backwoods people. With the aid of the spirited daughter of a renegade mountain family, the student succeeds in exposing the various attempts to use him, debunks the theories of the professor, thwarts the owner of the cider, and shares it with those from whom he is supposed to be protecting it.

The manuscript has never been published. In 1943 Earle Bernheimer had 96 copies privately printed of a facsimile of the dedication leaf and the first page of text to use for a Christmas card.

In Thompson's *Selected Letters* there are two letters from Frost to Bernheimer (nos. 383 and 385) that give historical background on the creation of the manuscripts: 'I am rather in need of about two thousand dollars right now and would like to sell you two of my most valuable manuscripts at one thousand dollars apiece. One would be the original manuscript of my only full length play to date ["The Guardeen"] with all its emendations crude upon it.' (no. 383, 1 June 1941). 'We have now two versions of the play ["The Guardeen"] ready for you in two volumes. The second is better because more compact. There may yet be a third. If so, you shall have it. From your point of view I know the more versions the merrier. I never have versions of a poem or hardly ever; so I will try to have as many versions of this play as I possibly can. (no. 385, 16 Dec. 1941).

A copy of *Bread Loaf Book of Plays* (Middlebury, Vt., 1941) in the Barrett/Frost collection is inscribed, 'To Earle: This may well have started me on my downward career toward playwriting. The first result is The Guardeen in your possession. R.'

E28   1941. AMSs. [A WITNESS TREE.] On the first manuscript leaf recto, 'New Poems toward the Next Book / To Earle Bernheimer / from Robert Frost / Time of the visit of Earle / at 88 Mt Vernon St in Boston. / February 21 / 1941'. A fair copy of 16 of the 44 poems printed in 1942 as *A Witness Tree*. Written in blue ink on rectos of 17 of 20 leaves of fine white wove paper stitched at the center fold and enclosed in a single fold of heavy light blue paper. Leaves measure 279 × 216 mm., edges trimmed. Order and textual variation are as follows:

leaf 1: dedication leaf as transcribed above

    2: 'The Silken Tent'. 1st ed., p. 13

    3: 'Come In'. 1st ed., p. 16

    4: 'Geode'. 'All Revelation' in 1st ed., p. 14

    5: 'Triple Plate'. 'Triple Bronze' in 1st ed., p. 42

6: 'To a Moth Seen in Winter'. 1st ed., p. 56. Beneath the poem, RF has written 'This is a very early treatment of a theme now / uppermost in the general mind. Date about 1900'.

7: 'Wilfull Homing'. 'Wilful Homing' in 1st ed., p. 28

8: 'A Considerable Speck—Microscopic'. 1st ed., pp. 57–58. line 14: With loathing] AWT; With horror] MS. line 25: Collectivistic regimenting love] AWT; Political collectivistic love] MS. Above the poem RF has written 'On almost the same theme as that the the Moth in Winter. / Date about 1938'.

9: 'A Cloud Shadow'. 1st ed., p. 29. Word 'Breeze' capitalized throughout. line 4: "There's no such thing!"] AMT; there's no such thing,] MS

10: 'Happiness Makes Up in Height for What It Lacks in Length'. 1st ed., p. 15. line 3: Around with] AWT; Around by] MS. Line 4 is lacking from manuscript.

11: 'A Loose Mountain—Telescopic'. 1st ed., p. 63

12: 'Trespass'. 1st ed., p. 79

13: 'A Serious Step Lightly Taken'. 1st ed., pp. 84–85. line 8: For only] AWT; For hardly] MS. line 14: On our cisatlantic shore] AWT; On the hither Atlantic shore] MS. line 16: We'll make it] AWT; Well, make it] MS. Between the third and fourth stanzas is a quatrain in the MS overscored and noted 'Omit— R. F.' The stanza reads 'And mean this time to stay / And make possession firm / For ourselves and if possible our descent / For a long old-fashioned term.'

14: 'In Praise of Waste'. 'November' in 1st ed., p. 61

15: 'To a Young Wretch'. 1st ed., pp. 44–45. line 9: have meant to me!] AWT; have been to me!] MS. line 15: opposing goods] AWT; conflicting goods] MS

16: Untitled ('The Gift Outright'). 1st ed., p. 41. line 4: In Massachusetts, in Virginia,] AWT; Our Massachusetts, our Virginia,] MS. line 9: Until we found it] AWT; Until we found out that it] MS

17: Untitled ('The Secret Sits'). 1st ed., p. 71. MS text: The Secret sits in the middle and knows; / While we dance round in a ring and suppose.'

E29   1941. TMSs. A WITNESS TREE. '[Front cover] A Witness Tree K[athleen] M[orrison]'s Book as she copied it out / for the publisher. Now presented by her to / Earle Bernheimer November 20 1942 in New / York City. R. F. for K. M. [beneath, in Kathleen Morrison's hand] Poems [overscored] / September 22, 1941 [overscored] / A WITNESS TREE / by / Robert Frost'. 80 leaves (75 typed; 5 in the holograph of Kathleen Morrison) of white wove bond paper, measuring 277 × 214 mm. Leaves laid loose in a single quarto fold of heavy light blue paper. Comprising all the poems but one printed in 1942 as *A Witness Tree*. Lacking is 'A Semi-Revolution.' Most corrections are in the hand of Kathleen Morrison, with numerous editorial (Holt) and printer's (Spiral Press) annotations. Robert Frost has made four corrections and signed three poems:

leaf 1: cover leaf, blank save for following notes: '[K.M.'s hand] HOLO-GRAPH / MAY BE. / HE'S UNCERTAIN / [Frost's hand] Decided against it now'

4–5: contents in K.M.'s hand. Variant reading: Title for 'November' is listed as 'For the Fall of Nineteen-Thirty-Eight'. On leaf 5, KM has written in pencil 'The little ones without title / he will place somewhere'; refers to 'A Question,' 'Assurance,' and 'An Answer' which are unlisted but present in the manuscript. 'A Semi-Revolution' not listed

7: signed 'Robert Frost' beneath the poem 'Time Out'

8: signed 'Robert Frost' beneath the poem 'To a Moth Seen in Winter.' Beneath the signature, also in his hand, 'Please excuse the printers marks on the copy and disregard / these except perhaps the circa 1900 which may very well be kept for several reasons.'

13: 'For the Fall of Nineteen Thirty Eight' ['November']

17: a note in pencil signed '[Leonard] Blizard / H[enry] H[olt]' on the section title 'Quantula': 'Spiral / This is to go / between section TIME OUT and OVER BACK / (Be sure it has a title / page of its own and that / it gets into the contents / page.)'

18: 'In a Poem'. Correction in Frost's hand, line 1: 'lightly' corrected to 'blithely', as in the 1st ed.

18: 'On Our Sympathy with the Under Dog'. Correction in Frost's hand, line 3: 'us under' to 'asunder' as in 1st ed.

41: 'The Silken Tent'. Correction in Frost's hand, line 5: 'central pole' corrected to 'central cedar pole' as in 1st ed.

68: 'The Gift Outright'. Correction in Frost's hand, line 9: 'Until we found it was' corrected to 'Until we found out that it was' as in 1st ed. Signed beneath the poem, 'Robert Frost'

E30   1942. AMSs. A WITNESS TREE. '[Front cover] A Witness Tree / R. F. / 1942 / This becomes the property of Earle Bernheimer / on the Twentieth of November Nineteen Hundred / and Forty-two / Given under the hand of his / November Guest / Robert Frost / New York City'. A fair copy of 27 of the 44 poems printed in 1942 as *A Witness Tree*. Written in blue ink on rectos (and two versos) of 26 leaves. Eighteen are leaves of fine white wove paper stitched at the center fold and enclosed in a single quarto fold of heavy light blue paper. Leaves measure 279 × 212 mm., edges trimmed. Six are leaves torn from a notebook and laid in (containing the text of 'The Literate Farmer and the Planet Venus'); white wove paper ruled in light blue with a red margin rule, numbered 89–100 (pp. 89, 91–95, 97, and 99 with Frost holograph), measuring 212 × 174 mm., edges trimmed. A single leaf of white wove bond paper (text of 'Beech' and 'Syca-more') measuring 277 × 214 mm. is also laid in. Following the fifth leaf of the 18-leaf gathering, a single leaf of cream wove loose-leaf binder paper (text of 'Carpe Diem'), measuring 240 × 152, is tipped in on the stub of an excised leaf. The order of the poems differs from that of the first edition and there are textual variation and corrections in the manuscript:

leaf 1: '[in Frost's holograph] Order / 1 A Silken Tent / 2 Happiness Makes up in Height / for What It Lacks in Length. / 3 Triple Plate / 4 To a Young Wretch / 5 Carpe Diem / 6 Geode / 7 It Took That Pause / 8 A Poem on Spring (A Cloud Shadow)'. In the 1st ed., 'Triple Plate' was titled 'Triple Bronze'; 'Geode' (title as originally printed in the *Yale Review* [Spring 1938]), titled 'All Revelation'; 'It Took That Pause,' titled 'Time Out'; 'A Poem on Spring (A Cloud Shadow),' titled 'A Cloud Shadow.' The poems listed all appear in holograph in this manuscript; all but 'Triple Plate' have the later titles.

2: 'The Silken Tent'. 1st ed., p. 13

3: ' Cloud-shadow'. 'A Cloud Shadow' in 1st ed., p. 29

4: 'Come In'. Variant reading (overscored and corrected to the 1st ed., p. 16, reading), line 7: To better its perch for the night,] AWT; To attempt to better its perch,] MS

5: 'Give All to Change' (final word overscored and altered to 'Time'). 'I Could Give All to Time' in 1st ed., p. 17. Variant readings, line 7 (uncorrected): Then eddies playing round a sunken reef] AWT; Then water playing round a sunken reef] MS. line 11 (corrected): I could give all to Time] AWT; I could give all to change] MS. line 12 (corrected): What I myself have held. But why declare] AWT; What I myself have [2-syllable verb, too heavily overscored to read]. Why declare] MS

6 (tipped-in leaf): 'Carpe Diem'. 1st ed., pp. 18–19

7: 'To a Moth Seen in Winter'. 1st ed., p. 56

8: 'Happiness Makes Up in Height for What It Lacks in Length.' 1st ed., p. 15

9: 'Time Out'. 1st ed . p. 55. Variant readings, line 13: That might be clamored at] AWT; That might be clamored for] MS. line 14: But it will have its moment to reflect.] AWT; But it would have its moment to reflect.] MS.
'Triple Plate'. 'Triple Bronze' in 1st ed., p. 42

10: 'Wilful Homing'. 1st ed., p. 28
'It Is Almost the Year Two Thousand'. 1st ed., p. 64

11: 'Telescopic—A Loose Mountain'. 'A Loose Mountain (Telescopic)' in 1st ed., p. 63

12: 'To a Young Wretch'. 1st ed., pp. 44–45, 'To a Young Wretch (Boethian)'

13: 'Never Again Would Birds' Song Be the Same'. 1st ed., p. 24. Variant reading, line (corrected) 2: in all the garden round] AWT; in all the country round] MS

14: 'Geode [overscored] All Revelation' in 1st ed., p. 14

15: 'A Considerable Speck'. 'A Considerable Speck (Microscopic)' in 1st ed., pp. 57–58. Variant reading, line 25 (corrected): regimenting love] AWT; regimented love] MS

16: 'The Gift Outright'. 1st ed., p. 41. Variant reading) line 9: (uncorrected): Until we found it was ourselves] AWT; Until we found out that it was ourselves] MS

17: 'An Admirer of the Flag'. 'Not of School Age' in 1st ed., pp. 82–83

18: ['The Secret Sits'], ['An Answer'], ['A Question'] 'On the Difficulty of Keeping Up in Sympathy', ['Assurance']. Titles in 1st ed. are those supplied in brackets; pp. 68, 69, 71, 74–75. 'On the Difficulty of Keeping Up in Sympathy' is titled 'On Our Sympathy with the Under Dog' in 1st ed., p. 68.

19: 'Making [overscored] the Most of It'. 'The Most of It' in 1st ed., p. 23

20 (single laid-in leaf): 'Beech', 'Sycamore'. 1st ed., p. 9

21 (1st of 6 laid in): 'The Literate Farmer and the Star [overscored, corrected to 'Planet'] Venus'. 'The Literate Farmer and the Planet Venus' in 1st ed., pp. 86–91. Variant readings: [subtitle] A Dated Popular Science Medley on the bane of War / (From Talks Walking)] MS; A Dated Popular-Science Medley / on a Mysterious Light Recently Observed in the / Western Sky at Evening] AWT. Text of lines 1–21

22 (2nd of 6 laid in, recto): lines 22–44. Variant reading, line 29: Serious] AWT; Serius]MS. line 34 (corrected): Will tell you it's] AWT; That tell you its] MS

23 (2nd of 6 laid in, verso): lines 53–57. Variant reading, line 56: The

condemned world] AWT; The whole damned world] MS. Manuscript
has 8 lines not included in AWT printing: 'They are so honest in di-
viding all / They breath and drink and eat what we would call / True
communists intent on staying brothers / Though flung together in rivalry by mothers / As all of us are flung in being born. / Nor can we
laugh their coming back to scorn / They're spreading east from Ari-
zona hogans / If not with war crys then with heavy slogans.' These
lines are lightly overscored.
24 (3rd of 6 laid in, recto): lines 45–75 [excepting lines 53–57]
24 (3rd of 6 laid in, verso): lines 89–90. Lines not included in AWT:
   'We know the universe is automatic / And any other doctrine is fa-
   natic'. Additional phrase, not used, 'sacredness of waste'
25 (4th of 6 laid in): lines 76–97 [excepting lines 89–90]
26 (5th of 6 laid in): lines 98–120
27 (6th of 6 laid in): lines 121–42
The poems not in this manuscript are:
                   The Wind and the Rain
                   The Subverted Flower
                   The Quest of the Purple-Fringed
                   The Discovery of Madeira
                   Our Hold on the Planet
                   The Lesson for Today
                   The Lost Follower
                   November
                   The Rabbit Hunter
                   In a Poem
                   Boeotian
                   An Equalizer
                   A Semi-Revolution
                   Trespass
                   A Nature Note
                   Of the Stones of the Place
                   A Serious Step Lightly Taken

E31   1942. AMSs. [A WITNESS TREE.] A fair copy of 7 of the 44 poems
printed in 1942 as *A Witness Tree*. Written in blue ink on rectos of 7 leaves
of white wove paper stitched at the center fold and enclosed in a single
quarto fold of heavy light blue paper. Leaves measure 217 × 140 mm.; top
edge uncut, fore- and bottom edges trimmed. From the Lawrance Thomp-

son collection and inscribed on the inside front wrapper, 'For Larry / [For] being so patient in waiting / [For] Robert'.

leaf 1: 'A Silken Tent'. 'The Silken Tent' in 1st ed., p. 13

  2: 'Give All to Change'. 'I Could Give All to Time' in 1st ed., p. 17. Variant readings (uncorrected), line 7: Then eddies]1st; Then water]MS. line 11: I could give all to Time]1st; I could give all to change]MS. line 12: What I myself have held.]1st; What I myself have cherished.]MS

  3: 'A Loose Mountain—Telescopic'. 1st ed., p. 63

  4: 'Come In'. 1st ed., p. 16. In line 6, RF misspells 'sleight' as 'slight'.

  5: 'A Fraction of One Percent'. 'Our Hold on the Planet' in 1st ed., p. 43. Variant readings, line 5: And just because we owned]1st; It didn't, because we owned]MS. line 17: wouldn't be steadily more,]1st; wouldn't be more and more.]MS

  6: 'Geode'. 'All Revelation' in 1st ed., p. 14. line 3: Or]1st; And]MS

  7: 'A Cloud Shadow'. 1st ed., p. 55. line 13: That may]1st; That might] MS. line 14: But it will]1st; But it would]MS

E32 1942. AMSs. 'The Subverted Flower'; 'Pride of Ancestry'. Cambridge, Mass., 1942. Written in pencil and ink on the rectos of 6 leaves of an 8-leaf book dummy bound in brown linen cloth. Leaves of cream laid paper with vertical chainlines 29 mm. apart. Leaves measure 216 × 132 mm., edges trimmed. On the front open endpaper recto is the inscription, 'To Larry / from / R. F. / January 5 1942 / Cambridge Mass'. The manuscript is from the Lawrance Thompson collection.

The manuscript of 'The Subverted Flower' (first printed in *A Witness Tree,* 1942) was written in pencil earlier than the inscription date; probably in 1938. It has a few ink corrections and variant readings from the printed version:

Title: The original penciled title, 'The Inverted Flower', has been inked out and 'Subverted' supplied.

between lines 4–5: MS has 'And she said the hand was hairy [inked out]'

between lines 24–25: MS has 'In field and forest thus, [inked out]. Alternative lines supplied in ink, 'And not just one alone / Is overtaken thus [also inked out]'

line 38: To see if he could hear / And would pounce to end it all]1st; To see if he would hear / And pounce to end it all]MS

between lines 53–54: MS has 'And that a lesser part,'

'Pride of Ancestry' was printed in *The Years of Triumph,* p. 473, and a note concerning this manuscript is at pp. 688–89. The manuscript was then

in the possession of Lawrance Thompson, for whom it was written out at
the date of the inscription.

E33   1942. TMSs. 'The Gift Outright'. N.p., n.d. [probably before 1942,
judging by the readings of lines 9 and 16]. 1 page typed on the recto of a
single leaf of white wove paper, measuring 224 × 198 mm.; edges trimmed.
Title supplied in holograph and signed beneath 'Robert Frost'. Frost has
also written at the foot 'Written before 1936'.
    Printed first in the *Virginia Quarterly Review* (Spring 1942) and col-
lected in *A Witness Tree* (1942). Variant readings:
line 9: Until we found it was] 1st, AWT; Until we found out that] MS
    16: she might become.] 1st, MS; she would become.] AWT

E34   1942. TMSs. 'The Gift Outright'. N.p., n.d. [probably before 1942,
judging by readings of lines 9 and 16]. 1 page typed on the recto of a single
leaf of white wove bond paper, measuring 277 × 216 mm.; edges trimmed.
Title typed as 'WE GAVE OURSELVES OUTRIGHT'. The first three
words overscored in ink and 'The Gift' supplied in Frost's hand. Signed
beneath with initials 'R. F.' and 'My history of the Revolutionary War
which / was the beginning of the end of Colonialism. / R. F.' Line 9 has
the later reading in type 'Until we found it was ourselves'; however, Frost
has inserted 'out that' between the third and fourth words, providing the
earlier reading 'Until we found out that it was ourselves'. Line 16 has the
early reading ' . . . as she might become.'

E35   1942. AMSs. ['Time Out'.] N.p., n.d. [*ca.* 1942]. Written in blue ink
on one side of a single leaf of white wove 3-holed loose-leaf paper, measuring 242 × 152 mm., edges trimmed.
    Printed first in the *Virginia Quarterly Review* (Spring 1942); collected
in *A Witness Tree* (1942). The MS text has a variant reading in line 13,
'might' for 'may'.

E36   1943. AMSs. 'Till the Day Breaks' ['In the Long Night']. N.p., n.d.
[*ca.* 1943]. Written in blue ink on one side of a leaf of white wove paper,
measuring 215 × 189 mm.; edges trimmed and rough-cut. A fair copy made
for Earle J. Bernheimer.
    First printed in *Dartmouth in Portrait 1944* (Hanover, N.H., 1943); col-
lected in *Steeple Bush* (1947) with the title 'In the Long Night.' This MS

appears to be an earlier version or a version done from memory, with readings that vary from both printed texts:

line 7: Or would file out crawling single] 1st; We would crawl out filing
single] SB; We would file out crawling single] MS

8: To observe the Northern Light.] 1st, SB; To admire the neon light.]
MS

9: If Etookashoo and Couldlooktoo] 1st, SB; If Eetookshoo and Couldlooktoo*] MS. *Note*: The asterisk refers to a note beneath '*To the best
of my recollection the names / of two who went with a famous explorer
[Dr. Frederick A. Cook, surgeon on Robert Peary's expedition who
reached the North Pole on 21 April 1908, a year before Peary] / to or
toward the North Pole.' On p. 21 of SB is the note 'Etookashoo and
Couldlooktoo who accompanied Dr. Cook to the North Pole.'

16: There will come another day.] 1st, SB; There at length will come
a day.] MS

E37   1944. AMSs. A MASQUE OF REASON. Written in ink on the
rectos of 25 leaves (some additions and corrections on versos) of a red and
black cloth-bound notebook, lettered in gilt on the spine '||| RECORD ||||
27 | R | 150 ||'. Leaves of white wove paper ruled in light blue, measuring
207 × 173 mm., edges trimmed. Pages numbered 33–152 with the text on
alternate pp. 33–81. The first sixteen leaves have been torn out. On the front
free endpaper verso, Frost has written 'To Earle Bernheimer / from /
Robert Frost / May 26 1944 / Ripton Vermont'.

With one exception on the final manuscript page, all variant readings in
the manuscript have been overscored and corrected by Frost to the reading
in the first edition text. Page and line designations following are from the
first edition:

page 3, line 7: As Waller says.] MOR; As Lovelace says.] MS

6, line 9: You wouldn't say she fared so very badly.] MOR; She didn't do
so very badly, did she?] MS

7, line 2: (*The throne collapses. But He picks it up*] MOR; (*He lets the
throne collapse but picks it up*] MS

7, line 10: let's not go *back* to anything] MOR; let's not go back to any-
thing] MS

9, line 15 *et seq.*: But God, I have a question too to raise. / (My wife gets
in ahead of me with hers.) / I need some help about this reason problem / Before I am too late to be got right / . . .] MOR; But God, a

word about this reason problem / Before I am too late to be got right /
. . .] MS

11, line 20: Wolsey should have said.] MOR; Shakespeare should have
said.] MS

12, line 2: Was to learn his submission to unreason;] MOR; Was learning
to submit to brute unreason;] MS

12, line 8: There's not much I can tell you.] MOR; There's nothing I can
tell you.] MS

12. Between lines 18 and 19, the manuscript has five lines: 'Mankind for
instance never seems to tire / Of getting reconvinced in bloody drama /
That Civilization and Utopia / Are opposites and mutually exclusive, /
so that they cannot both be had at once.' Another couplet on the page
facing (p. 56 of MS) has been discarded: 'There's something that is
playing for me now / And having a great run on more than Broadway.'

13, lines 1 and 3: 'breaks' for 'brakes' in MS

14. Between lines 5 and 6, the manuscript has the line 'You saw ahead.
Tell me you had a reason'.

14, line 13: To asking flatly for a reason—outright.] MOR; To asking
flatly for an outright reason.] MS

15, line 10: we seem to know enough to act on.] MOR; we seem to know
enough for action.] MS

15, last line: Your kingdom, yes, Your kingdom come on earth.] MOR;
Thy Kingdom come on earth for instance. What] MS

17, line 20: Job, you must understand my provocation.] MOR; You have
to understand the provocation.] MS

17, line 23: Of what . . .] MOR; For what . . .] MS

17, last line: He thinks he can . . .] MOR; He thought he could . . .]
MS

18, line 2: From what it is with his. Both serve for pay.] MOR; From
what it was with his. They both were true / For naught . . .] MS

18, line 3: Disinterestedness never did exist] MOR; Disinterestedness
does not exist] MS

21. Ten lines following line 4 have been excised and supplied later as
lines 17–25 of p. 23 with one textual change: (*Here endeth chapter
forty-three of Job.*)] MOR; Here ends the Forty third Chapter of Job]
MS

23, line 13 (uncorrected in MS): church carpet, sisal hemp,] MOR;
church carpet, rich and rare,] MS

Throughout the manuscript text, first letter of the words 'he', 'him', 'you', 'yourself' referring to God are not capitalized. In the first edition they are in upper case.

E38   1944. AMSs. [STEEPLE BUSH.] The first fair draft of 37 of the 43 poems printed in 1947 as *Steeple Bush,* and one poem, 'Ten-Thirty A.M.' (written twice), not included in the printed work. Written in blue ink on the rectos of 33 leaves of a notebook, black pebbled cloth back and green and black marbled boards. A white paper label pasted on the front cover on which Frost has written 'October 1944 / Ripton / Cambridge / Sent to California 1948'. The text fills the entire notebook from which 21 leaves have been excised. White wove paper, measuring 212 × 171 mm.; edges trimmed and stained red. The order of the poems differs from that of the first edition and there are textual variations or corrections in the manuscript: leaf 1: Untitled ['Ten-Thirty A.M.'] and dedication to Earle Bernheimer.
　　Text of the poem:

> How much rain can down pour
> To make the shingles roar
> The drain pipe metal ring
> And yet not change a thing
> Inside the house or me
> In any least degree

　　Dedication: 'Dear Earle / This book goes to you for a birthday present / on *my* birthday March 26 1948 and for / a sign of friendship which having lasted so long gives promise of lasting / forever. / R. F.'
　2-3: 'An Unstamped Letter in Our Rural Letterbox'. 1st ed., pp. 11–12. line 10: So regular that in the dark] SB; So orderly that in the dark] MS. line 16: Yet freely left me face to face] SB; Yet left me freely face to face] MS. line 46: And have occurred] SB; And too occurred] MS
　4: 'Blind Individualist'. 'Haec Fabula Docet' in 1st ed., p. 51. line 14: his own poor iliac] SB; his own poor ilium] MS. Following the final line is another version of the 'moral': 'Variantly / The moral is it hardly need be shown / All those who try to go it sole alone / Or with the independence of Vermont / Are absolutely sure to come to want.'
　5: 'To an Ancient'. 1st ed., p. 13
　6: 'On Being Idolized'. 1st ed., p. 41
　　'To the Right Person'. 1st ed., p. 62
　7: 'The Middleness of the Road / Blue and Green'. 'The Middleness of the Road' in 1st ed., p. 35
　8: 'Skeptic'. 1st ed., p. 37

9: 'On Our Deciding to Have Our Universe Smaller'; alternate title: 'They Decided on a Smaller Universe'. 'Any Size We Please' in 1st ed., p. 54. line 9: He thought] SB; He said] MS

10: 'A Young Birch'. 1st ed., p. 3. line 16: But now at last] SB; But now today] MS. line 20: When you were sick in bed] SB; When you were reading books] MS

11: 'Ten Thirty A.M.' Variant reading transposing the two final lines.

12: 'The Courage to Be New'. 1st ed., p. 30. line 13: They will] SB; They may] MS. Beneath, a discarded quatrain: 'No one cavils at their killing / And being killed for speed. / Why is anyone unwilling / They should do as much for creed.'

13: 'A Living on Hope / Something to Hope for'. 'Something for Hope' in 1st ed., pp. 4–5. line 12: And with] SB; And in] MS. line 17: A cycle we'll say] SB; A cycle of say] MS

14: 'The purport of the oldest document / I ever heard of, the Papyrus Prisse: / The Fear of God'. 'The Fear of God' in 1st ed., p. 26. Following line 6 in the manuscript is an asterisk, lines supplied below: 'And so disarming such malignancy / As may be smiling darkly on the side / in the wings'

15: 'Why Wait for Science'. 1st ed., p. 53
'No Holy Wars'. 'No Holy Wars for Them' in 1st ed., p. 57. last line: Can ever give us] SB; Can ever get up] MS

16: 'The Planners'. 1st ed., p. 56. line 5: That put an end to] SB; That interrupted] MS

17: Untitled ('A Steeple on the House'). 1st ed., p. 28. line 6: Nor need we] SB; Nor will we] MS. Two additional lines in MS between lines 6 and 7: 'It may not prove to be a time or place / To go to without immortality'
Untitled ('Innate Helium'). 1st ed., p. 28. line 5: To give them still more buoyancy in flight.] SB; To make birds still more buoyant in their flight.] MS

18: 'Etherealizing'. 1st ed., p. 52. line 1: A theory if you hold it hard enough] SB; A theory if we have it hard enough] MS. line 2: gets rated] SB; gets treated] MS

19: 'The Importer'. 'An Importer' in 1st ed., p. 55

20: 'The Cliff Dwelling'. 'A Cliff Dwelling' in 1st ed., p. 43

21: 'Astrometaphysical'. 1st ed., p. 36

22: 'Were I in Trouble with Night Tonight'. 'Were I in Trouble' in 1st ed., p. 18

23: 'A Case for Jefferson'. 1st ed., p. 46. line 5: It isn't because he's Russian Jew.] SB; It is because he's Russian Jew.] MS

24: 'Two Leading Lights'. 1st ed., pp. 38–39. line 26: Has brought] SB; So what has brought] MS

25: 'Bravado'. 1st ed., p. 19
'It Bids Fair'. 'It Bids Pretty Fair' in 1st ed., p. 44
'Beyond Words'. 1st ed., p. 45

26: 'The Night Light'. 1st ed., p. 17

27: 'The Ingenuities of Debt'. 1st ed., p. 60. line 11: Not even the] SB; Not all the] MS

28: 'The Common Danger The Fear of Man'. 'The Fear of Man' in 1st ed., p. 27

29: 'Upsilon Iota Subscript'. 'Iota Subscript' in 1st ed., p. 31. line 5: So small am I] SB; So small I am] MS

30: 'Nature I Loved and Next to Nature Art / or Lucretius Versus the Lake Poets'. 'Lucretius versus the Lake Poets' in 1st ed., p. 47. In line 7, the word 'Harvard' has been overscored and 'college' supplied, as in 1st ed.

31: 'A Mood Apart'. 1st ed., p. 25
'A Wish to Comply'. 1st ed., p. 42. MS lacks the two final lines and ends with line 11.

32: 'The Broken Drought But He Meant It'. 'The Broken Drought' in 1st ed., p. 61

33: 'In the Long Night.' 1st ed., p. 21. line 7: We would crawl out filing single] SB; We would file out crawling single] MS
'On Making Sure Anything Has Happened'. 'On Making Certain Anything Has Happened' in 1st ed., p. 20

The poems lacking are: 'One Step Backward Taken,' 'Directive,' 'Too Anxious for Rivers,' 'A Rogers Group,' 'Bursting Rapture,' and 'U.S. 1946 King's X.'

E39   1946. AMSs. 'Directive'. N.p., n.d. [before 1947]. 2 pp. written in blue ink on 2 leaves of white wove, 3-holed loose-leaf paper measuring 240 × 152 mm. At the top of the first leaf in Frost's hand 'To Russell [Alberts] from R. F.'

The poem was printed first in the *Virginia Quarterly Review* (Winter 1946) and later collected in *Steeple Bush* (1947). Variant MS readings:
line 12: keeping covered.] SB; keeping skirted.] MS
    29: Make yourself a cheering song] SB; Make up a reassuring song] MS

30: Someone's road home from work this once was,] SB; Someone's road home this once was,] MS

34: Of country where two village cultures faded] SB; Of country where one village culture ended,] MS

35: Into each other. Both of them are lost.] SB; Another one began. They both are lost.] MS

40: Now left's no bigger] SB; You see's no bigger] MS

47: Now slowly closing] SB; Now closing slowly] MS

50: of the house,] SB; of this house,] MS

62: beyond confusion.] SB; without confusion.] MS

E40   1946. AMS. THE CONSTANT SYMBOL. On the front cover in Frost's hand: 'August / 1946 / The Constant Symbol'. Written in blue ink on the rectos of 8 of 29 leaves (some notes, additions, and corrections on versos) of a notebook (gray and white marbled boards, dark green cloth back). Leaves of white wove paper ruled in light blue, measuring 257 × 194 mm. The text is on leaves 8–15 of the notebook.

The Constant Symbol was printed first as an introductory essay in the Modern Library edition of *The Poems of Robert Frost* (1946). It was reprinted as a Christmas keepsake in 1962 by Mr. and Mrs. Barrett with a facsimile of the first holograph leaf of the present manuscript.

The MS text has some few variant readings without alteration of the sense of the essay. On leaf 14 verso, however, is a paragraph (apparently considered as a closing paragraph, but discarded) that does not appear in the printed versions: 'I have said all this at ease without coming to / the point waited for and putting it in so many words / that poems together maintain the / constant symbol of the confluence of the flow of / the spirit of one person with the flow of the / spirit of the race. The figure of confluence without compromise. Like walking into an escalator / and walking with it. Like entering into the traffic / to pass and be passed'.

E41   1947. AMSs. 'On Being Shown a Cosmic Ray' ['A Wish to Comply']. N.p., n.d. [*ca.* 1947]. Written in blue ink on one side of a fragment of white wove 3-holed loose-leaf paper, measuring 90 × 152 mm. Inscribed at the foot 'R. F. to R. A.'

Printed first in *Steeple Bush* (1947) with the title 'A Wish to Comply.' The MS text has lines 3 and 4 transposed and ends with line 11, lacking the last two lines in SB.

E42   1947. AMSs. STEEPLE BUSH. '[Front cover] The MS of Steeple
Bush / Kathleen Morrison / made the copy from / that went to the publisher. / Presented to Earle Bernheimer, / at Beverly Hills March 26 1947.
/ Robert Frost.' Thirty-seven of the 43 poems printed in 1947 as *Steeple
Bush,* written in ink on the rectos of 13 of 20 leaves stitched at the center
fold and enclosed in a single quarto fold of heavy light blue paper. Leaves
of fine white wove paper measuring 280 × 215 mm., uncut at the fore-edge.
A fair copy written perpendicularly with lines running from bottom to top;
the poems arranged in two columns. The order of the poems differs from
that of the first edition, and there are some textual variations or corrections
in the manuscript:

leaf 1: 'But He Meant It' (title as in first printing *Atlantic Monthly* [April
   1947]). 'The Broken Drought' in 1st ed, p. 61
   'US 1946—King's X'. Manuscript contains ten additional lines not used
   in 1st ed., p. 59: 'The scientist is like the politician / He's never more
   than for a moment cruel / Anything he invents as ammunition / He
   soon converts into domestic fuel. / So everything if left to him is sweet.
   / But all the same the so called human race / About this so called bomb
   had better meet / In London Paris right off anyplace / And vote to
   have the ones who let it loose / Keep it from further military use.' The
   last two lines have been overscored in ink.
   'Bursting Rapture'. Variant reading in line 7, corrected by overscoring
   and emendation to 1st ed., p. 58, reading: The discipline of farming
   was so stern,] 1st; The mental discipline had been so stern,] MS
   'The Planners'. 1st ed., p. 56
   2: 'One Step Backward Taken'. 1st ed., p. 6
   'Why Wait for Science'. 1st ed., p. 53
   3: 'No Holy Wars'. 'No Holy Wars for Them' in 1st ed., p. 57
   'Etherealizing'. 1st ed., p. 52
   'To the Right Person'. 1st ed., p. 62
   'We Can Have It Any Size We Please'. 'Any Size We Please' in 1st
   ed., p. 54
   4: 'A Young Birch'. 1st ed., p. 3
   'A Mood Apart'. 1st ed., p. 25. Variant reading, line 8: a mood apart.]
   1st; a state apart.] MS
   'From the Papyrus Prisse (much the oldest document I ever heard of)'.
   'The Fear of God' in 1st ed., p. 26 (with an additional note on p. 63,
   'PAGE 26 The Fear of God—Acknowledgement to the / Payrus
   Prisse').

5: 'Something for Hope'. 1st ed., pp. 4–5. Variant readings, line 12: And with] 1st; And in] MS. line 15: wasteful weed] 1st; noxious weed] MS. line 18: foresight] 1st; patience] MS

'The Spire'. 'A Steeple on the House' in 1st ed., p. 28

'The Night Light'. 1st ed., p. 17

6: 'To an Ancient'. 1st ed., p. 13

'A Rogers Group'. 1st ed., p. 40

'Upsilon Iota Subscript'. 'Iota Subscript' in 1st ed., p. 31

7: 'In the Long Night'. 1st ed., p. 21

'A Wish to Comply'. The manuscript lacks the two final lines as they appear in 1st ed., p. 42.

'On Making Sure Anything Has Happened'. 'On Making Certain Anything Has Happened' in 1st ed., p. 20

8: 'Astrometaphysical'. 1st ed., p. 36. Variant readings, line 9: My love for] 1st; This love of] MS. line 12: Should be] 1st; Might be] MS

'Beyond Words'. 1st ed., p. 45

'A Cliff Dwelling'. 1st ed., p. 43

'Innate Helium'. 1st ed., p. 29. Variant reading, line 6: Some gas like helium must be innate.] 1st; There must be gas like helium innate.] MS

9: 'Two Leading Lights'. 1st ed., pp. 38–39. Variant reading, line 25: That changes] 1st; That can turn] MS

'The Importer'. 'An Importer' in 1st ed., p. 55

10: 'Her Fear'. 'The Fear of Man' in 1st ed., p. 27. Variant reading, line 13: her exposure.] 1st; her aloneness.] MS

'Bravado'. 1st ed., p. 19

'The Play'. 'It Bids Pretty Fair' in 1st ed., p. 44

'The Ingenuities of Debt'. 1st ed., p. 60

11: 'A Bed in the Barn'. Not published in *Steeple Bush* nor included in the poems collected by RF:

A Bed in the Barn

He said we could take his pipe away
To make him safe to sleep in the hay.
And here were his matches—tramp polite.
He said he wanted to do things right.
Which started him off on a rigmarole
Of self respect to shame the soul,
Much too noble a hard luck yarn
To pay for an unmade bed in the barn.

> I thought how lucky the one who stays
> Where other people can tell his praise,
> Such as it is however brief:
> That he isn't a firebug or thief.
> For you're sadly apt to overdo
> Your praise when wholly left to you.

12: 'The Courage to Be New'. 1st ed., p. 30. The manuscript has an additional quatrain not in the 1st ed.: 'Footnote: / No one cavils at their killing / And being killed for speed. / Then why are we unwilling / They do as much for creed?'
  'Skeptic'. 1st ed., p. 37

13: 'On Being Idolized'. 1st ed., p. 41
  'The Middleness of the Road'. 1st ed., p. 35
  'U S 1946 King's X'. 1st ed., p. 59
  'Haec Fabula Docet'. 1st ed., p. 51

Not included in this manuscript are the following poems printed in the first edition: 'Directive,' 'Too Anxious for Rivers,' 'An Unstamped Letter in Our Rural Letter Box,' 'Were I in Trouble,' 'A Case for Jefferson,' and 'Lucretius versus the Lake Poets.'

E43 1947. AMSs. A MASQUE OF MERCY. Written in ink on the rectos of 40 leaves (a few corrections on versos) of a red and black cloth-bound notebook, lettered in gilt on the spine '||| RECORD ||||| 2 || COOP |'. Leaves of white wove paper ruled in light blue with a red margin rule; leaves measuring 258 × 197 mm. Pages numbered 1–84, 91–144. Text is on pp. 11–84, 91–95. The hiatus between pp. 84 and 91 is presumed to be an ending that Frost discarded. On p. 8, facing the first page of text, Frost has written 'To E[arle]. B[ernheimer]. to keep and call his. It is the original / manuscript from which K[athleen]. M[orrison]. typed the copy / for the printers. R. F. / March 26 1948 / Cambridge Mass'.

Except as noted, all variant readings in the manuscript have been overscored and corrected by Frost to the reading in the first edition text. Page and line designations following are from the first edition:

page 3, line 11: levity:] MOM; flippancy:] MS
  6: between lines 3–4, MS has 'And The Rural New Yorker. When we get / Through here he says he's going to buy a farm.'
  7: between lines 13–14, MS has 'I mean the Flood that prophesied the Deluge.'
  9, line 3: I never] MOM; I haven't] MS

21, line 6: sacrilege,] MOM; irreligion,] MS

22, line 10 (uncorrected): Paul only means you make too much of justice.] MOM; I only say you make too much of justice.] MS

24, line 7: even as Keeper says.] MOM; even as I say.] MS

24, line 14: And if] MOM; Now if] MS

24, line 15: (And you've got to)] MOM; (And you have got to)] MS

25: following line 4, MS has 'Paul and I josh each other, but we're
friends. / Not everything I say is said in scorn. / I speak so you will
understand me wrong.'

25, line 6: Some people want you not to understand them.] MOM; Some
people write so you won't understand them.] MS

28, line 13: Lies] MOM; Seems] MS

28, line 16: His irresistible] MOM; His lofty irresistible] MS

29, line 5: In making] MOM; Is in making] MS

30, line 6: There is your way prepared.] MOM; There is your door prepared.] MS

31: following line 12, MS has 'The world seems crying out for a Messiah.'

31, line 20: The world seems] MOM; The world is] MS

32, line 1: Light, bring a light!] MOM; Light, give me light!] MS

32, line 18: the lesser gods] MOM; the ancient gods] MS

32, line 22: Nervous is all the great things ever made you.] MOM; Nervous is all thought ever makes some people.] MS

32, line 23: But to repeat and get it through your head:] MOM; And
once more to break through your inattention:] MS(1); Let me repeat
and get it through your head:] MS(2)

35, line 20: All of us get each other pretty wrong.] MOM; All of us get
each other wrong entirely.] MS

36: following line 7, MS has ' 'Till some attempt is made at summing up.'

39, line 18: As if I asked for one more chance myself.] MOM; As I myself might ask for one more chance.] MS

E44   1948. AMSs. [A BOY'S WILL.] N.p., n.d. [*ca.* 1948]. A fair copy of
29 of the 32 poems printed in 1913 as *A Boy's Will.* Written in blue ink on
34 leaves (rectos only) of white laid paper with vertical chainlines 24 mm.
apart, watermarked 'STRATHMORE EMBOSSARY TEXT USA'. Leaves
measure 234 × 153 mm., edges trimmed. Bound in black cloth-backed decorative red-brown boards (pattern like the covers of *A Witness Tree*). The
last leaf has an undated (*ca.* 1948) 33-line inscription to C. Waller Barrett,
at whose request Frost made this fair copy:

leaf 34 (full text of inscription):

> 'To Waller Barrett / since he would have it all / in my hand / Robert
> Frost / A Few Remarks and Acknowledgements / Exact dates are get-
> ting harder to be sure of. My / Butterfly was printed by 1894. I used to
> say it was the tenth / I ever wrote. That must be about right. Now
> Close the Windows / and Revelation were not written for English A
> (Har[vard]) but were / offered there in place of themes in 1897–8. I
> tried to write out / the idea of Trial by Existence while still in High
> School but failed / with it. The repetition of a line in Mowing and The
> Tuft of / Flowers shows how far apart these two poems must be. The
> / whole book was pretty evenly spread over twenty years. / I seem
> never to forget the least notice any poem gets from / a friend. Susan
> Hayes Ward of The NY Independent began / late in 93 with My But-
> terfly. She made Bliss Carman see it / and Maurice Thompson. There is
> a letter from Thompson / in existence urging her to stop me before it
> was too late / and save me from the cruel life of a poet. Pound was /
> first caught by In Neglect. Ghost House was published / in The
> Youth's Companion by Mark Howe who didn't / disclose himself till
> years afterward. Mrs. David Nutt was / the first to "see" the whole
> book. Then in England came William / Heinemann. He objected to
> my quotations, without / quotation marks in Love and a Question and
> Into My / Own. Charles Lowell Young said long ago the whole thing
> / began with the second stanza or paragraph in My / Butterfly, in the
> first two lines of that stanza to be exact. / Thomas Bird Mosher said
> Reluctance was all I had / ever written and all I needed to have writ-
> ten. Wind / and Window Flower pleased Stuart Sherman. A Tuft / of
> Flowers read aloud by someone else, Charles Merriam, / got me my po-
> sition (toe-hold) in Pinkerton Academy in 1905. / In America this
> book as a whole got no notice till after / Alfred Harcourt took up
> North of Boston for Henry Holt / in 1915. The Holts have been my
> sole publisher in this / country ever since!'

The poems not present are 'A Prayer in Spring,' 'Asking for Roses,' and
'A Dream Pang.' These were apparently present when the manuscript was
executed, for each hiatus is represented by a stub of the excised leaf. Aside
from a few differences in punctuation which were obviously Frost's errors
in copying or recollection, the manuscript follows the order and readings of
the first edition with the following exceptions:

leaves 1–2: 'Ghost House'. p. 2, line 4: the daylight falls] ABW; broad daylight falls] MS

12: 'In a Vale'. p. 21, line 17: And thus it is] ABW; And thus it was] MS

15: 'Going for Water'. pp. 26–27, line 15: a hiding new] ABW; to hide anew] MS

17–19: 'The Trial by Existence'. pp. 29–31, line 61: a flower of gold] ABW; a little flower] MS

20–21: 'In Equal Sacrifice'. pp. 32–33, line 10: The Douglas] ABW; Now the Douglas] MS. line 32: fighting over it perished fain.] ABW; fighting over it so was slain.] MS

22–23: 'The Tuft of Flowers'. pp. 34–35, line 12: a 'wildered butterfly,] ABW; a bewildered butterfly,] MS

27: 'The Demiurge's Laugh'. p. 41, line 16: It was something among the leaves I sought] ABW; It was some trivial thing I sought] MS

31–32: 'My Butterfly'. pp. 46–48, line 8: The gray grass is not] ABW; The gray grass is scarce] MS

33: 'Reluctance'. pp. 49–50, line 1: Out through the fields and the woods] ABW; Out through the woods and the fields] MS

E45   1949. AMS. Preface for a book by Hervey Allen (unpublished). N.p., n.d. [*ca.* 1949]. Written in blue ink on rectos of 2 integral leaves of white wove paper measuring 213 × 140 mm.; edges trimmed.

The use of the past tense with reference to Hervey Allen indicates that this preface was written after his death in 1949. It apparently was intended for a posthumous book of Allen's poetry that was never published. 'What begins as lyric may be counted on if not broken off by death or business to end as epic. The principle was never better exemplified than in the fine poems of Hervey Allen and through the years to a book heard round the world[.] it was translated from admiration into so many languages. The book was a novel in prose but only a poet could have written it and its very name rang with poetry. Unquestionably it is best regarded as just one more poem on top of all his others[,] longer than all the rest put together[,] an epic that had come in the disguise of prose to get past our modern prejudice against the epic. Hervey Allen would have wanted it taken as part and parcel of his life in poetry. He would live to regret it in the Elysian fields if it wasn't.'

E46   1951. AMS. 26 poems. '[p. 2:] This is a special selection of / poems made by Mr. Frost for Mr. Barrett on January / first, nineteen fifty one. / K[athleen]. M[orrison].' Fair copies written in blue ink on the rectos of 25 of 26 leaves of fine white wove paper stitched at the center fold and en-

closed in a single fold of heavy light blue paper. Leaves measure 280 ×
215 mm.; top and bottom edges trimmed, fore-edge uncut. The poems included are:

Never Again Would Birds' Song Be the Same
Against Thinking
Mowing
The Line-Gang
Closed for Good
Dust of Snow
The Tuft of Flowers
The Mountain
Blue-Butterfly Day
Reluctance
My November Guest
Hyla Brook
November
A Blue Ribbon at Amesbury
Astrometaphysical
Why Wait for Science
For Columbus Day
Choose Something Like a Star
Tree at My Window
Wanton Waste
Goodbye and Keep Cold
Something for Hope
A Young Birch
A Leaf Treader
The Lost Follower
The Gift Outright

E47   1953. AMSs. 'Down to Earth' ['One More Brevity']. New York, 23
November 1953. 3 pp. written in blue ink on the rectos of white wove bond
paper, watermarked 'OLD BADGER BOND . . .'. Leaves measure 277 ×
216 mm. On the third leaf, at the foot of the page, Frost has written 'One
of two first drafts / This for Al [Edwards] / from Robert / Nov 23 1953 /
N.Y.'

   The poem was printed as the 1953 Christmas card, 'One More Brevity';
later collected in *In the Clearing* (1962). Variant MS readings:
line 4: I said] 1st,ITC; I thought] MS

26: trouble-creased.] 1st,ITC; bother-creased.] MS

27: So I spoke] 1st,ITC; I spoke] MS

38: puzzled.] 1st; baffled.] ITC; puzzled,] MS

42: his right] 1st; in his right] ITC; in the right] MS

44: Next morning] 1st,ITC; Next day] MS

45: went to] 1st; was at] ITC,MS

46: As much as to say, "I have paid my call.] 1st; With an air that said, "I have paid my call.] ITC; As if he had no feeling at all.] MS

47: You mustn't be . . . all] 1st; You mustn't feel . . . all] ITC; As if he had no feeling at all.] MS

48–49: lacking in MS

52: Only a fraction] 1st,ITC; A fraction only] MS

58: I might even claim] 1st,ITC; I might like to claim] MS

60: greatest star,] 1st,ITC; brightest star,] MS

61–62: MS has two additional lines between 61–62: 'Who had taken into his head the notion / Of taking some notice of my devotion'.

62: Who made an] 1st,ITC; And made this] MS

63: To show by deeds] 1st,ITC; To show by action] MS

64: My profiting by his virtue so long,] 1st; My having depended on him so long,] ITC; My having admired him afar so long,] MS

65: Yet doing so little about it in song.*] 1st; And yet done nothing about it in song.] ITC; And yet done nothing * about it in song.] MS
Note: The asterisks in MS and 1st edition refer to a note beneath the poem that in MS reads, '*Little or nothing. But see The Great Overdog and Choose / Something Like a Star. The star chosen, fairest in sight, / might have been taken for a planet but that planets are / not fixed and fixity is the point of the poem.' In the 1st ed., the note reads, '*But see *The Great Overdog* and *Choose Some-/thing Like a Star,* in which latter the star could / hardly have been a planet since fixity is of the essence of the piece.'

69: And finding, was indisposed to speak.] 1st; And finding, wasn't disposed to speak.] ITC; And finding, might not decide to speak.] MS

E48   1957. TMSs. 'Kitty Hawk'. Ripton, Vt., 9 September 1957. Typescript on the rectos of 10 leaves of white wove bond paper, 280 × 216 mm. There are six ink corrections in the hand of Kathleen Morrison. At the end of the poem is the holograph subscription in Frost's hand, 'Robert Frost / For Elsie [Elizabeth Shepley] Sergeant / Ripton Vt / Sept 9 57'.
The poem with this title was printed first as the Christmas card for 1956.

A second and much longer version was printed in the *Atlantic Monthly* (Nov. 1957). It was developed further for inclusion in *In the Clearing* (1962), incorporating a 64-line poem, 'The Great Event Is Science . . . ,' that was printed in the *Saturday Review* (21 March 1959).

This MS is the second version and has the following variant readings keyed to the printed text in the *Atlantic Monthly:*

line 83: Man was] AM; Gas] MS

84: Like a kiss] AM; Off the earth] MS

following line 109: 2 lines not in AM, 'Anyway the thing / Is I didn't sing.'

line 147: themselves glad] AM; them feel glad] MS

344: That's how we became] AM; Was that how we came] MS

359: From] AM; And from.] MS

397: And this] AM; Yes this] MS

401: Of things on] AM; Keeping on] MS

418: scepter-baton] AM; sceptre-baton] MS

E49   1959. SERGEANT, Elizabeth Shepley. TMS. *Robert Frost: The Trial by Existence* (fragments, with holograph corrections in Frost's hand) N.p., n.d., [*ca.* 1959]. 22 typed pages on 22 leaves of white wove bond paper, 280 × 215 mm. Three holes punched in each leaf, as for insertion in a loose-leaf notebook.

This typescript is an early draft version of sections of the book. Few pages of text are consecutive, and those that are represent fragments of chapters 1, 2, and 3. Other pages bear no relation to one another. All were obviously chosen for the presence of Robert Frost's holograph. There are 31 corrections and single word comments and 8 notes of 3 to 12 lines. On the final typescript text page of Chapter 1 is the longest note about RF's father: 'To do him justice you should / get it in that he was an editorial writer / all his years out there [San Francisco] and among his / closest friends was Henry George. / My father and mother were both Single Taxers. / It is so hard to get a character like my fathers / . . . . His "consumption" was thought / to date from a six day walking match he got / into with the famous Dan OLeary (who of course / gave him a head start of I don't know how much / He was very athletic and a great swimmer. I thought of / myself as a walker and runner when young. Raced sometimes'.

E50   1960. AMSs [signed with initials]. 'Kitty Hawk' (fragment). Ripton, Vt., 28 August 1960. 6 lines in blue ink on one side of a fragment of lined paper torn from a spiral notebook, 142 × 135 mm.

Lines 219–24 of the final version of 'Kitty Hawk' in *In the Clearing* (1962):

> But God's own descent
> Into flesh was meant
> As a demonstration
> That the supreme merit
> Lay in risking spirit
> In substantiation.

Subscribed in holograph, 'R. F. / to / Elsie [Shepley Sergeant] / Aug 28 60 / Ripton Vt / The Cabin'.

E51   1960. AMSs. 'Away'. N.p., n.d. [*ca,* 1960]. 1 p. in blue ink written on the verso of a single sheet of white wove paper measuring 288 × 187 mm. On the recto is the printed letterhead, '[within a decorative rule frame] HOMER NOBLE FARM | RIPTON · VERMONT'

Printed first as the Christmas card for 1958; collected in *In the Clearing* (1962). A facsimile of this MS was made for illustration in Elizabeth Shepley Sergeant's *Robert Frost: The Trial by Existence* (1960). The only variant reading is in line 19: words] 1st; urge] ITC,MS.

F   Letters

F1   1872. FROST, William Prescott, Jr. (Robert Frost's father, 1850–1885). AMSs. N.p., 24 June 1872. 10 pp. written in brown ink on 5 leaves of white laid paper, horizontal chainlines, lined in pale blue with vertical red margin line. Leaves measure 245 × 195 mm., edges trimmed. Removed from a notebook. Signed on the final page 'William Prescott Frost Jr.' A note in black ink on p. 1 'Please return / to Robert Frost / Franconia N.H.' in Frost's hand. Unpublished.

   This is an autobiographical and genealogical account of William Prescott Frost, Jr., and the Frost family, dating from 1595 with Nicholas Frost, born in Devonshire, England, and located in this country in Kittery, Maine, in 1636. Five generations are detailed in addition to William Frost's maternal ancestry and his own education. This account was written when he was twenty-one years old and had just graduated from Harvard College with honors, Phi Beta Kappa. He was subsequently to serve as headmaster at the Lewistown Academy in Lewistown, Pennsylvania, and later to relocate in San Francisco as a journalist where Robert Frost was born in 1874. In conclusion, he writes 'My plans in life are as yet unshaped, though I shall probably go into either journalism or law. At present I am quite undecided as to which of the two to choose.'

F2   1873. FROST, William Prescott, Jr. ALs. To Isabelle Moodie. [Lewistown, Pa., *ca.* 1 February 1873.] Published, *Selected Letters*, no. I.

   The first love letter from William Frost to his future wife. He declares his feelings for her and makes a proposal of marriage. 'Your answer to this will mark a turning-point in my life. A person of my character cannot transfer his love at will. What is yours now is yours for life. You cannot reject it. You can only refuse to reciprocate it. Whatever your answer may be, you can lose nothing, but I—I—*everything,* I know; then, you will think well before you reply.'

F3   1873. Printed document accomplished in manuscript. Marriage cer-
tificate of William Prescott Frost and Belle Moodie. Lewistown, Pa., 18
March 1873.

The Rev. O. O. McClean officiated; the witnesses were S. Shaw and
M. S. Elder, presumably Mrs. George W. Elder, whose husband was president of the Board of Trustees of Lewistown Academy, at whose house the
marriage was performed.

F4   1873. FROST, William Prescott, Jr. ALs, To 'My Darling Wife' (Isabelle Moodie Frost). San Francisco, Calif., 13 July 1873. Incomplete, lacking
the final leaf or leaves. Published, *Selected Letters,* no. II.

William Prescott Frost, Jr., and Isabelle Moodie had been married four
months when this letter was written from San Francisco where William
had gone to find work as a journalist. In the letter he urges her to join him
in the West by telling her of the success he has had in selling articles to
newspapers after only four days in San Francisco. He gives her minute instructions on train travel from Columbus, Ohio, to California with changes
at Indianapolis, Peoria, Council Bluffs, Omaha, and Ogden. Mrs. Frost, already pregnant, arrived in San Francisco in November 1873, and Robert
Frost was born on 26 March of the following year.

F5   1874. FROST, William Prescott, Jr. 2 ALSs. To 'My Dear Grand-
mother' (Mary Blunt Frost). San Francisco, Calif., 25 October and 29 November 1874. Published, *Selected Letters,* no. III.

'We are all well, particularly the little boy, who, in fact, has never seen a
really sick day in his short life. Belle says she is going to have his picture
taken this week, and then you shall have a chance to see how much like his
father and grandfather he is. . . . It would be hard for us to lose little Bob
now, it would be much harder if he should be carried off after reaching
the age that Pres' little girl did. . . .'

F6   1876. FROST, Isabelle Moodie. ALs. To 'My Darling Husband' (William Prescott Frost, Jr.). Columbus, Ohio, 1 November [1876]. Published,
Selected Letters, no. IV.

Mrs. Frost had returned east with 2-year old Robert and, on 25 June 1876,
gave birth to Jeanie Florence Frost at the home of William's family in Lawrence, Mass. An account of this period can be found on pp. 13–17 in
Thompson's *The Early Years.* Mrs. Frost writes of her son, 'Bob is just as
queer as ever about some things. Scarcely looks at lady visitors but is most

happy to climb upon gents' knees. A young gentleman called this evening one of my old pupils and it was quite amusing to see the devotion of the little fellow.' She is also concerned that William will overwork in his efforts on behalf of Samuel J. Tilden, Governor of New York and the Democratic candidate for President, opposing Rutherford B. Hayes.

F7   1891. OLIPHANT, Charles H. (Pastor of the First Congregational Church of Methuen, Mass.) ALs. [To whom it may concern.] Methuen, Mass., 17 September 1897.
    'Robert L. Frost was a teacher in Methuen Grammar School No. 2 some three years ago, and as Chairman of the School Committee I found him able & efficient in that capacity. Mr. Frost has taught much of the time since then and I should regard him as deserving & competent in any capacity such as those which he has filled.'

F8   1899. BRIGGS, LeBaron Russell (Dean of Students, Harvard). TLs. To Robert Frost. Cambridge, Mass., 31 March 1899.
    'I am glad to testify that your dismissal from College is honorable; that you have had excellent rank here, winning a Detur as a result of your first year's work; and that I am sorry for the loss of so good a student. I shall gladly have you refer to me for your College record.'

F9   1915–1954. 75 ALSs. RF to Lesley Frost. Various places (as below), 1915 to 1954.
    Letters F9.1–68 of this group and the groups following from Mrs. Frost to Lesley Frost and from RF to his grandson, William Prescott Frost, have been recently published in *Family Letters of Robert and Elinor Frost* (Albany: State University of New York Press, 1972), edited by Arnold Grade. A brief listing with a quotation or précis of content is provided for the published letters. Letters F9.69–75, unpublished, are listed as a group out of chronological sequence and are transcribed in full.

    F9.1   [February 1915, New York, N.Y.] 'Dear Kids'. When the Frost family returned from England, Mrs. Frost and the children went on to Bethlehem, N.H., while RF remained behind in New York to attend to the affairs of Merfyn Thomas, the 15-year-old son of the poet Edward Thomas. Merfyn had traveled with the Frosts from England and was detained at Ellis Island for lack of visible means of support or patronage. The letter describes Merfyn's plight among the 'scum of the earth' and speaks of meeting the author of 'Scum o' the Earth,' Robert Haven Schauffler.

F9.2   26 September 1917, Franconia, N.H. Lesley Frost had enrolled as a freshman at Wellesley College, and this is the first of many letters from her father advising her in the adversities she encountered there. She remained as an undergraduate for only one year. For an account of this period, see Thompson, *The Years of Triumph*, pp. 115–17.

F9.3   3 December 1917, Amherst, Mass. Advice on composing poetry in French for her French class. 'You should have heard Wilfred [Gibson] confessing complete ignorance of the business [of prosody] to the assembled professors of Chicago University last winter. They thought none the less of him but rather more. Possibly that was because he was an Englishman and a reputation. They might had skun him alive if he had been a mere pupil in their classes.'

F9.4   9 December 1917, Amherst, Mass. Asking her to read one of Amy Lowell's books in case Miss Lowell invites Lesley to visit her. RF complains about teachers at Wellesley.

F9.5   [*Ca.* Spring 1918, Amherst, Mass.] Concerned over a contretemps during a tennis match at Wellesley in which Lesley was asked to leave the court for a game fault.

F9.6   [*Ca.* Spring 1918, Amherst, Mass.] Further advice to hold herself aloof from slights at Wellesley.

F9.7   18 March 1918, Amherst, Mass. 'This is the day in the week when I get a chance to do to others as still others do to you. I wonder if truth were told how many of my underlings suffer from my exactions as you suffer from poor Miss Drew's.' RF refers to the class he was teaching at Amherst.

F9.8   13 May 1918, Amherst, Mass. RF is in bed with influenza and regrets that the family will not be able to meet Lesley in Boston as planned. 'I get an honorary M. A. from Amherst. Then it is fixed that I am to do $\frac{1}{3}$ time for $\frac{1}{2}$ pay. . . . I haven't made myself particularly detested yet— that's all that means. Give me another year to get into trouble. . . .'

F9.9   18 October 1918, Amherst, Mass. Lesley Frost withdrew from Wellesley after her freshman year was completed and went to work in the Curtis aircraft factory near Marblehead, Mass. In this letter RF admonishes her for unnecessary risks she has taken having to do with planes and boats.

F9.10   24 October 1918, Amherst, Mass. Mr. and Mrs. Frost were apparently concerned about Lesley's growing enthusiasm for airplanes and flying. In this letter, which incidentally displays a considerable technical knowledge of flying, RF tries to dissuade her from this new interest by telling stories of the complexities and occasional disastrous consequences of piloting a plane. Envelope present.

F9.11   [5 November 1918, Amherst, Mass.] A fair copy of 'The Aim Was Song.' The poem was printed first in *The Measure* (March 1921) and collected in *New Hampshire* (1923). This is an early draft with readings that vary from the printed versions. It contains an additional quatrain between the first and third which was discarded:

> On every rough place where it caught,
> Mast, bridge, roof, steeple, tree, and hill,
> Only to wonder what it sought
> That left it discontented still.

Other variant readings:
line 2: untaught] 1st,NH; around] MS
  4: In any rough place where it caught.] 1st,NH; To satisfy the need of sound.] MS
  7: too hard—] 1st,NH; too much:] MS
  14: The wind the wind had meant to be—] 1st,NH; It answered every blowing need.] MS
  16:—the wind could see.] 1st,NH; the wind agreed.] MS

F9.12   [5 November 1918, Amherst, Mass.] *The Cow's in the Corn.* A fair copy of an early draft. The playlet was published in a limited edition of 91 copies in 1929 by James Raye Wells' Slide Mountain Press (see A13). Variant readings:
line 2: Behind an open paper] 1st; Hidden behind a paper] MS
  4: someone on] 1st; someone in] MS
  5: Johnny hear that?] 1st; Jimmy hear that!] MS
  6: I hear you] 1st; I hear him] MS

7: Why don't you go and drive her in the barn?] 1st; Why don't you
   drive her out since you were born?] MS
13: to him.] 1st; at him.] MS

F9.13   25 January 1919, Amherst, Mass. Writes of a projected trip to
Puerto Rico, Lesley's life in New York (as a student at Barnard College).
Of his publisher, he writes, 'I think it is better for us that [Alfred] Harcourt is staying with the Holts. Where would we be with our books spread
over three publishing houses. Of course I'd go out with Harcourt in a
minute.' Tells of a triumph Carol had over a bigger boy in a fight. Envelope present.

F9.14   17 February 1919, Amherst, Mass. A long, detailed letter advising
a technique of reading toward the composition of an essay. Envelope
present.

F9.15   24 March 1919, Franconia, N.H. Asks what Lesley is thinking of
'to want me to judge in a lyric contest in which you may be entered however unbeknownst to me. Consider the risk of your winning any prize I
had the disposal of. No one would believe I hadn't known what poem
was yours. . . . People would say it takes two Frosts, father and daughter
to win one prize—that is if we won it. And we ought to win it on such
a good poem as this you sent home.' He continues with a criticism of the
poem.

F9.16   3 April 1919, Franconia, N.H. The poem entered by Lesley in
the poetry contest was not given the prize. 'It may be good if you can take
the smash from those girls for the practice it gives you in not caring. . . .
It's not so important what they decide about you. Don't let them see how
you feel about it. . . . You have to remember it is not quite impersonal.
You labor under the personal disadvantage of being who you are. . . .'
In a postscript, he writes, 'Been reading some of Henry James short stories. Simply too good.'

F9.17   20 May 1919, Franconia, N.H. 'I have a letter from [Alfred]
Harcourt in script to tell me in confidence that he is leaving the Holts to
set up for himself. . . . He wants to know if we will go with him and I
suppose there is only one answer possible after what has passed between
us. . . . I am on the point of making changes here at Franconia too and

at Amherst I feel all at sixes and sevens. Out of general breaking up may come some new beginning that will be exciting and perhaps good and even great for us.'

F9.18   22 May 1919, Franconia, N.H. 'There must be Hell to pay in the Holt office. . . . Harcourt will set out to be the big publisher. He won't need much office help though for sometime I imagine. He'll succeed just the same. Someone will back him where he wants for capital. And I should say he had been the whole literary side of Henry Holt and Co and would take the whole literary side off with him. . . . He means to do it on the great. No petty publishing for him. . . . A great publisher with a flock of great authors—all American. That's his ambition.' Frost intended to go with Harcourt when Harcourt and Donald Brace left Henry Holt and Co. to form their own publishing company. Louis Untermeyer and Dorothy Canfield Fisher actually did so. However, Frost was reminded that Holt held the copyrights of *A Boy's Will, North of Boston,* and *Mountain Interval.* If Frost ever wanted to publish a volume of collected or complete poems under the Harcourt imprint, the contents of those three books could not be included.

F9.19   4 November 1919, Amherst, Mass. Describes a new teaching technique he has devised to replace the quiz. 'In "salon" the players come to class determined to show as wise, witty, and well-read (anything else, too, that counts in good company).' He mentions a speaking engagement to the Amherst language departments. 'Shall have to tell them that the mainstays in a language department should always be men who refuse to put a book to any use it wasn't designed for by the author. . . . Shall have to tell them a pedagogue is a person who has been willing to do violence to anything in himself or in the great books or even in the students for the sake of making the books pedagogically useful, laborious and disciplinary in class. . . . Speaking of books: ask Chapin will you to give you one of the new N[orth]. O[f]. B[oston].s with his autograph. Tell him I won't beg a book of . . . [Roland Holt] and I'm damned if I'll buy one. . . .'

F9.20   [1919, Amherst, Mass.] Lacking the first page. 'I'm sorry for [Sidney] Cox. I wish I could do something for him here. But we are full to the back balcony. It looks as if Percy Mackaye might teach with us. I like him and I'm glad in a way but it just cuts out William Benet whose name I have been proposing to Mr. Meikle [Alexander Meiklejohn, president of Amherst]. . . .'

F9.21   28 January 1920, Amherst, Mass. Including the poem 'Plowmen'; an early draft. It was printed first in *A Miscellany of American Poetry 1920* (New York, 1920) and collected in *New Hampshire* (1923). Variant readings:
line 1: I hear men say to plow the snow.] MS, 1st; A plow, they say, to plow the snow.] NH
    2: though—] MS, 1st; no—] NH

F9.22   8 February [1920?], Franconia, N.H. 'I write this snowed in by the greatest snow storm of all time. . . . We are running short of food fuel and water. How long we can last we are not experienced enough in rationing to calculate. . . . Rescuing parties have been by with teams of six and eight horses, but these are merely local and neighborly . . . they are not intended to establish communication with the outside world. . . .' Envelope present.

F9.23   11 March 1920, Franconia, N.H. It had become Frost's custom to send fair copies of new poems to Lesley in New York for typing and delivering to the editorial offices of periodicals in which they were to be printed. 'Don't let this MS out of your hands and don't let the typewritten copies go to Harpers till I say the word. . . . I'm thinking I ought to get seven or eight hundred dollars for the lot. . . .' Envelope present.

F9.24   18 March 1920, Franconia, N.H. 'The trouble with most people we know is . . . that they may be very good at catching on to the very latest style in thought but they never even think of such a thing as wanting to set the style themselves. . . . They have never even tasted the pleasure of starting an idea for themselves however small. They look on ideas as things to take up with and subscribe. They value themselves on the number they have heard of and the radicality of the ones they go partizan for.'

F9.25   23 September [1920], Franconia, N.H. Personal advice on the way best to handle two men who have been causing difficulties.

F9.26   [Fall 1920, Franconia, N.H.] A short note about Lesley's projected trip to Paris.

F9.27 [September 1920] Arlington, Vt. Frost's friend, the sculptor Aroldo du Chêne, had offered the use of his New York apartment to Lesley and Irma Frost for a few months. 'You may have to live with Irma a few days before Mama or I come down. Please take the way with her that will keep the peace. Remember that her strictness is part of her nature. Don't try to make her over. Some of it she will outgrow, but not all of it even by the time she is eighty. It has its beauty if you know how to look at it. . . .'

F9.28 14 October 1920, Arlington, Vt. The du Chêne apartment is infested with roaches. 'Mama is just home and . . . brought some news with her as that a menagery had broken loose in the Du Chene's and was running all round over Irma in the dark like bad dreams. . . . I could tell you if you asked me what to do to your co-occupants . . . to set them back temporarily if not to get rid of them entirely.' He writes of a woman whose poetry he dislikes, 'she's never nonsensical or strained or overprecious and literary as Carl Sandburg, in most respects greatly her superior, sometimes is (Read the dedication of his Smoke and Steel for the kind of thing: "Listener to new yellow roses." Awful stuff. It vitiates many a good poem in his book.). . . .'

F9.29 [Summer 1926, Ann Arbor, Mich.] In 1924 Lesley Frost had opened a bookstore, The Open Book Shop, in Pittsfield, Mass. RF sends her an account of his observations of bookstores in Ann Arbor for comparison.

F9.30 [Summer 1926, Ann Arbor, Mich.] Writes approvingly of James Dwight Francis, whom Lesley Frost later married. 'I take your word for it that he is really good—by which you mean, I suppose, that we could trust him to be good to you. It would have to be very good you understand.'

F9.31 [17 April 1926, Ann Arbor, Mich.] Telling Lesley of his intention to leave the University of Michigan and accept the English professorship at Amherst. Envelope present.

F9.32 [Summer 1926, Ann Arbor, Mich.] To 'Dear Kids' (proprietors of Lesley's Frost's Pittsfield, Mass., book shop). 'Your printed matter received. In reply am giving you a large order for one copy of [Dorothy]

Canfield's Made to Order Stories which please send promptly as not to a member of your family.' Signed 'R. F. D. Ph. D.'

F9.33   3 August 1928, South Shaftsbury, Vt. RF, Mrs. Frost, and Marjorie were preparing for a trip to England and France. He sends last minute instructions to Lesley before they sail from Montreal. Envelope present.

F9.34   21 August 1928, Paris, France. The Frosts' trip to France is not a success. 'I don't believe this can last long the way it is going. The French are at their worst, I should imagine, at this time of year with the Americans all over them. . . . You needn't publish it at home, but what we are most aware of is not the beauty of Paris, but the deceitful hate all round us.' He gives examples of French chicanery and avarice in theaters, shops, churches, and on the street. Envelope present.

F9.35   [1 September 1928, Paris, France.] Continuing dissatisfaction with the French trip: 'the French hate us as nationals though they may like us here or there in special cases as individuals. . . . our childish behaviour on the boulevards over pleased with ourselves for having reached furthest Paris and making fun of them and their poor depreciated money. . . . [Marjorie] maintains that three Americans have been mobbed and killed in Paris for their frank insolence—or insolence with the franc.' He describes varieties of American behaviour in France. 'I deserve to be punished [for coming to Paris]. Upon my soul I never saw anything to match this summer Paris for ugliness not even a White Mountain resort. . . . You may say another time we'll know better. Not necessarily. We're not the kind that can be taught. We know instinctively all we are going to know from birth and inexperience.' Envelope present.

F9.36   [11 September 1928] Gloucestershire, Eng. He writes of seeing the houses in which the Frost family lived in 1912–15. Gives Lesley the English literary gossip. '[Wilfrid] Gibson's stock as a poet is quoted very low right now. How he lives is a puzzle to his friends. His third of the income from Rupert Brook's [*sic*] books may be a big help. [Walter] De la Mare is not yet well from an operation that nearly killed him. He is the most prominent one of them all, getting out with both prose and verse to even the unliterary reader. W. H. Davies suffers his worst pangs of jelousy [*sic*] over de la Mare. Davies spends a good deal of his time talking about his own relative deserts. Everyone agrees or concedes that he still writes his best. He has married a very young wild thing of no definable class, but partly gypsy. John Freeman, a well to do head of an insurance firm, has climbed with some poetic prominence. . . . Freeman asked me with too obvious eagerness what I should say Hugh Walpole's article in "Books" on him rating him among the first six was likely to do for him in America. I told him almost anything: which is no more nor less than the truth. He wrote the article about me in The Mercury and I ought to be grateful. There is nobody new to take our place as the younger poets: or so I heard them lamenting with a false note in the Mercury office. The Sitwells and T. S. Eliot were pointedly left out of count. Lascelles [Abercrombie] has been too busy and recently too ill to write poetry. . . . [F. S.] Flint is I don't know where. [Harold] Monro has moved his book shop. . . . Mrs. Helen Thomas [Edward Thomas' widow] hasn't been heard from yet. She has entirely new friends. She plans more books about Edward. Nobody blames her too hard for that first one.' Envelope present.

F9.37   18 September 1928, London. Acknowledges Lesley's engagement and marriage to James Dwight Francis. Envelope present. Quoted in Thompson, *The Years of Triumph,* pp. 640–41.

F9.38   [Fall 1928, South Shaftsbury, Vt.] He is thinking of letting James R. Wells print six of the poems from *New Hampshire* (1923) and asks Lesley to have typed copies ready to send. He and Carol are preparing for sugaring in Vermont. *Note:* Wells printed *The Cow's in the Corn* in 1929, but not the poems.

F9.39   [*Ca.* 1929, South Shaftsbury, Vt.] Concerning Lesley's unsuccessful marriage. Final pages lacking.

F9.40   20 April 1934, Billings, Mont. RF writes of his daughter Marjorie's final illness while he and Mrs. Frost wait for the outcome. Marjorie was transferred to the Mayo Clinic, Rochester, Minn., where she died of childbed fever on 2 May 1934.

F9.41   [*Ca.* 1934.] Describes the very generous terms of a new Holt contract.

F9.42   [1934.] Lesley had accepted an engagement to speak on poetry at Cambridge, Mass. In this long letter, RF cautions her against any show of animus against other living poets, 'Remember you are my daughter.' He tells her about the new movement in poetry. 'Ezra Pound was the Prime Mover . . . and must always have the credit for what's in it. He was just branching off from the regular poets when we arrived in England. . . . Pound once wrote to me that John Gould Fletcher failed as a free verse writer because he failed to understand the purpose of free verse, which was namely, to be less free not more free, with the verbiage. Pound began talking very early about rhythm alone without meter. . . . For my part I should be as satisfied to play tennis with the net down as to write verse with no verse form set to stay me. . . . But whatever you do, do Pound justice as the great original.' He goes on to speak of Eliot, T. E. Hulme, Hart Crane, Gertrude Stein, Gerard Manley Hopkins, Robert Bridges, St. John Perse, Maurice Hewlett, William Butler Yeats. 'Last we come to who means the most, Pound or Eliot. Eliot has written in the throes of getting religion and foreswearing a world gone bad with war. . . . I doubt if anything was laid waste by war that was not laid waste by peace before. Claim everything for America. Pound, Eliot and Stein are all American though expatriate.'

F9.43   23 March 1935, Key West, Fla. RF and Mrs. Frost are disenchanted with Florida, and RF's casual remark has led to a rift with Dos Passos and Hemingway. He outlines a projected speaking tour and mentions an honorary degree he is to receive from St. Lawrence University.

F9.44   [8 October 1935, Amherst, Mass.] He writes of a trip to New York and meetings with Louis Untermeyer, the Harcourts, the Blumenthals. A book of Marjorie's posthumous poetry is contemplated for which RF will write a foreword. Marjorie Frost Fraser's posthumous book of poems, *Franconia,* was printed privately for the Frosts by the Spiral Press in 1936, but without a foreword by RF.

F9.45   [*Ca.* 1935.] To Lesley at Rockford College, advising her on continued formal education.

F9.46   [30 September 1937] Springfield, Mass. Describes Mrs. Frost's operation for cancer and makes plans for her recuperation. Envelope present.

F9.47 [25 October 1937, Amherst, Mass.] Remarks on Lesley's idea of moving to Mexico. Tells of Mrs. Frost's gradual recovery and their plans to go to Gainesville, Fla. Envelope present.

F9.48 7 September 1938, Concord Corners, Vt. After Mrs. Frost's death in March 1938, RF visited the Untermeyers. Lesley was to join him there and he asks for things he wants her to bring along.

F9.49 30 November 1938 [Boston, Mass.]. Kathleen Morrison has helped RF move into an apartment in Boston and he is considering an invitation from Norman Hall to visit Tahiti.

F9.50 [3 February 1939, Miami, Fla.] RF is visiting Carol and Lillian Frost in Florida and staying with the Hervey Allens. He is pleased that Lesley is writing for publication at last, 'You have me to get over.' He is miserable visiting other people, has written a preface for Holt's new edition of his collected poems ('The Figure a Poem Makes'). He advises her against carrying poems of her students to editors, 'Only the bullying power of an Ezra Pound ever thrust poems down a publisher's throat.' Envelope present.

F9.51 25 February 1939 [on the train from Florida to the North]. He writes of his deepening friendship with Hervey Allen. The Hemingways were friendly and he played tennis with Mrs. Hemingway, whom he liked. Describes a trip to Cuba with Paul and Mary Engle. He adds a postscript about Carol and Lillian Frost and his difficulty in relating to his son. Envelope present.

F9.52 [1939, Boston, Mass.] RF sends Lesley a letter of Mrs. Frost's found among his papers and writes a brief analysis of his wife's character and life. His daughter Irma has had a serious operation for a tumor, and his concern for her health is compounded by worry for the direction her life is taking, 'I am prepared for any sadness in the structure of the universe.' Envelope present.

F9.53 [*Ca.* 1940, Boston, Mass.] RF is relieved that Lesley's work in Washington has enabled her to proceed toward a higher degree. He describes his own difficulties on the 'ragged edge of the profession' through lack of degrees, though he considers them generally unecessary, 'It will be by knowledge or achievement you will make your mark.'

F9.54   [*Ca*. 1940] Coconut Grove, Fla. RF gives details of property purchased in South Miami, Fla., near Hervey Allen. Later RF had two prefabricated houses shipped from Dover, Mass., to serve as winter quarters on this site. Outlines a new lecture tour.

F9.55   [12 February 1941, Miami, Fla.] Sends Lesley a preface she had written, found after a search through boxes of family papers that appall him at their number and confusion, 'I put things away on some sort of principle but it isn't long before the principle goes out of my head.' He worries about how he is going to write the books ahead of him 'which will be nothing but a more or less orderly arrangement of things already said and thought.' Among the boxes he has also found a group of stories written by Lesley as a child. In the final paragraph he reviews the cause and result of his rift with Amherst. Envelope present.

F9.56   [17 November 1941] Cambridge, Mass. He sends Lesley fifty dollars before leaving for Ripton and remarks about a mismanaged banquet in Washington. Envelope present.

F9.57   8 October 1942, Cambridge, Mass. Political differences and attitudes toward the recent American-Russian alliance, attitude towards war.

F9.58   21 December [1942, Cambridge, Mass.]. Sends Christmas checks and discusses finances. Attitudes and opinions on the war, the value of wartime work for writers (he does not approve), the ambitions of Nazi Germany.

F9.59   [24 April 1943, Boston, Mass.] RF plans a visit to Lesley in Washington. Envelope present.

F9.60   9 July 1943, Ripton, Vt. Plans for Lesley's visit to South Shaftsbury. 'I shall have a slighter connection with Harvard next year and a very considerable connection with Dartmouth.' as Ticknor Fellow in the Humanities. He gives details of his affiliation with Dartmouth.

F9.61   14 October 1943 [Cambridge, Mass.]. He has sent the manuscript of a play (*A Masque of Reason?*) to Lesley. He is opposed to Prescott

Frost's applying for a government pension after his release from military training due to illness. 'Patriotism comes first and Lord, I'm sure Prescott is man enough to earn a living once he gets his start from his family.'

F9.62   [2 September 1944, Ripton, Vt.] Before Lesley leaves for Europe, RF wants her to arrange for Irma to stay with Vera Harvey rather than Lillian and Prescott Frost during Lesley's absence. Irma might benefit from treatment by a good analyst. He writes of Louis Untermeyer's marital problems.

F9.63   [December 1944, Cambridge, Mass.] Plans for Christmas. Lesley and her children are expected in Cambridge to join him and the Morrisons on Christmas eve.

F9.64   [Fall 1949, Ripton, Vt.] An enigmatic letter having to do with 'poet-politics' at the Library of Congress and Harvard. 'I have a vague sense of having had this year the height of my success.' He writes of his absolute satisfaction with Ripton and the improvements he has made about the farm.

F9.65   19 January 1951, South Miami, Fla. RF sends Lesley some early papers and old notebook leaves which show 'that I did keep a note book at times in spite of my distrust of writing anything down except in final form for keeps. . . .'

F9.66   20 June 1951, Ripton, Vt. An approving letter about Lesley's plan to move to Texas. '. . . I have to get my sense of being an All American out of having family representatives in New York Montana Washington D.C. and . . . Texas.'

F9.67   19 December 1951, Cambridge, Mass. A Christmas note. 'Let's think of all the pleasant things there are for Christmas.'

F9.68   [1 May 1954, Amherst, Mass.] Advice on property Lesley considers purchasing with her sister Irma. Envelope present.

F9.69   10 May 1917, Franconia, N.H. Unpublished. 'The weather here makes it hard to believe you can be within three weeks of your summer vacation. I can hardly get it through my head that you are on the verge of examinations. The weather is only partly to blame for that however.

You have said so little about anything but athletics and and [*sic*] magazines lately that I had forgotten you were still studying and going to classes. Boas and Pillsbury's Psychology seem things of the distant past.

'We have planted nothing except a few trees, some lettuce and radishes in a cold frame and a pound or two of onion sets. Carol fishes a good deal and the rest of the time works round with the hens. He and Wilfred caught two hundred perch, big ones, over in Streeter pond today. I think that is more fish than I have caught in my whole life. They gave them away right and left in the village and kept enough for themselves. Perch not trout. He has caught some trout, one really good string that made a meal for all of us. But the perch aren't to be despised just because they don't compare with trout. Down country where we saw no trout we thought pretty well of perch.

'There are two hens setting and we ought to have some white chickens when you get home if we hatch any and don't lose them all.

'I sent you a couple of poems a week ago. Suppose I send you one or two more with this. I ought to send you George Whicher's dispose of the May Amherst Monthly: it tells you so well if you know how to read it, of the conflict now on between the aesthetic anti-Puritan anti-American Meiklejohn-Youngs and the anti-aesthetic Puritan-American Frost-Whichers. It's a wallop in the mouth.

'You may remember an old bellows that lies rotting just inside the old road where it leaves the new road at the top of the hill above Lynch's. It has lain there for years. I thought when I was up there yesterday what a use it would be to put it [*word illegible*] if I should crate it and send it C. O. D. to Mr. Meiklejohn to run the college with.

'I'll have some more money somehow for you in a few days.

Affectionately
Papa'

F9.70   [*Ca.* 1918–1919, incomplete.] Unpublished. '. . . We laughed over the account of it all in The Post: the hypocrisy of making the decision of the judges so unanimous: and the idiocy of calling the first poem at once so original and so like Amy and Carl. I should suppose it very likely that the four "honorable mentions" meant that the judges each picked a different pair for the first two and compromised with Erskine [to let] his pair win if he would let theirs be given some credit. Erskine said that the moral of it was that Barnard should have some more money for teachers' salaries.

'To bad I couldn't get down to see you. I doubt if I shall get down in April either; though I shall be within a hundred miles of you farm-hunting in Connecticut. Brown (W. R. of Amherst) is going to carry me round in his automobile.

'I have a half wild impulse to go the other way, though, into Maine. There's a little 3,000 population town of small industries (snow shoes, toys, etc) called Norway over there among lakes and about forty miles from Portland. I shall probably not settle down anywhere else till I have had a look round it anyway. I suppose it is foolish to get too far away from our markets, both for poetry and for farm produce.

'To Hell with the Untermeyers if they don't ask you to see them. They are busy every minute they are awake talking of fame. They don't think of it any more than they talk of it because they talk of it all the time. The absurdity of it never strikes them. Don't think you are under one least single obligation to seek them. All I think is we must have no trouble or break with them after what has passed between us. Louis means to be a good backer. It's funny to watch him, though, when it's a question of Edward Thomas. He parts company with me there. He refused to like Thomas' poetry and he refuses to like my poetry to Thomas. Funny world.

Affectionately
Papa

'Just happened to run across this by Daniel Webster: "I had not then learned that all true power in writing is in the idea not in the style, an error into which ars rhetorica, as it is usually taught, may easily lead stronger heads than mine." Ideas ideas ideas. Of course emotional ideas. Senses and sentiments are what to get after.

'Carol will send a five pound can of sugar tomorrow'

F9.71   28 September 1918, Franconia, N.H. Unpublished. 'Not much to say this time but this much money (check for $25 enclosed) Irma has Boston Grippe, as her nurses prefer to call it there, and we are wondering if you haven't it too. We are anxious to hear from you. The taking care really just begins when you think you are getting well enough to go out. That's the time to stay in longer.

'But possibly your cold hasn't proved to be the Distemper. That would be great.

'I'll tell you next letter about Hendricks and how too much flying has sickened him of the air. It's a wild game up there—and yet not various

enough to fill the mind with the days work and keep it off the subject
of death.

Affectionately

Papa

'But I think we hear a noise like the Central Powers squealing.'

F9.72   29 March 1919, Franconia, N.H. Unpublished. 'I want you to
spend some money on entertaining people you like and I don't want you
to be niggardly about it till I call a halt. I hope you had my check in time
to seem free handed enough with Margaret White (Wha's the matter
with me—blunder struck)

'If that girl is mad about anything I should say it must be either because your poem is too good or because it is irreligious or rather un-
Christian. I don't see how she can know enough to know it is too good;
so I conclude she frowns on you as impious or something, though I con-
fess that seems improbable in these days and at a metropolitan college.
At Wellesley for certain you would be barred from any prize for un-
orthodoxy. The reason might, surely would, be suppressed, but you would
find your poem unconsidered. They would say why in Hell can't she
praise the Greek god without reflecting on the Christian God. They
wouldn't see that it was the church, the form of worship that you found
false. You say nothing against the One God. He is Pan in a manner of
thinking. He includes Pan anyway, whatever else he is more than Pan.

'We are in the hen business to the depth of fifteen hens and a rooster,
five of the hens and the rooster being aristocracy. We are better off than
last year by one small hen house Carol built. We are going to hatch a
slew of chickens.

'Irma and I and Carol captured about forty young wild apple trees just
over the wall on that slope going down to the Pooles spring house and
are setting out an orchard on the steepest slope behind the house in our
mowing field.

'We ordered $10.40 worth of seed of James J. H. Gregory & Son of
Marblehead Mass today, wondering all the time if we would get it back
out of the enormous crops we expect to raise this summer.

'Carol is into the sugaring with the Herberts. Most of us are surfeited
with the taste of maple in one form or another, sap, syrop [*sic*], snow-
candy, or sugar. Great sugar weather. Wild cold and snowy yesterday
and still going it. Furnace feels good.

'Won't it be rather difficult about all those boys you are going to the
Plaza with?

'Yes you'll have to allow yourself something to entertain good people with.

'I think Irma ought to look into New York this year. She seems to want to sit round in the art gallery. You could take her there get some beneficial glimpses yourself and leave her to meditate the masters.

Affectionately
Papa

'John Bartlet [*sic*] writes that Margaret has taken the poetry editorship of Farm Journal. Funny how things come round.'

F9.73   16 April 1919, Franconia, N.H. Unpublished. 'Just one detail of the games did we find in the Sunday Times and that was that the Torch Race was the excitement of the day, and that your class won it. I said I'd bet that was where you came in. And it seems I wasn't far wrong. I don't know whether it wouldn't have been too much for us if we had been there. It's a wild kind of race the Torch Race when you come third and have to stand waiting for a torch that is dropping gradually behind. I'll bet you almost wanted to run without waiting for the torch. And I'll bet you went when you went as if you'd been shot out of a cannon, far as cannon are from anything Greek. There's nothing I'm more suscep-tible to than victory in athletics. I should have gone crazy when your will to win carried you to the front and over the line. I can just see you put in and scoot. I wonder how Irma felt till you had got ahead.

'I was thinking Saturday afternoon about your taking the turns with your hoop. All I hoped was you wouldn't fumble and drop the hoop. Well you got a first with that too. And your class came out on top. Enough glory for once in a way.

'That was a memorable encounter you had with Miss Dotage. We'll keep the record of that for our educational novel when we write it. Why it sounds like the middle ages. Her use of will power for self-control sounds so old-fashioned. Will power is drive as we use it now-a-days. It is that in some people that simply won't be checked. Education can't install it like an engine in a Ford car. You have it or you don't have it. Education can at most steer it. At worst it can damage it so that it won't go. It is a kind of hunger, a hunger for victory, for art, for philosophy. It may be a hunger for money. We have to be thankful when it isn't for still worse things. And we have to know that when it is denied in good objects there is danger of its being diverted to bad objects. It takes an awful fool to risk trying to kill the will to poetry in a young person. Even if your aim should be scholarship anyone but a fool would know that the more creative speed you get up the more mere knowledge you will pick up and carry along with you. The beauty of Miss Dotage is her incredibility. I should have thought there was no such animal. Will wonders never cease in the education of you?

'But there is something to be said for what is known as self-control. You for instance will have to exercise a good deal of it as editor of a magazine. You mustn't print just anything of your own you happen to write. You'll have to be a good deal more on your guard than you realize at this moment. It was an unguarded thing to think of asking Irma to make the cover for a Columbian magazine. It would be as mistaken and would do you as much harm as Louis' folly (which was awful.) It would hurt Irma too. Head that scheme off at once. What you want is a Barnardian or Columbian artist in it. Nobody else would be appropriate. You ought to be able to find someone who goes in for art or architecture. Some of the faculty that does the good detail in architecture would come in here.

'Easy does it. You decide on what of your own you will print. But perhaps you had better let me have a glimpse of it for confirmation.

'Mama is up around but not as she should be. I guess we have got to think of her a good deal this year.

'I just learn that the end of school is not much more than six weeks away. We'll all be together again soon.

'By the way I wish you would ask Harcourt if he could help you get rid of 200 dollars worth of bonds. I shall have to have some more money for you and for the rest of us. Perhaps he can tell you where to take the bonds to sell. Miss Eayres might tell you or help you. Let me know what they suggest.

'Yes we must manage to be good to Louis somehow. He means well by us.

'Get up late if you have to but try to get your eight hours sleep. Sock it to the studies. Remember in your writing for yourself and for your teachers and magazine: Ideas and Imagination. Don't take any stock in Miss Doty except as a specimen.'

F9.74   6 March [1942, Miami, Fla.]. Unpublished. 'My telegram of yesterday meant I was still to [*sic*] hoarse and voiceless to risk undertaking anything for Saturday night. If I do the one in Richmond Tuesday it will be as an experiment to see how I stand the strain. Florida has been no special good to me this year. I have had two of its summer-like colds. My suggestion would be that you find out from Kathleen right off now when I am to be in New York for the Junior League and try to get St. Johns to have me not further than two days away from their date either before or after.

'Great luck the scarlet fever didn't come off.

'I have nothing but sorrow for Irma—and John too—yes and Jack and Harold. But for some reason they seem not to want my sympathy. At least they give me no chance to show it. No one writes to me to tell me anything. I send Jack five dollars a month. You'd think or rather I'd think they might have him sit down and practice writing on me if only to the extent of a few words of thanks. I shall send them a present to help out in this emergency. I see John sports a good looking letter head. I trust it means he is doing business.

'You have good friends in Gainesville. I could tell by the way they spoke of you there this week.

'You mustn't be too hard on the British in their day of adversity. I hate to hear them starting to free India under fire. If one were fanciful he might venture the figure that it sounds like the Empires death bed repentance. Neither do I quite like their fawning on us at such a time. Still it ill becomes a Frost not to sympathise with a nation that has done so much for our family. Possibly you calculate it has not been all good— good only for me and not for the rest of the family. I have no answer for that. Anyway I am on their side. But what would Rudyard Kipling say —Had he lived to see this day—of having his poems edited by worlds-end-whimper T. S. Elliot [*sic*] to rouse the spirit of the British to the Natzi [*sic*] level to meet the Natzi greatness?

'There are sarcastic things I could say to our own campaign. For instance: the New Deal has won one more victory than was to be expected of them in the field of internal politics (over the hearts of the proletariat); now let's see them win a victory or so in the field of external politics over real men. Churchill won't last much longer unless his affairs take a turn for the better: and if he goes it will be too bad for the Groton boys who love the mother country like a mother.

Affectionately
Papa'

F9.75   30 August 1948, Ripton, Vt. Unpublished. 'There's the American Novel, there's American Poetry and there's me R. F. That is according to you. And don't think I'm not touched and impressed by these marks so often repeated of your regard for me. I don't see how you can ever be cross with me when you really admire me so much. You have a special claim on me and my poetry: You typed at the age of twelve some of my earliest manuscript going into a book and you have campaigned for it ever since in bookstores and editorial offices and from the platform. You came along at just the right age to get some satisfaction out of my strange career. Not everybody in the family had the same luck. I can be very very sad for the little good Carol and Irma got out of being my children. Marjorie was in the way of profiting by being an artist child of an artist. But she missed by death. You alone are left to cheer me with your pleasure in what I do and your participation in it. I stay the same always in my belief in your ability and my patience with you in your deliberate self-expression. You may be having a book next year or the year after next. I hear of your projects now and then from Lee or Elinor. I sort of count on you for a novel someday. But if you should never venture out with one in my lifetime I shouldn't feel frustrated in my ambition for you. You are sharing with me the literary life with such heartiness I get all the fun I need as we go along. I like to be telling people where you are and into what now. I have never heard you lecture, have I? I know you must be good at it from the way you talk and write letters. Sometime I must hear you.

'You'd think I might have written like this months ago. I have practically given myself up for a dead-letter writer. I went by. I can still play baseball or tennis—at least I think I can and brag that I can. But I shrink from writing dead letters—that is letters that something in the back of my mind makes me afraid will end up in the dead letter office because they can't overtake you in your jumps from nation to nation. That only means that I am too ready to use any excuse for keeping off stationary. I wouldn't be able to write this if I had tried it on regular letter paper.

'I wonder where you are at the moment. While I felt more or less sure you were in Colombia I made myself your fellow traveller by reading a whole big book about it as the Gateway to South America by Kathleen Ramoli. A boy from there you may have met at the Middlebury Spanish School (we called him Tito) sent it to me and it might have laid unread forever if you hadn't given me an interest in it. It seems to be El Dorado or somewhere near that mythical place. I suspect El Dorado was merely the vague rumor of Mexico in Peru and of Peru in Mexico. The two great civilizations had reports of each other across the savage jungles.

'Kay and I are busier with my relations with Henry Holt and Com-

pany than we should have to be. They have had another palace revolution in the firm. You'd think it might be infirm after all its troubles. But
no, it has such a foundation of text books that nothing can shake it. The
sufferers are their trade book people. For almost a year now my Collected has been out of print. They didn't even tell me. Their minds were
somewhere else. We found it out from friends who tried to buy it and
at last by trying to buy it ourselves in the course of our natural presenta-
tions. I ordered six of it and six of a Masque from the firm. The Masques
came with the usual slip of charges that showed I wasn't charged for the
Collected because it was out of stock. Bill Sloane wouldn't have neglected
me that way. It would be fine to escape to him, both Kay and I think.
But escape is not so easy. We have found that out from experience. I tried
it when [Alfred] Harcourt went and when Lincoln [MacVeagh] went
and Kay and I made a big effort to get me away to Little-Brown when
Richard Thornton went. It matters too. And it's going to matter more
and more as I get toward a hundred.

'We hear good news from Prescott and Elinor. But as the world is said
to be, that generation with us seems to be having a good time. Lee must
be reveling in opportunities. What I envy you both in my half education
is your Spanish, a complete language besides your native.

Affectionately
R. F.

'Your picture cards just received telling me to direct this letter to Mexico
City.'

F10   1917–1938. FROST, Elinor. 65 ALSs. To Lesley Frost. Various places,
between 1917 and 1938.

The most important of these letters have been recently published in
Family Letters of Robert and Elinor Frost, edited by Arnold Grade. They
span the same period as the preceding group from RF to Lesley Frost to
the time of Mrs. Frost's death in 1938.

F11   1931–1962. 15 ALSs. and 1 TLs. RF to his grandson William Prescott Frost III. Various places (as below), 1931(?) to 17 August 1962.

F11.1   [*Ca.* 1931]. The letter is printed in large primary letters for easy
reading by a seven-year-old, but signed 'Grandpa' in Frost's characteristic
hand. 'You have lots to do this spring on your fathers farm. But I hope
you will find time to take care of my farm too. I don't mean for you to

do all the work on both places. . . . I wish Jack could help you. . . . He begins to be quite a talker. But a talker isn't always a worker. Perhaps if he didn't talk so much he would get more done. Some one must put a flea in his ear. . . .'

F11.2   11 May 1933, Amherst, Mass. Anticipating a visit from his grandson. 'Take a good look at the United States of America as you come. There may be some questions I want to ask you about the country. Notice particularly if it looks to you as if it were falling to pieces, opening up cracks between the states.' With original envelope.

F11.3   21 December 1933, Amherst, Mass. 'How you have come on! I guess I don't have to print you any more letters to read if you can write a letter like that. . . . I always think of you as three thousand miles from snow [the younger Frost family lived at that time in Monrovia, California]. You are not really more than ten or fifteen I suppose. Very likely you can see snow on Mt. Wilson right now.' With original envelope.

F11.4   22 February 1934, Amherst, Mass. 'I hear you have been going to school in an earthquake cellar in California. I don't see what good a cellar would do in an earthquake. . . . If I were you I should work hard and get promoted from the cellar. I don't take much stock in an earthquake cellar, to tell the truth. . . . You've missed the deepest and coldest winter [here] in forty years.'

F11.5   [23 February 1934, Amherst, Mass.] 'Just a word to tell you I have been within a third of the way to where you are this last week. Two thousand miles more and I should have been in California where the earth quakes like jelly. . . .' With original envelope.

F11.6   22 August 1935, Franconia, N.H. 'Last night we had a good rain and a little lightning that sucked the electric lights low every time it flashed. That reminded me of your lesson in electricity on Monday. . . . Electricity has come into use in my life time. When I came to New England in 1885, there wasn't a telephone in the city I lived in, Lawrence, Mass., and there wasn't an electric light. . . . The [telegraph] wires were everywhere even in San Francisco. We used to lose our kites on them. But most electrical developments have taken place with me looking on. . . . And still I haven't paid enough attention to the biggest thing in the present-day world to understand such a thing as a transformer or an electric metre. A radio sender is a complete mystery. You'll have to educate me in all this some day. What do you suppose happens when a lightning flash draws down the house lights?' With original envelope.

F11.7   8 April 1938, Gainesville, Fla. 'I seemed to mind the spring cold in the north less for having filled myself up with sunlight all winter in the south. I believe I have had enough of heat to last me for awhile. . . . I'm going to tell you something just this once for you always to remember. I shall never speak of it again. Not more than a month ago she [Elinor Frost] told me you were a great favorite of hers. She said you had a good mind and, more important still, a good nature. She never knew a boy or girl she liked better. She was going a long way out of her usual way to say all this. She was seldom outspoken in praise. Don't forget. We'll keep such things locked in our hearts and when we write each other a letter as we must once in awhile, we'll speak of the ordinary things. . . .' Mrs. Frost had died in Gainesville on 21 March 1938. Original envelope.

F11.8   [1 November 1939] Boston, Mass. Containing a long and detailed discussion of an eclipse of the moon and a religious sect in Florida that believed the world is a hollow ball and 'we are inside of it with all our sea and land and the sky in another sphere contained in ours. In their church there was a nice mechanical model of the universe inside the world like a stone in a fruit. . . . Hervey Allen said he was going to try to buy the model as a curiosity. That's not a very respectful way to treat other peoples religion. Queer religion—and I guess pretty well petered out.' With original envelope.

F11.9   12 October 1940, Boston, Mass. On 9 October 1940 Robert Frost's only son, Carol (Prescott's father), commited suicide by shooting himself after years of psychic illness. His 16-year-old son was alone with him at the time and the only witness to the act. This is the letter that Frost wrote to Prescott after Carol's death: 'Disaster brought out the heroic in you. You now know you have the courage and nerve for anything you may want or need to be, engineer, inventor or soldier. You would have had plenty of excuse if you had gone to pieces and run out of that house crying for help. From what Lesley reported to me of her talk with Lillian [Prescott's mother] in Pittsfield Friday I judge you were in actual danger there alone with your unhappy father—unhappy to the point of madness. You kept your head and worked your faculties as coolly as a clock on the shelf. You've been tried more than most people are in a whole lifetime. Having said so much, I shan't bring up the subject again (for a long time anyway) either of your bravery or the terrible occasion for it.' With original envelope.

F11.10   10 December 1940, Boston, Mass. 'Everything is straight ahead in front of us as much play as it is work and as much work as it is play. All I encounter turns into thinking. All you encounter turns into thinking of another kind—scientific.' With original envelope.

F11.11   29 September 1941 [Cambridge, Mass.]. 'Knowledge is of two kinds, one is acquired from other people and one you think up yourself. The first you can go about getting wholesale, the second you have to venture into very cautiously. It is of course possible to go wrong in the first. Many are doing so at the present moment in their easy acceptance of what the governments are ladling out to them for war purposes. But you can be made the biggest fool of by your own originality. It is the only knowledge that can lift you into the higher ranks; you have got to have some of it to be anybody at all in law science art or business. But it is the more dangerous and as I say must be stepped out into or onto as onto the thin ice of early winter. . . . You have got to get going and find yourself as a thinker by trial and error. That is if you don't want to be a mere servant of other minds and live obediently to their dictation.' With original envelope.

F11.12   1 February 1943, Coconut Grove, Fla. Prescott Frost had enlisted as a private in the Army Signal Corps, but was later given a medical discharge because of a bronchial ailment. Frost writes to his grandson about the high rate of enlistments from Vermont and from Texas. 'I wonder if the explanation isn't that Texas and Vermont were once nations by themselves. . . . A history like that is bound to linger in the minds of its people and show itself in their character. That winter we all lived in Texas I heard plenty of proud talk about the state: When I told a Texan I thought Vermonters hated the idea of Govt. relief, he said Texans were the same. Absolutely no one at first would volunteer to go on relief and a posse had to be organized to run someone down to be the first victim of Govt. paternalism.'

F11.13   16 January 1946, Cambridge, Mass. Enthusiasm for the Orange Bowl football game to which he had listened on the radio. He makes plans to visit Prescott after a lecture tour. 'If I should want to write a Negro dialect story, how much an hour do you suppose I would have to pay a Negro for talking to me so I could learn . . . [the] idiom the way you learned German at the Berlitz School?' With original envelope.

F11.14   [13 September 1947, Ripton, Vt.] 'I'm glad you and Phyllis [Prescott's wife] are warming the Acton house. There must be things you and she will enjoy doing with and for it. Here's a hundred dollars for your tuition and here's looking forward to seeing you soon: a student at Tech. Love to you both. R. F.* *What Lesley has taken to calling me'. With original envelope.

F11.15   17 August 1962, Ripton, Vt. Typed letter. 'You probably won't have heard because it is a sort of state secret not meant to get out in general that on August 28th I am off to Russia to live there ten days and then come back here not to go on anywhere else. . . . As you may guess, this is a sort of errand I am on, not a sight-seeing junket. I shall have an interpreter with me and Freddy Adams [Frederick B. Adams, Jr.] to keep me from falling out of the plane. And Stewart Udall will be on board on his way to Siberia. . . . I let myself in for getting into such a big thing by accidentally getting friendly with the Russian Ambassador. . . .' Signed 'R. F.'

F12   1912–1943. 50 ALSs. RF to John T. Bartlett (Frost's pupil at Pinkerton Academy and a lifelong friend until his death in 1947). Various places (as below), 25 December 1912 to 20 January 1943.
Most of the letters have been quoted from or printed in full in Margaret Bartlett Anderson's *Robert Frost and John Bartlett: The Record of a Friendship* (1963), and 29 (F12.1–F12.29) have been published in *Selected Letters.*

F12.1   25 December 1912 (SL 40)
F12.2   26 February 1913 (SL 44)
F12.3   *Ca.* 18 March 1913 (SL 45)
F12.4   *Ca.* 4 April 1913 (SL 46)
F12.5   *Ca.* 10 May 1913 (SL 48)
F12.6   *Ca.* 16 June 1913 (SL 52)
F12.7   4 July 1913 (SL 53)

F12.8   6 August 1913 (SL 58). RF encourages Bartlett to write a review of *A Boy's Will* for the *Derry News*, using the already published reviews in *Poetry, The English Review, The Academy, The Bookman,* and *Poetry and Drama* as source and for quotation. In the letter of 22 February 1914 (F12.14), he thanks Bartlett for the review. The Barrett Library holds a copy of the *Derry News*, 34, no. 2 (7 November 1913), which contains John Bartlett's review. In it he mentions a second volume of verse to be published by David Nutt with the title *Farm Servants and Other People.* This was the title as advertised in the Nutt catalogue, though RF briefly considered calling it *New England Hill Folk.* Ultimately the book was published as *North of Boston.*

F12.9   7 August 1913 (SL 59)
F12.10   30 August 1913 (SL 60)
F12.11   *Ca.* 5 November 1913 (SL 64)
F12.12   8 December 1913 (SL 67)
F12.13   *Ca.* 15 December 1913 (SL 69)
F12.14   22 February 1914 (SL 73)
F12.15   *Ca.* 20 April 1915 (SL 113)
F12.16   8 May 1915 (SL 116)
F12.17   *Ca.* 2 June 1915 (SL 120)
F12.18   *Ca.* 21 October 1915 (SL 138)
F12.19   2 December 1915 (SL 141)
F12.20   30 May 1916 (SL 148)
F12.21   13 February 1917 (SL 158)
F12.22   13 August 1917 (SL 167)
F12.23   *Ca.* June 1922 (SL 222)
F12.24   1 January 1926 (SL 254)
F12.25   26 May 1926 (SL 259)
F12.26   1 November 1927 (SL 267)
F12.27   *Ca.* 7 May 1931 (SL 291)
F12.28   5 December 1933 (SL 306)
F12.29   20 January 1943 (SL 395)

F12.30   20 May 1915, Littleton, N.H. Published, *RF & JB*, p. 92. 'Back here at the piled-up letters and the business of buying a farm. The letters are rather too much for me with my piled-up inexperience. . . . Just you hold on a bit till I know where I stand with my Boston friends and I will do so for you (and more also) as I needed someone to do for me when I was your age. . . .'

F12.31   8 June 1915, Franconia, N.H. 'I'm not going to talk of this farm yet, because it isn't paid for. . . . Still we're on it and planting it and prospecting round over it. . . .'

F12.32   17 June 1915, Franconia, N.H. Complains of not receiving money to pay for the farm from Wilbur E. Rowell, attorney for his father's estate. 'I may have to skip from this place in the dark. . . . Here would be a question for these fellows who think they know poetry: Could a man as farmer mow for weeds what as poet he calls buttercups and daisies? Chew it over.'

F12.33   8 August 1915, Franconia, N.H. *R. F. & J. B.* pp. 97–98. Deploring the circumstance that prevents them from seeing one another more frequently. 'I know I need you or someone like you dating back to the days when my friends were those who had brains enough to judge me for themselves. I have lately been piled on top of by a lot of people who mistake their appreciation of my reviews for an understanding of me. . . .'

F12.34   24 August 1915, Franconia, N.H. *R. F. & J. B.,* p. 99. 'You're a good one—and a deep. I don't pretend to have fathomed you on this visit. . . . All I say is, you'll do. We had good talks. I like you and everything about and around you.'

F12.35   9 September 1915, Franconia, N.H. *R. F. & J. B.,* pp. 100–101. '. . . After all I am but a timid calculating soul always intent on the main chance. I always mean to win. All that distinguishes me from the others that mean to win . . . is my patience. I am perfectly willing to wait fifty seventy five or a thousand years as the fates may decree. I might be willing to be cut off at almost anytime (I *might*) but it would have to be for something. I do nothing for nothing.'

F12.36   [January, *ca.* 1916, Franconia, N.H.] *R. F. & J. B.,* p. 109–10. Describing speaking engagements. 'The Dartmouth Dinner was for the politicians. I felt rather lost with my brief poem in all the smoke and noise. I would do better another time; for I would bargain for an early place on the program and should know from experience how to make more of my voice and manner. I wasn't particularly good at the New York Dinner either. There I struck too serious a note. Dinners are all new to me.'

F12.37   28 September 1916, Franconia, N.H. *R. F. & J. B.,* pp. 108–9. Letter of concern for Bartlett's health.

F12.38   25 April [1917], Amherst, Mass. *R. F. & J. B.,* pp. 112–13. Advice to John Bartlett on his writing career and the scheduling of his time.

F12.39   [Letter fragment, perhaps summer 1919.] *R. F. & J. B.,* pp. 123–24. 'I never wrote to write right: I wrote for the fun of it. That's all I can hope to write for. For the fun of it in the large sense—for the devil of it. . . .'

F12.40   7 April 1919, Franconia, N.H. *R. F. & J. B.,* pp. 119–23. 'The year for us at Amherst was unsatisfactory what with all this sickness and the unsettlement in college due to the war. We came away with a bad enough conscience about the money we had taken for no work to speak of. . . . Maybe we could have been writing something if we hadn't been killing time down there on salary. I have gone rather easy on the writing for the two years last past. Breath-weight [William Stanley Braithwaite] had no choice in the matter of taking or leaving any poetry of mine for his anthology. There was none. Nary a drop. I have shown not a poem to an editor since I gave The Ax Helve to The Atlantic summer before last. . . . Not that I've absolutely stopped writing. I do a little and let it lie around where I can enjoy it for its own sake. . . . By and bye we will show ourselves again. No hurry. Wait till the fools have had time to try themselves on An Old Man's Winter Night and The Gum Gatherer. It's up to them to read as much as it is to me to write.'

F12.41   [*Ca.* August 1920 (?), Franconia, N.H.] Planning a meeting by way of a speaking engagement. 'If we decide I ought to come, I'll do it for anything you say, but if it's left to me to say, really for my self-respect I should ask for rather more than $600. I say self-respect when I mean the public respect. It is a miserable business being a poet among professors and business men. The only way to make them respect you is to make them pay.'

F12.42   16 October 1920, Arlington, Vt. 'For two summers running we had frosts on our gardens there in July and August and we decided not to give the place another chance. It was too much like murder in the state. . . . we couldn't think of going west or any further west than the western boundary of New England because I have to be where I can earn a little money by lecturing at colleges especially now that I have chucked Amherst. I served my time at Amherst (four years), the same as at Pinkerton . . . to show that as the father of a family I could do what I had to and then turned to something I liked better.'

F12.43 [20 December 1921] Ann Arbor, Mich. *R. F. & J. B.*, pp. 126–27. 'You may have heard how I am a guest of the University of Michigan this year. . . . I have averaged about three public speeches a week. . . . There have been long poems of mine you might or might not like to see in The Yale Review for October, The Century for November and there'll be one in Poetry for January.'

F12.44 11 December 1925, Ann Arbor, Mich. *R. F. & J. B.*, p. 134. 'Don't you get too ready to have . . . [Carol Frost] for Christmas company. He will be moved to act slowly if at all. . . . His heart is in his Vermont projects. . . . It will come hard to break off and start all over. He has something of my father in him that won't own up sick. It's from no ideal of gameness either. He's just naturally self-disregardful. He rather dispises [*sic*] frail careful people. But never mind he may listen to us in the long run.'

F12.45 23 December 1926, South Shaftsbury, Vt. 'I'm sprinkling a few poems around again—just a few, in the New Republic, Yale Review etc. They are my product for the last three years. Most of them have some age on them. I'm the same old slow poke.'

F12.46 [*Ca.* June 1928, South Shaftsbury, Vt.] Anticipating a meeting after ten years.

F12.47 [Winter 1928, Amherst, Mass.] *R. F. & J. B.*, pp. 149–50. Bartlett had written a review of *West-Running Brook*. This letter is Frost's gesture of thanks for what he considered a fine review. 'You brought it off with perfect discretion. I might have dreaded it from anyone else I ever raised by hand. I knew you could be trusted to flatter me unsentimentally—you old hard-head.'

F12.48 [*Ca.* September 1931, South Shaftsbury, Vt.] *R. F. & J. B.*, pp. 159–60. 'The enclosed picture of Cal[vin Coolidge] in his smock and

boots ought to make you more of an American if not a New Englander.
There is something so touching in seeing a Republican try to pose as a
Democrat. Signs like this (pretenses and poses) tell us that the Bolsheviki
are coming; the reality has gone out of the old order we grew up in and
gave our hearts to. But never mind; we're not politicians: we don't care
too much. It isn't as if we had signed the Declaration and voted for the
Constitution. It's no frame-up of ours. Let it all go to pieces. There's
still the comparative climate of Vermont, Colorado and California to
think of. Did you see Menken's statistical guest [*sic*] of the worst state
in the Union in the last Mercury?' Photograph enclosed.

F12.49   [1 January 1935, Key West, Fla.] *R. F. & J. B.*, pp. 182–84.
'. . . there was a government once that began to put itself into the people,
the object of its activity, to stiffen them so that there would be sure to be
something there to govern. It kept doing for them out of the taxes till a
day came when there [was] nothing positive enough left to tax. The last
known it was making farmers pay taxes on any abandoned farms in their
neighborhood as well as on their own. It was forcing the rich into the
office of tax collector so that they could pay out of their own means what
they failed to collect. The thing ran awhile longer before it went to pieces
and began all over. The pieces were a long time lying around loose. I can
just see a little boy named Freddy Ordway looking at me in the class
where we studied about that country. A government must feel a funny
lost feeling when it has nobody but its own reflection to govern. . . .'

F12.50   15 June 1945, Ripton, Vt. *R. F. & J. B.*, pp. 203–4. '. . . whether
we like the philosophy or not we can't refuse the comfort of knowing
that any time we please we can loaf six months of a year at twenty five
dollars a week. Twenty five a week is more than I ever earned till I was
forty. We old-time shoe-string starters mustn't ask everybody to be
like us.'

F13   1912. Autograph drawings. 'Three-Acre Desideratum' (fanciful map
of land near Vancouver, B.C.). [Beaconsfield, Bucks., Eng., *ca.* 1912.] In
pencil on two oblong leaves of white wove paper measuring 183 × 307 mm.;
edges trimmed. Published in *R F & J B* (illus.).

   John and Margaret Bartlett had moved to Vancouver, British Columbia,
where Bartlett worked for the two daily papers and became acting editor
of the Point Grey *Gazette,* a weekly. Frost was intrigued by the idea of

Vancouver and seriously considered joining the Bartletts there. He drew
these fantasy maps of the adjacent land he and the Bartletts would acquire.
Acre A was to be the Bartletts' property centered by 'Salmon Trout Brook'
with 'Bridge of Size'; on one side 'Palatial Residence with Mansard Roof.
Home of Acting Editor of Point Grey Gazette.' On the other, 'Gate to
Knowledge. Exact Replica of Gate to Harvard Yard', 'Cider Orchard', 'Bee
Hives. Honey for Bears', 'Four-Bear Den' in a 'Rocky Fastness' with the
note 'Bears of a kind not addicted to faring on children over 6 years old,
i.e., paying half or whole fare.' Farther to the left a 'Chinese Joss House.
Religious Advantages'; also, 'Hydrant fire protection', 'Electric Carline 5¢
fare to Vancouver', and 'I am willing to pay $100 for the front acre. The
others ought not to cost so much.' The other map, 'Acre B', represents his
own more modest requirements: 'Lean-to Sanctuary (My study)', 'Cow
Pasture', 'Gold Diggings', 'Grove of Sequoia or Redwoods', 'Undismal
Swamp (No Mosquitos)', 'Potato Patch', 'Nine Bean Rows (See poem by
Yates [*sic*] in Oxford Book of Verse.)'

F14   1913–1915. FROST, Elinor. 3 ALSs. To Margaret [Mrs. John]
Bartlett. [Beaconsfield, Bucks., Eng.] 18 March and 3 July 1913 [and Beth-
lehem, N.H., *ca.* June 1915]. All published, *Selected Letters,* nos. 45a, 52a,
120a.

F15   1947 and 1949. 2ALSs. RF to Margaret [Mrs. John] Bartlett. Cambridge, Mass., 26 December 1947 and 22 November 1949. Both published,
Selected Letters, nos. 412, 418.
    Answering Mrs. Bartlett's request to publish the correspondence between
Robert Frost and John Bartlett. Frost asks her to wait until he is dead to
publish.

F16   1912–1915. 6ALSs. RF to Thomas Bird Mosher. Various places (as
below), 1912 to 1915.

F16.1   19 February 1912, Plymouth, N.H. Published, *Selected Letters,*
no. 34. With the letter is included a fair copy of 'Reluctance' (printed
first in *Youth's Companion,* 7 November 1912) which had yet to be published when this letter was written. The poem was seen in manuscript by
Mosher, who wrote to Frost requesting permission to purchase it for one
of his publications. Mosher did use the poem as a prelude to a catalogue

of Mosher imprints in 1913, after it had been collected in *A Boy's Will* (1913).

F16.2   4 March 1912, Plymouth, N.H. Published, *Selected Letters,* no. 35. The letter tells Mosher 'my whole story of the poem Reluctance. It was The Atlantic that had returned it and left me in that dejection your letter lifted me out of. . . . The Companion took the poem. Following hard upon that piece of good luck The Forum took another poem which I call My November Guest. . . . I do not say that either of them heralds a new force in literature. Indeed I think I have others still under cover that more nearly represent what I am going to be. . . .'

F16.3   20 January 1914, Beaconsfield, Bucks., Eng. Published, *Selected Letters,* no. 71. RF writes of the publication of *North of Boston* and urges Mosher not to give up publishing *The Bibelot:* 'I sometimes dream you may use it yet to foster something very American in literature. . . . "Poetry" (Chicago) hasn't done anything but foster Pound and a few free-verse friends. I wonder if you noticed the comparison [Ford Madox] Hueffer instituted in it between [Walter] De La Mare and F. S. Flint. . . . Flint belongs to Pound's clique. Hueffer patronizes it en bloc.' He complains of Mrs. Nutt's strictures against publishing without reference to the firm of David Nutt as intermediary.

F16.4   27 July 1914, Ledbury, Eng. Published, *Selected Letters,* no. 83. RF writes of reviews of *North of Boston* and of being an American poet almost unknown in his own country.

F16.5   October 1914, Gloucestershire, Eng. Published, *Selected Letters,* no. 89. Arranges terms for a publication with Mosher, 'All I have in mind is to reach through you an American public. So long as you get me read I shall ask no questions about royalties. Mrs. Nutt however is another matter. She would say that as one of her indentured poets I have no right to be corresponding with an American publisher even in friendship.'

F16.6   22 March 1915, Littleton, N.H. Unpublished. Proposing a meeting.

F16a   1915–1916. 6 ALSs. RF to Walter Prichard Eaton (dramatic critic, essayist, poet). Franconia, N.H., 1915–1916.

F16a.1   15 July 1915, Franconia, N.H. Published, *Selected Letters,* no.
125. RF praises Eaton's *Barn Doors and Byways* and hopes to make his
acquaintance since the Eatons summer near Franconia. '. . . if left to its
own tendencies, I believe in time . . . [poetry] would exclude everything
but love and the moon. That's why it's none the worse for a little rough
handling once in a while. Do it a violence, I say, if you have to make it
aware of what's going on around it. . . .'

F16a.2   18 September 1915, Franconia, N.H. Published *Selected Letters,*
no. 135 '. . . You don't mention my having had a whole article to myself
in The Atlantic as among my signal honors; from which I infer that you
don't like the article. I wonder why. Others seem to ignore it on purpose.
I wonder what's the matter.' Suggests a meeting for lunch in New York.

F16a.3   31 August 1915, Franconia, N.H. Unpublished. 'I hope it is to be
as you lead me to expect, if for no other reason, because I had so much
rather talk than write to you. I will write if I have to, but oh circumstances have conspired of late to make letter writing a burden like the
grasshopper. I shall be on the look out for you on the road that comes up
from Willow Bridge. And as Shelley says Come soon.'

F16a.4   25 November 1915, Franconia, N.H. RF sends Eaton a fair copy
of 'Putting in the Seed' (MI, 1916) with a covering note hoping for another meeting. The poem has two variant readings from the published
text:
   line 11: On through] 1st; And with] MS
   12: soil] 1st; ground] MS

F16a.5   [8 February 1916, Franconia, N.H.] Unpublished. '. . . This
house has been twice warmed by word from you once in the friend's letter you sent and once in the Christmas card and still no thanks from me.
I'm a bad person. But I don't want to write letters: I want to see you
you . . .'

F16a.6   [15 July 1916, Franconia, N.H.] Unpublished. 'The Ann Arbo-
reals seem less bent on Williams than they were on you. We know what's
good for them, however, and must see that they get it. Don't you want to
write me a little note about Williams that I could show Burton [Marion

LeRoy Burton, President of the University of Michigan]? I mean one free from Barkis jokes.'

F17   1915–1918. 3 ALSs. RF to Alice Brown (New England prose writer). Various places, dates (as below). Unpublished.

F17.1   15 January 1915, Methuen, Mass. RF thanks Miss Brown for a letter, 'It is less in need of an answer now that Miss [Amy] Lowell has arranged matters with you. As I understand it, several of us are to read to you on Feb. 2. Count on me to do my best with pleasure.'

F17.2   26 May 1916 [Franconia, Mass.]. Thanks Miss Brown for one of her books with a fulsome inscription.

F17.3   2 November 1918, Amherst, Mass. 'I must accept your congratulations though you are tardier with them than I am with the books I was going to inscribe. But we are both poets and I don't know what easement belongs to us as such if it isn't from being punctual. Yes, I have been a full professor at Amherst from the moment I came here year before last.'
    Amy Lowell had compared RF's poetic tales with Alice Brown's prose stories and rather tactlessly added that Miss Brown had 'a rare sense of humor,' implying that RF had none.

F18   1924–1938. 11 ALSs. and 1AMSs. RF to Robert Silliman Hillyer (American poet). Various places (South Shaftsbury, Vt.; Amherst, Mass.; Monrovia, Calif.; Franconia, N.H.; Key West, Fla.; San Antonio, Tex.; Concord Corners, Vt.), 25 January 1924 to 12 August 1938. Unpublished.
    Robert Frost and Robert Hillyer met in Cambridge, Mass., about 1917, just before the Harvard Press published Hillyer's first book, *Sonnets and Other Lyrics*. The two poets adopted the habit of taking long walks together, and it was Hillyer who proposed Frost's walking tour through northwestern Connecticut. Later, in 1935, Hillyer arranged a reading by Frost in the Morris Gray series at Harvard. In the August 1936 issue of *Atlantic Monthly*, Hillyer published a poem entitled 'A Letter to Robert Frost,' an embarrassingly fulsome work that inspired Granville Hicks' parody, 'A Letter to Robert Hillyer.' The parody was turned down by Bernard de Voto, then editor-in-chief of *Saturday Review of Literature*, because of certain unfavorable comments concerning himself. Hicks' poem was published as a review of 'A Letter to Robert Frost' in *New Republic* (20 October

1937). In 1934 Hillyer was awarded the Pulitzer Prize for collected verse. He was long associated with the English Department of Harvard.

F18.1   [25 January 1924] South Shaftsbury, Vt. Frost grants Hillyer's request for a copy of 'The Census-Taker.' 'You made no mistake with me in singling it out from my others. It's one I have had complacent moments over. . . .' Typescript of the poem present, signed at the end 'Robert Frost'.

F18.2   [12 March 1924] Amherst, Mass. Reply to a request that he should read at the New England Poetry Series for the 1924 / 1925 season. 'But don't tell me you want me to read in public for you. Not really. Why, you wouldn't come yourself. . . .'

F18.3   24 July 1924, South Shaftsbury, Vt. Accepts the invitation to read in October 1924.

F18.4   [4 February 1931] Amherst, Mass. Frost is annoyed that Holt will not send Hillyer a copy of *Collected Poems* (1930) for review. 'What's the use of writing books if my publishers aren't going to let anybody see and review them? But patience to prevent that murmur soon replies, You used stoutly to maintain that you wrote your books for yourself: you didn't care whether anybody else read them or not. If I said that I lied. And then you have to remember that when I said it, if I said it, nobody else did read my books or seemed likely to read them. I can't be held [for] lofty sentiments wrung from me by suffering.'

F18.5   [28 September 1932] Monrovia, Calif. The holograph poem, 'A Restoration':

A Restoration

In the dark moment on the Eastern Stairs,
I had one of my characteristic scares.
On feeling in my soul I missed my name.
(I'd swear I had it on me when I came)
'Twas when the gods began to brag of theirs.
Without my name in this place, I could see

I should be no one—simply nobodee.
Incontinently I became outpourous:
O Ra Rah Rah, Osiris and O Horus,
Oh let my name be given back to me!
'You're sure you didn't lose it through a hole,'
Osire suggested. 'N'Osire it was stole.'
A female voice piped up 'What's all the crisis?
Is something missing?' I replied 'Aye, Aye—sis,
My name is missing. Someone's picked my soul.'
On the last staircase, my but what a row.
Someone to calm me asked me with a bow
Was this nym I was after just my pseudo.
I only shouted louder 'No, my Kudo.
I want my name back and I want it now.'
The Ra Rah Rah King summoned Robert Hillyer.
'Do something to abate this clamor will yer?
Find and restore this fellow's Kudonym.'
And Robert did it, glory be to him.
Oh what a friend to have for my familiar.

                                                    R. Frost

The inspiration for this comic poem was Hillyer's *The Coming Forth by Day* (1922), a metrical arrangement of parts of *The Book of the Dead* with a prefatory essay on Egyptian religion. Hillyer had sent Frost a copy, and this poem, in retaliation, is based on the concept that the one essential necessary to achieve immortality in Egypt was recollection of one's name as a staircase between the two worlds.

F18.6   5 September 1934, Franconia, N.H. A letter of congratulations to Hillyer on his receipt of the Pulitzer Prize and his election to the American Institute of Arts and Letters. 'I have cared for your poetry a long time now. It must be nearly twenty years ago that I visited Kent School with a volume of yours in my hand to get me into the president's office. So your reward from the Pulitzers was in some sense my reward also.'

F18.7   22 March 1935, Key West, Fla. Accepting Hillyer's invitation to read in the Morris Gray series at Harvard, 17 April 1935. 'It is good of you not to let Harvard forget the old regular poet whom she taught Latin and Greek. I was just thinking I might have to resort to eccentricities if I hoped to attract her attention.'

F18.8   9 February 1937, San Antonio, Tex. The chief matter of this letter is Hillyer's rescue of Frost after his failure to keep an engagement to read the Phi Beta Kappa poem at the time of the Harvard Tercentenary. Hillyer read his 'Letter to James Buell Munn' as a quick replacement. 'I have been on the point of thanking you all fall for coming to my rescue if it could be called to *my* rescue. I'll bet it didn't keep many of the starchy stiffs from crossing me off for an Ethelred the Unready. . . .'

F18.9   16 June 1937, South Shaftsbury, Vt. Congratulating Hillyer on his appointment to the Boylston Professorship at Harvard and pointing out the similarity of their poetic ideals. 'We must try to keep in step with each other and the music if only to show how much not writing free verse has done to preserve our time sense. . . . We mustn't strut in our latest honors and we mustn't in our triumph over the Imagists.'

F18.10   15 September 1937, Concord Corners, Vt. Thanks and appreciation for a copy of Hillyer's book, *A Letter to Robert Frost.* 'The book is too much mine for my praise of it to be of value. . . . The whole scheme is a felicity. It yields what they call a good time. Odd, but in the days when I first knew you, I kept telling George Browne (of Browne & Nichols) there ought to be some more epistolae. . . . My point is that while Browne and I were vainly looking about for someone to write us our epistolae there you were under our very noses the very one to have written them as is proved by your having written them now.' George Browne has also recommended to Frost that he use the spelling 'intervale' for the title of *Mountain Interval.*

F18.11   20 July 1938, South Shaftsbury, Vt. The last two letters are concerned with a plan to have Frost join the faculty of the Harvard Latin Department. 'I feel as if I might find rest there if anywhere this side of urn burial. It is a dream: but one to the realization of which there is at least one great obstacle. I mean my having been elected to the Board of Overseers. I have it plainly in writing that no one not even a seer can be at once an Overseer and an employee of the University. I am prepared to hear you say next, as I am always hearing in this irregular life of mine, that probably an exception could be made in my case. But I am tired of living outside the law. . . . So that unless we can think of waiting a year or so and then proposing my resignation from the Board I should say it was all off. . . . I had in mind a half course in all the small Latin poems that get translated into English verse. It would be for boys who had had not less than three years of Latin and who could make their own translations preferably into verse or at worst free verse. The course would be designated: Translation of Latin Poems into English verses not to be preserved. . . . My attitude in the reading would of choice and perforce be worldly rather than scholarly. But there's the rub and the second obstacle. . . . First off the Latinists might think they were willing to adopt me for the cheap public support I might bring them in their decline . . . but will they in their fastidious scholarship be able to stand me on my terms for any length of time? You understand the whole point of my plan would be to treat the Latin poems as if they were still a rather accessible off hand pleasure for a number of people. . . .'

F18.12   12 August 1938, South Shaftsbury, Vt. 'Listen! I have scared myself with what I have set going. It won't do for me to profess Latinity. I have been warned off already. . . . The course I propose may not belong in the Latin Department anyway. What a pity I didn't think of it for the English Department. It could have been the very same thing, Latin verse treated worldly rather than scholarly. . . . It would have looked quaint in the catalogue as the one course in English with a prerequisite of three or four years of Latin. But it is too late to talk of this now. The Latin Department has been roused up and now it is the Latin Department or nothing. Let it be nothing. . . . I must not bedevil my declining years with a wantonly falsified position anywhere. I am in a reckless mood and a dangerous one not least of all to myself left thus lying around loose in the world. Take care of me because I am   Very much yours   Robert'.

F19   1925–1959. 4 ALSs and 1TLs (RF) and 2 ALSs (Elinor Frost). To Elizabeth Shepley Sergeant (author of *Robert Frost: The Trial by Existence* [New York, 1960]). Various places (as below), 1925 to 1959.

F19.1   RF to Elizabeth Sergeant. [Spring 1925, South Shaftsbury, Vt.] Quoted in *RF: The Trial by Existence*, p. xx. Elizabeth Sergeant had written a literary portrait of RF, 'A Good Greek out of New England,' for the *New Republic* (30 Sept. 1925). Before it was submitted, she sent the manuscript to him for approval. This letter is his response to the article, 'Done with absolute discretion and as by one intellectual being for another. . . . If you err at all it is on the right side, i. e., in my favor. I shan't think less of you for that. . . . I like particularly the way you got round my recantations of my confession to being a sensibilitist. Now things are beautifully mixed up—the way I always like to leave them. . . . Keep the crooked straightness whatever you drop for the editor. A crooked straightness in character is my favorite just now—an absolutely abandoned zigzag that goes straight to the mark. . . .'

F19.2–3   EWF to Elizabeth Sergeant. 1 September and [21] September [1927], Sugar Hill, N.H. In both letters Mrs. Frost makes plans for Elizabeth Sergeant's visit to them in South Shaftsbury. They have just given up the idea of going abroad. 'We had stayed on in the hay fever region about two weeks longer than usual, and joyfully saw, from day to day, that Robert was not having it much of any. Just the merest touch. But because of that touch . . . we drove up yesterday.' When the Frosts return to South Shaftsbury they will try to find a farm where she can stay for a month or two. 'Marjorie's health is still a great anxiety, and the reason why we are uncertain what we ought to do, and that we do not have any real peace anywhere.'

F19.4   RF to Elizabeth Sergeant. [*Ca.* September 1927, South Shaftsbury, Vt.] Quoted in *RF: Trial by Existence,* p. xxi. Inviting her to come for a visit, 'we will knock on our heads . . . and see what we can scare up in the way of people to review and buy your book [*Fire under the Andes* (1927), in which the RF portrait was reprinted] and mine [probably *West-Running Brook,* as yet unpublished]. We've got to start right now and get some publicity for ourselves and publisher.' He writes of alienation from many of his friends, 'And some of them get into such tragic messes that I feel as if it were my proverbs failing me and not just my friends. . . . My prophetic soul told me I was in for it forty five years ago come yesterday on the Cliff House beach at San Francisco. Is it not written in a poem of mine ['Once By the Pacific']. The one thing I boast I can't be is disillusioned. Anything I ever thought I still think. Any poet I ever liked I still like. It is noticeable. I go back on no one. It is merely that others go back on me. I take nothing back. I don't grow. My favorite theory is that we are given this speed swifter than any stream of light time or water for the sole purpose of standing still like a water beetle in any stream of light time or water off any shore we please.'

F19.5   RF to Elizabeth Sergeant. 28 July 1935, Boulder, Colorado. Unpublished. In the summer of 1935, Miss Sergeant had arranged for RF to give a poetry reading in Santa Fe, N.M., where she was doing Pueblo Indian research. The Frosts' daughter Marjorie had died the year before. RF writes of the coming trip to Santa Fe, '. . . I'm as sure to disappoint my rivals for your friendship as you are sure to have over advertised me with them. You have to remember they are not disinterested. They have plenty to gain in being disappointed. Never mind. One of the nicest things about me is my willingness not to do very well on trial. Who am I that I should always expect to succeed. A truly modest person can even accept being an anticlimax. . . . I have half hoped to bring Elinor with me, but she is not up to more than what she is in Boulder for, namely to be a few days with the child of the daughter we lost. The whole world has sadder associations than she can bear. . . . Never mind this either. We have a toughness. We mean to get over it just in time to die ourselves.' Envelope present.

F19.6   RF to Elizabeth Sergeant. [26 April 1941] Kenyon College, Gambier, Ohio. Unpublished. 'I had become bad enough as a letter writer when Shuster's Best Letters of All Time [M. L. Schuster (ed.), *A Treasury of the World's Great Letters* (New York, 1940)] finished me off entirely with self-consciousness. . . . I'm a four-weeks trespasser on the preserve of the Kenyon-Review-Southern-Quarterly combination. To render me nugatory they keep driving me with overwhelming southern courtesy to professional ball games however inaccessible. . . . It all grew out of a weakness I have for not correcting any impression people may have that I was once an athlete. The dramatist Terrence had that effect on me. Not a thing a me alienum puts. All the same I am never as much at home among clixters as I am in a ball park.' Envelope present.

F19.7   RF to Elizabeth Sergeant. TLS. 11 September [*ca.* 1959], Ripton, Vt. Unpublished. Written at the time Miss Sergeant was preparing the text of *Trial by Existence*. 'Isn't it lucky we caught such a serious error as that about Preston Shirley. He was my greatest and only very intellectual friend at Dartmouth in 1892. Though a frail boy and always a sufferer from ailments, he was the life of the place in many ways, full of old family and Dartmouth traditions. . . . We sat up all night carrying on and saying good-bye to each other the night before I ran away. He was the only person I said good-bye to. . . . I don't know how I misled you into confusing him with Louis Cox who was no special friend of mine at all. Louis Cox became Chief Justice of the Supreme Court in Massachusetts. . . . I am tempted to go and write Preston Shirley's biography now.'

F20   1936–1948. 16 ALSs, 2 TMSs, 1 document. The letters: RF to Earle J. Bernheimer. Various places (Amherst, Boston, Cambridge, Mass., and Ripton, Vt.), dated between 2 March 1936 and 10 September 1948.

In *Selected Letters of Robert Frost,* Thompson provides an account on pp. 442–43 of the variable friendship between Robert Frost and the collector Earle J. Bernheimer. Ten of the letters (F20.1–F20.10) in this group were published in *Selected Letters.*

F20.1   19 April 1937. From Elinor Frost (SL 339-a)
F20.2   18 November 1939 (SL 376)
F20.3   1 June 1941 (SL 383)
F20.4   22 March 1944 (SL 397)
F20.5   7 March 1944 (SL 402)
F20.6   10 June 1944 (SL 404)
F20.7   8 August 1945 (SL 405)
F20.8   14 January 1947 (SL 407)
F20.9   16 October 1947 (SL 411)
F20.10   10 September 1948 (SL 414)

F20.11   2 March 1936, n.p. Unpublished. 'I have as many addresses as some rascals have aliases. That bibliography is being done by the Jones Library of Amherst Mass. Charles Green and Shubrick Clymer are at work on it. Carefulness makes them slow.'

F20.12   8 November 1938, Boston, Mass. Unpublished. 'One serious thing or another has kept me from writing you. . . . The most serious has been my total disinclination to do anything life-like. But I shall get going again. . . . I of course want to do anything I can to make my books more interesting to you.'

F20.13   22 March 1944, Cambridge, Mass. Unpublished. 'I sent you a telegram yesterday. . . . The Western Union girl said we couldn't use a word like "joke" in a war time telegram; said "joke" made it social. Big row. Kathleen [Morrison] scolded, then I took the telephone and scolded some more. Wanted to know who was to decide for us about the American language. Result: telegram was accepted but sullenly so I was afraid it might not go forward. . . . Ray Nash is slow with his catalogue but you shall have your Masque of Reason pretty soon. . . .' The telegram is with the letter: 'Had begun to think something like that so don't worry. Good joke between friends.'

F20.14   [*Ca.* May–June 1944] Cambridge, Mass. Unpublished. 'The Dartmouth people are anxious enough to get your collection—never doubt that. . . . They will be found just as appreciative of what you can bestow as the United States Government in the person of Joseph Auslander. . . . I will mark on your list the items I particularly want them to see at this time and you can send them . . . to Mr. Ray Nash. . . . He is the great authority up there on all such matters and the one who had had most to do with my having been made the George Ticknor Fellow in the Humanities. I will add to the exhibit in your name the original manuscript . . . of the new blank-verse Mask [*sic*] of Reason which you haven't read yet.'

F20.15   14 December 1944, Cambridge, Mass. Unpublished. 'Here is a real rarity for you for Christmas [an early draft of 'Provide, Provide' (not present)]. . . . The Holts are doing a last minute card for Christmas ['An Unstamped Letter in Our Rural Letter Box'] of which I will save you all the imprints. . . .'

F20.16   [*Ca.* March 1947] N.p. Unpublished. '. . . We and the Holts and Joe Blumenthal are out with a new book [*Steeple Bush*]. . . . The second Masque [*A Masque of Mercy*] is in the hands of the Holts and The Atlantic Monthly who will publish it simultaneously in October [printed in the November 1947 issue]. We are reading the proofs this very day. The manuscript from which Kay typed the copy . . . is to be yours as I promised. . . . Let's not talk about absolute first drafts. There's no such thing I suspect. I know I always wipe my traces out behind me. What you get will be a first in the true sense, in my sense, of the word. . . .'

F20.17   26 October 1945. TMSs. 'A Preface to "The Death of the Hired Man" for Whit Burnett High School Textbook' (title supplied at the foot in Kathleen Morrison's hand). Signed, 'R. F.', with the note, 'I don't know whether this was used / or not.' in Frost's hand.

Text: 'In asking me to preface my poem, Mr. Burnett's idea is no doubt to have me bring it up to date by connecting it with some such thing as National Labor Relations. I am always glad to give my poems every extraneous help possible. The employee here depicted is no longer numberous enough to be dealt with statistically by the Departments of Economics and Sociology. Nevertheless I should like to flatter myself that it is at least partly for his sake that the revolution is being brought on. In conclusion I beg to protest that it was with no such thoughts as these that the poem was written. By the way, it's in blank verse, not free verse.'

Whit Burnett was editor of *This Is My Best* (New York: Dial Press, 1942; New York: World Publishing Co., 1945) and *The World's Best* (New York: Dial Press, 1950) in which selections of RF's work were included.

F20.18   16 May 1946. TMSs. [A tribute to Ernest Silver.] Signed, 'Robert Frost' with the note, 'Mr. Ernest Silver was head of Pinkerton Academy / at Derry when I taught there and went to be head of Plymouth / N.H. Normal School taking me with him. / Robert Frost'. 9-line text.

F20.19   26 April 1943. Printed document accomplished in manuscript, informing Robert Frost of his election to membership in *The Saturday Club*. Inscribed at top, 'For Earle to keep for me R. F.'

F21   1937–1938. 14 ALSs. RF to Robert S. Newdick (professor of English at Ohio State University). Various places (as below), 8 June 1937 to 12 February 1939. Unpublished, excepting letter 20 July 1938.

With Robert Frost's approval, Professor Newdick was gathering material for the poet's biography. Newdick died suddenly while the work was still in an early stage.

F21.1   [8 June 1937, Amherst, Mass.] 'I just want to ask you to look sharply into the question of the Class Hymn [Lawrence High School, class of 1892]. You are probably right, but my recollection would have been that the [Lawrence High School] Bulletin with the poem and all our graduation essays in it wasn't out till after the exercises were over; in which case it would be in behind the Order of Exercises by a nose. My wife's mother wrote the music for the Hymn.' A copy of the program of graduation exercises in the Barrett Library (C1) attributes the music to Beethoven. RF must mean that Mrs. White made the arrangement by setting his words to Beethoven's music.

F21.2   20 September [1937], Concord Corners, Vt. '. . . I feel disposed to make you an offer about those poems and letters in Huntington [Library, San Marino, Calif.]. . . . I will write you a free pass to visit them if you will go out there and pass critically not only on the handwriting, but on the paper water mark (if any) and general physique of the poem, I had a love once. (What a name! What a subject!) Nothing not really important could bother me more than to have that thing accepted of fools as mine. Photostat copies wont do what I want. The emergency calls for detective work. . . .' The Huntington Library had acquired in 1929 some manuscript material from the files of *The Independent* that purported to be the work of Robert Frost. Most annoying to Frost were two poems, 'Sea Dream' and 'I Had a Love Once'; the latter with the signature 'Robert Lee Frost'. Prof. Newdick examined the manuscripts at Frost's instigation and pronounced them to be spurious; however, there is still some question of their possible authenticity (*cf.* Thompson, *The Early Years,* pp. 530–32). With original envelope.

F21.3   11 October 1937, Amherst, Mass. 'Now you make me feel like a green apple you boys are determined to eat. I warned [Wilbert] Snow and [Lawrance] Thompson I wasn't ripe enough. But I suppose they are the first threat can claim an option on me. You have poor luck. Never mind, remember all the literature Dante got out of the Peach he couldn't have. I hate being hard on a friend. Needs must.' With original envelope.

F21.4   [26 November 1937, Amherst, Mass.] 'I forgot to say how confident you are of my infallability. Why don't you assume that I may be mistaken about Memphis? I wouldn't intend to be. I hate the definition of poetry that it is just mistakes—licensed mistakes . . . perhaps I shan't be proved as wrong in the end as one who sets up to be no scholar and no authority deserves to be.' With original envelope.

F21.5   14 December 1937, Gainesville, Fla. 'I must write you a word of reassurance before you set out on your errand of mercy in far California [to examine the manuscripts at Huntington]. I don't want to trouble you too much about your thoughts of me, but I want to trouble you enough to make them long long thoughts. You mustn't let your partizanship hasten you to heroic conclusions. Slow slow. . . . You must be religiously careful not to make me anything but what I am. Of course I know you are resolved on that. But permit me to caution you. . . . The great test is going to be your handling passim my literary quality. You can see what a confusion the critics make of it in my Recognition [*Recognition of Robert Frost* (New York: Holt, 1937), edited by Richard Thornton] How without seeming to notice it are you going to bring order out of that chaos?' With original envelope.

F21.6   [November 1937.] The letter is written on a typed copy of a poem, 'Death Song of the Last American Indian,' sent to Frost by New-dick with a note appended, 'Isn't this poem yours?' The poem is imitative of the style and meter of Longfellow's *The Song of Hiawatha*. Beneath, Frost has written, 'No, I didn't write this, nor does it seem at all like me. I am unaware of ever having deliberately taken up another person's jingle. You must be very careful in your ascriptions. . . . And in other ascriptions too. I feel the great danger of what you are trying to do with me. The word "deeply" for example in your last inquiry. What books of Tacitus was I so deeply studying. I never did anything deeply. 'Tis ever thus with the biographer: he will be making the most of everything. You are going to have me a classical scholar. I'm no scholar. You're one. You must be slow enough with your biography to get the real me through your head. No fabrications good or bad. Sorry I can't be dead and out of your way. Having me alive to deal with must make your task so very much harder. What guess work all appreciation is. In the Recognition book [*Recognition of Robert Frost* (1937). A Barrett copy (593052) has the inscription, 'For Hilda and Vera [Harvey] / if they will please remember / that I didn't write it or even / edit it.—Their Uncle Rob / Gainesville, Florida / December 25 1937'.] you will read that I have no sense of humor, that I have a sense of humor. That I have no philosophy, that I have a philosophy. I am praised for having and for not having both. Also I am blamed. Cheer up, you can go no further wrong than the best of them. . . . The older you are the better you will understand my foolishness.'

F21.7   [28 December 1937] Gainesville, Fla. Frost refers again to the two poems in the Huntington Library and offers a solution to their authorship. 'It is of course preposterous to ascribe either Sea Dreams or I Had a Love Once to me. They are not in my handwriting, they are not in my wife's handwriting, I didn't sign them, she didn't sign them and I deny having written them. That ought to be enough for gentlemen though scholars. You know how to talk their technical language to these specialists and I miss my guess if you don't get them to throw the two damned spuriosa out of the Huntington Library or at least separate the two from the poems undeniably and admittedly mine. . . . You can't tell what might happen in a house like the Wards' [editors of *The Independent*] where the editor [the Rev. William Hayes Ward] and his two spinster sisters [one, Susan Hayes Ward, was poetry editor] were all sentimental about poems and poets for the Independent: but my guess is the two sisters took turns in taking possession of the manuscript spoils from the office and when there was something so good (in their opinion) they both wanted it, one kept the original and the other made a copy. They may have been careless about the authors names and written some in later even years later from memory when the author got famous. . . . The fact is I didn't write the poems and you are in a fair way to establish it. I wonder if either of the poems ever appeared in print in The Independent. That might be amusing to look into. . . . To find either printed as by someone else would be a fine blow to Huntington pride.' Lawrance Thompson believes the poems to be very early ones of Frost and the manuscripts, in the hand of Elinor Frost who sent these fair copies to *The Independent*. Frost remained adamant in his denial of authorship. With original envelope. Together with a carbon typescript of the two poems made by Prof. Newdick.

F21.8   18 January 1938, Gainesville, Fla. Newdick found other of Frost's early poem manuscripts in the Huntington collection and sent him a list. 'The only poems in your list I should be curious to see are Clear and Colder, Genealogical, Poem incomplete, and To a Moth Seen in Winter. . . . I have a faintly pleasant recollection of at least two, Clear and Colder and To a Moth Seen in Winter. The last is in blank verse isn't it? Or is it in rhymed couplets? I made it walking down a foggy icy mountain one thaw in March the year we were at Plymouth. Not everything is as easy to date as that. I wonder which version of A Black Cottage you found out there. I did two versions, in and around 1905–6, one in rhyme which I lost on purpose as a failure and the other that came down with some changes into North of Boston. . . . As a matter of fact a number of my poems could have three or four dates apiece on them. Reluctance except for one very important change (which wouldn't you like to know!) is a very old poem. Most of your list is recognizable through the disguise of tentative titles. What's A Summer's Garden? A Girl's Garden? Then 1897 is a funny date for it.'

It is curious that Frost did not recall 'Clear and Colder' with more certainty; it was printed in *Direction* (Autumn 1934) and collected in *A Further Range* (1936). He was apparently pleased with 'To a Moth Seen in Winter,' which was subsequently printed in the *Virginia Quarterly Review* (Spring 1942) and collected in *A Witness Tree* (1942). 'The Black Cottage,' as noted, was printed in *North of Boston* (1914), and 'A Girl's Garden,' in *Mountain Interval* (1916). Perhaps it was the earlier versions that Frost did not remember. 'Genealogical' is printed in *Selected Letters,* pp. 604–6. With original envelope.

F21.9   2 June 1938, Amherst, Mass. Arranging for a meeting with New-dick to be combined with speaking engagements in Ohio. With original envelope.

F21.10   2 June 1938, Amherst, Mass. 'I should be glad if Mr. Hamlin would let you have copies of any letters of mine he may have in his keeping. I can't help wondering what they are like myself. I have said all sorts of careless things in my letters till lately.' With original envelope.

F21.11   [20 July 1938, South Shaftsbury, Vt.] This letter is quoted in Thompson, *The Years of Triumph,* pp. 702–3, having to do with Frost's resignation from the Amherst faculty in 1938, of which Thompson writes in detail on pp. 700ff. The version offered Newdick in this letter promulgates the notion that President Stanley King of Amherst had been supplementing Frost's salary anonymously out of his own pocket and had come to regret that gratuity. 'King has been so mysterious both in his determination to get me out and in refusing to give his reasons that I have arrived at him as my guess as to what rich alumnus was my keeper. . . . He is done with me partly because I haven't shown my appreciation by coming to hear him talk in Chapel and faculty meeting. . . .' Thompson has proved this to be an erroneous account of the actual circumstances.

F21.12   17 September 1938, Elizabethtown, N.Y. 'I'm afraid I couldn't
let you do what you propose to do with my poems on the radio. It would
drive me crazy to have parts of them turned into prose. It can't be you
quite realize what a poem is. Any translation hurts it. And there is absolutely no excuse for translating a poem into other and worse words in its
own language. What's more I am not ambitious to use the radio in the
present state of its programs for the spread of my work. I have a very low
opinion of the people running it, which is only confirmed by the neces-
sity you are no doubt under of mangling my work to make an education
hour after their hearts. . . .' With original envelope.

F21.13   2 December 1938 [Boston, Mass.] Outlining his lecture schedule
and thanking Newdick for a mutually successful meeting in Ohio. 'The
point I tried to make was that I was a very hard person to make out . . .
I might easily be most deceiving when most bent on telling the truth.'

F21.14   12 February 1938, Coconut Grove, Fla. Describing a trip to
Cuba with the poet Paul Engle and his wife. 'I am still at a loss what
harmless to do with myself. Perhaps I had better seek money. . . .' With
original envelope.

F22.1–6   1941–1951. 6 ALSs. RF to his nieces Hilda and Vera Harvey.
Various places (Cambridge, Boston, Ripton, Vt.), December 1941 to December 1951. Unpublished.
    The correspondence is primarily concerned with Christmas greetings,
thanks for gifts, and inscribing of books for his nieces.

F23   1912. FROST, Elinor. ALs. To Mrs. Harry Brown. Beaconsfield,
Bucks., Eng., 25 October 1912. Unpublished.
    Robert Frost had brought his young family to England in September
1912 and found a cottage for them in Beaconsfield. Mrs. Frost describes the
town, the house, and the surrounding countryside to her friend, Mrs.
Brown. She describes her impression of the English people, 'The people are
very polite, but they are very different from Americans. I would say that
the majority I have had an opportunity to observe seem inferior to me, if I
was not afraid of being prejudiced. . . . Lesley and Irma are attending a
private school, and I am teaching Carol and Marjorie myself. . . .' This
letter was written the day before the MS of *A Boy's Will* was accepted for
publication by David Nutt and Company, London.

F24   1913. ALs. RF to Harold Monro (poet and editor of *Poetry and Drama*). Beaconsfield, Bucks., Eng., 25 November 1913. Unpublished.

Two of Frost's poems, 'The Fear' and 'A Hundred Collars,' were printed in *Poetry and Drama* (Dec. 1913); later collected in *North of Boston* (1914). Frost writes to the editor, Harold Monro, about line 67 of 'The Fear': 'About the MS. The proof is beautifully clean. I agree with you that the line you stumble over ought to contain the word seemed. But *"Nothing." It seemed to come from far along the road,* is too long by a foot. The original MS. read *"Nothing." It seemed to come from far away*. What would you think of that? *"Nothing." It came from well along the road,* I have thought of to keep certain solid words I like, but I object to "well". Without more ado, will you let me ask you to decide for me?'

The poem as printed in *Poetry and Drama* had the second suggested reading; however, the version printed in *North of Boston* had the third reading, ' "Nothing." It came from well along the road.'

F25   1914. FROST, Elinor. ALs. To her sister, Leona White Harvey. Gloucestershire, Eng. [*ca*. 20 June 1914]. Published, *Selected Letters,* no. 80a.

Mrs. Frost sends copies of *A Boy's Will* and *North of Boston* to her sister. 'The second book has been out five or six weeks. . . . There have been . . . good reviews. . . .' She describes their 350-year-old house, Little Iddens, and the surrounding countryside of Ledbury. She speaks of their friends and neighbors: Wilfrid Gibson and Lascelles Abercrombie, the 'Georgian' poets, and Robert Frost's great friend, Edward Thomas, 'who is a very well known critic and prose writer. . . . Rob and I think everything of him. He is quite the most admirable and lovable man we have ever known.'

F26   1915. ALs. RF to Lascelles Abercrombie. Franconia, N.H., 21 September 1915. Published, *Selected Letters,* no. 136.

The poet Lascelles Abercrombie had guided Frost in the original publication of his books. After Frost's return to the United States he continued a lengthy correspondence with Abercrombie. At the time of this letter, Abercrombie was trying to get Frost out of the disastrous contract he had signed with his first publisher, Mrs. Nutt. 'I never had one penny or one word of accounting from Mrs Nutt and I should like nothing better than just to cry Havoc and let you work on her. . . . I am seeing my American publisher's lawyer in New York this week to find out what can be done to save me from the fool's contract I signed. What do you say if when we are ready on this side and I say the word, you strike from that?'

F27   1915. ALs. RF to 'My dear Mr. Brown' (Boston bookseller). Franconia, N.H., 27 October 1915. Unpublished.

Apologizes for neglecting the books he had promised to inscribe for Mr. Brown. 'I have had to end ignominiously by copying you out a poem or two that I care a little for. . . . I did so want to add something to the books to make them at least worth the publisher's price. I wonder if I shall ever dare to look in on you at your store when I am in Boston.'

F28   1916. ALs. RF to Mrs. Edith H. Blaney. Franconia, N.H., 15 October 1916. Unpublished.

RF agrees to autograph some of his books for Mrs. Blaney. 'And if autographs are anything, you must let me send you an autographed copy of North of Boston. . . .' He promises to visit Mrs. Blaney next time he is in Boston, '. . . but I have become so mercenary that I believe I have lost the art of going anywhere except on business. Envelope present.

F29   1918. ALs. RF to 'Mr. Van Loon'. N.p., n.d. [*ca.* 1918–1920]. Unpublished.

'I am afraid there is not poetic idea enough in your poems to distinguish them. Striking comparisons, similes, metaphors, analogies are about all that counts as poetry in this world. Write down your luckiest comparison simply and unaffectedly enough and you can hardly help having poetry. That's the whole game. Don't use other people's phrases such as "The world is too much with us," "we are not as other men," "master hand," . . . etc. That's about all I could tell you if you came to see me. Make one good distinct figure of speech that's all your own and you are started on the road to poetry. Started.'

F30   1919. ALs. RF to Lola Ridge (American poet, editor of *Others* and *Broom*). Franconia, N.H., 24 April 1919. Unpublished.

Frost refuses Lola Ridge's request for a poem from him for *Others*. 'Taking a poem out of me now would be like taking out a swallowed fish hook. Not only my heart (which might not be so bad) but my lungs might have to come with it. I have wrestled with this business since your letter came. But it makes it easier between us that I am an individualist in the premises. You of all people won't want me to behave as anything else. . . .'

F31   1920. ALs. RF to 'My dear Mrs. Mansfield'. Amherst, Mass., 20 January 1920. Unpublished.

Responding to Mrs. Mansfield's request for a speaking engagement. 'Of course if you are going to say pleasant things about my talk at Garden City, I shall have no choice in the matter: I shall have to accept your invitation to talk in New York too. March 17th will be right for me. . . .'

F32   1920. ALs. RF to 'My dear Mrs. Penniman'. Franconia, N.H., 17 March 1920. Unpublished.

'. . . I am many times more the loser than you if my delay keeps you from using my play [*A Way Out*]. By all means use it if you like. What I get for it is not important for the present. Someday I hope to make money with plays. Till then——Let me ask that you will try to have the two characters pretty well matched and your light low enough for the last part of the scene.'

F33   1921. 2 ALs. RF to Grace Walcott (Hazard) Conkling (American poet). Unpublished.

F33.1   28 June 1921, South Shaftsbury, Vt. 'I am grateful that you should have thought to link Edward Thomas' name with mine in one of your lectures. You will be careful, I know, not to say anything to exalt either of us at the expense of the other. . . . Anything we may be thought to have in common we had before we met. When Hodgson [Ralph Hodgson, English poet] introduced us at a coffee house [St. George's Restaurant] in London in 1913 I had written two and a half of my three books he had written all but two or three of his thirty. The most our congeniality could do was confirm us both in what we were. There was never a moment's thought about who may have been influencing whom. The least rivalry of that kind would have taken something from our friendship. We were greater friends than almost any two ever were practicing the same art. . . . He gave me standing as a poet—he more than anyone else, though of course I have to thank [Lascelles] Abercrombie, [Ford Madox] Hueffer, [Ezra] Pound and some others for help too. I dragged him out from under the heap of his own work in prose he was buried alive under. . . . I made him see that he owed it to himself and the poetry to have it out by itself in poetic form where it must suffer itself to be admired. It took some time. I bantered, teased and bullied all the summer we were together at Leddington and Ryton. . . .

It was plain that he had wanted to be a poet all the years he had been writing about poets not worth his little finger. . . . I had about given him up, he had turned his thoughts to enlistment and I mine to sailing for home when he wrote his first poem. The decision he made in going into the army helped him make the other decision to be a poet in form. And a very fine poet. And a poet all in his own right. . . .'

F33.2   29 Dec. 1921, Ann Arbor, Mich. Frost declines to write a preface for a book of poetry by Mrs. Conkling's prodigy daughter, Hilda. 'Hilda needs me not. I think you underestimate her strength to go alone. She is sure to succeed by sheer force of poetry, and that's the way I should like to see her for the dignity of the art. . . .'

F34   1925. ALs. RF to 'Mr. Tewson'. 'On my own trail', 25 August 1925. Unpublished.
'For sheer usefulness in every modern encounter, I consider "So I have heard and do in part believe" the most beautiful single line of English verse. It should be found early in the first act of Hamlet, Horatio speaking. Your letter has just reached me. I am in the woods a fugitive from everything and all but cut off from mail.'

F35.1–2   1926. 2 ALSs. RF to 'My dear Miss Lamb'. South Shaftsbury, Vt., 10 July and 6 August 1926. Unpublished.
Both letters extend to Miss Lamb permission to 'use *Reluctance*'. 'I have a special feeling for that poem from the way it bound me in friendship to Tom Mosher. . . . I hope all goes well with you in the little shop up off the street.'

F36.1–2   1927. 2 ALSs. RF to Elizabeth Tarney (New Hampshire poetess). Amherst, Mass., n.d. and 25 January 1927. Unpublished.
The undated letter was to provide Miss Tarney with a signature to insert into a 'scissor-and-paste' book she was making up. 'It wouldn't be right for me to sign a book so much of your making. . . .'
The letter of 25 January thanks Miss Tarney for sending some of her poems. 'I was one New Hampshire poet. Then you wrote some poems and now there are two of us.'

F37   1928. ALs. RF to Padraic Colum (Irish-American poet). London, 18 September 1928. Published, *Selected Letters,* no. 269.
Frost hopes that Colum will act as his guide in Ireland on a forthcoming

visit. 'Nobody ever talked Ireland to me as intimately as you did that day lying by the side of a road in Pelham (near Amherst) ten years ago.'

F38   1932. ALs. RF to John Hall Wheelock (American poet and poetry editor of Charles Scribner's Sons). Amherst, Mass., 15 December 1932. Unpublished.

Recommending the availability for a speaking engagement of David McCord, a young poet and alumnus of Harvard. 'He has been reading into the infant mind some gratuitous oddities that I know nothing at all like. . . . They are of a wiry configuration that might easily wind themselves into the minds of a considerable public. . . . I'll bet a real publisher could get them going.'

David McCord was responsible for bringing Frost to Harvard for a reading in 1935 which resulted in his appointment at Harvard in 1938.

F39   1933. ALs. RF to 'Mr. Bird'. South Shaftsbury, Vt., 7 June 1933. Unpublished.

A response to an invitation to make a lecture tour of California in the winter of 1933–1934. 'You intend to distribute me humanely over some weeks, devote me largely to the undergraduates and protect me from too much hospitality. . . . Do you think I would like the January February March weather in California?' Ill health prevented the trip in 1933 and the death of the Frost's daughter Marjorie in May 1934 put an end to the plan.

F40   1933. ALs. RF to Mr. Hazlett (editor of the *American Mercury*). Amherst, Mass., 15 December 1933. Unpublished.

'You asked me for poems when I didn't have any except in process. I didn't answer at the time for fear of bad luck from talking about intentions. I write now to ask if you would still like something of mine. . . .'

With the letter is a typescript of 'Lost in Heaven' on a single leaf of bond paper, with 'The American Mercury' stamped in red at top and printer's marks in pencil. In spite of the fact that the *American Mercury* apparently accepted the poem for publication, it was never printed there. The first printing was in *Saturday Review of Literature* (Nov. 1935); later collected in *A Further Range* (1936). Text conforms with the first printing, having 'I warned the clouds, by opening on me wide.' in line 11.

F41   1935. ALs. RF to 'Dear Mr. Grover'. Amherst, Mass., December 1935. Unpublished.

'I'm not the authority I should be on my own editions. . . . The rough brown Boy's Will came first. The parchment with the red stripe came second. Mr. Charles Green of the Jones Library at Amherst Mass will presently be publishing an absolutely perfect bibliography of my works. I believe he would tell you this order. . . .'

F42   1936. ALs. RF to Lawrance Thompson (Frost's biographer). Cambridge, Mass., 26 March 1936. Unpublished.

'Can I do anything to help you? You are so very kind. I'd like to contribute the enclosed remnant of manuscript if I knew who would act as repository. . . . It is a sample of what most of my note books get reduced to in the process of revision. . . .' Envelope present.

The 'remnant of manuscript' was a group of four poems later printed in *A Further Range* (1936): 'A Stone Missive,' 'The Truth of It,' 'Two Tramps in Mud-Time,' and 'A Record Stride.' The notebook containing these manuscripts is represented in the Manuscripts section of this catalogue.

F43   1937. ALs. RF to Cyril Clemens (cousin of Samuel L. Clemens and author). Amherst, Mass., 13 April 1937. Unpublished.

'No I am neither mason of any degree nor carpenter, but only just a husbandman. I would say keep the pin and wear it yourself if I didn't assume you were a Knight of Columbus. . . .' In 1940 Cyril Clemens published a book, *A Chat with Robert Frost,* with a foreword by Hamlin Garland. Clemens was the founder and president of the International Mark Twain Society.

F44.1–2   1937. 2 ALSs. RF to Robert Partridge (English poet and librarian of the Passmore Edwards Public Library, London). San Antonio, Tex., 21 January 1937 and Amherst, Mass., 20 April 1937. Unpublished.

In response to Partridge's inquiry about the first edition of *A Boy's Will.* 'Several people know more about my first editions than I. My publisher used not to think it good for me to know how many of my books were printed or even how many were sold. . . .' He recommends Charles R. Green, John Kohn, and J. W. Haines as sources of information. Of Haines he writes, 'He has my reputation in his keeping and he may have some of my firsts up his sleeve. . . .'

The second letter accompanied a copy of *A Boy's Will* in one of the later bindings sent by Frost to Partridge, 'The Amherst Jones Library Frost Bibliography (if you get all that) makes the enclosed copy a first printing in the fourth covers. . . . My wife has the only copy of Twilight in existence. There were two copies printed but we destroyed one of them years ago.'

F45   1937. ALs. RF to John Hall Wheelock (American poet and editor of Charles Scribner's Sons). Amherst, Mass., 21 November 1937. Unpublished.

'I doubt if I ought to turn preface-writer yet awhile. But don't be sorry you asked me to preface Edith Wharton's Ethan Frome. I am a great admirer of that Yankee-rustic grotesque [Frome, not Mrs. Wharton]; and nothing flatters me more than to have it assumed that I could write prose— unless it be to have it assumed that I once pitched baseball with distinction. Van Wyck [Brooks] is your man, isn't he? Just as well you weren't at the Book Fair to see us poets humiliated by the last-minute injection of H. G. Wells into the program. I don't say it didn't do us good.'

F46   1938. ALs. RF to John S. Van E. Kohn (American bookman and poet). Concord Corners, Vt., 2 September 1938. Published, *Selected Letters,* no. 366.

In a letter of 24 August (*Selected Letters,* no. 365), Frost asked Kohn, then proprietor of The Collector's Bookshop, New York, to supply him with first editions of *A Boy's Will* and *North of Boston* at the going price. Lacking copies in stock, John Kohn responded by sending copies from his personal collection to accommodate the poet. Kohn did not charge Frost what the books were then worth and in this letter Frost remonstrates with him for this act of generosity, 'you are not to be allowed the only price-fixing. . . . The destination of the books is such and my obligation for favors so great there, that the more I pay for the books the more my gratification. . . . The transaction flatters me I suppose.'

F47   1943. Telegram with ANs. New York, N.Y., 4 May 1943. Unpublished.

The telegram, from Frank D. Fackenthal, provost of Columbia University: 'Take pleasure in advising you award to "A Witness Tree" by trustees of Columbia University of Pulitzer Poetry Prize. Announcement press Tuesday morning. Hearty Congratulations.' Beneath the message, Frost has written a draft of his reply, 'Getting it for the fourth time rather stops me from saying anything against a fourth term as president. R. F.'

F48   1954. ALs. RF to Roy V. Thornton (Frost collector). Amherst, Mass., 11 November 1954. Unpublished.

Asking Thornton to do him the favor of letting Clifton Waller Barrett 'look with envy on the little book called Twilight you have made so famous by paying so much for it. . . .' Thornton had purchased *Twilight* in the sale of Earle J. Bernheimer's books (Parke-Bernet Galleries, 11 and 12 December 1950) for $3,500. With Robert Frost acting as intermediary, Mr. Barrett later purchased the copy directly from Roy Thornton.

F   ADDENDUM THE LAWRANCE THOMPSON COLLECTION— A Calendar

1. Correspondence between Robert Frost and the executor of his grandfather's estate, Wilbur E. Rowell; correspondence between Jeanie Frost (RF's sister) and Rowell, and related correspondence.
FROST, Robert. 29 ALSs to Wilbur E. Rowell. Various places: Amherst, Mass. (2), Beaconsfield, Bucks., Eng. (4), Franconia, N.H. (14), Little Iddens, Gloucestershire, Eng. (3), Plymouth, N.H. (2), South Shaftsbury, Vt. (4); 25 June 1912–21 November 1931. Nine letters are published in *Selected Letters,* nos. 36, 37, 50, 56, 72, 76, 80, 194, and 224. The others are unpublished.
FROST, Elinor. ALs to Rowell. Sugar Hill, N.H., 3 September [1925].
FROST, Jeanie Florence. ALs to RF. Augusta, Maine, n.d.
FROST, Jeanie Florence. 81 ALSs to Wilbur E. Rowell. Various places, 1905–1920. Two letters published in *Selected Letters,* nos. 75a and 96a. Others unpublished.
ROWELL, Wilbur E. 22 TLSs to RF. Lawrence, Mass., 1912–1927.
ROWELL, Wilbur E. 3 TLSs and 20 carbon TLS to Jeanie Frost. Lawrence, Mass., 1913–1920.
Ca. 25 letters and documents from Louie Merriam, various doctors, to and from Wilbur E. Rowell, relating to Jeanie Frost's commitment to the State Hospital in Augusta, Maine; RF's real estate transactions, the W. P. Frost estate, etc.

2. Correspondence between Lawrance Thompson and Robert Frost, Mrs. Theodore Morrison, and others in connection with the biography.
FROST, ROBERT. 10 ALSs and 4 TLSs to Lawrance Thompson. Various places: South Shaftsbury, Vt., Gainesville, Fla., Ripton, Vt., Cambridge, Mass., Miami, Fla., Amherst, Mass.; 14 July 1937–15 August 1962. Eleven letters are published in *Selected Letters,* nos. 351, 375, 388, 392, 401, 414, 438, 428, 431, 455, 462. Others unpublished.
FROST, Robert. Telegrams to Lawrance Thompson. Ten sent between 1938–1943.

MORRISON, Mrs. Theodore (Kathleen). *Ca.* 80 ALSs and TLSs to Law-rance Thompson. Various places, between 1939 and 1962.

SNOW, Wilbert. 5 TLSs to Lawrance Thompson. Wesleyan University, Middletown, Conn., 1936.

STEVENS, Wallace. A.Poem.s. ['The Virgin Carrying a Lantern'.] Key West, Fla., 25 Feburary 1940. A holograph copy made for Lawrance Thompson as payment of a bet that Thompson could not recite the poem. The bet occurred during a meeting between RF and Stevens in the Casa Marina Hotel, Key West. On this occasion, Stevens said to RF, 'The trouble with you, Frost, is that you write about *things*,' and RF answered, 'The trouble with you, Wallace, is that you write about—bric-a-brac.' The poem was printed in *Harmonium* (1923).

3. The Robert Frost / Earle J. Bernheimer correspondence and related ma-terial.

FROST, Robert. 1 ALs, 5 TLSs, and 2 typewritten telegrams to Earle J. Bernheimer. Various places, 1941–1950. Five letters are published in *Selected Letters,* nos. 385, 399, 406, 419, 420. Others unpublished.

BERNHEIMER, Earle J. Draft TLs to RF. [Beverly Hills, ca. 27 March 1950.] An early draft with autograph corrections.

COHN, Capt. Louis Henry. 9 TLSs to Earle J. Bernheimer. New York, 1938–1945.

BAUM, George K. (partner of Earle J. Bernheimer in the firm of Baum, Bernheimer & Co.). Carbon telegram to RF. 8 January 1940. Announces transmittal at request of Bernheimer of $4,000 in payment for *Twilight*. In-scribed by Bernheimer.

4. FROSTIANA: photographs, pamphlets, catalogues, programs, menus, photostats, invitations, newspaper clippings and reviews, miscellaneous cor-respondence, comprising about 400 separate items. Single items of unusual importance are:

   Two school themes written by Helen Melville Moody, corrected in pencil by RF. *Ca.* 1913.

Catalogue of Pinkerton Academy, 1910–1911, with four tickets advertising plays directed by RF.

Leaflet (4 pp.) of critical praise for RF, published by David Nutt for *North of Boston*.

The Old Farmer's Almanac, 1906. Signed by RF on pp. 1 and 13 (calendar for April containing a line from 'Mending Wall' that good fences make good neighbors.

5. The Lawrance Thompson / Elizabeth Shepley Sergeant correspondence, consisting of 12 ALSs from Elizabeth Sergeant to LT. Peterborough, N.H., and Piermont, N.Y., 1955.

6. The Lawrance Thompson notebooks. 6 loose-leaf folders, 5 ledger books, 6 parcels of unbound typescript, comprising the journal kept by Thompson of his day-to-day relationship with Robert Frost from 1939 to 1963 and his extensive notes for the biography to 1972.

7. Other Robert Frost manuscripts and letters in the Lawrance Thompson collection.
FROST, Robert. ALs to Mrs. Marion Parris Smith. Pittsfield, Mass. [*ca.* 1924]. Thanking Mrs. Smith for the gift of a rug. '. . . we were called away from our little old colonial house . . . in Michigan by the serious illness of one of our daughters here in Pittsfield. We have made very bad work of our divided life so far this year. This attempt (bold at our age) to be about equally eastern and western may defeat itself like trying to sit on more than thirteen to fifteen eggs at once. It may addle the eggs and give the hen a nervous breakdown. Life has never been a choice for me. I can honestly say I have seen but one thing presented to do at a time. Until now anyway. Wouldn't it be terrible if in old age life should turn on me and begin to present itself to me in alternatives and nothing but alternatives? That would be just like life which by definition is that which carefully prepares you for one thing and then confronts you with something else.'
FROST, Robert. AMS [signed later]. 'Barriers'. 2 pp. written in brown ink on the recto and verso of a single leaf of cheap, wove yellow paper. [Amherst, *ca.* 1918.] Inscribed in the upper left corner, 'Aug 30 1952 / Notes made after / class talk the day Wilson's / Fourteen Points came out / R. F.' The notes are in the form of questions to be asked his students: 'If an idea is a good idea what difference if any does it make to you whether it is your own or someone elses? Is it permissable to erect barriers against the intrusion of other peoples thought on our own thinking? What are some of the barriers? On what ground do we ask to be let alone when we are engaged with a piece of work? Discriminate between the kinds of egotism involved. What is this prejudice in favor of keeping people off us with their suggestions while we are in process? What barriers does Pres Wilson refer

to in his third point and what does he mean by his proposal to remove them as far as possible? Why were they ever erected? If barriers against foreign trade why not also against foreign art? Do you know of any trade barriers against foreign art or literature? Would literary barriers against foreign literature be any better than trade barriers against it? Is all this or any of it a question of friendship and peace between nations?'

FROST, Robert. AMS. ['Questioning Faces'] and prose fragment. A single leaf of white wove paper torn from a blank publisher's dummy. The poem is a fair copy written in ink; the prose fragment in pencil, 'By the lessons of poetry in prose or verse we are brought to see that the whole of thinking is metaphor'. Beneath are pasted two drug-container labels from the O. K. Drug Store in Coral Gables, Fla. These were placed there by Lawrance Thompson to identify the occasion as 'Miami-and-pneumonia'. The labels are made out to RF by Dr. Franz Stewart; one for Darvon, the other for Declomycin capsules. Both are dated 1 February 1962.

Bibliography
Index

Bibliography

Anderson, Margaret Bartlett. *Robert Frost and John Bartlett: The Record of a Friendship*. New York, Chicago, San Francisco: Holt, Rinehart and Winston, 1963.

Bowers, Fredson T. *Principles of Bibliographical Description*. New York: Russell & Russell, 1962.

Byers, Edna Hanley (ed.). *Robert Frost at Agnes Scott College*. Decatur, Ga.: McCain Library, Agnes Scott College, 1963.

Clymer, W. B. Shubrick, and Charles R. Green. *Robert Frost: A Bibliography*. Amherst, Mass.: The Jones Library, 1937.

Cook, Reginald L. *The Dimensions of Robert Frost*. New York, Toronto: Rinehart and Co., 1958.

Cox, Sidney. *A Swinger of Birches*. New York: New York University Press, 1957.

Grade, Arnold (ed.). *Family Letters of Robert and Elinor Frost*. Albany: State University of New York Press, 1972.

Lathem, Edward Connery (ed.). *Interviews with Robert Frost*. New York, Chicago, San Francisco: Holt, Rinehart and Winston, 1966.

Lathem, Edward Connery (ed.). *The Poetry of Robert Frost*. Barre, Mass.: Imprint Society, 1971.

Lymen, John F. *The Pastoral Art of Robert Frost*. New Haven: Yale University Press, 1960.

Mertins, Louis and Esther. *The Intervals of Robert Frost*. Berkeley and Los Angeles: University of California Press, 1947.

Mertins, Louis. *Robert Frost: Life and Talks—Walking*. Norman: University of Oklahoma Press, 1965.

Sergeant, Elizabeth Shepley. *Robert Frost: The Trial by Existence*. New York: Holt, Rinehart and Winston, 1960.

The Spiral Press through Four Decades: An Exhibition of Books and Ephemera. With a commentary by Joseph Blumenthal. New York: The Pierpont Morgan Library, 1966.

Thompson, Lawrance. *Robert Frost: The Early Years, 1874–1915*. New York. Chicago, San Francisco: Holt, Rinehart and Winston, 1966.

——. *Robert Frost: The Years of Triumph, 1915–1938*. New York, Chicago, San Francisco: Holt, Rinehart and Winston, 1970.

—— (ed.). *Selected Letters of Robert Frost*. New York, Chicago, San Francisco: Holt, Rinehart and Winston, 1964.

Index

References are to items, not to pages. Principal descriptive entries for titles are indicated by boldface type. Square brackets indicate the entry is inferred for some aspect of the description—the text content, for example. Such minor variations in titles as differing initial articles, spelling, and hyphenation are not reflected in the index.